W0042864

The State of the Art
in Computational Intelligence

Advances in Soft Computing

Editor-in-chief
Prof. Janusz Kacprzyk
Systems Research Institute
Polish Academy of Sciences
ul. Newelska 6
01-447 Warsaw, Poland
E-mail: kacprzyk@ibspan.waw.pl
http://www.springer.de/cgi-bin/search-bock.pl?series=4240

Esko Turunen
Mathematics Behind Fuzzy Logic
1999. ISBN 3-7908-1221-8

Robert Fullér
Introduction to Neuro-Fuzzy Systems
2000. ISBN 3-7908-1256-0

Robert John and Ralph Birkenhead (Eds.)
Soft Computing Techniques
and Applications
2000. ISBN 3-7908-1257-9

Mieczysław Kłopotek, Maciej Michalewicz
and Sławomir T. Wierzchoń (Eds.)
Intelligent Information Systems
2000. ISBN 3-7908-1309-5

Peter Sinčák · Ján Vaščák
Vladimír Kvasnička · Radko Mesiar (Eds.)

The State of the Art in Computational Intelligence

Proceedings of the European Symposium
on Computational Intelligence
held in Košice, Slovak Republic,
August 30–September 1, 2000

With Forewords by
Lotfi A. Zadeh, David E. Goldberg and Kunihiko Fukushima

With 130 Figures
and 41 Tables

Physica-Verlag

A Springer-Verlag Company

Ass. Prof. Dr. Peter Sinčák
Dr. Ján Vaščák
Technical University of Košice
Faculty of Electrical Engineering and Informatics
Letna 9/B
040 00 Košice
Slovakia
E-mail: sincak@tuke.sk
         vascak@tuke.sk

Prof. Dr. Vladimír Kvasnička
Slovak University of Technology Bratislava
Faculty of Chemical Technology
Radlinskeho 9
812 37 Bratislava
Slovakia
E-mail: kvasnic@cvt.stuba.sk

Prof. Dr. Radko Mesiar
Slovak University of Technology Bratislava
Faculty of Civil Engineering
Radlinskeho 11
813 68 Bratislava
Slovakia
E-mail: mesiar@vox.svf.stuba.sk

ISSN 1615-3871

Die Deutsche Bibliothek – CIP-Einheitsaufnahme
The state of the art in computational intelligence: with 41 tables / Peter Sinčák, Ján Vaščák, Vladimír Kvas-nič\ka, Radko Mesiar (eds.). With Forew. by Lotfi A. Zadeh... -- Heidelberg; New York: Physica-Verl., 2000
    (Advances in soft computing)
    ISBN 978-3-7908-1322-7   ISBN 978-3-7908-1844-4 (eBook)
    DOI 10.1007/978-3-7908-1844-4

This work is subject to copyright. All rights are reserved, whether the whole or part of the material is concerned, specifically the rights of translation, reprinting, reuse of illustrations, recitation, broadcasting, reproduction on microfilm or in any other way, and storage in data banks. Duplication of this publication or parts thereof is permitted only under the provisions of the German Copyright Law of September 9, 1965, in its current version, and permission for use must always be obtained from Physica-Verlag. Violations are liable for prosecution under the German Copyright Law.

Physica-Verlag Heidelberg New York
a member of BertelsmannSpringer Science+Business Media GmbH
© Physica-Verlag Heidelberg 2000

The use of general descriptive names, registered names, trademarks, etc. in this publication does not imply, even in the absence of a specific statement, that such names are exempt from the relevant protective laws and regulations and therefore free for general use.

Softcover Design: Erich Kirchner, Heidelberg

SPIN 10773231   88/2202-5 4 3 2 1 0 – Printed on acid-free paper

Forewords

written by   **Lotfi A. Zadeh**
                         David E. Goldberg
                         Kunihiko Fukushima

The Role of Fuzzy Systems in Computational Intelligence

Computational Intelligence was born close to two decades ago, at a time when there was a growing consensus that traditional AI was too deeply anchored to Aristotelian logic, and intolerant of uncertainty, imprecision and partial truth.

Today, Computation Intelligence, or CI, for short, is generally viewed as a consortium of methodologies which play important roles in the conception, design and utilization of information/intelligent systems. The principal members of the consortium are: fuzzy logic (FL); neuro computing (NC); evolutionary computing (EC); probabilistic computing (PC); chaotic computing (CC); and parts of machine learning theory (ML). What is important about these methodologies is that, for the most part, they are complementary and synergistic, rather than competitive. A common theme is the principle: Exploit the tolerance for imprecision, uncertainty and partial truth to achieve tractability, robustness, low solution cost and better rapport with reality.

Within CI, fuzzy set theory or fuzzy system theory, or fuzzy logic – which is the label in common use today – provide a conceptual framework for dealing with partiality of truth, possibility and dependence. Thus, fuzzy logic cuts across other methodologies and provides a common foundation.

A source of frequent misunderstanding is that the term "fuzzy logic" has two distinct meanings. In a narrow sense, fuzzy logic is a logical system which underlies the modes of reasoning which are approximate rather than exact. But in a wide sense – which is in dominant use today – fuzzy logic is much more than a logical system; it is, in effect, coextensive with fuzzy set theory.

More specifically, fuzzy logic in its wide sense, FL, has four principal facets which overlap and have unsharp boundaries.

The first facet, FL/L, is the logical facet – a facet which is coextensive with fuzzy logic in its narrow sense. The second facet, the set-theoretic facet, FL/S, is the part of FL which is concerned with classes which have unsharp boundaries. My 1965 paper on fuzzy sets dealt with this facet. Today, most papers in the mathematical literature on fuzzy sets relate to the set-theoretic facet.

The third facet, the relational facet, FL/R, is concerned with representation and analysis of imprecise dependencies. Most applications of fuzzy logic, especially in the realms of consumer electronics, industrial systems and control fall within the province of this facet.

The fourth facet, the epistemic facet, FL/E, is concerned with knowledge, meaning and information. Possibility theory is a part of this facet, as is possibilistic logic, which is shared with the logical facet.

The core of FL is centered in two basic concepts: fuzzification and granulation, along with their conjunction, fuzzy granulation. Fuzzification, or f-generalization, is a mode of generalization in which a set is replaced by a fuzzy set. Fuzzy granulation, or f.g-generalization, is a mode of generalization in which a fuzzy set is partitioned into fuzzy granules, with a granule being a clump of points (objects) which are drawn together by indistinguishability, similarity, proximity or functionality. For example, the fuzzy granules of a face are the nose, chin, cheeks, lips, etc. Fuzzy granulation plays a pivotal role in fuzzy logic and its applications; it underlies the two most important concepts in FL, namely, the concepts of a linguistic variable and fuzzy if-then rule sets.

A new and important direction in fuzzy logic is related to what may be called the computational theory of perceptions (CTP). This theory, which is based on fuzzy logic, provides a machinery for processing of information which is perception-based, e.g., "it is likely to rain later in the evening," "most Swedes are blond," etc. Existing scientific theories do not have this capability.

By providing a machinery for computation with perceptions, CTP opens the door to a major enlargement of the role of natural languages in scientific theories, especially in probability theory, decision analysis and control. A countertraditional move in this direction has the potential for leading to a significant paradigm shift in both basic and applied sciences.

The Proceedings of the ESCI Symposium serves an important function by providing a broad and authoritative exposition of the constituent methodologies of CI. What is of particular importance is inclusion of contributions which describe so-called hybrid systems, that is, systems in which the constituent methodologies are used in combination rather than in a stand-alone mode. In coming years, hybrid systems are likely to be the norm rather than exception. Such systems are certain to have a much higher MIQ (Machine IQ) than those we can design today. We are entering the age of information/intelligent systems – an age in which computational intelligence will play a principal role.

Lotfi A. Zadeh
Berkeley, CA April 24, 2000

A Meditation on Computational Intelligence and Its Future

It is an honor for me to have been asked to write a foreword for the proceedings of the 2000 European Symposium on Computational Intelligence in Slovakia. The rise of computational intelligence (CI) as an alternative to earlier artificial intellegence (AI) paradigms is reflected in the submitted paper statistics. Of the 106 papers that were submitted, 35 were devoted to neural networks, 25 involved fuzzy systems, 10 were devoted to genetic and evolutionary computation, six were devoted to artificial life, and 20 involved hybrids of the constituent methods. Indeed, the symposium organizers should be congratulated on having assembled such a diverse collection of interesting and useful papers, but as I scan the statistics, I can't help wonder about the larger lessons of this symposium for the field and its future. In the remainder of the foreword, I reflect on the rise of CI, wonder whether CI will ultimately be successful in influencing the course of human events, and then briefly discuss perhaps the single most important requirement for CI systems of the future.

The rise of CI. Computational intelligence has been on the rise whether viewed individually from the perspective of the constituent disciplines—neural computation, fuzzy systems, and genetic and evolutionary computation (GEC)—or from the perspective of joint activities such as this one. In my own discipline, genetic and evolutionary computation, a recent on-line listing contained exactly 50 workshops, symposia, and conferences between now (April 2000) and next March. In other words, one could do nothing but traipse around the world and attend GEC-related events every week of the year if one was so inclined, and this growing popularity is remarkable. Not long ago there was only one GEC conference, the first International Conference on Genetic Algorithms (1985), and all of about 60 people attended. By way of contrast, last year the Genetic and Evolutionary Computation Conference (GECCO-99) in Orlando drew 619 attendees, so the growth in both numbers of events and attendees per event has been substantial. .

Is CI successful? But our success in numbers—our success in talking amongst ourselves—has not yet translated to having influence in the most prestigious academic departments, organizations, and industries. With rare exception, these positions are still held by those who grew up with artificial intelligence as their guiding technology. This situation reminds me of a story told of the German physicist Max Planck. A friend approached him and asked him how the acceptance of the new physics was going. The great man is reputed to have said, "Fine, lots of funerals." Our situation is simultaneously similar and dissimilar to that of the new physics. A substantial mind makeover is required to accept the differences in philosophy and outlook of CI versus the earlier AI, but the time rate of discovery of new knowledge is no longer well matched to the funeral rate of earlier thinkers.

Of course I should be quick to point out that I am not suggesting that this problem is one we should actively try to solve through an increase in the number of homicides or unexplained accidental deaths. But it *is* an interesting question for the survival of the field, as we must imagine a pathway to both intellectual and political success if the field of computational intelligence and its constituent disciplines are to survive and continue to influence the course of human events. Certainly, the growth of the field is itself a remarkable fact given the low levels of corporate or governmental support driving our study. Ours is an insurgency led by passionate researchers, and we should not underestimate the power of passion in the promotion of important ideas. But the pathway to wider acceptance takes more than passionate commitment, and I believe the pathway for widespread CI ascendance is presenting itself to us in the form of (1) scalable results, (2) with practical import, using (3) *little* or *economic* models or theory.

Scalable results. The AI winter following the bust of the expert systems bubble in the 1980s was the result of systems that worked well in the pilot stages, but were too brittle as they were tried on larger, real-world systems. CI has been more concerned with results that scale well from its very inception, and fielded CI systems continue to grow and prosper; we have not yet "hit the wall" on the growth of these systems in practice.

Practicalilty. Moreover, it seems to me that CI has been tied more closely to practice from its beginnings with real problems tackled earlier and more often. Early AI was characterized by the solution of "blocks world" types of problems, but early fuzzy, neural, and genetic systems have been solving complex simulation, optimization, and control problems for some time, and the trend seems likely to continue.

Little or economic models. Additionally, the growth of CI has been accompanied by a concomitant interest in applicable theory or what I have called *little models* or *economic models*. Where early AI seemed content with the firewall that exists in the computer science curriculum between the rigor of algorithm theory on the one hand and fielded systems on the other, CI seeks out scaling laws, bounding theories, or equations that are only complex enough to advance the state of CI design. Some may decry the loss of rigor this suggests, but I view it as an advantage of CI, plain and simple, and elsewhere in this proceedings and at the symposium I discuss this view in more depth. Simply stated, the use of *scaling laws* is extraordinarily helpful in the design of complex CI systems. The Wright brothers used lift coefficients and drag coefficients to build Flyer I, but they did not use the Navier-Stokes equations. Likewise, we must use models to design complex CI systems, but the models must be simple enough to be tractable in design usage at the same time they are sufficiently predictive to answer the design questions that arise.

The coming integration in our CI future. These three factors, I believe, bode well for the future of our field. As more people come to the party, it is essential that our systems scale well, are practical, and are guided by solid and appropriately complex theories or models. Many of the papers of this volume reflect these values, and better understanding and articulation of CI's competitive advantage in the marketplace of ideas can only help future researchers and practitioners to accentuate these matters in their own work. But as we turn to the future, one conference statistic stands out as a harbinger of things to come. Recall that some 20 of the 106 submitted papers involved a hybrid of two or more of the constituent methods of CI, and this, I believe, is our collective future.

Individually the constituent methods of computational intelligence are powerful. Each has a driving metaphor, a driving logic, and a driving base of successful application, but the future of our field lies in the *integration* of the best of the constituent technologies. Some of this drama is being played out today on the pages of this very proceedings through simple *combinations* of neural-fuzzy, neuro-genetic, fuzzy-genetic, or fuzzy-neuro-genetic systems, but the careful integration of our methods into autonomously intelligent systems goes beyond simple combinations. Subtle integration of the abstraction power of fuzzy systems, the associative powers of neurocomputing, and the innovating power of genetic systems requires a design sophistication beyond our current means and a better sense of economy of hybridization than has been recognized heretofore. Some of these matters are now receiving attention, and their study will grow. Nonetheless, the integration of the constituent technologies into powerful competent systems is off on a not-too-distant horizon. This proceedings represents a few more steps toward that now-visible goal, and I urge the contributors to and readers of this volume to join together to hasten the day when that goal shall be reached.

David E. Goldberg
University of Illinois at Urbana-Champaign
Urbana, IL 61801

Computational Intelligence and Modeling Neural Networks

Computational Intelligence is a challenging research area, which aims to design and construct systems that behave intelligently like human beings. It constitutes an interdisciplinary area, ranging from brain sciences to industrial applications. It includes many different fields, such as computer sciences, mathematics, cognitive sciences, neurophysiology, psychology, electronics, control engineering, robotics, physics, and many others. It has a wide variety of industrial applications. One of the important aims of this symposium would be to promote interaction among different fields.

Although interdisciplinary research is indispensable for the development of this field, I would like to mention here the importance of modeling neural networks of the biological brain. Since we want to design systems like human brain, it is important to understand the mechanism of the brain and learn from its real biological basis.

Scientific efforts towards understanding architectures and functional mechanisms of neural networks in the brain, however, are confronted with an almost unsurpassable level of complexity that cannot be solved by conventional neurophysiological and psychological experiments only. The development of basic concepts and general principles of operation is therefore of crucial importance in guiding the way of thinking and defining working hypotheses for further investigations. For that reason, neural networks modeling form an essential tool in studying the consequences of these basic ideas in a rigorous way.

To be more concrete, in the modeling approach, we study how to interconnect neurons to synthesize a brain model, or a network with the same functions and abilities as the brain. When synthesizing a model, we try to follow physiological evidence as faithfully as possible. For parts that are not yet clear, we construct a hypothesis and synthesize a model that follows the hypothesis. We then analyze or simulate the behavior of the model, and compare it with that of the brain. If we find any discrepancy in behavior of the model and the brain, we change the initial hypothesis and modify the model. We then test the behavior of the model again. We repeat this procedure until the model behaves in the same way as the brain. Although we must still verify the validity of the model by physiological experimentation, it is probable that the brain uses the same mechanism as the model, because both respond in the same way. The relationship between modeling neural networks and neurophysiology resembles that between theoretical physics and experimental physics.

The modeling approach is therefore of increasing importance in neurophysiological and psychological experimentation, where testable hypotheses are in great need. With mathematical models it can convincingly be shown how complex behavior can emerge even from very simple rules of operation. Basic ideas concerning information processing in biological neural networks may lead to new design principles for computational intelligence.

Although I stressed the importance of modeling neural networks here, I never think light of other approaches. Nevertheless, interdisciplinary cooperation of many different fields is indispensable for the progress of computational intelligence.

This ESCI-2000 symposium would provide us a place for interaction and discussions among researchers and engineers of different fields from all over the world. It will give us a large step to the development of computational intelligence for the future.

Kunihiko Fukushima
The University of Electro-Communications, Japan

Preface

Computational Intelligence is a very dynamic domain of modern information society, and represents a unique proof to the usefulness of technology to human kind. The desire of constructing an artificial human being that would be able to help people solve many difficult problems is still very far ahead, but many important applications are in use worldwide. The basic and applied research in this area is very important and will determine the level of technological development of society. The level of intelligence of human-made machines, is and will be, an important indication of the level of the information society in the 21st century. People working in the area of research, technological development and practical applications feel a responsibility for the future of society. It is considered a great challenge for us to contribute to leading edge technology that will be able to put more intelligence into machines and artificial human-made systems. Important scientific meetings concerning computational intelligence take place all over the world. The Euro-International Symposium on Computational Intelligence, organized in Košice, Slovakia had a great response and is proof that there is great potential and interest concerning computational Intelligence in region of Central Europe.

In this book are three forewords from leading scientists in the fields of fuzzy systems (Prof. Zadeh), evolutionary computations (Prof. Goldberg) and neural networks (Prof. Fukushima). These forewords confirm some important tendencies in computational intelligence's future.

The book is organized in six parts as follows: Neural networks, Fuzzy Systems, Miscellaneous CI Techniques, Hybrid Systems and Applications and Case Studies. The last part consists of short information on posters' abstracts presented at the Symposium. Each paper went through a review process with selected experts from the CI domain.

More than 100 papers were submitted to the symposium integrating communities of neural networks, fuzzy systems, evolutionary computation, and artificial life. A great number of hybrid techniques are presented. There is clear tendency to use integration of various techniques to achieve better and more effective technology to solve a given task. There is no longer a pure neural solution or pure fuzzy approach. We live in a very competitive environment and therefore, the results are much more important than the technology and method used in application. There are a number of tools based on computational intelligence, which have some biological inspirations. It is extremely important to learn and grab know-how of biological systems, and to apply them in technology on an every day basis. Let me express a strong belief that this symposium is a useful contribution to the worldwide effort for pushing leading edge technology towards the usefulness of society. I am strongly convinced that the creator of mankind, **our Lord,** is supporting our mission and supervising our paces not to misuse technology against human kind in the future. Computational Intelligence should be about helping people and society to solve tasks easier and effectively in every domain of our life.

Firstly, I would like to express a cordial thankfulness for support of this Symposium to EU for its program **"High Level Scientific Conferences"** and sponsoring the meeting through financial support for keynote/invited speakers and young EU's researchers on the symposium. I also thank all our sponsors of the Symposium for their support. The invited and keynote speakers' papers and some selected papers were published by Physica-Verlag in a different book under the title **"Quo Vadis Computational Intelligence?"**, by Peter Sincak, Jan Vascak (Eds.) and with a fascinating foreword written by Prof. James Bezdek. The book contains papers of leading persons in the CI field as Zadeh, Carpenter, Hirota, Fukushima, Kacprzyk, Kasabov, Koczy, Moraga, Adeli, Takagi, Gedeon and many others. I am sure that this meeting is a European contribution to the worldwide effort to progress in intelligent information systems development.

I would like to express my gratitude to all authors and reviewers preparing this multi-author book. I also thank Prof. Janusz Kacprzyk and the people from Physica-Verlag for encouragement during the editing of this book. Finally, I would like to thank all my colleagues and my PhD and MSc. students for their help during the Symposium preparation.

Dr. Peter Sinčák

Technical University of Košice, Slovakia

August, 2000

Contents

Forewords

The Role of Fuzzy Systems in Computational Intelligence   vi
Lotfi A. Zadeh

A Meditation on Computational Intelligence and Its Future   viii
David. E. Goldberg

Computational Intelligence and Modeling Neural Networks   xi
Kunihiko Fukushima

Preface

    xiii

Peter Sinčák

Part 1 : Neural Networks

    1

Discovering Common Features in Software Code Using Self-Organizing Maps   3
Alvin Chan, Tim Spracklen

Graded Signal Functions for ARTMAP Neural Networks   9
Norbert Kopčo, Gail A. Carpenter

Incremental Approximation by Layer Neural Networks   15
Gabriela Andrejková

Efficient Training of MLP with Training Step Rate Estimation   21
*Vladimir Golovko, Yuri Savitsky, Theodore Laopoulos,
Anatoly Sachenko, Lucio Grandinetti*

Self-Organizing Maps for Representing Structures 27
Igor Farkaš

Invariant Representation of Images by Pulse Coupled Neural
Network 33
Radoslav Forgáč, Igor Mokriš

Detection of Ischemic Episodes with a Combination of
Unsupervised and Supervised Learning 39
*Stergios Papadimitriou, Liviu Vladutu, Severina Mavroudi,
Anastassios Bezerianos*

Spatial Distribution of Patterns and the Hopfield Network
Phase Space Geometry 44
Marek Jaszuk, Wiesław A. Kamiński, Alexander D. Linkevich

Switched Capacitor-Based Integrate-And-Fire Neural
Network 50
Daniel Hajtáš, Daniela. Ďuračková, Graham Benyon-Tinker

A Neural Network Algorithm for Digital Circuits Test
Generation 56
Juraj Štefanovič

The Parallel Bayesian Optimization Algorithm 61
Jiří Očenášek, Josef Schwarz

Application of Heuristic Programming to Dynamic System
Stabilization 68
Dušan Krokavec, Anna Filasová

First Order Dynamic Instance Selection 74
Peter Géczy, Shiro Usui, Ján Chmúrny

Part 2 : Fuzzy Systems

79

Toward an Enlargement of the Role of Natural Languages in
Information Processing, Decision and Control 81
Lotfi A. Zadeh

Notes on Fusion of Uncertain Information 83
Mourad Oussalah

Fix-Mundis for Fuzzy IF-THEN Rule Bases with T-Norm
Based Compositional Rule of Inference Interpretation 89
Karl-Heinz Temme, Madjid Fathi

Computational Problems of Constrained Fuzzy Arithmetic 95
Mirko Navara, Zdeněk Žabokrtský

Linear Regression with Fuzzy Variables 99
Štefan Varga, Michal Šabo

Fuzzy-Petri Net Reasoning System and Transfering of
Knowledge to the Markov Chain 104
Zoran M. Gacovski, Georgi M. Dimirovski, Stojce Deskovski

Fuzzy Conceptual Graphs: A Language for Computational
Intelligence Approaching Human Expression
and Reasoning 114
Tru Hoang Cao

A New Heuristic Measure for Learning Rules from Fuzzy
Data 120
*Francisco Botana, José Ranilla, Ricardo Mones,
Antonio Bahamonde*

On the Role of Transitivity in Fuzzy Relational Calculus 127
Bernard De Baets

Project Network Planning on the Basis of Generalized Fuzzy
Critical Path Method 133
Anatoliy Slyeptsov, Tatyana Tyshchuk

Flexible Querying - Data Structures Unification 140
Peter Marcinčák, Marcel Matula

New Connectives for (Full) Fuzzy Resolution 146
Dana Smutná, Peter Vojtáš

Learn the Ranking of Precedence Cases 152
István Borgulya

Sugeno-Type Fuzzy Predictor of the MPEG Video Stream..... 162
Agnieszka Chodorek

Part 3 : Miscellaneous CI Techniques

169

Biological Inspiration for Multiple Memories Implementation
and Cooperation 171
Frédéric Alexandre

Optimization as a Multistage Decision Making 175
Jiří Pospíchal

Can Computers Be Conscious? Methodological
Considerations from the Standpoint of the Humanities 182
Marek Dobeš

Part 4 : Hybrid Systems

189

GA-FIS for Dynamic Environment 191
Radek Matoušek, Pavel Ošmera, Jan Roupec

Genetic Method for Optimization of Fuzzy Neural Networks
Structure 197
Vladimír Olej, Jiří Křupka

A Reverse Neural Model of a General Planar Transmission
Line 203
Zbyněk Raida

Fuzzy Sets and the Theory of Neuronal Group Selection for
the Problem of Interpretation 209
Savely Girshgorn

Neuro-Fuzzy Architectures with Various Implication
Operators 214
Danuta Rutkowska, Robert Nowicki, Leszek Rutkowski

Fuzzy Cluster Identification Using Neural Networks 220
Peter Sinčák, Marcel Hric, Norbert Kopčo, Ján Vaščák

Part 5 : Applications and Case Studies

231

Soft Computing Applications Developed by ECANSE ....
Roman Blaško
233

Tetris Player: Strategy Driven Algorithm 238
Martin Lukáč, Paul Bourgine

Electrical Daily Load Forecasting Using Artificial Neural
Network in the Power System of Slovak Republic 243
Peter Szathmáry, Michal Kolcun

Practical Approach to Prediction of Plant Technological
Parameters with Missing Data 250
Marián Hrehuš, Štefan Figedy

Application of Artificial Neural Networks to Represent the
Rainfall-Runoff Process for Flow Forecasting 256
Pavel Fosumpaur

Using Neural Network in Cryptography 262
Eva Volná

Application of Artificial Neural Network Strategies in
Process Control 268
Alojz Mészáros, Anton Andrášik, Anton Rusnák

Design of a Fuzzy Adaptive Autopilot 276
Ján Vaščák, Peter Kováčik, František Betka, Peter Sinčák

Mobile Robot Control Using BP Based Adaptive Critics 282
Rudolf Jakša, Miroslav Hudec, Peter Sinčák

Computational Intelligence Controllers for Lego Robots -
Comparison Study 288
Marian Gavalier, Rudolf Jakša, Miroslav Hudec, Peter Sinčák

Document Clustering with Neural Networks 296
Rastislav Lences

Dual-Tone Multiple Frequency Detection Using Adaptive
Filters and Neural Network Classifiers 302
Georgi Iliev, Nikola Kasabov

An Experiment with Feed-Forward Neural Network for
Speech Recognition 308
Bohumir Jelinek, Jozef Juhar, Anton Cizmar

Increase the Pattern Capability in System for Flying Object
Recognition 314
Radosław Semkło

Personal Verification with Hand Shapes Using a Modular –
Type Neural Network with RBF Output Units 318
Seiji Ishihara, Takashi Nagano

A Soft Measurement Technique for Searching Significant
Subsets of Prostate Cancer Prognostic Markers 325
*Huseyin Seker, Michael O. Odetayo, Dobrila Petrovic,
Raouf Naguib, Freddie Hamdy*

Application of an Adaptive Hybrid Neural Network
to Medical Diagnosis 329
*Chee Peng Lim, Poh Suan Teoh, Phaik Yean Goay,
Robert F. Harrison*

Reliability of Artificial Neural Network Predictions – A Case
Study in Drug Release Profile Predictions 337
Siow San Quek, Chee Peng Lim, Kok Khiang Peh

An Island-Based Evolutionary Algorithm for Maximizing
Schedule Reliability 344
Piotr Jędrzejowicz, Aleksandr Skakovski

Using of Genetic Algorithms (GA) in the Operating Control
in Power System of Slovak Republic 350
Ľuboslav Pribičko, Michal Kolcun

A Population Learning Algorithm for Solving the
Generalized Segregated Storage Problem 355
Dariusz Barbucha, Piotr Jedrzejowicz

Using Support Vectors Machine for Classification of
Remotely Sensed Images.. 361
Marek Bundzel, Peter Sinčák, Norbert Kopčo

Posters

371

Application of Neural Network for Stress Classification 373
Milan Šorf, Vladimír Eck, Ladislava Janku, Lenka Lhotská

Solvability and Stability of Fuzzy Relation Equations 376
Martin Gavalec

Hybrid Evolutionary – Tabu Search Algorithm for
Scheduling Multiple-Variant Tasks 380
Piotr Jedrzejowicz, Ewa Ratajczak, Henryk Szreder

Self-Adaptation in Evolutionary Design of Neural
Networks 382
Bohdan Macukow, Maciej Grzenda

Genetic Algorithms Efficiency in Neural Network Learning .. 384
Radosław Semkło, Zbigniew Światnicki

Using Genetic Algorithm for Fuzzy Filter Optimisation 386
Csaba Stupák, Stanislav Marchevský

An Approach to Mobile Robot Learning 388
Vladimir Golovko, Oleg Ignatiuk, Rauf Sadykhov

Reactive Agents Based Autonomous Transport System 390
Milan Schmotzer

Mathematical Notes on Neural Networks 392
Ivan Daňo

Entropy of Fuzzy Dynamical Systems 394
Beloslav Riečan

Neural Extension of Fuzzy Prolog 397
Martin Lieskovský

Part 1

Neural Networks

Discovering Common Features in Software Code Using Self-Organizing Maps

Alvin Chan and Tim Spracklen

Electronics Research Group, Engineering Department,
University of Aberdeen, Scotland AB24 3UE

Abstract: The self-organizing map is discussed as an unsupervised clustering method. Its ability to form clusters indicates similar features in a data set. Based on this property, it is demonstrated that a self-organizing map is capable of identifying features within software code by grouping procedures with similar properties together. This allows us to identify potential objects, abstract data types or classes. In experiments with a simulation package Pascal_SIM (a procedural oriented implementation) as the data set, features were identified and a feature matrix constructed that served as the input to the self-organizing map. The results obtained were clusters on the map that indicated procedures with similar features being grouped together. This demonstrates that the self-organizing map is potentially a viable tool in intelligently automating the discovery of common features and groupings within code.

1 Introduction

In today's age of software technology, organizations are forced to operate in the ever fast changing business environment. The systems that the organizations depend on are also dependent on the changes that keep them competitive and dynamic in the market. The sort of systems that are generally needed are driven by object oriented technology.

The object oriented platform is well known for its benefits in software maintenance, reusability and ability in identifying system objects in a natural sense. However, replacing legacy systems with a new object-oriented system poses issues that need addressing. A legacy or existing software is the result of large investments and possibly years of maintenance. Maintenance that has been carried out may not have any documentation relating to it. Even the original software may have no available documentation and the developers will probably no longer be available for consultation. Therefore the knowledge and expertise that is available to solve this problem is largely stored in the original code itself. Thus the fundamental starting point for any migration process is by identifying features that will help in a better understanding of the code in order to aid the reverse engineering process.

In this paper, we address the issue of not only extracting features but a way in which knowledge can be gained from these features in a manageable sense. We illustrate the feature identification process using a simulation package Pascal_SIM[3] which is a procedural oriented implementation as our test case. Based on the features identified, a feature matrix is constructed and used in the self-organizing map (SOM)[4] to identify groupings of procedures or functions that have similar features. These groupings provide valuable knowledge in identifying potential abstract data types, classes and objects. Thus the SOM provides a valuable insight into similar features within legacy code and allows a more manageable way in which knowledge can be gained from the code.

2 Related Work

In [2], the approach adopted is by identifying objects which are centered around persistent data stores (e.g. files and tables in a database) while programs and subroutines are candidates to implement the object methods. The assignment of programs and subroutines is done while minimising the coupling between the objects identified. The approach adopted was of a top-down one, where the system was analysed as a whole, by considering programs as single entities, then decomposing programs that cannot be associated as methods of a single object. A case study was done on a COBOL software system. In [9], they used a similar approach as well, their analysis tool, named OBAD, recovers abstract data types (ADTs) and object instances. This is done by using Abstract Syntax Tree representation of a program. Again, it is based on identifying objects which have persistent state and procedures that operate on this state.

The works described, are centered on the analysis of legacy code, and with rules and methods, decides on the potential objects identified. Nevertheless, some form of user intervention is required. The remaining parts of this paper, provides an alternative of grouping similar procedures together using the SOM and demonstrates the ability of the SOM to perform some of the tasks by replacing or aiding human intervention to make decisions on groupings of procedures or identification of classes within legacy applications.

3 Self-Organizing Map Approach

In our SOM approach to identifying common features, we began by constructing an appropriate input. A feature matrix was required as the input that was made up of features from the procedural code. In this study, the simulation package, Pascal_SIM, a procedural implementation was used as our test case.

3.1 Feature Identification

The first stage in determining similar procedures or functions, starts by identifying features. This poses the following questions:

- "What should be identified?"
- "How should the features identified be encoded in a manner that is suitable as the input for the SOM?" and
- "How could the procedural code be suitably represented in a feature matrix such that the representation is still valid?"

Inspired by the work done in digital libraries for software reuse and information retrieval [1][5][6][7][8], we have adopted a similar approach to creating a feature matrix. Although these works are centered on information retrieval, they are very similar in the work presented. In [1], they promote software reusability by using the SOM to address the issue of lack of appropriate methods and tools for representing reusable software. They demonstrated using UNIX commands and attributes, where a binary encoding scheme was used as the training input to the SOM. The trained SOM which showed the groupings of commands with similar properties, is then used to provide query results. Resulting in the return of commands that are most likely to match the query. A similar approach was done in [7], where DOS commands and a C++ library of classes were used as test cases. In both cases, they demonstrated the ability of structuring software libraries according to the similarities of the stored software components. In these works, the idea of grouping or structuring similar software components together, provided the inspiration of this paper in which, software structuring is studied using the SOM. Instead of organising software at the component level, we look at structuring software at the procedural level.

Retrieving relevant information from legacy code is the key process in enabling the SOM algorithm to work successfully. Therefore, this stage is deemed crucial for subsequent stages to work correctly. Four key elements are defined that needed to be identified and that contribute towards building up the feature matrix.

- Global variables used.
- Type casted variables used.
- Procedures called.
- Other procedures that used the procedure in question.

By analysis, and identifying the four key elements, abstract information for each individual procedure within the legacy code were identified.

The next step was to determine a suitable format in which the SOM algorithm would be able to handle and produce desirable results. In our test case, we identified 54 procedures/functions in the Pascal_SIM library with a total of 59 different features. Although, 54 procedures/functions were identified, only 49 of them were used. This was because the 6 procedures did not have any features that seem relevant to our feature matrix. Therefore, the size of the feature matrix was 49 by 59.

We adopted a binary approach to encoding the feature matrix that was used as the training data set for the SOM. Basically, a "1" is put in the vector element column if the associated feature is present in the procedure and a "0" otherwise. Each row coincides with one of the 49 procedures/functions and each column represents a feature extracted. An example is illustrated in table 1.

Table 1. Example of a Section of the Feature Matrix

category	procedure	entity	class_num	queue	make_queue
entity	make_class	0	0	1	1
queue	give	1	0	1	0
queue	take	1	0	1	0

3.2 Results

In our test case, a standard 10X10 single layer SOM was used to produce the results as shown in figures 1 and 2. Inspecting figure 1 manually, labeled with the procedures that fired neurons, it is noticeable that procedures with very similar features fired the same neuron.

Using the same map, but overlaid with labels of procedures according to their categories defined in the Pascal_SIM documentation in figure 2, shows indications of procedures performing similar functions being grouped together. This is an obvious visual case with procedures that are categorized under entity and queue.

rnd	normal negexp uniform sample	poisson	run		set_background reset_colors	gotoxy	write_entity		move_v move_h
log_normal					delay				write_queue
									write_block
make_histogram log_histogram			make_sim			make_bin acquire return		branch	
	reset_histogram								
print_histogram				enter_class	set_foreground		count		cause
make_sample			make_class_table					make_class	
make_streams			remove_entity			dis_entity			
		calendar_top picture					take_top	take_tail	
new_entity	sim_error initialize			make_queue empty		give_top give_tail			give take

Fig. 1. Standard SOM Labeled with Procedures

random_generator_streams (1)	samp_distribution (4)	samp_distribution (1)	simulation_executive (1)		screen_control (2)	screen_control (1)	visual_display (1)		visual_display (2)
samp_distribution (1)					visual_display (1)				visual_display (1)
									visual_display (1)
histogram (2)			timing_executive (1)			resource (3)		process_executive (1)	
	histogram (1)								
histogram (1)				visual_display (1)	screen_control (1)		entity (1)		timing_executive (1)
samp_distribution (1)			visual_display (1)					entity (1)	
random_generator_streams (1)			process_executive (1)			entity (1)			
		timing_executive (1) user_written_routines (1)					queue (1)	queue (1)	
entity (1)	error_messages (1) user_written_routines (1)			queue (2)		queue (2)			queue (2)

Fig. 2. Standard SOM Labeled with Categories

4 Discussion and Future Work

Based on the results obtained in 3.2, instead of having to make visual decisions based on the map, the process of automating the detection of closely related procedures can be done by calculating the euclidean distance between the fired neurons and finally, arranging them into their similar groups. These groups can then be classes, abstract data types or potential objects. The idea and motivation of this paper is to relieve the analyst the tedious work of grouping these procedures that are similar. An example of what a SOM system that groups procedures together might be is illustrated in figure 3.

Further research is required using SOMs in the area of software reverse engineering. To further this work presented, SOMs in different architectural structures, for example in its hierarchical form and how it may represent potential object classes in line with inheritance, could also be used.

5 Conclusion

In conclusion, this paper presents the idea of using SOMs in the area of software reverse engineering, where it can be used to aid a programmer in the reverse engineering process. This is done, by suggesting potential groups of procedures that could lead to objects, classes and abstract data types, based on their similarities. This idea, though trivial in its implementation, is presented in hope to stimulate further research into the use of SOMs in this area.

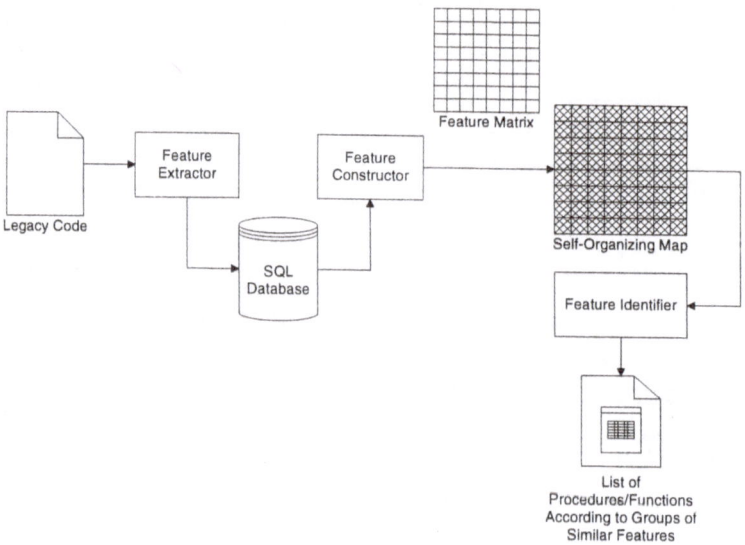

Fig. 3. SOM System to Group Similar Procedures

References

1. Sushil Acharya and R. Sadananda. Promoting software reuse using self organizing maps. *Neural Processing Letters*, 5(3):219–226, 1997.
2. A. Cimitile, A. De Lucia, G.A. di Lucca, and A.R. Fasolino. Identifying objects in legacy systems. In *5th International Workshop on Program Comprehension (WPC'97)*, Dearborn, MI, 1997. IEEE Computer.
3. Ruth Davies and Robert OKeefe. *Simulation Modelling with Pascal*. Prentice Hall International (UK) Ltd, 1989.
4. Teuvo Kohonen. *Self-Organizing Maps*. Information Sciences. Springer, second edition, 1997.
5. Dieter Merkl. Structuring software for reuse - the case of self-organizing maps. In *International Joint Conference on Neural Networks*, volume 3, pages 2468–2471, Nagoya Congress Center, Japan, 1993. IEEE.
6. Dieter Merkl. Self-organizing maps and software reuse. *Computational Intelligence in Software Engineering, World Scientific*, 1998.
7. Dieter Merkl, A Min Tjoa, and Gerti Kappel. Structuring a library of reusable software components using an artificial neural network. In *2nd International Conference on Achieving Quality in Software*, pages 169–180, Venice, Italy, 1993.
8. Dieter Merkl, A Min Tjoa, and Gerti Kappel. A self-organizing map that learns the semantic similiarity of reusable software components. In *5th Australian Conference on Neural Networks (ACNN'94)*, pages 13–16, Brisbane, Australia, 1994.
9. Alexander S. Yeh and David R. Harris. Recoverying abstract data types and object instances from a conventional procedural language. In *2nd Working Conference on Reverse Engineering (WCRE'95)*, pages 227–236, Toronto Ontario, Canada, 1995. IEEE Computer Society.

Graded Signal Functions for ARTMAP Neural Networks

Norbert Kopčo and Gail A. Carpenter

Department of Cognitive and Neural Systems, Boston University
677 Beacon St., Boston, MA 02215, USA
{kopco, gail}@cns.bu.edu

Abstract. This study presents an analysis of a modified ARTMAP neural network in which a graded signal function replaces the standard choice-by-difference function. The modifications are introduced mathematically and the performance of the system is studied on two benchmark examples. It is shown that the modified ARTMAP system achieves classification accuracy superior to that of standard ARTMAP, while retaining comparable complexity of the internal code.

Keywords. ARTMAP, fast learning, graded signal function, neural network

1 Introduction

Adaptive Resonance Theory (ART) was introduced by Grossberg [1] as a theory of human cognitive information processing. Based on the theory, a series of real-time neural network architectures for unsupervised and supervised learning have been developed. These networks combine fast learning with stable category coding and are a suitable tool for many pattern recognition problems. The ART models for unsupervised learning include ART 1, ART 2, fuzzy ART, and distributed ART. ARTMAP, a family of supervised ART architectures developed for classification problems, includes the fuzzy ARTMAP and distributed ARTMAP neural networks. A collection of papers on ART models can be found in [2], and more recent models are summarized in [3].

The present paper focuses on the process of search for a best category code in response to a given input in ARTMAP networks. Specifically, a new signal function is proposed that enables the system to find near-optimum discrimination curves between categories in complex input space. The modified signal function is introduced mathematically, then evaluated by implementing it in a fuzzy ARTMAP system and analyzing its performance on two benchmark problems.

2 Description of Fuzzy ARTMAP Dynamics

This section gives a brief summary of the fuzzy ARTMAP [4] algorithm. The **inputs** of the fuzzy ARTMAP system are usually normalized by complement coding, which converts an M-dimensional input vector $a = (a_1,...,a_M)$ $(0 \leq a_i \leq 1)$ into $2M$-dimensional input pattern $I = (a, 1-a) = (a_1,..., a_M, 1-a_1,...,1-a_M)$. The pattern is normalized since $|I| = M$, where $|I| \equiv \sum_{i=1}^{2M} |I_i|$ is the city-block norm.

When a new input is presented, the system **searches** for a candidate coding node within its coding layer. In ART systems, the j-th coding node defines a hyper-rectangle R_j, or *coding box*, in the M-dimensional input space, described by the weights $w_{i,j}$ leading to that node. The hyper-rectangle reduces to a rectangle in two dimensions or to an interval in one dimension (Figure 1). For every input pattern, the ARTMAP search mechanism chooses the smallest coding box that is covering the input, or the box that is closest to the input, based on the activation of the *choice-by-difference* (CBD) signal function T_j [5], now used in a majority of simulations. The CBD signal function is defined as:

$$T_j = M(2-\alpha) - d(R_j, a) - \alpha |R_j| = |w_j \wedge I| + (1-\alpha)(2M - |w_j|). \quad (1)$$

In this equation, α is a parameter (usually $\alpha = 0^+$), $d(R_j, a)$ represents the city-block distance from the input pattern a to the coding box R_j, and $|R_j|$ represents the size of R_j. The J-th coding node is chosen as a candidate code if its signal function T_J has the maximum value.

The candidate node is then compared with the input pattern according to a **match rule**. The candidate **resonates** if $|I \wedge w_J| > \rho |I|$; or it is **reset** if the inequality does not hold, where $\rho \in [0,1]$ is called a *vigilance* parameter. If reset occurs, a search for a new candidate is initiated, or a new coding node is created. If the candidate node resonates, the system checks whether the node is associated with the correct output class (always satisfied for new nodes). If the node is associated with an incorrect category, a process of **match tracking** is initiated, i.e., ρ is increased just enough so that the current candidate will not resonate any more and a search for a new candidate is initiated.

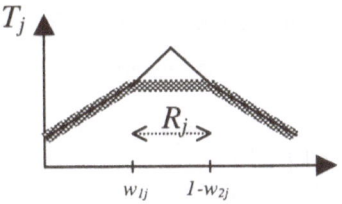

T_j

R_j

w_{1j} $1-w_{2j}$

Figure 1 Choice signal for standard CBD ($\overset{***}{}$) vs. graded CBD ($-$) in one input dimension

Once a coding node is found that satisfies all the requirements, **learning** is initiated that updates all the weights leading to the J-th node, defined by

$$w_J^{(new)} = \beta\left(I \wedge w_J^{(old)}\right) + (1-\beta)w_J^{(old)}. \tag{2}$$

Fast learning is usually chosen, obtained by setting $\beta=1$.

3 Definition of Graded Signal Functions

In general, the ARTMAP search for the internal code that best matches the presented input pattern can be accomplished by choosing one of many different signal functions, used to determine the activation of the coding nodes. Most current ARTMAP systems use the *choice-by-difference* signal function (CBD, [5]), which implements the idea of minimum fast learning. For the CBD function the signal is independent of the position of the input pattern if the input is located within the coding box, as shown for one dimension in Figure 1. In the present paper, a new signal function is introduced, called a *graded choice-by-difference* function, or graded CBD, which makes the choice signal dependent on the input position even when the input lies within the category box. Namely, an input near the center of the box R_j generates a larger signal T_j than an input near the boundary of the box (Figure 1).

The activation in the graded CBD signal function is defined by:

$$T_j = M(2-\alpha) - d(R_j, a) - \alpha\left|R_j\right|(1-\eta\gamma_j) \tag{3}$$

where η is a parameter that defines by how much the activation at the center of the box is increased relative to the box boundaries. When $\eta=0$, graded CBD reduces to standard CBD (1). In (3), γ_j specifies the minimum of graded activations across dimensions $i=1...M$:

$$\gamma_j = \min_{i=1..M}\left[1-\left[\frac{2\left|a_i - c_{j,i}\right|}{1 - w_{j,i+M} - w_{j,i}}\right]^+\right]^+ \tag{4}$$

In (4), $c_{j,i} \equiv (1 - w_{j,i+M} + w_{j,i})/2$ denotes the center of the j-th coding box in the i-th dimension, and $\left[a\right]^+ \equiv \max(a,0)$ is a rectification operator. Note that $\gamma_j = 1$ at the center of R_j and $\gamma_j = 0$ at any point a on the boundary of R_j. In order to ensure that the same input would choose the same category if it were immediately re-presented (direct access), the ART match rule was also modified, to better correspond to the new choice rule. In addition to the match criterion defined above, the new match rule essentially simulates the process of weights-update (2) followed by re-presentation of the current input. Then, the J-th node resonates only if the simulated update led to the desired choice of the winning node by direct access. The resulting graded signal function system has the capacity to create more accurate decision boundaries, especially when these boundaries are not parallel to the input space axes (Figure 2).

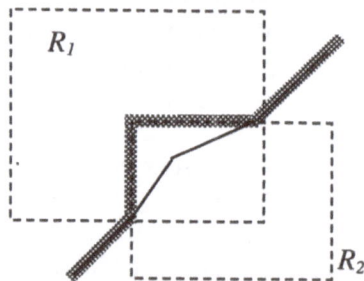

Figure 2 Decision boundaries between two category boxes (R_1 and R_2) with standard CBD (▦) vs. graded CBD (—)

4 Results on Benchmark Data and Discussion

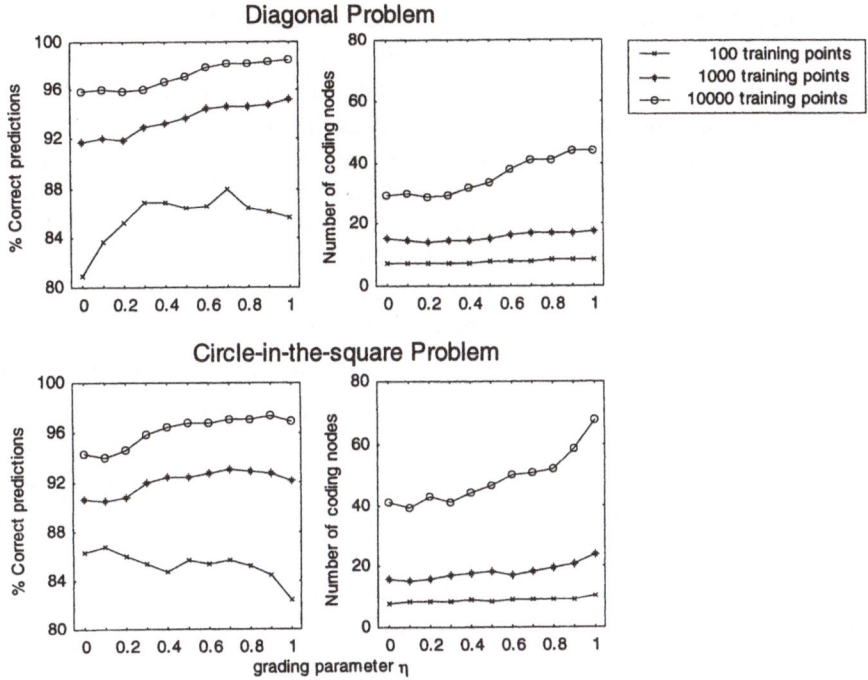

Figure 3 Simulations of fuzzy ARTMAP with standard CBD ($\eta=0$) and with graded CBD signal function ($\eta>0$). The upper row shows results of simulations with the diagonal data set, the lower row contains data for circle-in-the-square simulations

The performance of a fuzzy ARTMAP system with the graded CBD signal rule was evaluated on two benchmark problems, the circle-in-the-square (CIS) problem and a diagonal problem. Data sets for both problems consist of 2-dimensional uniformly distributed points, with the values in each dimension ranging from 0 to 1. Each data set has two output classes. In CIS, a point $a=(a_1,a_2)$ is in the class C_{out} if $(a_1 - 0.5)^2 + (a_2 - 0.5)^2 > \dfrac{1}{2\pi}$, otherwise it is from the class C_{in}. In the diagonal data set a point is from the class C_{lower} if $a_1>a_2$, otherwise it is from the class C_{upper}. Simulations with training sets of different sizes (100,

1000, or 10,000 points) were performed. The testing set size was fixed to 10,000 points.

The results of simulations of the two benchmark problems are shown in Figure 3, which shows percent correct predictions and number of coding nodes as functions of the value of the graded signal parameter η. In the graphs, $\eta=0$ corresponds to the standard CBD rule. Each point in Figure 3 corresponds to an average of 10 simulations with randomized order of inputs. For each of the conditions, application of the graded signal function led to improved performance, accompanied in some conditions by a slight increase in the internal code complexity. This improvement is mainly due to the improved ability of the new signal function to approximate decision boundaries not parallel to the axes of input feature space (Figure 2).

These results indicate that ARTMAP systems with the graded CBD signal rule can be used for many types of pattern recognition problems, especially when the data from individual classes are not easily separable, which may lead to many overlapping category boxes. More simulations are necessary, especially with noisy data, to better understand the behavior of the system in complex environments.

[This research was supported by grants from the Office of Naval Research and the Defense Advanced Research Projects Agency (ONR N00014-95-1-0409 and ONR N00014-1-95-0657).]

References

1. Grossberg, S. (1976) Adaptive pattern recognition and universal recoding, II. Feedback, expectation, olfaction, and illusions. Biological Cybernetics. **23**, 187-202

2. Carpenter, G.A., Grossberg, S. (1991) Pattern Recognition by Self-Organizing Neural Networks. M. I. T. Press, Cambridge Massachusetts

3. Carpenter, G.A., Milenova, B.L., Noeske, B.W. (1998) Distributed ARTMAP: a neural network for fast distributed supervised learning. Neural Networks. **11**, 793-813

4. Carpenter, G.A., Grossberg, S., Markuzon, N., Reynolds, J.H., and Rosen, D.B. (1992) Fuzzy ARTMAP: A Neural Network Architecture for Incremental Supervised Learning of Analog Multidimensional Maps. IEEE Transactions on Neural Networks, **3**: 698-713.

5. Carpenter, G.A., Gjaja M.N. (1994) Fuzzy ART choice functions. In Proceedings of The World Congress on Neural Networks (WCNN). **4**, 133-142

Incremental Approximation by Layer Neural Networks

Gabriela Andrejková

P. J. Šafárik University, Faculty of Science
Department of Computer Science, Jesenná 5,
041 54 Košice, Slovakia

Abstract: We study incremental algorithms operating on one- and two-hidden-layer neural networks with linear output units in such way that in each iteration, some new hidden units are put in the first or in the second hidden layer. The weight parameters of the new units are determined and output weights of all units are re-calculated. We apply the algorithms to the special class of functions (for predictions of geomagnetic storms). [1]

1 Introduction

Kůrková [5] showed that assumption that the activation function is essentially Heaviside is necessary and gave examples of functions that can be approximated with any accuracy by networks with a fixed number of hidden units heaving a differentiable activation function. In [7], [8] has introduced concept of variations with respect to a family of functions and characterized sets of functions of d variables, for which incremental approximants converge with with bounded rate independently of the number of variables.

Kůrková and Beliczynski [6] developed incremental algorithms operating on one-hidden-layer neural networks with a linear output unit in such a way that in each iteration, parameters of one new hidden unit are determined and output weights for all hidden units are calculated. It means, any $\mathcal{L}_2$-function f ($|f|^2$ has the integral on the set X with $\mathcal{L}_p$ norm: $\|f\| = \left[\int_{x \in X} |f(x)|^p dx \right]^{\frac{1}{p}}$) can be approximated within any accuracy by a sufficiently large networks.

Beliczynski [3] presented an incremental algorithm of discrete functions approximations by using one-hidden-layer neural networks, where functions were represented by a set of $(input, output)$ pairs.

In our paper, we describe approximations of *special class of functions* which are interesting in practice (e. g. physics - predictions of geomagnetic storms, Andrejková, Azorová, Kudela [1]) according to neuron numbers in hidden layers of neural networks. Incremental algorithms are used in two phases: (1) for the approximation of functions from some subset of $C_s \langle a, b \rangle^d$ and (2) for the approximation of the rest functions from $C_s \langle a, b \rangle^d$ on the base of results in the step (1).

---

[1] This research was supported by Slovak Grant Agency for Science VEGA, project No. 1/7557/20

2 Basic definitions

Let $C_s\langle a, b\rangle^d$ will be the class of functions. Function $f \in C_s\langle a, b\rangle^d$ if fulfills the following properties:

- f is defined in bounded interval $\langle a, b\rangle^d, a, b \in \mathcal{R}$,
- f, f' are continuous in $\langle a, b\rangle^d$,
- f has a minimum $c_{min} \in \langle a, b\rangle^d$,
- $f(c_{min}) \geq M_{min}, M_{min} \in \mathcal{R}$,
- $f(x) \leq M_{max}, M_{max} \in \mathcal{R}$,
- $f(x)$ is decreasing in $\langle c_t, c_{min}\rangle^d, c_t \in (a, c_{min})^d$

$C_s\langle a, b\rangle^d$ is a subset of all continuous functions $C\langle a, b\rangle^d$ and $C_s\langle a, b\rangle^d$ is not linear subspace of $C\langle a, b\rangle^d$. We will work with the interval $\langle a, b\rangle^d$ but if is it necessary then $\langle a, b\rangle^d$ will be transformed to the interval $\langle 0, 1\rangle$.

The convergence results will be stated for inner product spaces and applied to Hilbert space $\mathcal{L}_2(J^d)$, where J^d is a closed d-dimensional cube. J denotes the interval $\langle 0, 1\rangle$ and $\mathcal{N}$ denotes the set of positive integers. Let $(\mathcal{X}, \cdot)$ be a real linear space with an inner product and let $\|\cdot\|$ denote the norm induced by this inner product and let $\mathcal{G}$ be subset of $\mathcal{X}$ and n be a positive integer. We denote by $conv_n(\mathcal{G})$ the set of all convex combinations of n elements of $\mathcal{G}$, i. e. $conv_n \mathcal{G} = \{\sum_{i=1}^{n} a_i g_i; (\forall i = 1, \ldots, n)(a_i \in J \& g_i \in \mathcal{G}) \& \sum_{i=1}^{n} a_i = 1\}$, by $conv(\mathcal{G})$ convex hull of $\mathcal{G}$ and by $cl(conv(\mathcal{G}))$ the convex closure of $\mathcal{G}$, i.e. the closure with respect to the topology induced by norm $\|\cdot\|$ of the convex hull of $\mathcal{G}$.

Let $f \in \mathcal{X}$. We call a sequence $\{f_n; n \in \mathcal{N}_+\} \subset \mathcal{X}$ G-incremental convex approximations of f if the following recursion is satisfied:

(i) $f_1 = g_1, g_1 \in \mathcal{G}$,
(ii) $f_n = (1 - a_n)f_{n-1} + a_n g_n$ where $a_n \in J$ and $g_n \in \mathcal{G}$

For $f \in \mathcal{X}$ we call a sequence of $\mathcal{G}$-incremental approximants *best, nearly best,* resp. $\mathcal{G}$-incremental approximants of f, if in each iteration the parameters $w_{n1}, \ldots, w_{nn}$ and $g_n \in \mathcal{G}$ are chosen to minimize, almost minimize, resp. $\|f - f_n\|$, i.e. $\|f - f_n\| = min\{\|f - (1 - a)f_{n-1} - ag\|$, $\|f - f_n\| \leq inf\{\|f - (1 - a)f_{n-1} - ag\|, a \in I, g \in \mathcal{G}\} + \varepsilon_n$, where $lim_{n\to\infty}\varepsilon_n = 0$, and the recursion is initialized by $f_1 = g_1$, where $g_1 \in \mathcal{G}$ is chosen to satisfy $\|f - f_1\| \leq inf\{\|f - g\|; g \in \mathcal{G}\} + \varepsilon_1$.

Jones's result on incremental approximations was improved by Barron [2], [4] and it can be formulated as follows:

Let $(\mathcal{X}, \|\cdot\|)$ be a Hilbert space, B a positive real number and $\mathcal{G}$ a subset of $\mathcal{X}$ such that for every $g \in \mathcal{G}$ $\|g\|_2 \leq B(\|\cdot\|_2$ is Euclidean norm), $f \in cl(conv(\mathcal{G})), c > B^2 - \|f\|_2^2$ and $\{f_n; n \in \mathcal{N}_+\}$ be a sequence of nearly best $\mathcal{G}$ incremental convex approximant of f with tolerance $\{\varepsilon_n; n \in \mathcal{N}_+\}$ satisfying for each $n \in \mathcal{N}_+$ $\varepsilon_n \leq \frac{\delta c}{n(n+\delta)}$, where $\delta = \frac{c}{B^2 - \|f\|_2^2} - 1$. Then for every $n \in \mathcal{N}_+$ $\|f - f_n\|_2 \leq \sqrt{\frac{c}{n}}$.

3 Construction of convex incremental approximations

We describe *incremental algorithms*, the design which is based on the proofs of
Jones and Jones-Barron theorems. The algorithms will have some properties
they follow from properties of the given class of functions.

Let $C_s \langle a, b \rangle^d = \bigcup_{j=1}^{2} CN_s^j \langle a, b \rangle^d, CN_s^1 \langle a, b \rangle^d \cap CN_s^2 \langle a, b \rangle^d = \emptyset$.

The partition into two above described classes is done on the base of the
following ideas:

(a) The functions in $C_s \langle a, b \rangle^d$ are presented as measured values in given
points, e.g. (*input, output*) pairs. It should be better to have their analytical expressions or a computation model that computes them (for
example, a neural network). Along the modeling of the neural networks
can be established the class $C_s^1 \langle a, b \rangle^d$. It will be established according to
condition for the number of units in the first hidden layer.

(b) If we have the analytical expressions for functions or we have neural
networks for the approximation of functions in $C_s^1 \langle a, b \rangle^d$ then it is possible
to use the results of Jones-Barron theorem to construct a neural network
for computation of the convex hull of $C_s^1 \langle a, b \rangle^d$ (or convex hull of some
subset of $C_s^1 \langle a, b \rangle^d$ according to given conditions).

According to previous definitions and results we will present:

- The incremental algorithm $\mathcal{A}_1$ with the restricted number of units in the
first hidden layer to the subclass $C_s^1 \langle a, b \rangle^d$ as can be seen in Figure a). The
neural network NN_f^1 will be developed to each function $f \in C_s^1 \langle a, b \rangle^d$.
The NN_f^1 computes the function $\overline{f}$ that is an approximating function for
f with some accuracy.
- The incremental algorithm $\mathcal{A}_2$ for computing of convex hull of functions
in $\mathcal{G}^2 = \{\overline{f} : \overline{f} \text{ is computed by } NN_f^1\}$ as can be seen in Figure b). $f \in$
$cl(conv(\mathcal{G}^2))$ will be approximated by $\{f_n; n \in \mathcal{N}_+\}$ according to Jones-
Barron theorem.
- The relation between $cl(conv(\mathcal{G}^2))$ and $C_s^2 \langle a, b \rangle^d$.

3.1 Algorithm $\mathcal{A}_1$.

Input to the algorithm is the function $f \in C_s \langle a, b \rangle^d$ presented as the set of
pairs $\{(\overline{x}^1, f(\overline{x}^1)), \dots, (\overline{x}^r) f(\overline{x}^r))\}, \overline{x}^k = (x_1^k, \dots, x_d^k)$, the values $0 \leq f(\overline{x}) \leq$
1, r is the number of training values.

We suppose that $B_{max} = max\{\|f\|, f \in C_s \langle a, b \rangle^d\}$ and $B = \frac{B_{max}}{2}$. $\mathcal{G}^1$ will
be the set of functions which will be used for an incremental approximation
in the first step, $\mathcal{G}^1 = \{g_j^1; \|g_j^1\| \leq B, g_j^1(\overline{x}) = \sum_{i=1}^{d} w_i^j x_i), j = 1, 2, \dots\}$ (g_j^1 is
the function computed by one unit).

Let β be the value for an accuracy of approximation, it means we require
$\|f - f_m\| \leq \beta$ for the maximal number of units N. The following relation has
to be fulfilled: $B^2 < \beta^2 \cdot N$.

18

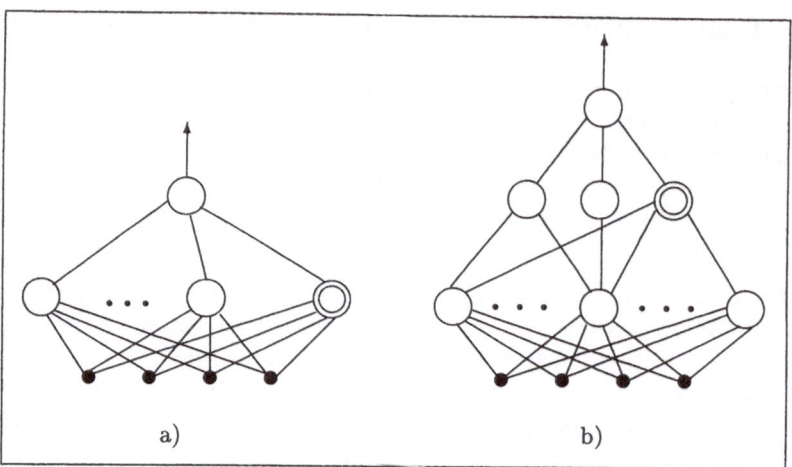

Fig. 1. The structure of a) one-hidden-layer incremental algorithms, b) two-hidden-layer incremental algorithms.

The algorithm works in the following steps (developes the NN_f^1 which computes $\overline{f}$ to the function f):

1. $f_1 := g_1^1; n := 2;$
2. while $n \leq N$ do
3. begin
4.   select $\{g_n^1$ from $\mathcal{G}^1; a_n$ from $J\};$
         {The main problem is in the selection of a_n and g_n^1}
5. $f_n := (1 - a_n)f_{n-1} + a_n g_n^1;$
         {It means that the previous weights will be corrected too.}
6. end;

The step for the selection of $\{g_n^1$ from $\mathcal{G}^1; a_n$ from $J\}$ gives the space for heuristics. We use one of them:

- g_n^1 to select according to inequality $\|f_{n-1} - g_n\| > \|f - f_{n-1}\|$
- $a_n \geq \frac{\|f - f_{n-1}\|}{\|f_{n-1} - g_n^1\|}$

3.2 Algorithm $\mathcal{A}_2$.

Let $f \in C_s^2 \langle a, b \rangle^d$. We would like for f to be in the convex hull of functions in $\mathcal{G}^2 = NN_f^1$. It means the neural network NN_f^2 with two hidden layers will be developed on the base of functions in $\mathcal{G}^2$.

The function $f \in C_s^2 \langle a, b \rangle^d$ is the input to the algorithm $\mathcal{A}_2$. f is proposed by the set of pairs as in the algorithm $\mathcal{A}_1$. $\mathcal{G}^2 = \{g_j^2; \|g_j^2\| \leq B, g_j^2 \in NN_f^1\}$, β is an accuracy of approximation, e. g. $\|f - f_m\| \leq \beta$ for some current number of units in the second hidden layer.

The algorithm can be described in the following steps:

1. $f_1 := g_1^2; n := 2; q := true;$
2. while q and $(n \leq M)$ do
3. begin
4.   if selection for g_n^2 does not exist then $q := false$ else
5.   begin select $\{g_n^2$ from $\mathcal{G}^2; a_n$ from $J\};$
          {*The main problem is in the selection of a_n and g_n^2*}
6. $f_n := (1 - a_n)f_{n-1} + a_n g_n^2;$
          {*It means that the previous weights will be corrected too.*}
7.   end
8. end;

The step for selection can be applied on the base of the previous heuristic but the selection should be unsuccessful, because the function $g \in \mathcal{G}^2$ may not exist. In the case, the following two possibilities exist:

- to be satisfy with the current accuracy for the function f (but it breaks our requirements), or
- to put some new functions (one-hidden-layer networks) to $C_s^1 \langle a, b \rangle^d$ (but it should increase B and N).

3.3 The relation between $C_s \langle a, b \rangle^d$ and $cl(conv(\mathcal{G}^2))$

$f \in C_s^1 \langle a, b \rangle^d$ implies $f \in cl(conv(\mathcal{G}^2))$. It should be constructed the two-hidden-layer neural network NN_f^2 (which computes an approximating function $\overline{f}$) to each $f \in C_s^2 \langle a, b \rangle^d$ but sometimes with the lower accuracy than we required.

4 Results of the application

Practical results of the first algorithm $\mathcal{A}_1$ application show that for the approximation of some $f \in C_s \langle a, b \rangle^d$ is necessary to use too big number of neurons in the hidden layer as it is shown in Table 1). In *the application of the algorithms for the prediction of Geomagnetic Storms (GMS)*. As a first step, we try to predict the GMS in time interval $\langle t, t + q \rangle$ for $q = 4$ by one-hidden layer network.

The developed networks have been used for GMS predictions with input parameters n, v, B_z and σ_{B_z} (n – the plasma density of solar wind, v – the bulk velocity of solar wind, B_z – z-component of the interplanetary magnetic field, σ_{B_z} – the fluctuation of B_z). To prepare the training and testing samples we used the data from years 1980 and 1981, because we had the continued values of parameters n, v, B_z, σ_{B_z} and D_{st}, which are measured at each hour and relatively few measured values were missing.

Results of the preparing phase: We used $d = 32, \beta = 0.05$. The numbers of neurons in the one-hidden-layer networks for the chosen functions are in the

Table 1. *The results of the incremental algorithm $\mathcal{A}^1$ to develop one-hidden-layer networks*

Numbers of units	Success in 1980	Success in 1981
33	28%	31%
52	45%	43%
72	55%	63%
98	82%	75%
116	82%	81%

first column of Table 1. The success of the prediction (approximation) of the rest functions are in the second and third column of Table 1.

On the base of the results in Table 1 we decided to choose the value N from interval $70 - 80$. For the approximation the rest function will be used second algorithm $\mathcal{A}_2$ and approximation will be done by two-hidden-layer neural network, where the subclass $C_s^I \langle a, b \rangle^d$ constructed by the algorithm $\mathcal{A}_1$ is the base of functions for the algorithm $\mathcal{A}_2$. The new computed results are much better than results computed for $N = 32$ and $M = 29$ in [1].

References

1. Andrejková, G., Azorová, J., Kudela, K.: Artificial neural networks in prediction of D_{st} Index. Proceedings of the 1-th Slovak Neural Networks Symposium, Vol. II, Herlany, 1996, 51–59
2. Barron, A. R. (1993) Universal approximation bounds for superposition of sigmoidal function. IEEE Transactions on Information Theory **39**, 930–945
3. Beliczynski, B. (1996): An almost analytical design of incremental discrete functions approximation by one-hidden-layer neural networks. In Proceedings of WCNN'96, 988-991, Lawrence Erlbaum, San Diego.
4. Jones, L. K. (1992) A simple lemma on greedy approximation in Hilbert space and convergence rates for projection pursuit regression and neural network training. Annual of Statistics, **20**, 608–613
5. Kůrková, V. (1995) Approximation of Functions by Perceptron Networks with Bounded Number of Hidden Units, Neural Networks, Vol. 8, No. 5, 745–750
6. Kůrková, V., Beliczynski, B. (1995) Incremental approximation by one-hidden-layer neural networks. In proceedings of ICANN'95, pp. I.505-510, Paris: EC2& Cie.
7. Kůrková, V. (1998) Incremental approximation by neural networks. In *Complexity: Neural Network Approach*. Eds. K. Warwick, M. Kárny, V. Kůrková, Springer, 177-188.
8. Kůrková, V. (2000) Incremental Approximation by Neural Networks, Proceedings of NC'2000, Berlin, p. 12.

Efficient Training of MLP with Training Step Rate Estimation

Vladimir Golovko[1], Yury Savitsky[1], Theodore Laopoulos[2], Anatoly Sachenko[3], Lucio Grandinetti[4]

[1] National Academy of Sciences, Belarus, cm@brpi.belpak.brest.by

[2] Aristotle University of Thessaloniki, Greece, laopoulos@physics.auth.gr

[3] Ternopil Academy of National Economy, Ukraine,sachenko@cit.tane.ternopil.ua

[4] University of Calabria, Italy, lugran@unical.it

Abstract: A new computational technique for training of multilayer feed-forward neural networks with sigmoid activation function of the units is proposed. The proposed algorithm consists two phases. The first phase is an adaptive training step calculation, which implements the steepest descent method in the weight space. The second phase is estimation of calculated training step rate, which provide reach a state of activity of the units on the each training iteration. The simulation results are provided for the test example to demonstrate the efficiency of the proposed method, which solves the problem of training step choice in multilayer perceptrons.

Keywords: Multilayer Perceptrons, Backpropagation, Adaptive Training Step

1   Introduction

Multilayer perceptrons (MLP) form a wide set of feed-forward neural networks. They have a wide variety of applications in different areas: classification, control, pattern recognition, function approximation, prediction etc. Adaptability of the neural models for any application provides by training procedures. The most commonly training methods in MLP is error backpropagation (BP) algorithm [2], [3]. In spite of the fact that BP is successfully used for various kind of tasks, it have lacks such as slow convergence, non-stability of convergence and local minimum problems [4].

In this paper a new method is developed for efficient training of MLP by combining BP, adaptive training step calculation (ATS) technique [1] and training step size estimation (SSE) method. The ATS is used to find an optimal training step, which minimizes the neural unit training error. The SSE is used to validation the training step size for guaranteeing of neural unit training adaptability. This technique along with BP allows to solve the problems of optimal learning rate choice and to advance of MLP adaptability.

2 Using the ATS Technique in Back Propagation for MLP Training

The most popular training algorithm for MLP is BP and is described in brief with the following notations.

$y_j^{[l]}$ Output of the j th unit in layer l.

$S_j^{[l]}$ Weighted sum of input activity of the j th unit in layer l.

$w_{ij}^{[l]}$ Weight connecting i th unit in layer $l-1$ to j th unit in layer l.

x^p Input p th training sample.

d^p Desired p th training sample.

L Number of layers.

N^l Number of units in layer l.

P Number of training patterns.

t Number of current training iteration.

In this notations $w_{0j}^{[l]}$ represents weight connecting i th unit in the bias layer to j th unit in layer l and $y_0^{[l-1]} = -1$.

BP implements a gradient search technique to find the network weights, that minimizes the squared error function given below:

$$E(t) = \sum_{p=1}^{P} E^p(t) = \sum_{p=1}^{P} \sum_{k=1}^{N^{[L]}} \left(y_k^{[L]}(t) - d_k^{[L]} \right)^2 \tag{1}$$

The weights of MLP are updated iteratively according to following rule:

$$w_{ij}^{[l]}(t+1) = w_{ij}^{[l]}(t) - \alpha \frac{\partial E^p}{\partial w_{ij}^{[l]}}, \quad \frac{\partial E^p}{\partial w_{ij}^{[l]}} = \frac{\partial E^p}{\partial y_j^{[l]}} \frac{\partial y_j^{p,[l]}}{\partial S_j^{p,[l]}} \frac{\partial S_j^{p,[l]}}{\partial w_{ij}^{[l]}} = \gamma_j^{p,[l]} g'(S_j^{p,[l]}) y_i^{p,[l-1]}, \tag{2}$$

$\alpha > 0$ is a constant, called training step, and g is sigmoid activation function.

In BP there is a problem of choice of an optimal training step [5]. For choice of adaptive step it is possible to use a method of steepest descent [1]. According to it, the training step $\alpha^{p,[l]}(t)$ for layer l is selected by minimizing a square error $E^p(t)$ for training sample p as given below:

$$\alpha^{p,[l]}(t) = \min E^p(y_j^{p,[L]}(t+1)), \quad j = 1, N^{[L]} \tag{3}$$

The expression for ATS calculation, considered in [1], is follows:

$$\alpha^{p,[l]}(t) = \frac{\sum\limits_{j=1}^{N^{[l]}} (\gamma_j^{p,[l]})^2 g'(S_j^{p,[l]})}{g'(0) \cdot (1 + \sum\limits_{i=1}^{N^{[l-1]}} (y_i^{p,[l-1]})^2) \sum\limits_{j=1}^{N^{[l]}} \gamma_j^{p,[l]^2} (g'(S_j^{p,[l]}))^2} \tag{4}$$

In expression (4) was used decomposition of activation function g under the Tailor series and limitation by first two members. Therefore this is approximate method of ATS definition for nonlinear activation functions. For MLP efficient training using ATS it is necessary to limit the ATS size [1]. The limitation size is defined empirically. Therefore there is a problem to definition of acceptable bounds of the training step.

Let's consider the next problem connected with incorrect choice of the training step size. During training phase all neural units of MLP are divided on subset of neural units with small training efficiency and on subset of neural units with large training efficiency. The training efficiency for the neural unit j on the layer l is defined by size of activation function derivative $g'(S_j^{p,[l]})$. For sigmoid nonlinearity it is defined as

$$g'(S_j^{p,[l]}) = \frac{\partial y_j^{p,[l]}}{\partial S_j^{p,[l]}} = g(S_j^{p,[l]})(1 - g(S_j^{p,[l]})) = y_j^{p,[l]}(1 - y_j^{p,[l]}) \qquad (5)$$

When training step size is too large, it provides in the most cases to form output activity closely to 0 or to 1 for the next training iterations. In this cases there is reduction of training adaptability of this units, as $g'(S_j^{p,[l]}) \to 0, \Rightarrow \partial E^p / \partial w_{ij}^{[l]} \to 0.$

As result there is reduction of the training efficiency and reduction adaptability of MLP. For solving of described above problems consider below the developed in this paper the technique of ATS validation.

3 SSE Technique

As criterion for definition of acceptable bounds of the training step in this work is used minimum acceptable of activation function derivative rate ε. During the training it is necessary to provide the next inequality:

$$g'(S_j^{p,[l]}(t+1)) > \varepsilon \qquad (6)$$

Solve this inequality for sigmoid nonlinearity according $\alpha^{p,[l]}$:

$$y_j^{p,[l]}(t+1)(1 - y_j^{p,[l]}(t+1)) > \varepsilon \qquad (7)$$

where $y_j^{p,[l]}(t+1) = g\left(S_j^{p,[l]}(t+1)\right)$

Along the expression (7) we can get:

$$\frac{1}{2} - \frac{1}{2}\sqrt{1 - 4\varepsilon} < y_j^{p,[l]}(t+1) < \frac{1}{2} + \frac{1}{2}\sqrt{1 - 4\varepsilon} . \qquad (8)$$

As sigmoid function is increasing and monotonic, it is possible to transformation this inequality to the next form:

$$g^{[-1]}\left(\frac{1}{2} - \frac{1}{2}\sqrt{1 - 4\varepsilon}\right) < S_j^{p,[l]}(t+1) < g^{[-1]}\left(\frac{1}{2} + \frac{1}{2}\sqrt{1 - 4\varepsilon}\right), \tag{9}$$

where $g^{[-1]}$ is inverse function, defined as $g^{[-1]}(y) = \ln(y/(1-y))$
Then the expression (9) can be presented as follows:

$$\ln\frac{1 - \sqrt{1 - 4\varepsilon}}{1 + \sqrt{1 - 4\varepsilon}} < S_j^{p,[l]}(t+1) < \ln\frac{1 + \sqrt{1 - 4\varepsilon}}{1 - \sqrt{1 - 4\varepsilon}} \tag{10}$$

Final solving for inequality (6) is follows:

$$\begin{cases} \dfrac{S_j^{p,[l]}(t) - \ln\dfrac{1 - \sqrt{1 - 4\varepsilon}}{1 + \sqrt{1 - 4\varepsilon}}}{\displaystyle\sum_{i=0}^{N^{[l-1]}} y_i^{p,[l-1]}\dfrac{\partial E^p}{\partial w_{ij}^{[l]}}} > \alpha^{p,[l]}(t) > \dfrac{S_j^{p,[l]}(t) - \ln\dfrac{1 + \sqrt{1 - 4\varepsilon}}{1 - \sqrt{1 - 4\varepsilon}}}{\displaystyle\sum_{i=0}^{N^{[l-1]}} y_i^{p,[l-1]}\dfrac{\partial E^p}{\partial w_{ij}^{[l]}}}, & \text{if } \displaystyle\sum_{i=0}^{N^{[l-1]}} y_i^{p,[l-1]}\dfrac{\partial E^p}{\partial w_{ij}^{[l]}} > 0; \\[40pt] \dfrac{S_j^{p,[l]}(t) - \ln\dfrac{1 - \sqrt{1 - 4\varepsilon}}{1 + \sqrt{1 - 4\varepsilon}}}{\displaystyle\sum_{i=0}^{N^{[l-1]}} y_i^{p,[l-1]}\dfrac{\partial E^p}{\partial w_{ij}^{[l]}}} < \alpha^{p,[l]}(t) < \dfrac{S_j^{p,[l]}(t) - \ln\dfrac{1 + \sqrt{1 - 4\varepsilon}}{1 - \sqrt{1 - 4\varepsilon}}}{\displaystyle\sum_{i=0}^{N^{[l-1]}} y_i^{p,[l-1]}\dfrac{\partial E^p}{\partial w_{ij}^{[l]}}}, & \text{if } \displaystyle\sum_{i=0}^{N^{[l-1]}} y_i^{p,[l-1]}\dfrac{\partial E^p}{\partial w_{ij}^{[l]}} < 0. \end{cases} \tag{11}$$

Let's consider in detail application of the given expression for SSE. In (11) the expression $\displaystyle\sum_{i=0}^{N^{[l-1]}} y_i^{p,[l-1]}\dfrac{\partial E^p}{\partial w_{ij}^{[l]}}$ specifies the direction of gradient search for

$S_j^{p,[l]}$ during training. If $\displaystyle\sum_{i=0}^{N^{[l-1]}} y_i^{p,[l-1]}\dfrac{\partial E^p}{\partial w_{ij}^{[l]}} < 0$ this implyies that

$S_j^{p,[l]}(t) < S_j^{p,[l]}(t+1)$ and correspondingly that $y_j^{p,[l]}(t) < y_j^{p,[l]}(t+1)$
for unit j of layer l. In this case it is necessary to use the next limitation for
$\alpha^{p,[l]}(t)$:

$$\alpha^{p,[l]}(t) < \left(S_j^{p,[l]}(t) - \ln\frac{1 + \sqrt{1 - 4\varepsilon}}{1 - \sqrt{1 - 4\varepsilon}}\right) \Bigg/ \left(\sum_{i=0}^{N^{[l-1]}} y_i^{p,[l-1]}\frac{\partial E^p}{\partial w_{ij}^{[l]}}\right) \tag{12}$$

In other case, if $\displaystyle\sum_{i=0}^{N^{[l-1]}} y_i^{p,[l-1]}\dfrac{\partial E^p}{\partial w_{ij}^{[l]}} > 0$ then after next training iteration

$S_j^{p,[l]}(t) > S_j^{p,[l]}(t+1)$ and correspondingly $y_j^{p,[l]}(t) > y_j^{p,[l]}(t+1)$. In
this case it is necessary to use the next limitation for $\alpha^{p,[l]}(t)$:

$$\alpha^{p,[l]}(t) < \left(S_j^{p,[l]}(t) - \ln\frac{1 - \sqrt{1 - 4\varepsilon}}{1 + \sqrt{1 - 4\varepsilon}}\right) \Bigg/ \left(\sum_{i=0}^{N^{[l-1]}} y_i^{p,[l-1]}\frac{\partial E^p}{\partial w_{ij}^{[l]}}\right) \tag{13}$$

So, the SSE method includes the phase of analyzing of $\sum\limits_{i=0}^{N^{[l-1]}} y_i^{p,\,[l-1]}(\partial E^p / \partial w_{ij}^{[l]})$

and phase of application of expression (12) or (13) for ATS validation in BP.

4   Simulation Results and Discussion

To assess the performance of the proposed learning technique experiments were conducted on standard problems of parity. Here the output of the MLP is required to be '1' if the input pattern contains an odd number of '1' and '0' otherwise. In this problem the most similar patterns which differ by a single bit require different answer. For simulation a three-layer MLP of size 4-4-1 is considered. The training set contains 16 samples. Ten different series of experiments are considered for various training conditions. The simulation results demonstrate the efficiency of SSE technique for ATS validation in the BP computational algorithm (see Table below).

5   Conclusions

In this paper a new algorithm based on combining the adaptive training step technique and training step size estimation technique in backpropagation is proposed. The SSE is used to validation the training step size for guaranteeing of neural unit training adaptability. This technique along with BP allows to solve the problems of optimal learning rate choice and to advance of MLP adaptability. The testing example demonstrates efficiency of proposed method of the training step size estimation.

Table 1. Table showing the simulation results for various training conditions: 1) using constant training step; 2) using ATS technique with various constant limitations; 3) combining the ATS technique and SSE technique. NIT - number of training iterations; MSE - mean square error.

NIT	MSE	Type of training step	Size of the training step	ATS validation	ε
2010	0.0241	Constant	0.099	-	-
2350	0.0067	Constant	0.50	-	-
2140	0.0941	Constant	0.99	-	-
2500	0.091	ATS	-	<0.50	-
1990	0.078	ATS	-	<0.99	-
2090	0.0096	ATS	-	<1.99	-
2050	0.267	ATS	-	<2,50	-
2100	0.0052	ATS	-	SSE	0.099
2250	0.0051	ATS	-	SSE	0.05
2310	0.0292	ATS	-	SSE	0.0099

Acknowledgments

This paper is supported by INTAS program "INTAS OPEN 97-0606". The authors express gratitude to the European Union for financial support.

References

[1] Vladimir Golovko, Yury Savitsky, "New Approach of the recurrent Neural Network Training", Proc. of the Int. Conf. on Neural Networks and Artificial Intelligence ICNNAI'99, 12-15 October 1999, Brest, Belarus, - pp. 32-35

[2] G. E. Hinton, "How neural networks learn from experience," *Sci. Amer.,* pp. 145-151, Sept. 1992.

[3] D. E. Rumelhart, G. E. Hinton, and R. J. Williams, "Learning representations by backpropagating errors," *Nature,* vol. 323, pp. 533-536, 1986.

[4] R. Beale and T. Jackson, *Neural Computing: An Introduction.* Bristol, U.K.: Inst. Phys., 1992.

[5] X.-H. Yu and G.-A. Chen, "Efficient backpropagation learning using optimal learning rate and momentum." *Neural Networks,* vol. 10, no. 3, pp. 517-527, 1997.

Self-Organizing Maps for Representing Structures

Igor Farkaš

Institute of Measurement Science, Slovak Academy of Sciences, Bratislava, Slovak Republic

Abstract: We propose a novel neural network model for representing data structures. The model consists of a hierarchy of Self-Organizing Maps (SOMs) equipped with leaky integrating units. Each of the maps is thus designed to represent sequences of data in a fashion resembling Barnsley's iterated function system. Each data structure is decomposed into a hierarchy of sequences where in all but the lowest levels a special symbol is substituted to represent corresponding subtrees. The advantage of this representation is that it is directly computable, and if neurally implemented using SOMs, it is computationally unexpensive. Preliminary simulations using simple symbolic tree structures demonstrate that obtained representations have the required property of systematic order.

1 Introduction

In most artificial intelligence tasks such as language processing and reasoning the need arises to represent data structures such as sequences and trees. Originally, these tasks were predominantly tackled using symbolic approaches, while neural networks were claimed to lack this representation power [1]. However, to face this critisism, during the last decade a number of architectures and algorithms were designed demonstrating the capability of connectionist approaches to generate structured representations as well. The best known examples include recursive autoassociative memory [2], tensor-product-based approaches [3,4] and systems using synchrony of firing to perform binding [5,6].

In this paper, we propose an alternative structure-representing model which incorporates the concept of *self-organization* (SR-SOM). It is based on a hierarchy of modified self-organizing maps with leaky integrating units. The key idea is that each data structure is decomposed (using some external parsing module) into a hierarchy of sequences each of which is represented separately in a map.

First we describe how symbolic sequences can be represented and learnt using the SOM. In recent years, there have appeared various attempts to enhance the standard, static map with ability to represent sequences of data. Existing approches can be classified into two groups.

The first group can be characterized as a *sequence mapping* by SOM, where every sequence of input patterns becomes represented by a subsequent firing of winners in the map. In proposed models (e.g. [7–9]), due to distributed representation of a sequence, the SOM units themselves do not become sequence recognizers, however.

The second group was introduced by Kohonen as *operator SOMs*, where each unit serves as a sequence processor (operator). In addition, neighboring units in the map are supposed to be sensitive to similar sequences (according to some similarity measure). In our approach, we employed *leaky integrator* SOM units, which were previously shown to be capable of topologically representing sequences [10,11]. The latter model [11] overcomes some limitations of the former (it works for longer sequences than the former) and was also employed in our model.

2 The model

Leaky integrating symbolic sequences with SOM formally corresponds to an Iterated Function System (IFS) introduced by Barnsley [12]. IFS is defined by a collection of affine contraction mappings

$$i(s) = \mu s + (1 - \mu)x_i, \quad x_i \in \{0,1\}^N, \quad x_i \neq x_j \quad \text{for} \quad i \neq j \qquad (1)$$

functioning on a unit hypercube $X = \langle 0,1 \rangle^N$, with[1] $N = \lceil \log_2 M \rceil$, where M is the number of symbols in input alphabet, $s \in X$ and using contraction coefficient $\mu \in (0,.5)$. The number of mappings is equal to M, the center $\{\frac{1}{2}\}^N$ of the hypercube is the starting point. IFS leads to spatial representation of symbolic sequences (for rigorous analysis published recently see [15]). IFS representation has a nice ordering property in that two sequences with common suffices are mapped close to each other in X. In Fig.1a, considering symbols $A = [0,0], B = [1,0], C = [0,1]$ and $D = [1,1]$, we show IFS representations of a few sequences.

Learning to represent sequences. Training SOM with leaky integrating units proceeds as follows. With each presentation of a symbol $\mathbf{x}$, every unit i in the map updates its input as

$$\mathbf{z}_i(t) = \mu \, \mathbf{z}_i(t-1) + (1 - \mu)(\mathbf{x}(t) - \mathbf{w}_i(t)) \, ,$$

where $\mathbf{w}_i$ is the classical weight vector associated with unit i. At the beginning of each sequence, $\mathbf{z}_i = 0, \forall i$. Sequences are parsed sequentially, symbol by symbol. As in standard SOM, units compete for the current symbol and the winner c satisfies the condition

$$\mathbf{z}_c(t) = \min_i \{\|\mathbf{z}_i(t)\|\} \, ,$$

where $\|.\|$ denotes the Euclidean norm. Weight adaptation in winner's neighborhood is based on the rule

$$\mathbf{w}_i(t+1) = \mathbf{w}_i(t) + \alpha(t)h_{ic}(t)\mathbf{z}_i(t) \, ,$$

---

[1] for $x \in \Re$, $\lceil x \rceil$ denotes the smallest integer y, such that $y \geq x$

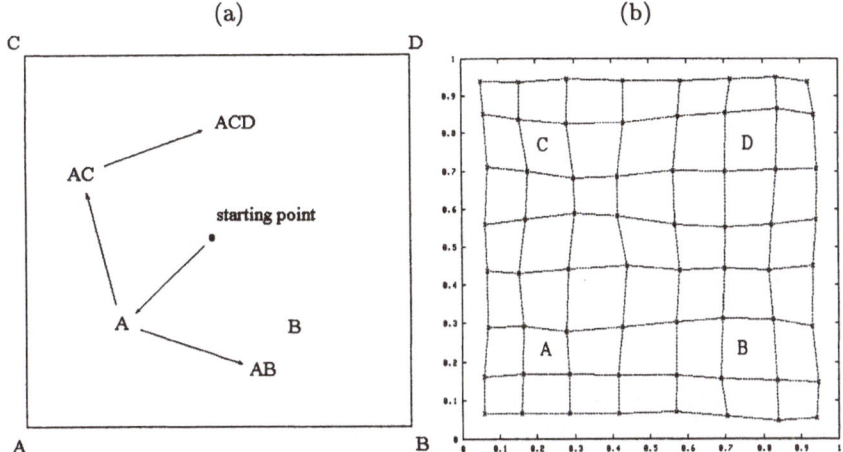

Fig. 1. (a) Examples of IFS sequence representations from the symbol set $\{A, B, C, D\}$ and for coefficient $\mu = 0.5$. (b) Ordered SOM with 8×8 leaky integrator units trained on all sequences with length ≤ 3, presented with equal probability. Symbol A shown denotes the surrounding area of 4×4 units representing all sequences having suffix A; similarly for other suffices. Due to fractal structure of this arrangement, the analogical subdivision applies to lower levels as well.

where parameters $\alpha(t)$ and $h_{ic}(t)$ have standard meanings of the decreasing learning rate and neighborhood function, respectively. As the SOM attempts to approximate the distribution of training data, we can obtain a nicely ordered map of sequence representations, such as the one shown in Fig.1b. It was trained on sequences with limited length, from 4-symbol set, where each symbol was selected with equal probability.

Note that due to linearity of encoding, the underlying sequence reconstruction is straightforward. Given the weight $\mathbf{w}(\tau)$, we repeatedly apply the formula inverse to eq. 1 until we end in the center of X or in its vicinity. The extracted symbol $\mathbf{x}_c$ in each iteration τ must satisfy the equation $x_c = \arg\min_l\{\|\mathbf{w}(\tau) - \mathbf{x}_l\|\}$.

Representing structure. Using the hierarchy of SOMs, one map per level, we can decompose each structure into a hierachy of sequences. At each level of this hierarchy, we can have one or more sequences to be represented in SOM. The difference between level 1 and all higher levels is that whereas in level 1 the sequences can contain only symbols belonging to input alphabet, in higher levels the sequences contain a symbol Δ which serves as substitution of a lower subtree (e.g., structure A(AB) becomes decomposed to AB in level 1 and AΔ in level 2).

During decomposition, it happens that two or more sequences need to be simultaneously represented in one map. To have the "multi-sequence" representation capability, the representation is taken as a global activity of the

(a)

(b)

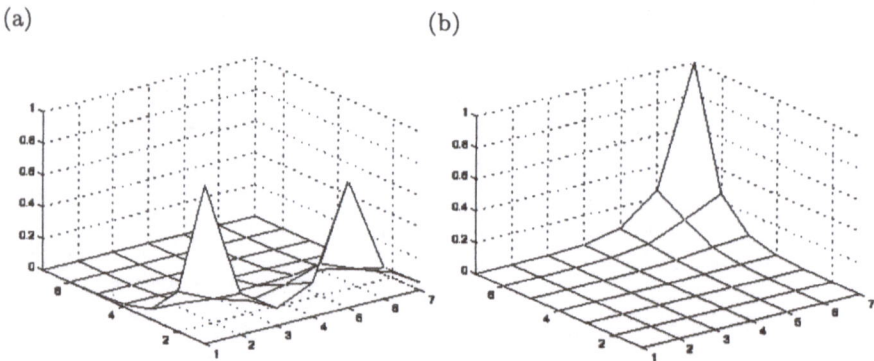

Fig. 2. Example of structure representation using SR-SOM. Structure (AB)(AA) is decomposed into sequences AB ⊕ AA in level 1 (figure a) and to ΔΔ in level 2 (figure b). Both maps have 7 × 7 units. For explanation see the text.

map. This choice is justified by observation that if topographic order exists in terms of units' positions in the map, it remains preserved if the output is taken as a global map activity having gaussian shape with a peak centered around the winner [13]. For that purpose, every unit has the RBF-like input-output function of the form

$$y_i = \exp(-\|\mathbf{r}_c - \mathbf{r}_i\|^2/\sigma) \;,$$

where $\mathbf{r}_j$ is the position of unit j in the map, and σ determines the sharpness of the Gaussian surface. The overall SOM output is thus taken as vector $\mathbf{Y} = [y_1, y_2, ..., y_K]$, with K denoting the number of units. In order two distinguish between two structures containing the same sequences but in different order, such as (AB)(AA) and (AA)(AB), the corresponding peaks are combined in one SOM in leaky integrating fashion. This means that the earlier the sequence occurs in the structure, the lower the height of its peak will be ($y_i \leftarrow k y_i, k < 1, \forall i$). Fig.2 shows an example of representing a structure (AB)(AA). SOM in level 1 (SOM$_1$) has two peaks: one corresponding to the sub-sequence AA (left), the other for AB (smaller peak on the right, $k = 0.8$). SOM$_2$ in figure b has one peak corresponding to the sequence ΔΔ, where we considered $\Delta \equiv D = [1, 1]$ for convenience.

For structure representations it is important that they themselves must be structured to allow structure-sensitive processing [14]. To check this property of SR-SOM representations, we have generated all 2-symbol sequences having one of the templates {(xx)x,x(xx),(xx)(xx)}. Each structure was represented by a 7 × 1 SOM$_1$ and a 7 × 7 SOM$_2$ as a concatenated vector $\mathbf{Y} = [\mathbf{Y}_1, \mathbf{Y}_2]$. SOM$_1$ had only one input (because there are only 2 symbols), whereas SOM$_2$ needed to have two inputs (because we have symbols A, B and Δ). From these representations, the hierarchical cluster diagram was calculated and plotted

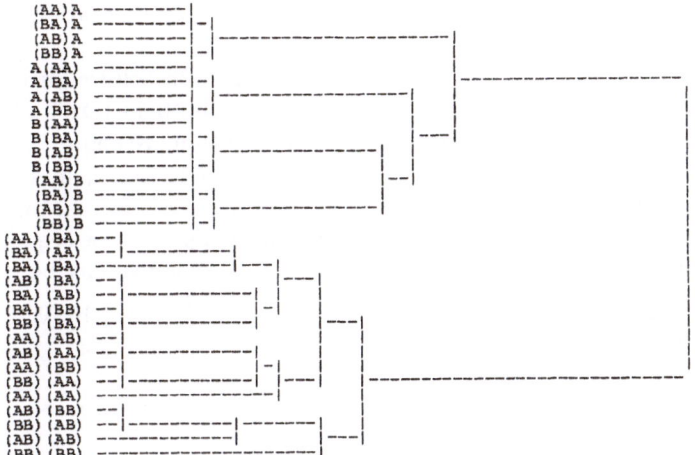

Fig. 3. A hierarchical cluster diagram of SR-SOM representations of simple sequences contaning two symbols. Distances fall in range from 0.3 to 3.2.

to show the similarities.[2] It can be seen from Fig.3 that obtained representations indeed show a nice property that similar structures are similar also in terms of their SR-SOM representations $\mathbf{Y}(s_i)$.

3 Discussion

Preliminary experiments show that at least in case of simple structures consisting of a few symbols, the obtained SR-SOM representations appear to be structured. The similarity between two structures is induced by the property of IFS in which the longer common suffix of the two sequences, the more similar are their representations.[3] It can also be observed in the dendrogram (Fig.3), where e.g. structure (BA)(AA) is more similar to (BA)(BA) than to (BA)(AB). The advantage of these representations is their computational efficiency (to the contrary with RAAM) and transparency. The computational efficiency practically equals that of a SOM, because all training consists in learning subsequences, which result from structure decomposition.

Regarding the type of representation, SR-SOM appears to possess features of both classical, symbolic systems as well as connectionist systems. On the system level, the representation is *spatially concatenative* (using terminology in [17]), because individual map representations are concatenated together. At the same time, the representation at a particular level is maintained by a SOM which produces *distributed representations* associated with two inherent dimensions in the data. In our setting, the neurons are considered to be

---

[2] i.e., for two sequences s_1, s_2 their difference is taken as $\|\mathbf{Y}(s_1) - \mathbf{Y}(s_2)\|$

[3] This differs from Kohonen's symbol maps which employ "spatially well-balanced" similarity measure between strings [16].

overlapping *value units*, which enable simultaneous representation of multiple values in one map.

What needs to be further tested is how this approach scales with larger symbol set as well as more complex structures (both in terms of "height" and "width"). The core of SR-SOM applicability to more complex structures resides in our assumption that if we have more than 4 symbols in input alphabet (which increases the dimensionality of input space), in real tasks not all sequences appear in the data. This implies that mapping these sequences onto a 2-dimensional SOM while preserving local relationships may be feasible.

Acknowledgement: The work has been supported in part by VEGA grant No. 2/5088/2000.

References

1. J.A. Fodor and Z.W. Pylyshyn. Connectionism and cognitive architecture: A critical analysis. *Cognition*, 28:3–71, 1988.
2. J.B. Pollack. Recursive distributed representations. *Artificial Intelligence*, 46(1-2):77–105, 1990.
3. P. Smolensky. Tensor product variable binding and the representation of symbolic structures in connectionist systems. *Artif. Intelligence*, 46:159–216, 1990.
4. T. Plate. Holographic reduced representations. *IEEE Transactions on Neural Networks*, 6(3):623–641, 1995.
5. L. Shastri and V. Ajjanagadde. From simple associations to systematic reasoning. *Behavioral nad Brain Sciences*, 16(3):417–494, 1993.
6. J.E. Hummel and K.J. Holyoak. Distributed representations of structure: a theory of analogical access and mapping. *Psych. Review*, 104(3):427–466, 1997.
7. D.J. James and R. Miikkulainen. Sardnet: a self-organizing feature map for sequences. In *Advances in Neural Information Processing Systems 7*, 1995.
8. K. Kopecz. Unsupervised learning of sequences on maps with lateral connectivity. In *ICANN'95*, pages 431–436, Paris, France, 1995.
9. J. Göppert and W. Rosenstiel. Dynamic extensions of self-organizing maps. In *Proceedings of ICANN'94*, pages 330–333, 1994.
10. G.J. Chappell and J.G. Taylor. The temporal Kohonen map. *Neural Networks*, 6:441–445, 1993.
11. T. Koskela et al. Time series prediction using recurrent SOM with local linear models. *Int. Journal of Knowledge-Based Intell. Eng. Systems*, 2:60–68, 1998.
12. M. Barnsley. *Fractals Everywhere*. Academic Press, 1988.
13. I. Farkaš. Invariance of gaussian-vector mapping using a self-organizing map. *Neural Network World*, 7(2):153–159, 1997.
14. L. Niklasson and M. Bodén. Representing structure and structured representations in connectionist networks. In A. Browne, editor, *Neural Network Perspectives on Cognition and Adaptive Robotics*, pages 20–50. IOP Press, 1997.
15. P. Tiňo. Spatial representation of symbolic sequences through iterated function systems. *IEEE Trans. on Systems, Man and Cybernetics*, 29(4):386-392, 1999.
16. T. Kohonen. Self-organizing maps of symbol strings. *Technical report A42*, Helsinki University of Technology, Espoo, Finland, 1996.
17. N.E. Sharkey Connectionist representation techniques. *Artificial Intelligence Review*, 5:143-167, 1990.

Invariant Representation of Images by Pulse Coupled Neural Network

Radoslav Forgáč[1], Igor Mokriš[1]

[1] Matej Bel University, Faculty of Finance, 974 01 Banská Bystrica, Slovakia

Abstract: The goal of this contribution is analysis of rotation, dilation and translation invariance of PCNN for drab images with similar features. A set of tested images contains face and verso of coins that satisfy this property.

Keywords: Pulse Coupled Neural Network (PCNN), feature extraction, drab image recognition

1. Introduction

This contribution is continuation of papers [3] and [4] on Pulse Coupled Neural Network (PCNN) which were used for recognition of images with sharp edges. The paper [3] is focused to the PCNN pre-processor that extracts invariant features from input images with sharp edges. In the paper [4] is designed image recognition system that uses the distributed neural network. The described system consists of PCNN pre-processor and classifier based on back-propagation neural network. The distributed neural network was tested for the images with sharp edges. The results were positive and correctness of used method was acknowledged. This paper deals with analysis of PCNN invariance of drab images with similar features.

For unique coin identification is needed to recognise and compare the mean and thickness of a coin, weight of coin and recognition its image of face and verso. The problem starts by coin image recognition because a selected method must satisfy several criteria. One of the main criteria is the recognition time, which is influenced by the raster of input images and dimension of feature set which depends on training set. Dimension of feature set can be reduced by invariance of image representation, which is used for the feature extraction. Therefore the rotation invariance of coin within interval <0°, 360°> and at the same time translation invariance must be analysed in the area that is used for recognition. The image dilatation of coins is not possible in this case. Neural networks can solve the coin recognition problem. On the other side the mean, thickness and weight of coin can be determined easily by classical methods of measurement.

2. Structure of Pulse Coupled Neural Network

The PCNN is based on biologically motivated processing model developed by Eckhorn [2], who explained the experimentally observed synchronous activity in the cat visual cortex. This model was more described by Johnson [7, 8] and hardware implementation was done by Frank, Hartmann [5], Kinser and Lindblad [9]. Mathematical foundations of pulse coupled models were presented by Izhikevich [6].

The structure of PCNN is direct connected with structure of an input image. If input image is a matrix with $m \times n$ image pixels, then structure of PCNN is matrix with $m \times n$ neurons. Each neuron in the PCNN is directly coupled with an image pixel. The neuron receives input signals from corresponding input image pixel and at the same time from outputs of neighbouring neurons, i.e. from linking and feeding areas. Linking area of corresponding neuron is given by linking radius r_0, which determines the number of neurons in the linking area. For example, if $r_0 = 1$ (or 1.5, 2, 3, etc.), then linking area consist of 4 (or 8, 12, 28, etc.) linking neurons. The value of linking radius r_0 is equal for every PCNN neurons. The weight of neurons depends on implementation of PCNN kernel which can be described for example by the Gaussian or $1/r$ distribution.

The PCNN is used as the pre-processor for invariant feature extraction. The grey input image, which is presented by two-dimensional matrix, is through PCNN transformed to a sequence of temporary binary images. Each of these binary images is a matrix with the same dimension as an input image matrix and is generated by group of pixels with similar intensity. The PCNN can segment not only intensity regions but also intensity gradient regions. The sum of the outputs of neurons gives a one-dimensional time signal function at every iteration time. This coded time signal is advisable for classification using conventional neural networks or the other recognition methods.

The standard model of PCNN is described by iteration by the following equations:

$$F_{ij}(n) = S_{ij} + F_{ij}(n-1) \cdot e^{-\alpha_F} + V_F \cdot (M * Y(n-1))_{ij} \tag{1}$$

$$L_{ij}(n) = L_{ij}(n-1) \cdot e^{-\alpha_L} + V_L \cdot (W * Y(n-1))_{ij} \tag{2}$$

$$U_{ij}(n) = F_{ij}(n) \cdot (1 + \beta \cdot L_{ij}(n)) \tag{3}$$

$$\Theta_{ij}(n) = \Theta_{ij}(n-1) \cdot e^{-\alpha\Theta} + V_{\Theta} \cdot Y_{ij}(n-1) \tag{4}$$

$$Y_{ij}(n) = \left\{ \begin{array}{l} 1 \text{ if } U_{ij}(n) > \Theta_{ij}(n) \\ 0 \text{ otherwise} \end{array} \right. \tag{5}$$

where F_{ij} is the feeding input, L_{ij} is the linking input, n is an iteration step, S_{ij} is constant input stimul (e. g. intensity of pixel i, j in the input matrix). W and M are the weight matrices, * is the convolution operator, Y is the output of the neuron, V_L and V_F are potentials, α_L and α_F are decayed constants, U_{ij} is the internal activity, β is the linking coefficient and Θ_{ij} is the dynamic threshold.

The basic principle of PCNN is as follows: Let the initial values equal to zero. When $n = 1$ (i.e. first iteration) and the internal activity U_{ij} is greater than the dynamic threshold Θ_{ij}, neurons produce pulses on the output (i.e. $Y_{ij} = 1$). After the pulse, the dynamic threshold is raised with the amount to Θ_{max}. Since Θ_{max} is always larger than U_{ij}, the output of the neuron changes back to zero value. The internal activation U_{ij} will reach a stable level and threshold Θ_{ij} will decay until internal activation U_{ij} is again greater than threshold Θ_{ij}. Thus the pulse generator of a neuron can produce a single pulse at its output in every iteration step n. The pulses from all activated neurons in the iteration step n give the temporary binary image. The time signal, generated from the sum of sums of outputs Y_{ij} in every iteration step n is defined as:

$$G(n) = \sum_{ij} Y_{ij}(n) \tag{6}$$

The PCNN as pre-processor has three advantages for feature extraction. First is large reduction of number of features for image recognition in relation to the number of pixels of recognised image. Second advantage is invariance of time signal against rotation, dilatation, translation, noise of images and their combinations. Third advantage is that PCNN don´t learn.

3. Results of Experiments

Experiments described in this paper were realised on images of Slovak coins. The set of images contained coins with nominal values 1 Sk, 2 Sk, 5 Sk and 10 Sk (see

Fig. 1). The image raster was 217 x 224 pixels, density 72 dpi and 24 bits represent one image pixel. All experiments were performed in the adjustment PCNN simulator [1] in Matlab under Windows 95. The images were rotated within interval <0°, 360°> and at the same time they were translated.

A modified version of PCNN was used. This version does not include the exponential item for feeding input and convolution in equation (1), i.e. feeding input for a neuron consists of an image pixel intensity only. The advantage of this version of PCNN model is elimination of time for feature extraction. The efficiency of recognition remains comparable with standard model of PCNN. Parameters of PCNN were set as follows: the linking coefficient $\beta = 0.2$, the linking radius $r_0 = 1.5$, the decayed constants: $\alpha_L = 1$, $\alpha_\Theta = 5$, potentials $V_L = 2$, $V_\Theta = 10$ and the number of iterations $n = 30$. $1/r$ distribution is used for PCNN kernel development.

Fig. 1. The training set of images that contains coins with nominal values 5 Sk (left upper), 2 Sk (right upper), 10 Sk (left down) and 1 Sk (right down).

The images of coins are relatively simple, but saliencies are dull. The transformation of images of coins from three-dimensional space to two-dimensional space (e.g. by scanner or camera) more reduces these saliencies. The other negative property is monotony of coin colour, where coins 1 Sk and 10 Sk are relative colour similarly and coins 2 Sk and 5 Sk are colour identical. One of way to eliminate these absences of saliencies was done by increasing of iterations of PCNN to 50. The increase of iterations will cause three series of nonzero amplitudes of time signal for this case. In this manner PCNN generates more features to image recognition. On the other side time of feature extraction is longer and is needed classifier with more complicated structure.

Recognition of coins requires rotation and at the same time translation invariance of features. Previous experiments for simple images [8] and sharp images from real scene [3, 4] confirmed that PCNN is invariant against rotation, dilatation and translation of images. The time signal determines, whether an image was rotated, translated or dilated. If two time signals are alike, but translated each other, then comparable images are not identical. If two time signals are alike, but amplitudes are less or bigger, then it is the same image, but dilated.

The time signals for the same but translated images are identical. It comes to this, that representation of translated images of coins is identical to representation of image in the basic position.

The time signals of rotated images are soft deformed in compare with time signal of image in basic position. The representation of rotated images is approximately equal in entire interval $<0°, 360°>$.

The PCNN is invariant against dilatation of images, too. This property is paradoxical unsuitable for Slovak coins recognition. If input images are scale down, then the amplitudes of time signal are smaller. If input images are, scale up, then the amplitudes of time signal are greater. The time signal remains identical in all cases of dilatation in compare with time signal of basic position. This paradox is typical for coins 2 Sk and 5 Sk, where the verso is identical for both coins (see Fig. 1). In addition, the colour of both coins is identical, too. The representation of these coins is very identical and good recognition depends on measurement of mean, weight and width of these coins.

The similarity of face representation of 10 Sk and verso representation of 1 Sk suggests, that PCNN is sensitive on sharp features, e.g. edges or colour composition of images. The PCNN is not able to recognise all drab details. This problem can be partially eliminated, when resolution of images will be increased.

4. Conclusion

The goal of this contribution is analysis of invariant feature extraction for face and verso of coin recognition by PCNN that represents group of drab images. The experiments confirmed rotation and at the same time translation invariance of PCNN. Very good invariance against dilatation of images had negative effect for this type of application. Even through the PCNN is a few sensitives on details of the image. It is possible to claim that PCNN is suitable for invariant feature extraction of drab images but this approach needs better classifier.

References

1. Becanovic, V. (1998): PCNN Toolbox for MATLAB ver. 3.1.3. http://msia02.msi.se/~vlatko/Pub/pcnn313.zip

2. Eckhorn, R. et al. (1990): Feature Linking via Synchronization among Distributed Assemblies: Simulations of Results from Cat Visual Cortex. Neural Computation **2**, 293-307

3. Forgáč, R., Mokriš, I. (1999): Contribution to Invariant Image Recognition Using PulseCoupled Neural Networks. In: MENDEL'99 – 5th International Conference on Soft Computing, Brno, 351-355

4. Forgáč, R., Mokriš, I. (1999): Invariant Image Recognition Using Distributed Neural Networks. In: INES'99 - 3rd IEEE International Conference on Intelligent Engineering Systems, Stará Lesná, 105-109

5. Frank, G. - Hartmann, G. (1995): An Artificial Neural Network Accelerator for Pulse-Coded Model Neurons. In: ICNN95 - International Conference on Neural Networks, Perth, 2014-2018

6. Izhikevich, E. M. (1999): Class 1 Neural Excitability, Conventional Synapses, Weakly Connected Networks, and Mathematical Foundations of Pulse-Coupled Models. IEEE Trans. on Neural Networks **10**, 499-507

7. Johnson, J. L., Ritter, D. (1993): Observation of Periodic Waves in a Pulse-coupled Neural Network. Optics Letters **18**, 1253-1255

8. Johnson, J. L. (1994): Pulse Coupled Neural Nets: Translation, Rotation, Scale, Distortion and Intensity Signal Invariance for Images. Applied Optics **33**, 6239-6253

9. Kinser, J. M., Lindblad, T. (1999): Implementation of Pulse-Coupled Neural Networks in the CNAPS Environment. IEEE Trans. on Neural Networks **10**, 584-590

Detection of Ischemic Episodes with a Combination of Unsupervised and Supervised Learning

Stergios Papadimitriou, Liviu Vladutu, Severine Mavroudi , Anastassios Bezerianos

Department of Medical Physics, School of Medicine, University of Patras, 26500 Patras, Greece, *tel:* +30-61-996115, *fax:* +30-61-992496
email: bezer@patreas.upatras.gr

Abstract : The paper presents a novel neural network architecture for the effective detection of ischemic episodes. This architecture combines unsupervised learning for the simple regions and supervised for the difficult ones in a two stage learning process. The unsupervised learning approach extends and adapts the Self-Organizing Map (SOM) algorithm of Kohonen. The supervised learning has the objective of improving the decision boundaries at some parts of the state space (i.e. at the ambiguous regions). This combination of learning paradigms allows to realize the classification performances of advanced supervising learning approaches with the use of significantly less computational resources.

Keywords: *Myocardial Ischemia, Self-Organizing Maps (SOM), Principal Component Analysis, Radial Basis Functions (RBF), Support Vector Machines (SVM).*

1   Introduction

In this paper a new neural network architecture for the classification of ischemic episodes is presented. This architecture combines unsupervised and supervised learning in a two stage learning process. The unsupervised learning is based on a modified Self Organizing Map (SOM) algorithm of Kohonen [1,3] with dynamic insertion/deletion of nodes in a bidimensional lattice of neurons. This unsupervised algorithm performs well at discriminating the ischemic from the normals over a large part of the state space while at the same time is computationally efficient. However, there remain some parts of the state space that require the enforcement of complex decision boundaries. These parts are detected at the unsupervised phase and a supervised learning paradigm is explored in order to cope with the difficult regions of the state space. Since the new architecture combines the modified SOM algorithm with supervised neural network models is called the Network Self-Organized Map (NetSOM).

The NetSOM therefore is consisted of:

-The internal SOM, i.e. the modified SOM based unsupervised learning network.

-The Supervised Expert network.

The second component, the Supervised Expert network operates over the subspaces where the internal SOM cannot perform unambiguous decisions. Among the different supervised approaches that we have tested for the implementation of the Supervised Expert, the Support Vector Machines (SVM) gave the best results.

2 Methods

2.1 The Preprocessing Phase

Information about ischemia exists in the ST-T Segment of the ECG signal. We used for our study the ECG signals of the European ST-T Database, which are a set of long-term Holter recordings provided by eight countries.

The original data space consisted from the ECG signal samples undergoes a *dimensionality reduction* as the feature space is constructed. This is accomplished with the *Principal Component Analysis* (PCA) method that retains about 98.1% from the energy of the original signal within 5 PCA coefficients.

The PCA projection coefficients are fed to the NetSOM nonlinear device in order to perform the complex (and highly nonlinear) classification decision about the category pertaining to each analysis case (i.e. normal, abnormal).

The PCA transformation describes the original vectors (ST-T Segments) according to the direction of maximum variance reduction in the training set. The latter information is obtained by analyzing the data covariance matrix.

2.2 The Network Self-Organizing Map (NetSOM)

The NetSOM is consisted of two components: the *internal SOM* and the *supervised expert network*.

The internal SOM is based on the SOM training algorithm. The SOM algorithm creates a *feature map* that is *topologically ordered*. This neural network model can effectively display the important statistical characteristics of a high dimensional input space over the topologically ordered lattice of neurons [3].

The ambiguous neurons i.e. those neurons for which the uncertainty of class assignment is significant, are identified with an entropy based criterion [1]. Afterwards, training and testing sets are created for the training of the supervised expert. These sets consist only of the patterns that are represented by the ambiguous neurons. The classification task proceeds by feeding the pattern to the internal SOM. If the winning neuron is one that is-not ambiguous, the internal SOM classifies by using the class of the winning neuron. In the other case, the supervised expert is used to perform the classification decision.

2.3 The Supervised Expert Network

We have chosen two types of neural networks that are of a local approximation type and also incorporate formalism in their design in order to obtain adequate generalization performance: the Radial Basis Function (RBF) [2] and the Support Vector Machine (SVM) [6].

The RBF networks explore the Tikhonov's regularization theory for obtaining generalization performance[1, 2, 5]. The NetSOM has been configured to grow adaptively until about 2000 patterns map onto the ambiguous neurons. This size of the training set is appropriate for a RBF solution by means of a numerically effective approach. Specifically, m fixed centers are selected at random from the training patterns. Their spread σ is common and is computed according to the empirical formula $\sigma = d_{max}/\sqrt{2m}$, where d_{max} is the maximum distance between the chosen centers. Finally, the only parameters that need to be learned are the linear weights of the output layer, which are computed with the *pseudoinverse* method [1]. The number of centers that yielded good generalization performance is m=500 and the regularization parameter λ at the range 0.1 to 0.3.

Recently, a new class of neural networks, the Support Vector Machines (SVM) have been developed that can access the generalization performance within a formal framework. The SVMs exploit a relatively new type of supervised learning that is based on the principle of Structural Risk Minimization developed within the Vapnik's Statistical Learning Theory [6]. The decomposition of the problem at the context of NetSOM to an unsupervised part and a supervised one is similar to the case of Radial Basis Functions.

3. Results

We took a training set of approximately 5,000 ST-T complexes extracted from 3 records (different from those used at the testing set). The two main classes (i.e.

normal and ischemic) are represented by an approximately equal number of samples. The evaluation of the SOM and the NetSOM models has been performed on another 15 records out of the 90 records of the European ST-T database. The testing sets have been constructed from these records. The whole test set contains principal component projection coefficients from approximately 120,000 ECG beats.

The table below displays the results of the average performance of ischemic episode detection evaluated with the three network types. The second column displays the sensitivity while the third one the predictivity of episode detection. As it is expected from the beat classification results, the NetSOM with SVM as supervised expert yields a better average for the episode detection performance.

Table 1. The average ischemia episode detection performance evaluated with the corresponding networks (i.e. SOM, NetSOM with RBF as supervised expert and NetSOM with SVM as supervised expert).

Network Type	Ischemia Episode Sensitivity	Ischemia Episode Predictivity
SOM	74.9%	73.7%
NetSOM/RBF	79.5%	77.6%
NetSOM/SVM	82.8%	81.3%

4. Conclusions

This work has proposed a new supervised extension to the Self-Organizing Map (SOM) model [3,4] that is called the Network Self-Organizing Map (NetSOM). This model exploits the ordering potential of the SOM in order to split the global state space in two subspaces. The first subspace corresponds to regions over which the classification task can be performed directly with the unsupervised SOM algorithm. However, for the second subspace complex decision boundaries should be enforced and the generalization performance should be explicitly designed. The SOM algorithm is not appropriate for this task and therefore supervised training networks capable of achieving good generalization performance (i.e. Radial Basis Functions [1,2] and the Support Vector Machines [1,6]) are used. The Support Vector Machines have obtained the best discrimination capability for the ambiguous regions. This combination of unsupervised and supervised learning yields an architecture that is simple, performs well and is computationally effective.

References

[1] Simon Haykin, Neural Networks, Prentice Hall International Inc, Second Edition, 1999

[2] T. Poggio and F. Girosi, "Regularization algorithms for learning that are equivalent to multilayer perceptrons", Science 247, pp. 978-982, 1990.

[3] Teuvo Kohonen, "Self-Organized Maps", Springer-Verlag, 1997.

[4] Helge Ritter, Thomas Martinetz, Klaus Schulten, Neural Computation and Self-Organizing Maps, Addison-Wesley, 1992.

[5] Christopher M. Bishop, Neural Networks for Pattern Recognition Clarendon Press-Oxford, 1996.

[6] Vapnik., V. N., Statistical Learning Theory, New York, Wiley, 1998.

Spatial Distribution of Patterns and the Hopfield Network Phase Space Geometry

Marek Jaszuk[1], Wiesław A. Kamiński[1], and Alexander D. Linkevich[2]

[1] Maria Curie-Skłodowska University, Division of Complex Systems Physics, Radziszewskiego 10, 20-031, Lublin, Poland
[2] Polotsk State University, Blokhin 29, 211440 Novopolotsk, Belarus

Abstract: It is well known that complex dynamical systems exhibit a rich variety of interesting nonlinear phenomena that could be used for information processing. One of those promising issues has originated from the attractor neural network models [1,2]. In this paradigm, any piece of information stored in the system is represented by an attractor in the phase space of a neural network (NN), and information processing is considered as the time evolution of the NN state. Such an approach is based on the observation that the state of a dissipative nonlinear dynamical system converges asymptotically toward an attractor, whose type, shape, location and size differs depending on values of the system parameters. Investigation into the phase portrait of NN, i.e. what attractors exist and what their properties are, is therefore of great importance. Despite the progress achieved in analytical treatment of dynamical systems, computer simulations are still the main tools for exploring the phase space of such complex systems.

The aim of the present paper is to study numerically phase spaces of Hopfield's analog NN with emphasis on memorization of patterns (MP's) and their spatial distribution influencing the geometrical structure of attraction basins. Special attention is paid to the phase space geometry changes with rotation and shifting eithe single pattern or their whole set.

1 Formulation of the NN model and the learning problem

We consider a neural network composed of N neuron-like elements labeled by index i $(i = 1, \ldots, N)$. The state of the neuron i at time moment t is defined by the membrane potential $x_i(t)$ with time evolution obeying the current conservation law [2]:

$$\dot{x}_i = F_i(\mathbf{x}) \equiv -\gamma_i x_i + \sum_{j=1}^{N} T_{ij} f_j(x_j) + I_i, \tag{1}$$

where the vector $\mathbf{x} = (x_1, \ldots, x_N)$ describes the state of NN and the positive constant γ_i characterizes dynamics of an isolated neuron i. The synaptic efficiency T_{ij} determines influence of the output signal $f_j(x_j)$ of neuron j on the state of neuron i with f_j being the transfer input-output function. I_i means an external (sensory) current entering the neuron. In this paper we take $tanh(\beta_j x_j)$ with $\beta_j = const > 0$ as the transfer function. Type of information processing we consider here is autoassociative memory. According to the Hopfield approach [1] it can be treated as follows.

Every piece of information μ to be stored in the system is encoded by the stationary state $\xi^\mu = (\xi_1^\mu, \ldots, \xi_N^\mu)$ in a way ensures that eq. (1) is compatibile with the conditions

$$T\mathbf{y}^\mu - \mathbf{z}^\mu = 0 \qquad (\mu = 1, \ldots, p), \tag{2}$$

where p is the number of memorized patterns. Vectors $(\mathbf{y}^1, \ldots, \mathbf{y}^p)$ and $(\mathbf{z}^1, \ldots, \mathbf{z}^p)$ are easily expressed through $\xi^1, \ldots, \xi^p$. For $\mathbf{y}^\mu = (y_1^\mu, \ldots, y_N^\mu)$ and $\mathbf{z}^\mu = (z_1^\mu, \ldots, z_N^\mu)$ we have $y_i^\mu = f_i(\xi_i^\mu)$, $z_i^\mu = \gamma_i \xi_i^\mu - I_i^\mu$, $(\mu = 1, \ldots, p, \quad i = 1, \ldots, N)$. If network state $\mathbf{x}^0 = (x_1(t^0), \ldots, x_N(t^0))$ at the initial time moment t^0 is close enough to a memorized pattern ξ^μ then, due to intrinsic dynamics of the system, the state $\mathbf{x}(t)$ should converge to the fixed point ξ^μ. In other words a distance $d(\mathbf{x}(t), \xi^\mu)$ between the points $\mathbf{x}(t)$ and ξ^μ vanishes as $t \to \infty$. Because $\mathbf{x}(t)$ is a continuous function, an infinitely large time is necessary to achieve exact coincidence of the state $\mathbf{x}(t)$ and the desired point ξ^μ. However, all real computations are performed with a finite accuracy and such a behaviour is not actually required. It is enough therefore to demand that the network state reaches a prescribed ε-neighborhood of the fixed point ξ^μ. This means there exists a time moment t_ε such that $d(\mathbf{x}(t), \xi^\mu) \leq \varepsilon$ for all $t \geq t_\varepsilon$. We will say in this case that the memorized pattern ξ^μ has been retrieved by the network with the accuracy ε after the time instant t_ε.

To achieve the desired behavior of the network, the synaptic matrix T_{ij} should be appropriately adjusted whith a learning algorithm.

2 A learning algorithm based on outer products of vectors

Due to linearity of eqs. (2) the general solution T can be represented in the form

$$T = R + BH, \tag{3}$$

where R is a particular solution of eqs. (2), H is a solution of the corresponding homogeneous equations $H\mathbf{y}^\mu = 0$, and B is an arbitrary $N \times N$ matrix. To find the matrices R and H, we use the projection learning algorithm [3–5] which yields the equation

$$R_{ij}^\mu = R_{ij}^{\mu-1} + \left(\sum_{k=1}^N r_k^{\mu-1} y_k^\mu \right)^{-1} \cdot \left(z_i^\mu + \sum_{k=1}^N R_{ik}^{\mu-1} y_k^\mu \right) r_j^{\mu-1} (\quad \mu = 1, \ldots, p). \tag{4}$$

The analogous formula for H^μ_{ij} may be easy written. Vectors $\mathbf{r}^\mu$ have to satisfy the conditions $\sum_k r^{\mu-1}_k y^\alpha_k = 0, for \alpha = 1,\ldots,\mu-1$ and $\sum_k r^{\mu-1}_k y^\mu_k \neq 0$.

This learning method allows to memorize a number of patterns p not exceeding the number of neurons N. Patterns used in this method are constructed of any real numbers. The only restriction that patterns have to be linearly independent.

3   Numerical examination of the phase space geometry

To illustrate properties pertaining to the geometrical structure of the NN phase space made up of the neuronal variables $x_1,\ldots,x_N$, we use graphical representation. For the task of our simulations we have choosen a system consisting of $N = 2$ neurons which can memorize no more than 2 patterns. The neurons parameters, the same for all neurons and fixed during simulations, were following: $\gamma = 1.0$, $\beta = 1.0$ and $I = 0.0$. The phase space for this simple system is only 2-dimensional one and therefore it is easy to analyse its properties. The simulations are extendable to higher dimension networks but our restricted imagination makes it difficult to understand phenomena occuring in more than three dimensions.

After the learning procedure is applied all patterns from the training set become fixed points of the network dynamics. Apart from memorized patterns, an additional set of "spurious" fixed points appears. All these points can be attractors, saddle points or repulsive points. A kind of a particular fixed point depends on the pattern spatial position.

To represent geometrical properties of the phase space of the system we draw some figures using the following prescription. By different shades of grey we indicate regions belonging to different basins of attraction: white and light grey points belong to the MP's basins of attraction, while black and dark grey represent basins of the spurious attractors. Moreover, the fixed points are marked by black and white dots indicating their belonging to the training and spurious sets, respectively.

In this analysis we search for how the pattern position influences the shape of particular basins of attraction. For this purpose we carried out simulations of pattern rotation around the origin of coordinates of the phase space. We have also looked for the effect of pattern scaling.

Fig. 1 shows a few examples of patterns rotation around the (0,0) point counter clockwise. The patterns are orthogonal and of the same length equal to 1. One can notice that for the rotation angle equal to or smaller than $\alpha = 25°$ (Fig. 1(a-b)), the whole space is divided into four parts, each of them being basins of attraction of four spurious attractors. Simultaneously the memorized patterns are saddle points lying on the borders of different basins of attraction. The middle point of the picture, the origin, is a repulsive point. In this case the network is useless as an associative memory because the points from the training set are not attractors. For $\alpha \geq 26°$ MP's become attracting points (see. Fig. 1(c-d)) and it is possible to usie the network as an associative memory. Especially, the case of $\alpha = 45°$ (Fig. 1(d)) seems to be optimal for this task. For the rotation angle $\alpha \geq 64°$ the picture becomes similar to that shown in Fig. (1(a-b)).

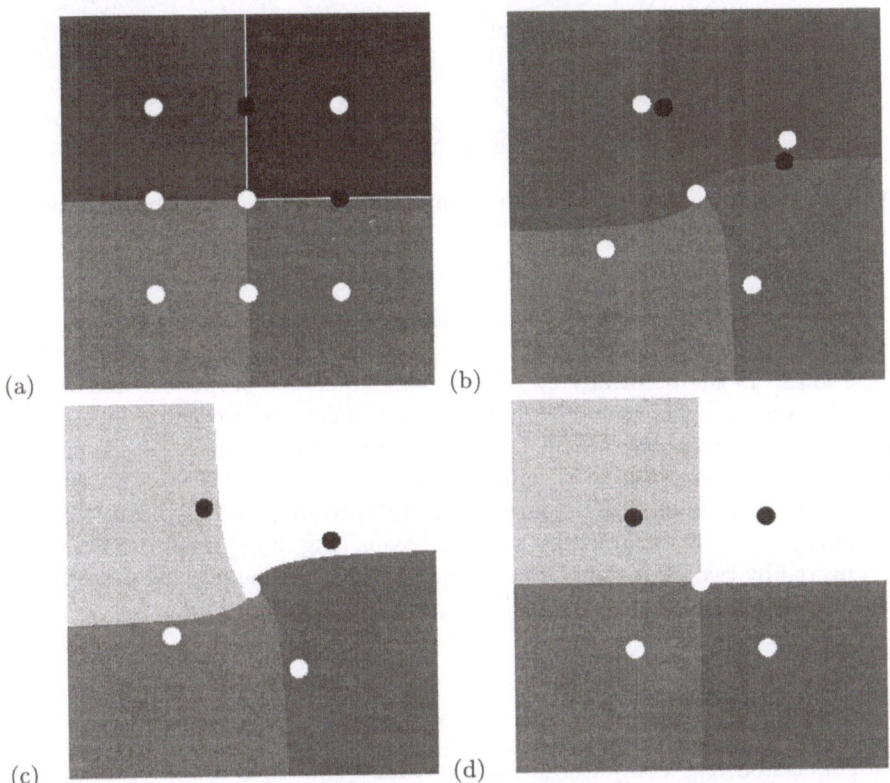

Fig. 1. Example of rotaion of two patterns around the orgin: (**a**) starting position; (**b**) rotation angle $\alpha = 20°$; (**c**) rotation angle $\alpha = 30°$; (**d**) rotation angle $\alpha = 45°$

We have also analysed the relative pattern position. We choose position of one pattern such as the system will display the best associative memory properties, what refers to rotation from the starting position by $\alpha = 45°$. Then we rotate the non-fixed pattern changing the angle between it and the fixed pattern from $0°$ to $180°$. We have obtained in the symulations that the moved pattern can also be represented as an attractive point if the angle between both patterns is in range $65° \leq \alpha_1 \leq 155°$ (see Fig. 2(b)). For other values the pattern represented by a saddle point (Fig. 2(a)).

48

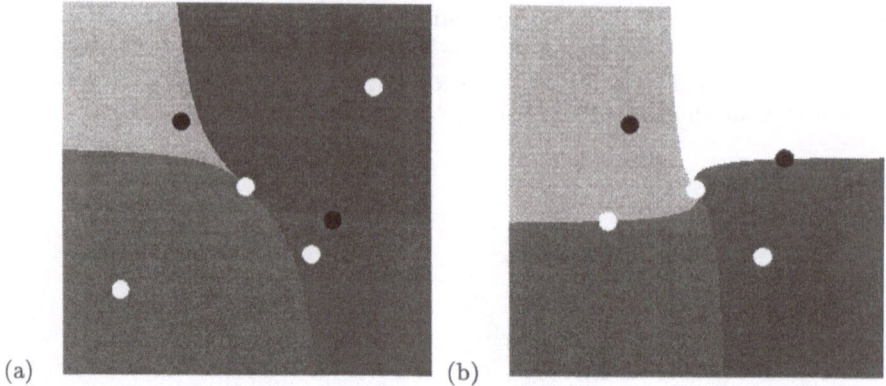

(a) (b)

Fig. 2. Examples of rotation of single pattern around the orgin with angle α_1 between patterns: 155° (**a**) and 115° (**b**)

Influence of the patterns relative distance from the origin of coordinates was also studied As previously we fixed one of the patterns in the optimal position from the point of view of associative memory properties and shifted another one. Results of such computer experiment are presented in Fig. (3). One observes that the smaller distances from the origin result in smaller basin of attraction (Fig. 3(b)) until it vanishes completely (Fig. 3(a)). On the contrary increase of the distance effects in spreading of this basin through regions previously occupied by another basins (Fig. 3(c)) until the full space is covered by two basins only: one connected with the memorized pattern and the second one with the spurious attractor (Fig. 3(d)).

4   Conclusions

In conclusion, the computer simulations have shown that the optimal conditions for exploiting the Hopfield's analog neural network as the asociative memory pattern are orthogonality and rotation according to the system axes by an angle eqall to 45° . The length of patterns measured by the distance from the origin is not restricted but shuld be the same for all patterns. If the restrictions are fulfilled only approximately the network still works correctly.

References

1. Hopfield J. J. (1982) Proc. Natl. Acad. Sci. USA **79**, 2554
2. Hopfield J. J. (1984) Proc. Natl. Acad. Sci. USA **81**, 3088
3. Kapelko V. V., Linkevich A. D. (1996) Phys. Rev. E **54**, 2802
4. Kartynnick A. V., Linkevich A. D. (1994) Optical Memory and Neural Networks **3**, 329

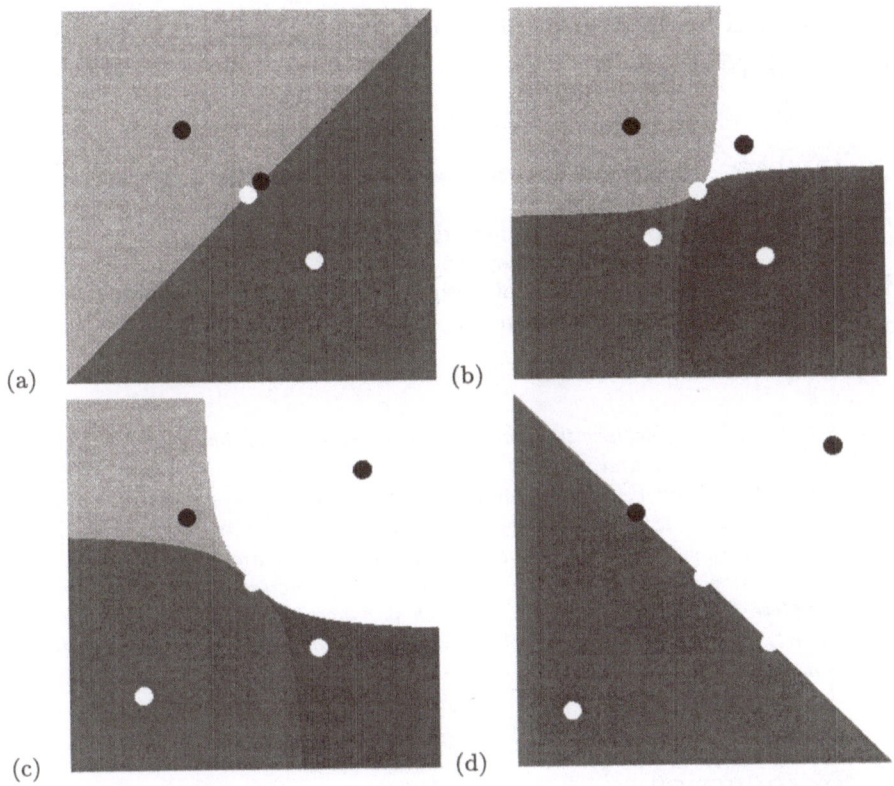

(a)

(b)

(c)

(d)

Fig. 3. Example of shifting one of the patterns along its direction for scaling factor
(a) $d = 0.45$; (b) $d = 0.7$; (c) $d = 1.7$; (d) $d = 2.0$

5. Linkevich A. D. (1993) Proc. Second Seminar "Nonlinear Phenomena in Complex Systems", Polotsk, February 15 - 17, ed. V.I. Kuvshinov and D. W. Serow (PIYaF, Saint-Petersburg, 1993) 373

Switched Capacitor-Based Integrate-And-Fire Neural Network

D. Hajtáš[1], D. Ďuračková[1], and G. Benyon-Tinker[2]

[1] Slovak University of Technology, dept. of Microelectronics,
   Ilkovičova 3, 819 12 Bratislava, Slovakia
[2] Bournemouth University, School of Design, Engineering and Computing,
   Fern Barrow, BH 125BB Bournemouth, U.K.

Abstract: This article deals with an analog implementation of the functional parts of an Integrate-and-fire neural network. The designed parts would be used as leaf cells with automated layout generation for a complex Integrate-and-fire neural network with built-in analog learning and weight storage. The most important cell is the synapse, which includes a postsynaptic forming block, learning and weight storage, which makes it possible to give individual output characteristics to each synapse in a complete neural network. This approach is conceptually close to its biological counterpart. The design uses a switched capacitor technique to achieve a significant reduction in silicon area.

1   Introduction

In many neural network applications a synapse with built-in learning is required. The following neuron and synapse parameters should be taken into account: neuron hyperpolarisation threshold, time constant of after-hyperpolarisation sensitivity recovery, time constant of exponential decrease of post-synaptic potential (PSP), learning rate for up and down learning, and external NMDA potential. It is important for each synapse to have a specific output signal characteristic (time constant of PSP discharge is assumed in our case). Therefore a PSP circuit is needed on the output of each synapse.[1], [4]

In this paper, the design of a circuit for the realisation of a neuron and a learning synapse is presented. In order to achieve an efficient implementation of the synapse from the area point of view, a switched capacitor (SC) technique was employed for the design. Moreover, in an SC circuit the synapse output and neuron after-hyperpolarisation characteristic of each synapse and neuron can be easily and accurately tuned by capacitance ratio. Finally, the time dependencies are defined by the number of clock cycles and therefore they do not depend on the clock signal frequency. This offers the possibility to use the solution over a wide frequency range.

2 Realisation

The basic computing elements of the network are the neurons and the synapses providing interconnections between them. In a biological network, the neuron consists of a body (soma), an input path (dendritic tree with synapses) and an output path (axon with synapses). The synapse is the point where information (a burst of pulses) is electrochemicaly transfered from the output of one neuron to the input of another. The influence of a synapse on a neuron strongly depends upon the distance between the synapse and the body of the neuron (weight). The neuron pulses are transformed to the post-synaptic soma potential (PSP) with an exponential time characteristic, which allows the integration of signals over time. When the PSP exceeds the input threshold of a neuron it causes hyperpolarisation of the neuron and the neuron "fires". This is followed by the recovery period (afterhyperpolarisation) when the neuron is unable to fire.

In this approach the neuron has an analogue current input and a binary (logical) voltage output, with vice versa for the synapse. It is necessary to use a special neuron with an analogue voltage input for the input layer of a complete network.

2.1 Neuron

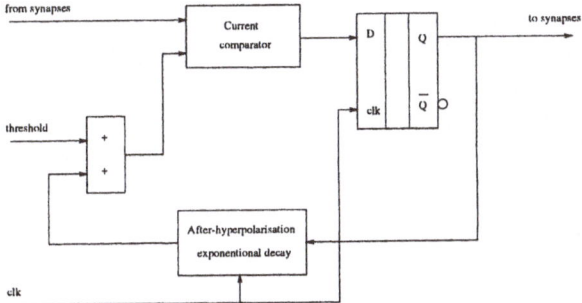

Fig. 1. A block diagram of a neuron for a neural network with learning synapses.

Each neuron has a simple current comparator at its input, which compares the current flowing in from the dendritic tree with an adjustable threshold. It provides also after-hyperpolarisation of the neuron by increasing the threshold value. In this part two voltage-to-current converters are used. The output of the current comparator is fed to a dynamic D flip-flop controlled by a common clock signal. The dynamic D flip-flop consists of four inverters with long channel transistors, two buffers and two single transistor switches, which takes less area than a standard D flip-flop. This part performs output signal shaping to produce a pulse with a fixed width of one clock cycle.

The neuron contains also the switched capacitor based circuit for timing the after-hyperpolarisation started by the output pulse. (Fig. 1). Several neurons were designed with different input sensitivities (maximum input currents are 40 μA, 20 μA, and 10 μA and minimal thresholds are 2 μA, 1 μA, and 0.5 μA respectively). The type of neuron used in a design depends on the number of the synapses conected to the input of the neuron.

2.2 Synapse

The basic functions of the synapse are weighting of the neuron output signal, PSP-like shaping of its output signal, and analogue weight storage and weight refreshment [2]. A voltage adder computes a new start-value for the PSP circuit continuously (NewValue = PSP + Weight). After the "spike" from a transmitting neuron arrives this computed value is sent to the PSP circuit via a transfer gate. The PSP circuit consists of an array of 54 minimum value (unity) capacitors and two single transistor switches controlled by the main clock signal on opposite phases. The time constant of exponential decay of the PSP is given by the ratio of capacitors created within the array (the ratio is set by connecting the capacitors together). The output of the PSP circuit is fed through a V-to-I converter to the dendritic tree.

In addition to this each synapse also provides a self-learning capability (weight changing depending on specific conditions). All these parts of the synapse use switched capacitor based circuits, instead of analogue memory. For example the soma potential capacitor and the auxiliary capacitor (used for shaping the PSP) using this technique have a value of 250 fF and 5 fF respectively (compared to tens of pF in non-SC design [1], [3]). The circuit for changing weight works on the principle of Hebb's learning rule, where the value of the change depends on the time difference between the output pulses of the transmiting and the receiving neuron, connected by the synapse.[1]

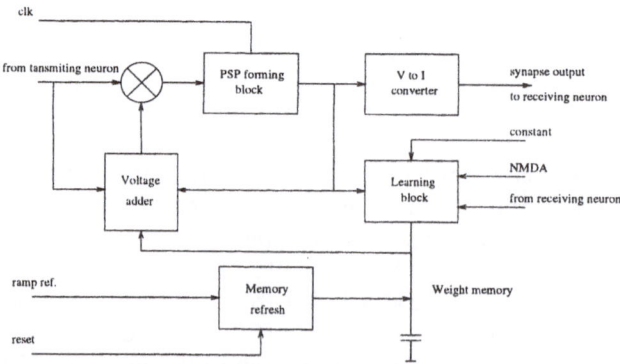

Fig. 2. A block diagram of a synapse with built-in Hebb's learning and current output.

There are basically two kinds of synapses: excitatory, which may cause hyperpolarisation of a neuron and inhibitory, which suppress the postsynaptical activity at the input of a neuron. The maximum synapse output current is approximately 2 μA in both directions. The block diagram of a synapse is shown in Fig. 2.

3 Simulation Results

Each part of this design was simulated with the Cadence Analog Artist tool using SpectreS and SpectreSVerilog. The models of the transistors were taken from the AMS-0.8 μm library version 3.12.

The synapse (Fig. 3) was simulated with a 500 kHz main clock signal, an initial memory value of 0.7 (when 1 is the maximum) and a capacitor ratio in the SC PSP circuit of 52:2 (number of unity capacitors of the PSP and auxiliary capacitor respectively). The NMDA learning threshold and the learnig constant for the down learning were 1 V above the analogue ground.

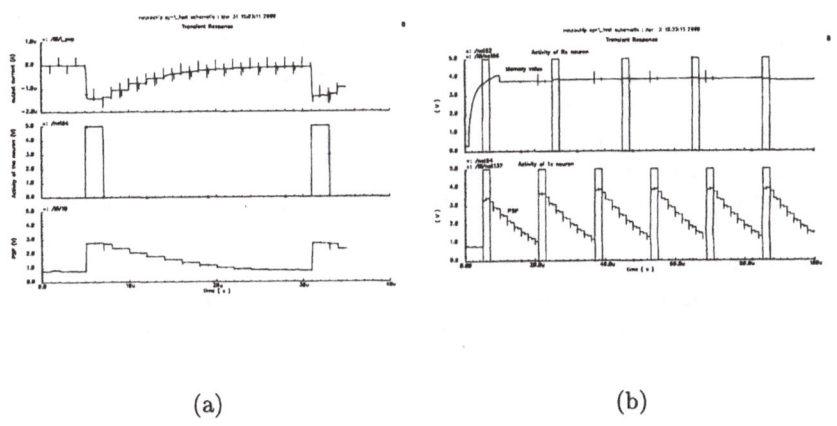

(a) (b)

Fig. 3. In figure **(a)** the function of the PSP circuit is shown. During activity of the neuron, the value stored in memory is added to the present value on the PSP capacitor and the circuit starts the discharging process. **(b)** The simulation of the learning circuit function, responsible for changing the value stored on the memory capacitor.

The neuron was simulated with the same clock rate as the synapse above, the ratio of the SC afterhyperpolarisation block was 62:2, the input threshold was set to 0 V and the dendritic input emulating the soma potential was 1 μA (Fig. 4a). The behavior of the same neuron with the same settings across different input currents (1 μA; 2 μA; 3 μA) is depicted in Fig. 4b.

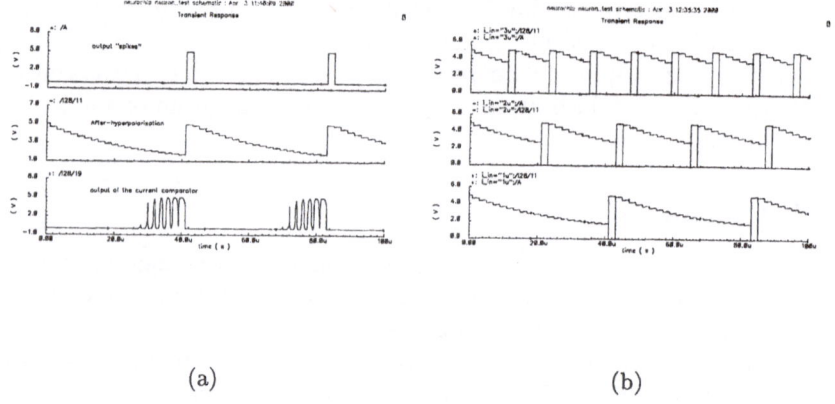

(a)   (b)

Fig. 4. Simulation of the neuron: **(a)** The neuron response with internal signals: the after-hyperpolarisation and the output of the current comparator. **(b)** Simulations with different input currents.

4 Fabrication

For fabrication within a multi-project chip a test design has been constructed, consisting of two neurons with different input current sensitivity and one learning synapse connected between them. The total design area (without the area of the padring cells) is 266 x 200 μm^2. Figure 5 shows the layout of the two neurons, one synapse between them, and some boundary circuits above them providing buffering of the clock signal and the analogue ramp voltage.

The main system clock and the analogue voltage ramp for memory refresh are generated in cells in the padring of the chip. The total number of pads for providing measurements on the neurons and the synapse is 12 including power supply, ground and analog ground.

5 Conclusion

In this paper an analogue design of a complete Integrate-and-Fire neural network using a leaf cell design technique is presented. Each cell is described also by a mathemathical model for faster simulation of a complete network. The total design area in the AMS 0.8 μm process is approximately 155x155 μm^2 for each synapse and 55x155 μm^2 for each neuron. The neuron and synapse were realised using a switched capacitor technique which significantly reduces the design area, and this makes it feasible to include a PSP in each

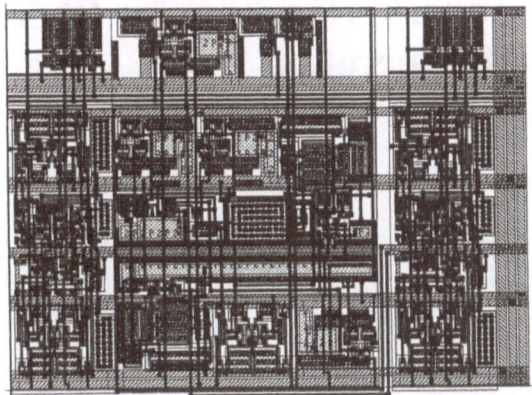

Fig. 5. The layout of the test-circuit.

synapse. Therefore it is possible to define a unique output characteristic for each synapse, which is closer to the biological model.

Acknowledgement

This work was supported by the Socrates / Erasmus project and Ministry of Education of the Slovak Republic under Grant No: 1/6096/99

D. Hajtáš is a visitor at the School of Design, Engineering and Computing at Bournemouth University.

References

1. Zahn T., Izak R., Trott K. (1997): Mixed analog-digital neurochip for acoustical attention. Europian workshop on neuromorphic systems, Stirling, U.K.
2. Vittoz E., Oguey H., Maher M. A., Nys O., Dijkstra E., Chevroulet M. (1991): Analog storage of adjustable synaptic weights. In VLSI Design of Neural Networks, Kluwer Acad. Publ., 47 - 63.
3. Glover M. A., Hamilton A., Smith L. S.(1998): Analogue VLSI Integrate and Fire Neural Network for Clustering Onset and Offset Signals in Sound Segmentation System. In Neuromorphic Systems, Engineering Silicon from Neurobiology, Progress in Neural Processing, vol. 10, World Scientific Pub Co, ISBN: 9810233779
4. Izak R., Hajtas D., Durackova D. (1998): Analog neuromorphic VLSI system with Integrate and Fire Neurons and on-chip learning Synapses, in Proceedings of 43. IWK, vol.2, 76 - 81.
5. Ismail M., Fiez T. (1994): Analog VLSI Signal and Information Processing, McGrow - Hill Series in Electrical and Computer Engeneering
6. Gregorian R., Temes G. C. (1986): Analog MOS Integrated Circuits for Signal Processing, John Wiley & Sons, ISBN: 0471097977

A Neural Network Algorithm for Digital Circuits Test Generation

Juraj Štefanovič

Departement of Computer Science and Engineering,
Faculty of Electrical Engineering and Information Technology,
Slovak Technical University, Ilkovièova 3,
812 19 Bratislava, Slovakia.
e-mail: stefanovic@dcs.elf.stuba.sk

Abstract: This work is a contribution to the methods of ATPG (Automatic Test Pattern Generation) for digital circuits, using neural network model. Some studies have already been devoted to the ATPG using neural networks at the logical level of circuit description. In this work, the behavioral level of circuit description is examined. The proposed method is based on Hopfield's neural network model utilisation: the digital circuit description (behavioral statements) is converted to the neural network and the network simulation produces the input circuit signals. This network showed a small efficiency for ATPG purposes yet, though it might be as an useful method to construct network by using higher description language.

Keywords: digital circuits, test patterns, neural networks.

1 Introduction

An ATPG algorithm using Hopfield's neural network model is presented in [1], [2] and [3]. The structure of digital circuit model is transformed to the neural network model. The transformation is as follows: each logical (electrical circuit) gate is translated to the elementary neural network where the attractor states have the correspondence to the logical truth table vectors. Such elementary neural networks are connected via LEGO principle following the logical structure of given logical circuit. Moreover, the two circuits: fault free and faulty one, are connected together and their outputs are set to be non equal. The simulation of this created neural network should finish in some point attractor state, where the input signals are a test pattern for digital circuit. The successful test pattern distinguishes the faulty and fault free circuit by observing their outputs.

2 Problem specification

The research papers mentioned above were discussing logical level circuit models. Our goal is to transform behavioral digital circuit model to the corresponding neural network of Hopfield's type. The behavioral model is described by VHDL (Very High Silicon Integrated Circuits High Description Language), with restriction to the architecture behavioral, *data flow* (no loops inside). On Fig. 1 there is a relation between the behavioral circuit description (left side) and the neural network under research (right side). The set of logical truth table vectors of the left side should correspond to the set of point attractors of the right side.

```
if(A) then C
     else if(B) then D
                 else E
```

=

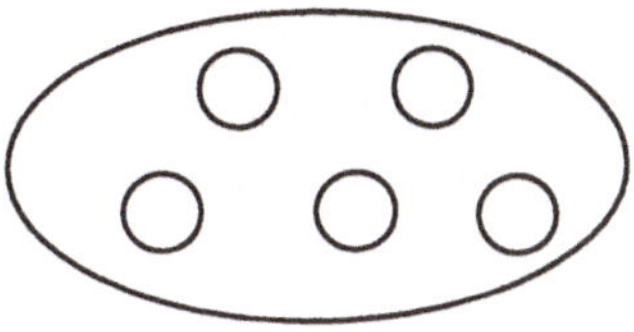

$\mathbf{X}_{out} = F\,(A,B,C,D,E,\mathbf{X}_{in})$ $E = f\,(\mathbf{X}_{in},\mathbf{X}_{out},\ldots)$

Fig. 1. A transformation problem of behavioral description (left, circuit function F) to the neural network (right, energy function f)

3 Solution

On Fig. 2, there is a possible relation between behavioral description and the neural network architecture. The **ABC** and **AB´D** paths are constructed from neurons. The paths are exciting their own neurons and an inhibition of the opposite path is added too. There is a hypothesis, that the point attractors of this network are corresponding to the left side function description.

```
if(A) then
          if(B)   then (C)
          if(B´)   then (D)
```

=

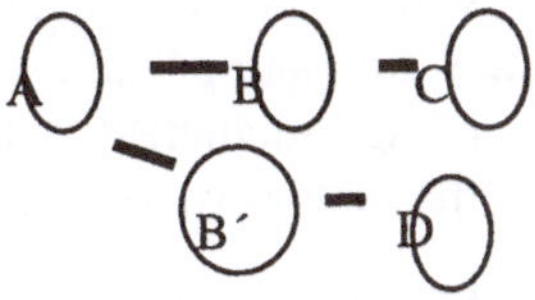

Fig. 2. VHDL statements on the left, neural network nodes on the right

The proposed architecture of neural network is a superposition of two networks: the network of nodes they represent VHDL conditional expressions (C - nodes) and the nodes they represent VHDL statements (A - nodes). Their output activity corresponds to the relation between circuit state and desired VHDL assertion. The energy of proposed network is computed by:

$$E = \min \{ E(ABC), E(AB\,D), ... \} \qquad (1)$$

4 Experiment

On Fig. 3, there is a part of construction of small neural network, which should correspond by its behavior to the given left side description.

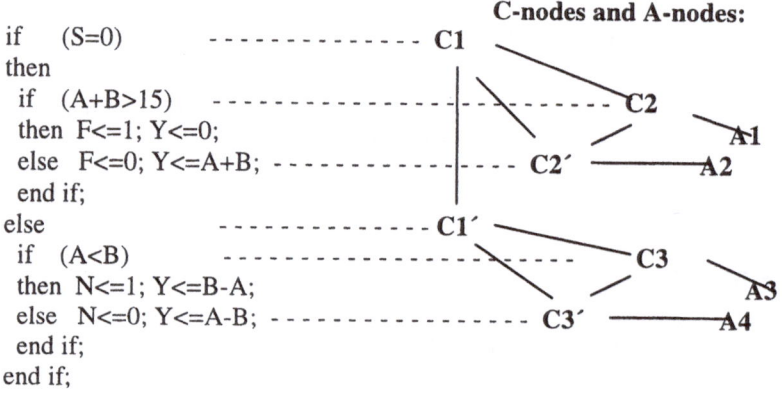

Fig. 3. A behavioral description transformed to the neural network

The transformation of network above is proposed as an algorithmic method, which can produce a network of any description of a such class. The A-nodes are computing entities they control the signal states (S,A,B,F,Y,N) via corresponding assignment statements on the left side (Fig. 3). The C-nodes are doing in the same way, via corresponding conditional statements.

On Fig. 4, the proposed network is shown as a formal superposition of two networks they work together: the network of nodes activities computes the consistency among statement branches (which branch is going to win) and the network of signal activities computes the consistency between states of signals and all expressions. These two networks are tight connected.

C,A nodes input, time T   C,A nodes activity, time T+Δ

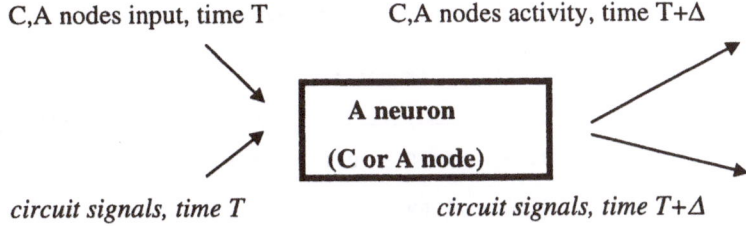

circuit signals, time T   *circuit signals, time T+Δ*

Fig. 4. A two networks superposition in one: the network of C,A nodes activities and the network of signal activities

On Fig. 5, there is an example of C,A nodes modeling principle. The cut and step functions are doing the network incrementation details. On Table 1, there is an example of network simulation. From the first column: the starting temperature T is high (1), the energy E is probably medium, the circuit signal states are chosen randomly in <0-15> or <0-1> responses. The "**A4-**" state means: the C-nodes state shows A4 attractor state (the A4 statement wins) but the A-node state there does not match (the signal values are not good enough). "**A3+**" state appears twice in simulation history and the energy reaches some local minimum value there.

```
float nodeC2 (float input) {
  if(random(2)) {  /*A+B>15*/
    if(random(2)) A=cut(A+input*inc(A+B-15.0));
    else          B=cut(B+input*inc(A+B-15.0));
    }
  return(rel(A+B-15.0));  /*node activity*/
  }
float nodeA3 (float input) {
  if(random(2)) N=cut(N+input*step(1.0-N));    /*N<=1*/
  if(random(2))
    switch(random(3)) {
      case 0: Y=cut(Y+input*step((B-A)-Y)); break; /*Y<=B-A*/
      case 1: A=cut(A+input*step((B-Y)-A)); break; /*A<=B-Y*/
      case 2: B=cut(B+input*step((Y+A)-B)); break; /*B<=Y+A*/
      }
  return(0.5*( eq0(N-1.0) + eq0(B-Y-A) ));   /*node activity*/
  }
```

Fig. 5. A principle of C,A nodes modeling

Table 1. An example of 10 000 iterations of given neural network

T	-E	A	B	Y	S	F	N	State
1.0	0.45	8.45	7.88	12.0	0.72	0.69	1.00	A4-
0.9	0.51	4.94	4.38	8.62	0.22	0.67	1.00	A2-
0.7	0.80	0.71	2.70	1.74	0.88	0.01	1.00	A3+
0.6	0.50	3.16	2.91	10.0	0.74	0.82	1.00	A4-
0.5	0.64	7.37	12.9	3.93	0.10	0.72	1.00	A1-
0.4	0.75	12.4	9.22	1.99	0.57	0.61	1.00	A4-
0.3	0.83	1.54	6.60	1.54	0.71	0.28	1.00	A3+
0.2	0.86	1.85	3.03	0.05	0.47	0.71	1.00	A2-

5 Conclusions

The proposed neural network architecture has a good statistical correspondence to the source behavioral description from the attractor set's point of view. The more complicated descriptions are not very successful, though the [1], [2] and [3] are optimistic. The use of the proposed method as a simple network behavioral description tool can be interesting too. This work was supported by Slovak Science Grant Agency: G1/7611/20 grant.

References

1. Bannino J., Santucci J.F. and Floutier D. (1995) A.T.P.G. for Combinational Circuits using Neural Methods. In: *Proc. of ATW'95 - Fourth Annual Atlantic Test Workshop*, Corsica, France, pp. 1-19

2. Chakradhar S.T., Agrawal V.D. and Bushnell M.L. (1994) Energy Minimization and Design for Testability. In: *Journal of Electronic Testing*, Kluwer Academic Publishers, vol.5, No.1, pp. 57-66

3. Zhang Z., McLeod R.D. and Pedrycz W. (1993) A Neural Network Algorithm for Testing Stuck-Open Faults in CMOS Combinational Circuits. In: *Journal of Electronic Testing*, Kluwer Academic Publishers, vol.4, No.3, pp. 225-235

The Parallel Bayesian Optimization Algorithm

Jiří Očenášek, Josef Schwarz

Brno University of Technology
Faculty of Electrical Engineering and Computer Science
Department of Computer Science and Engineering
CZ - 61266 Brno, Božetěchova 2
e-mail: ocenasek@dcse.fee.vutbr.cz, schwarz@dcse.fee.vutbr.cz

Abstract: In the last few years there has been a growing interest in the field of Estimation of Distribution Algorithms (EDAs), where crossover and mutation genetic operators are replaced by probability estimation and sampling techniques. The Bayesian Optimization Algorithm incorporates methods for learning Bayesian networks and uses these to model the promising solutions and generate new ones. The aim of this paper is to propose the parallel version of this algorithm, where the optimization time decreases linearly with the number of processors. During the parallel construction of network, the explicit topological ordering of variables is used to keep the model acyclic. The performance of the optimization process seems to be not affected by this constraint and our version of algorithm was successfully tested for the discrete combinatorial problem represented by graph partitioning as well as for deceptive functions.

1   Introduction

The proposed algorithm belongs to an EDA class of algorithm (Estimation of Distribution Algorithm) [1], based on probability theory and statistics. They use statistical information contained in the set of selected parents to detect gene dependencies. The estimated probability model is used to generate new promising solutions according to this distribution. The process can be described as follows:

Generate initial population of size **M** (randomly);
Repeat
    Select parent population of **N** individuals according to a selection method ($N \leq M$);
    Estimate the distribution of the selected parents;
    Generate new offspring of size **N'** according to the estimated model;
    Replace some individuals in current population by generated offspring;
Until termination criteria is met

2 Sequential BOA

BOA (Bayesian Optimization Algorithm) [2] uses Bayesian network (BN) to encode the structure of a problem. In the chromosome of length n each gene is treated as a variable and represented by one node in the dependency graph. For each variable X_i it is defined a set of variables Π_{X_i} it depends on, so the distribution of individuals is encoded as

$$p(X) = \prod_{i=0}^{n-1} p\left(X_i \mid \Pi_{X_i}\right) \tag{1}$$

Generally, the existence of oriented edge from X_j to X_i in the network implies the belonging of the variable X_j to the set Π_{X_i}. To reduce the space of networks, number of incomming edges into each node is limited to k.

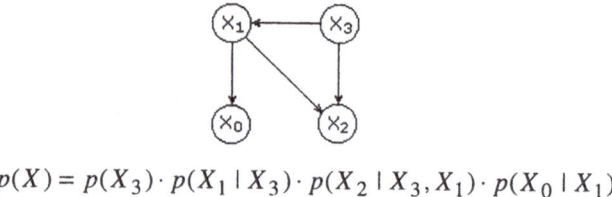

$$p(X) = p(X_3) \cdot p(X_1 \mid X_3) \cdot p(X_2 \mid X_3, X_1) \cdot p(X_0 \mid X_1)$$

Fig.1 Example of Bayesian network for joint probability distribution of 4 variables

The Bayessian Dirichlet metric (BD) [3] is used to measure the quality of the network. A special case of BD metric, so-called K2 metric, is used when no prior information about the problem is available.

Many algorithms can be used to build up the network. The optimal search is NP-hard, so in the sequential implementation [4] a simple greedy algorithm was used with only one edge addition in each step. The algorithm starts with an empty network B and for each edge that can be added it computes the K2 metrics of the network B' that can be constructed from B by adding this edge. The edge giving the highest improvement is then added to the network B. This process is repeated until no more addition is possible. By the term 'edge can be added' we mean the test whether the edge keeps the network acyclic, meets the limit of incoming edges and does not belong to the network yet.

After network construction new individuals are generated. First, the variables (genes) are ordered in the topological order and each iteration, the nodes whose parents are already determined are generated using the conditional probabilities. This is repeated until all the variables are generated. Since the sequence of generation should be defined, the dependencies between variables must be acyclic.

3 Parallel approach

As shown in [2], the overall time to construct the Bayesian network using the greedy search driven by BD metric is $O(k2^k n^2 N + kn^3)$, where n is the length of a chromosome, k is the limit of incoming edges into each node and N is the size of parent population. The time complexity for generating N' new individuals (offspring) is only $O(knN')$, where N' is proportional to the number of parents N. The time complexity for offspring evaluation depends on the complexity of fitness computation itself and in the case of additively-decomposable functions is $O(nN')$.

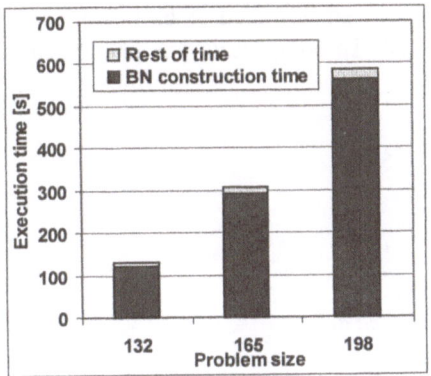 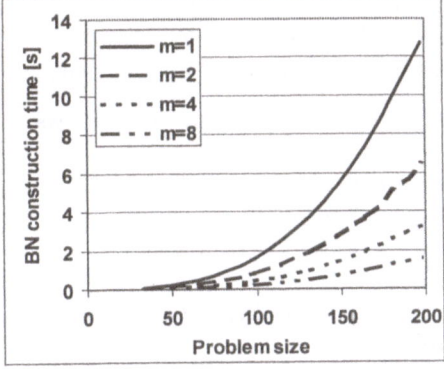

Fig.2 The BOA time complexity profile   Fig.3 BN construction time for m processors

Fig.2 shows the empirical confirmation of the time-complexity terms stated above: nearly all the execution time of sequential BOA is spent to find the structure of Bayesian network. The remaining time includes fitness computation, parent selection and offspring generation. In comparison to the construction of Bayesian network all of those remaining tasks are easy to be done in parallel, but they take only less than 5% of the overall time. Fig.3 shows the time of Bayesian network construction using one processor of Sun Enterprise 450 server; for the case of m=2,4,8 the time was estimated with no communication overhead considered. Both experiments were done for $f_{3deceptive}$ function [2].

4 Proposed solution

The goal is to utilize more processors when searching for a good network. Our consolation is that the BD metric is separable and can be written as a product of n factors, where i-th factor expresses the influence of edges ending in the variable X_i. It is possible to use up to n processors, each processor corresponds to one variable and it examines only edges leading to this variable (it has its own local copy of parent population).

The addition of edges is parallel, so we need an additional mechanism to keep the network acyclic. The most simple way how to do it is to predetermine the topological ordering of nodes in advance. At the beginning of each generation, the random permutation of numbers $\{0,1,...,n-1\}$ is created and stored in the **perm** array. Each processor generates the same permutation (the initial seed of permutation generator is distributed via set of processors in the initial phase). The direction of all edges in the network should be consistent with the ordering, so the addition of an edge from X_j to X_i is allowed if **perm**[j] < **perm**[i]. Evidently, the variable X_i with **perm**[i]=0 has no predecessor and is forced to be independent, thus the space of possible networks is reduced. To compensate this phenomenon we use new permutation for each generation.

The algorithm can be written as follows:

Start with an empty network B;
Generate the permutation array perm;
for i := 0 **to** (n - 1) **do in parallel**
begin
  while *any edge ending in the variable X_i can be added* **do**
  begin
    for *each possible start of new edge (variable X_j having perm[j]<perm[i])* **do**
    begin
      Compute the local increase of K2 metrics after adding edge (X_j,X_i);
    end
    Add the edge (X_j,X_i) giving the highest improvement to the network B;
  end
end

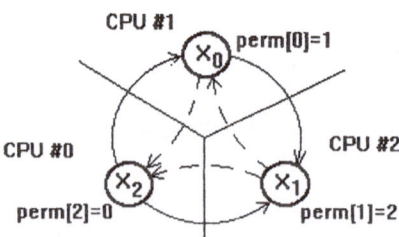

Fig. 4 Example with $n=3$ and **perm**=(1,2,0). The dashed edges are not allowed, so the three processors do not have to communicate to keep the network acyclic.

Moreover, the explicit ordering of nodes enables the generation of new individuals in a linear pipeline way. If we use n processors, then the i-th processor receives from (i-1)-th processor the chromozome with i positions fixed and generates the value of variable X_k, where **perm**[k] = i.

5 Time complexity for parallel BOA (PBOA)

When using only m processors ($m \leq n$), the time complexity of the greedy search for a network structure is $O(\lceil n/m \rceil (k2^k nN + kn^2))$ and the time for generating N' new individuals in a pipeline is $O(\lceil n/m \rceil (kn + kN'))$. This algorithm requires no cooperation between processors, so the time estimation shown in Fig.3 is valid. When we use $m=n$ processors, the time complexity is decreased roughly from $O(n^3)$ to $O(n^2)$.

6 Experimental results

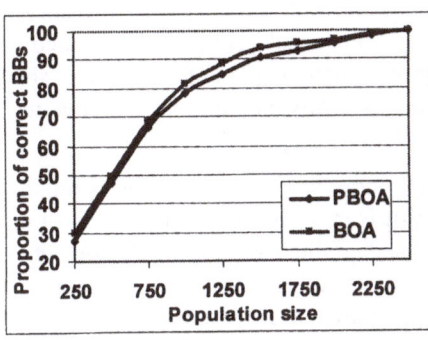
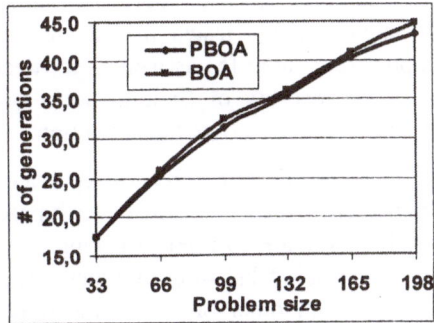

Fig.5 Proportion of correct BBs   Fig.6 Number of generations until convergence

In Fig.5 and Fig.6 the experimental results for $f_{3deceptive}$ function [2] are shown. The population size needed to get the same quality of solution as well as the number of generations until successful convergence is similar for both BOA and PBOA. The same conclusion we obtained for $f_{5deceptive}$ function [2].

Table 1. The results of grid graphs bisection [5]

Graph name	Grid 100.2 with bottleneck	Grid 100.10
BOA: Min. population size for 90% success	2500	2400
PBOA: Min. population size for 90% success	2600	2500
BOA: Avg. # of generations until convergence	47,9	57,9
PBOA: Avg. # of generations until convergence	51,2	66,3
BOA: Average # of fitness evaluations	119750	138960
PBOA: Average # of fitness evaluations	133120	165750

The values in the Table 1 indicate that for real problems like graph bisectioning the PBOA needs slightly higher population size and number of generations, but this is not critical because PBOA reduces the additional time by the parallel processing too.

7 Conclusion and future work

This paper is focused on the parallelization of the original (sequential) Bayesian Optimization Algorithm [4] – namely on the parallel construction of Bayesian network. The proposed approach with predetermined topological ordering of BN nodes keeps the network inherently acyclic, so the time complexity of parallel BN construction is linearly reduced by the number of processors. The performance of the algorithm was tested for the discrete combinatorial problem represented by graph bisectioning [5] as well as for deceptive functions [2] and our results show that the capability of finding global optima is really not affected by the used simplification of network construction.

We have also described how to generate new individuals using the linear pipeline architecture with n processors - each processor is responsible for generation of one variable. We are currently working on a coarse-grained version of PBOA, where the cluster of workstations and message passing techniques are used. Each process receives from other processes the remaining parts of Bayesian network and is responsible for generation, evaluation and distribution of its portion of population. This helps us to overlap the communication latency between workstations.

Acknowledgement

This research has been carried out under the financial support of the Research intention No. CEZ: J22/98: 262200012 – "Research in information and control systems" and it was also supported by the Grant Agency of Czech Republic grant No. 102/98/0552 "Research and Application of Heterogeneous Models".

References

[1] Muehlenbein, H., Rodriguez, A. O.: Schemata Distributions and Graphical Models in Evolutionary Optimization. GMD Forschungs Zentrum Informationstechnik, 53754-St. Augustin, 1998, pp.1-21.

[2] Pelikan, M., Goldberg, D. E., Cantú-Paz, E.: Linkage Problem, Distribution Estimation, and Bayesian Networks. IlliGal Report No. 98013, November 1998, pp. 1-25.

[3] Heckerman, D., Geiger, D., Chickering, M.: Learning Bayesian networks: The combination of knowledge and statistical data, Technical Report MSR-TR-94-09, Redmond, Microsoft Research, 1994, pp. 1-53.

[4] Pelikan, M.: A Simple Implementation of Bayesian Optimization Algorithm in C++(Version1.0). Illigal Report 99011, February 1999, pp. 1-16.

[5] Schwarz, J., Očenášek, J.: Experimental study: Hypergraph partitioning based on the simple and advanced genetic algorithms BMDA and BOA, 5th International Mendel Conference, 1999, FME VUT Brno, Czech Republic, pp. 124-130.

Application of Heuristic Programming to Dynamic System Stabilization

Dušan Krokavec and Anna Filasová

Technical University of Košice, Faculty of Electrical Engineering and Informatics, Department of Cybernetics and Artificial Intelligence, Letná 9/B, SK-042 00 Košice, Slovak Republic

Abstract: The paper is devoted to application of linear quadratic (LQ) control principles for dynamic system stabilization by heuristic programming in neuro-control. This idea seems to be suitable for learning in noisy and nonlinear environments using dynamic programming generalization for neural reinforcement learning approaches. The main emphasis was on combination of these with shift of the dominant state matrix eigenvalues. The effectiveness of the technique is demonstrated by its application to the problem of transient process stabilization in power system.

1   Introduction

To handle special situations arising in modern industry systems various versions of linear, adaptive, nonlinear or artificial intelligence based control have been suggested. Linear control, using linearized models, is fully justified for small disturbance operation around a fixed operating point. When the system is subjected to large disturbances, there needs to be a mechanism to adapt the controller to the new operating conditions. However, in highly structured systems, assuming the model is unknown, is losing too much information. So it is still interesting to use some adaptation of the model based familiar ideas and to combine them with artificial intelligence implementation algorithms. One from this is a combination of the dominant eigenvalue system matrix shifting and the heuristic dynamic programming. The paper present the basic principle of this combination for large scale structured plants, like the power systems are. The most applicable publications which have dealt with the above mentioned problem are [2], [4], [9], [11], in [6], [8] are proposed the basic techniques for dealing with them.

2   Disturbed System Motion

Generally, large systems are given by differential and algebraic equations

$$\dot{\mathbf{x}}_1(t) = f_1(\mathbf{x}_1(t), \mathbf{x}_2(t), \mathbf{p}(t), q(t)), \tag{1a}$$

$$\mathbf{0} = f_2(\mathbf{x}_1(t), \mathbf{x}_2(t), \mathbf{p}(t), q(t)) \tag{1b}$$

where $x_1(t)$ is the dynamic state vector, $x_2(t)$ is the algebraic state vector and the time function $q(t)$ represents sudden changes of system operating conditions due to large disturbances. Vector $p(t)$ is a vector of controlled parameters (including any parameters which can be varied in tuning and control) which elements are normally bounded by some physical constrains.

If $p(t)$ and $q(t)$ are piecewise constant function of time, which have step breaks at certain moments of time depending upon system disturbances and control action, system (1a), (1b) can be considered as autonomous within same intervals and sudden changes of $p(t)$ and $q(t)$ at the break points result in new system initial conditions at the begin of every interval.

If the algebraic Jacobian matrix be nonsingular, there exists a locally defined function $x_2(t) = \Psi(x_1(t), p(t), q(t))$ for constant $p(t)$, $q(t)$ that satisfies $0 = f_2(x_1(t), \Psi(x_1(t), p(t), q(t)), p(t), q(t))$ and for $x_1(t) = x(t)$ the system can be locally represented as follows

$$\dot{x}(t) = f_1(x(t), \Psi(x_1(t), p(t), q(t)), p(t), q(t)) = f(x(t), p(t), q(t)) \quad (2)$$

If the state matrix of (2) calculated at a fixed point $(x(t), p(t), q(t))$

$$A(x(t), p(t), q(t)) = \frac{\partial f_1(x_1(t), x_2(t), p(t), q(t))}{\partial x_1} -$$
$$- \frac{\partial f_1(x_1(t), x_2(t), p(t), q(t))}{\partial x_2} \left[\frac{\partial f_2(x_1(t), x_2(t), p(t), q(t))}{\partial x_2} \right]^{-1} \frac{\partial f_2(x_1(t), x_2(t), p(t), q(t))}{\partial x_1} \quad (3)$$

has at least one eigenvalue with positive real part, the system is locally unstable. Using substitution $\Delta x(t) = x(t) - x_0(t)$, where $x_0(t)$ is the undisturbed motion, (2) can be transformed to equation of disturbed motion

$$\Delta \dot{x}(t) = f(\Delta x(t) + x_0(t), p(t), q(t)) - f(x_0(t), p(t), q(t)) =$$
$$A(x_0(t), p_0(t), q_0(t))\Delta x(t) + B(x_0(t), p_0(t), q_0(t))\Delta u(t) + o(\Delta x(t), \Delta u(t)) \quad (4)$$

where $o(\Delta x(t), \Delta u(t))$ does not contain linear terms of $\Delta x(t)$ and $\Delta u(t)$.

Elementary manipulation of (4) gives for small sampling period t_s and zero-order-hold inputs the discrete-time state-space description of the system

$$x(i+1) = F(x_0(i), p_0(i), q_0(i))x(i) + G(x_0(i), p_0(i), q_0(i))u(i) + \quad (5)$$
$$+ O(t_s, \Delta x(t), \Delta u(t))$$

where $O(t_s, \Delta x(t), \Delta u(t))$ does not contain linear terms of t_s, $\Delta x(t)$, $\Delta u(t)$.

3 Heuristic Dynamic Programming for LQ Control

The control objective is to construct a feedback controller $u(i) = -K(i)x(i)$ to the system (5) such that the quadratic performance index

$$J = \sum_{i=0}^{\infty} x^T(i)Qx(i) + u^T(i)Ru(i) \quad (6)$$

is minimized. This problem is equivalent to finding the control function $\mathbf{u}(i)$ and the Lyapunov function $V(\mathbf{x}(i))$ of special structure. Assuming, that

$$f(\mathbf{x}(i), \mathbf{u}(i)) = \mathbf{F}\mathbf{x}(i) + \mathbf{G}\mathbf{u}(i) = \mathbf{x}(i+1) \tag{7a}$$
$$V(\mathbf{x}(i+1)) = \mathbf{x}^T(i+1)\mathbf{P}(i)\mathbf{x}(i+1) \tag{7b}$$
$$r(\mathbf{x}(i), \mathbf{u}(i)) = \mathbf{x}^T(i)\mathbf{Q}\mathbf{x}(i) + \mathbf{u}^T(i)\mathbf{R}\mathbf{u}(i) \tag{7c}$$
$$g(\mathbf{x}(i)) = -\mathbf{K}(i)\mathbf{x}(i) = \mathbf{u}(i) \tag{7d}$$

from the Pontryagin minimum principle implies $\mathbf{u}(i)$ must be such, that

$$\frac{\partial V(\mathbf{x}(i))}{\partial g(\mathbf{x}(i))} = \frac{\partial r(\mathbf{x}(i), \mathbf{u}(i))}{\partial g(\mathbf{x}(i))} + \frac{\partial V(\mathbf{x}(i+1))}{\partial \mathbf{x}(i+1)} \frac{\partial f(\mathbf{x}(i), \mathbf{u}(i))}{\partial g(\mathbf{x}(i))} = 0 \tag{8}$$

and target for an action minimization can be defined as

$$\mathbf{e}_a(i) = 0 - \frac{\partial V(\mathbf{x}(i))}{\partial g(\mathbf{x}(i))} = 0 - \left(\frac{\partial r(\mathbf{x}(i), \mathbf{u}(i))}{\partial g(\mathbf{x}(i))} + \frac{\partial V(\mathbf{x}(i+1))}{\partial \mathbf{x}(i+1)} \frac{\partial f(\mathbf{x}(i), \mathbf{u}(i))}{\partial g(\mathbf{x}(i))} \right) \tag{9}$$

Using the criterion $W_a(i) = \frac{1}{2}\mathbf{e}_a^T(i)\mathbf{e}_a(i) = \frac{1}{2}\sum_{h=1}^{M} e_{ah}^2(i)$ for the action neural network training, a steepest-descent discrete gradient method, using error backpropagation algorithm, can be applied to solve this minimization, i.e.

$$\Delta w_{rs}(i) = -\mu_a \frac{\partial W_a(i)}{\partial w_{rs}(i)} = -\mu_a \left(\frac{\partial r(i)}{\partial \mathbf{u}(i)} + \frac{\partial V(i+1)}{\partial \mathbf{x}(i+1)} \frac{\partial \mathbf{x}(i+1)}{\partial \mathbf{u}(i)} \right) \frac{\partial \mathbf{u}(i)}{\partial w_{rs}(t)} =$$
$$= -\mu_a \sum_{k=1}^{M} \left(\frac{\partial r(i)}{\partial u_k(i)} + \sum_{j=1}^{N} \frac{\partial V(i+1)}{\partial x_j(i+1)} \frac{\partial x_j(i+1)}{\partial u_k(i)} \right) \frac{\partial u_k(i)}{\partial w_{rs}(t)} \tag{10}$$

where $\frac{\partial x_j(i+1)}{\partial u_k(i)}$ is calculated from analytical equation of the system model, $\frac{\partial V(i+1)}{\partial x_j(i+1)}$ is approximated by the critic, $\frac{\partial r(i)}{\partial u_k(i)}$ is calculated as a derivative of (7c) and N, M is the number of state and input variables, respectively.

The critic neural network is trained using the assumption of the optimal response $V(\mathbf{x}(i)) \doteq V(\mathbf{x}(i+1)) + r(\mathbf{x}(i), \mathbf{u}(i))$ which gives for the jth desired output of the critic neural network

$$c_j^0(i) = \frac{\partial V(i)}{\partial x_j(i)} = \frac{r(\mathbf{x}(i), \mathbf{u}(i))}{\partial x_j(i)} + \frac{r(\mathbf{x}(i), \mathbf{u}(i))}{\partial \mathbf{u}(i)} \frac{\partial \mathbf{u}(i)}{\partial x_j(i)} + \frac{V(\mathbf{x}(i+1))}{\partial \mathbf{x}(i+1)} \frac{\partial \mathbf{x}(i+1)}{\partial x_j(i)} =$$
$$= \frac{r(i)}{\partial x_j(i)} + \sum_{k=1}^{M} \frac{\partial r(i)}{\partial u_k(i)} \frac{\partial u_k(i)}{\partial x_j(i)} + \sum_{h=1}^{N} \frac{\partial V(i+1)}{\partial x_h(i+1)} \frac{\partial x_h(i+1)}{\partial x_j(i)} +$$
$$+ \sum_{k=1}^{M} \sum_{h=1}^{N} \frac{\partial V(i+1)}{\partial x_h(i+1)} \frac{\partial x_h(i+1)}{\partial u_k(i)} \frac{\partial u_k(i)}{\partial x_j(i)} \tag{11}$$

where $\frac{\partial x_h(i+1)}{\partial u_k(i)}$ is calculated from analytical equation of the system model, $\frac{\partial V(i+1)}{\partial x_h(i+1)}$ is approximated by the critic and $\frac{r(i)}{\partial x_j(i)}$, $\frac{\partial r(i)}{\partial u_k(i)}$ are calculated as a derivative of (7c), respectively. The value $\frac{\partial u_k(i)}{\partial x_j(i)}$ is given as the product of synaptic weights from jth input to kth output of the action network.

The training criterion and the optimization procedure for critic neural network can be than $W_c(i) = \frac{1}{2} \sum_{i=1}^{N} (c_j(i) - c_j^0(i))^2$, $\Delta w_{rs}(i) = -\mu_c \frac{\partial W_c(i)}{\partial w_{rs}(i)}$. It is evident, that the basic strategy to update the neural nets can be given by the straight application of the above presented equations. The better critic neural network approximate criterion the better the action neural network will approximate an optimal control. The system matrix eigenvalue shift is given by appropriate choosing of matrix $\mathbf{Q}$.

4 Direct Shift of a System Matrix Eigenvalue

The modern stability theory has not yet provided a general criterion to judge whether systems are stable for a variety of initial conditions, disturbances and uncertainties. LQ control, as well as heuristic dynamic programming, is based on the basis of the Lyapunov's functions. But unfortunately only one partial form based on simplified linearized system model is used there and has many limitation in discrete events and constraints applied parameters limits. It seems the minimization technique used to minimize the system eigenvalue real parts along the system trajectory be able to present or predict the stabilizing actions.

The jth eigenvalue of the matrix (3) satisfies equation

$$\mathbf{w}_j^T \mathbf{A} \mathbf{v}_j = \lambda_j \tag{12}$$

and the positions of the dominant eigenvalues along the real axis can be describe as

$$W_\lambda(i) = \frac{1}{2} \sum_{\lambda_j > \lambda_0} (\lambda_j(i) - \lambda_0)^2 \tag{13}$$

Minimization of $W_\lambda(i)$ leads to a movement of $\lambda_j(i)$ toward their reference point. Using the steepest descent optimization procedure the gradient of (13) gives a direction of changing of $\mathbf{p}(i)$ at each iteration. Elements of the sensitivity vector and a direction of changing of control $\mathbf{p}(i)$ during the optimization can be compute using the well known formula

$$\mathbf{p}(i) = \mathbf{p}(i-1) - \mu_p \left(\frac{\partial W_\lambda(i)}{\partial \mathbf{p}(i)} \right)^T \tag{14a}$$

$$\frac{\partial W_\lambda(i)}{\partial \mathbf{p}(i)} = \sum_{\lambda_j > \lambda_0} (\lambda_j(i) - \lambda_0) \frac{\partial \lambda_j(i)}{\partial \mathbf{p}(i)} = \sum_{\lambda_j > \lambda_0} (\lambda_j(i) - \lambda_0) \Re \left\{ \frac{\mathbf{w}_j^T \frac{\partial \mathbf{A}(i)}{\partial \mathbf{p}(i)} \mathbf{v}_j}{\mathbf{w}_j^T \mathbf{v}_j} \right\} \tag{14b}$$

where $\mathbf{w}_j^T$ and $\mathbf{v}_j$ are left and right eigenvector of the state matrix $\mathbf{A}$.

This technique can be used to evaluate the utmost changes of damping when some system parameters are unknown but varied within their ranges $p_{in} \leq p_i \leq p_{im}$.

5 Experimental Results

The purpose was to demonstrate whether the proposed methods are able to achieve the system stability with emphasis on disturbed system motion. The tests were conducted for a power system model to present a neural network technique for stabilizing power system transient processes. The single machine infinite bus power system model [1] was studied to reveal load uncertainty influence on power system stability. The mathematical model of the system consists of four differential equations, which cover both generator and load dynamics.

The continuous-time nominal control acts in such a way that the system is stabilized, i.e. its state matrix has eigenvalues with negative real parts. Points of the dynamic stability boundary (both oscillatory and aperiodic ones) are corresponding to the eigenvalue $\lambda_h = 0 \pm j\omega$ (Hopf bifurcation) and $\lambda_h = 0$ (saddle node bifurcation) of the state matrix (3), respectively. Singularity induces aperiodic bifurcation is caused by singularity of the algebraic sub-matrix. Besides revealing the type of instability the constraint set determine the frequency of critical oscillatory mode. The eigenvectors determine sensitivity of the real part eigenvalues and observability and excitability of the critical oscillatory mode.

The system LQ control was simulated using an action neural network and a critic neural network where analytical equations were used to compute system model outputs and the utility function in the training stage. Both the action and critic neural networks have feedforward architecture with one hidden layer. The neural network structures used were {4 MP (linear), 2 MP (tanh), 1 MP (ktanh)} for action neural network and {4 MP (linear), 4 MP (tanh), 4 MP (linear)} for critic neural network (format : {input, hidden, output} layers). These networks were trained using the basic backpropagation algorithm, where the single-stage process strategies to train the critic desired outputs were used [6]. To combine LQ control with eigenvalue shift algorithm the action neural network structure was {4 MP (linear), 4 MP (tanh), 1 MP (ktanh)}. Further the scaling of the state-space variables was applied and bias term in critic and particularly in the action neural network were used. The number of MP were specific to the system model [1].

6 Conclusion

This paper has describe a framework for neural network application in system stability evaluation and control. Tests have showed impressive generalization capability of the controllers designed via heuristic programming process. It has been discovered that the unknown load parameters result in the damping uncertainty and by varying the control parameter, to provide dominant eigenvalue shift along the integral trajectory, better damping of the resulting process can be reached. The results obtained provide some non-trivial penetration on the future studies on the large-scale system control actions.

Acknowledgements

The work presented in this paper was supported by Grant Agency of Ministry of Education and Academy of Science of Slovak Republic VEGA under Grant No. 1/6270/99.

References

1. Chiang, H.D., Dobson, I., Thomas, R.J., Thorp, J.S., Lazhar, F.A. (1990) On voltage collapse in electric power systems. IEEE Trans. on Power Systems. **5**, No. 2, pp. 601-611
2. Gruzdev, I.A., Toroptzev, E.L., Ustinov, S.M. (1986) Optimization of automatic control devices tuning for a variety of power system operating condition. Elektrichestvo, No. 4, pp. 11-15 (in Russian)
3. Filasová, A. (1997) Robust controller design for large-scale uncertain dynamic systems. Preprints of the 2nd IFAC Workshop on New Trends in Design of Control Systems, pp. 127–132, Smolenice, Slovakia
4. Krokavec, D., Filasová, A. (1999) Action dependent heuristic dynamic programming from the point of discrete-time control. Proceedings of the 12th Conference Process control '99, Vol. 1, pp. 202–206, Tatranske Matliare, Slovakia
5. Kučera, V., Kraus, J. (1999) How to shift an individual eigenvalue by quadratic criterion. Proceedings of the 12th Conference Process control '99, Vol. 2, pp. 1–5, Tatranske Matliare, Slovakia
6. Lendaris, G.G., Paintz, C. (1997) Training strategies for critic and action neural network in dual heuristic programming method. Proceedings of the IEEE International Conference on Neural Network ICNN'97, pp. 712–717, Houston
7. Ljung, L. (1977) Analysis of recursive stochastic algorithms. IEEE Trans. Automat. Contr. **AC-22**, No. 4, pp. 551–575
8. Makarov, Y.V., Popovič, D.H., Hill, D.J (1998) Stabilization of transient processes in power systems by eigenvalue shift approach. IEEE Trans. on Power Systems. **13**, No. 2, pp. 382-388
9. Prokhorov, D.V., Santiago, R.A., Wunsch, D.C. (1995) Adaptive critic design: A case study for neurocontrol. Neural Networks, **8**, No. 9, pp. 1367–1372
10. Solheim, O.A. (1972) Design of optimal control systems with prescribed eigenvalues. Int. J. Control, **15**, No. 1, pp. 143–160
11. Werbos, P.J. (1990) Consistency of HDP applied to a simple reinforcement learning problem. Neural Networks, **3**, pp. 179-189

First Order Dynamic Instance Selection

Peter GÉCZY[1], Shiro USUI[1], and Ján CHMÚRNY[2]

[1] Toyohashi University of Technology, Toyohashi 441-8580, Japan
[2] Military Academy, Liptovský Mikuláš, SK-03119, Slovakia

Abstract: Training of adaptable systems such as neural networks indispensably depends on the training exemplar set. The most promising training algorithms utilize dynamic instance selection. Dynamic instance selection technique is capable of selecting instances dynamically at each iteration of adaptation procedure. Adaptable system is thus at each iteration presented with appropriately selected set of learning instances that can vary in size and content. Variability of the selected exemplar set contributes to the speed of learning and lowers its computational cost. Benefit of dynamic instance selection can also be found in improved properties of trained adaptable systems.

1 Introduction

Dynamic instance selection techniques [1]–[5] feature high flexibility in selecting instances for adaptable systems. Training instances are selected dynamically at each iteration of the adaptation procedure. Selected set of instances can vary in size as well as in content from iteration to iteration. Dynamic instance selection techniques are not inherently linked to particular adaptation techniques. Selection of instances can be random or according to the certain distribution until the specific conditions are satisfied. Stopping condition(s) for selecting instances are derived with close consideration of the dynamics of adaptable systems. This gives the dynamic instance selection techniques potential for improving the convergence speed and quality of adaptation.

Static Instance Selection [6], [7], and *Stochastic Instance Selection* [8] approaches indicate reasonable improvement of adaptation phase in cases when the ratio of instances to free parameters (denoted in further text as I-FP ratio) is close to 1. Small improvements were indicated also for the values of I-FP ratio around 2 and 3. However, the techniques appear to be ineffective for higher values of the I-FP ratio. *Dynamic Instance Selection* techniques have been reported to increase convergence speed of adaptation even at the value of I-FP ratio 15 (and possibly even more) [2].

2 Adaptable Systems, Mapping, and Training

Adaptable system essentially contains a set of adaptable parameters, realizes mapping, and is capable of adapting its parameters with specified adaptation procedure - training. Considering these facts, the adaptable system and its elements are defined as follows.

Adaptable System: *Adaptable system is triple $\mathcal{AS} = (\mathbf{u}, \mathcal{F}, \mathcal{A})$ where $\mathbf{u}$ denotes a set or vector of adaptable parameters, $\mathcal{F}$ is a mapping given the parameters $\mathbf{u}$, and $\mathcal{A}$ is an adaptation procedure (also referred to as training or learning). An adaptable system $\mathcal{AS}$ with adaptation procedure $\mathcal{A}$ having linear or superlinear convergence rates and utilizing only the first order information about the system is called first order adaptable system.*

Mapping of Adaptable System: *A mapping $\mathcal{F}(\mathbf{u}, \mathbf{x})$, $\mathcal{F} : \Re^{N_I} \to \Re^{N_O}$, where N_I is the dimensionality of the input space, N_O is the dimensionality of the output space, $\mathbf{u} \in \Re^{N_F}$ is N_F-dimensional real valued vector of adjustable parameters of $\mathcal{F}$, and $\mathbf{x} \in \Re^{N_I}$ is N_I-dimensional real valued input vector, is said to be a mapping of an adaptable system.*

Training in Adaptable Systems: *Let $T = \{[\mathbf{x}, \mathbf{y}] | \mathbf{x} \in \Re^{N_I} \wedge \mathbf{y} \in \Re^{N_O}\}$ be a training set with cardinality N_P. Each pair $[\mathbf{x}, \mathbf{y}]$ contains the input pattern $\mathbf{x}$ of the dimensionality N_I, and the expected output pattern $\mathbf{y}$ of the dimensionality N_O. Let $\mathbf{u}$ denote a set of free parameters of adaptable system, and the objective function $E(\mathcal{F}(\mathbf{u}, \mathbf{x}), \mathbf{y})$ belongs to the class C^1. Training of adaptable system is a process of minimizing the objective function E, $\arg\min_{\mathbf{u}} E(\mathcal{F}(\mathbf{u}, \mathbf{x}), \mathbf{y})$, given a finite number of samples $[\mathbf{x}, \mathbf{y}] \in T$ drawn from an arbitrary sample distribution.*

3 Theoretical Concept

In the instance selection task it is beneficial to distinguish two important sets of instances: representative instances: $\mathcal{RI} = \{[\mathbf{x}_i, \mathbf{y}_i] \in T \mid m(\mathbf{u}, \mathbf{x}_i, \mathbf{y}_i) < \mathcal{L}\}$, and critical instances: $\mathcal{CI} = \{[\mathbf{x}_i, \mathbf{y}_i] \in T \mid m(\mathbf{u}, \mathbf{x}_i, \mathbf{y}_i) \geq \mathcal{L}\}$. Sets $\mathcal{RI}$ and $\mathcal{CI}$ are defined with respect to the measure, $m(\mathbf{u}, \mathbf{x}_i, \mathbf{y}_i) = ||\nabla E(\mathcal{F}(\mathbf{u}, \mathbf{x}_i), \mathbf{y}_i)||_2$, where $|| \cdot ||_2$ denotes l_2 norm. Measure m enables dynamic categorization of instances at each iteration of adaptation procedure of $\mathcal{AS}$.

Search direction of line search optimization techniques (whether steepest descent or conjugate gradient) is primarily formed of instance sub-gradients. Each instance contributes to the formation of search direction. Selected set of instances will thus generally form a different search direction than the complete set of instances. It is therefore appropriate to evaluate the expression of the normed search direction.

Theorem 1. *(l_2 Norm of Search Direction for Superlinear First Order $\mathcal{A}$)*
Let $\mathcal{A}$ be superlinear first order line search optimization technique, $\mathbf{s}^{(k)}$ be a search direction at the state $\mathbf{u}^{(k)}$, $\alpha^{(k)}$ be a scaling factor of the search direction at the state $\mathbf{u}^{(k)}$, $\nabla E(\mathbf{u}^{(k)})$ be a gradient vector at the state $\mathbf{u}^{(k)}$, and $\mathbf{u}^*$ be the optimum point. The following holds:

$$||s^{(k)}||_2 = \frac{|E(\mathbf{u}^*) - E(\mathbf{u}^{(k)})|}{|\alpha^{(k)}| \cdot ||\nabla E(\mathbf{u}^{(k)})||_2} \equiv PI^{(k)}.$$

The fastest convergence rates a first order technique can achieve are superlinear. Assumption of superlinear convergence rates leads to the above suitable expression that allows single-step calculation of normed search direction. This is computationally very effective.

4 Instance Selection Algorithm and its Demonstration

To avoid ill-conditioning and assure asymptotic behavior, the following function on the minimum required number of selected instances is introduced:

$$N_{SP} = N_P - (N_P - N_{TP}) \cdot \frac{\frac{1}{Iter} \sum_{k=1}^{Iter} PI^{(k)}}{PI^{(1)}} , \tag{1}$$

N_{SP} is the minimum required number of selected exemplars, N_P is cardinality of training set T, N_{TP} is pre-determined minimum number of exemplars in order to keep the optimization problem well-posed, and $Iter$ is given iteration. Function (1) increases as the adaptation converges to the equilibrium state. Thus it limits the number of eliminated instances so as to satisfy the asymptotic behavior.

Considering the introduced theoretical material the dynamic instance selection algorithm can be formulated. The proposed algorithm selects a training set suitable for adaptation of $\mathcal{AS}$ at each iteration. Adaptation procedure then forms search direction of the instance sub-gradients contained in the selected set $T^{(k)}$ and accordingly adapts the parameters of $\mathcal{AS}$.

Dynamic Instance Selection (set $\mathcal{CI}^{(k)}$, set $\mathcal{RI}^{(k)}$, iteration k)
{
    variables: set $T^{(k)}$;   *// set of selected instances*
                       sample S;   *// single instance*
    Calculate$PI^{(k)}$;
    CalculateN_{SP}(k);
    while (($\mathcal{CI}^{(k)}$ or $\mathcal{RI}^{(k)}$ are not empty) $\wedge$
        (($||\mathbf{s}_{T^{(k)}}^{(k)}||_2 < PI^{(k)}$) $\vee$ ($|T^{(k)}| < N_{SP}$)))
    {
        if ($\mathcal{CI}$ is not empty) **then** S=GetNextInstanceFrom($\mathcal{CI}^{(k)}$);
            else S=GetNextInstanceFrom($\mathcal{RI}^{(k)}$);
        PutSampleIn$T^{(k)}$(S);
    }
    return($T^{(k)}$);
}

Functionality of the algorithm is demonstrated on the neural network training task with I-FP ratio equal to 15. The neural network was trained on the well-known benchmark data set IRIS [9]. Artificial neural network consisted of three layers of computing units with structure 4-2-1 (linear input units, nonlinear sigmoidal hidden units, and linear output unit). Units were fully, layer-by-layer, interconnected with real valued connections initialized randomly in the interval $< -0.1, 0.1 >$. This initialization corresponded to the steepest part of the nonlinear sigmoidal function of hidden units. Back-propagation (BP) adaptation of neural network was terminated when the value of the objective function decreased below 0.013. Ten simulation runs were done for each value of learning rate, ranging from 0.5 to 0.9 in 0.1 increments, with different random initialization of network's adaptable parameters. Obtained results were averaged. BP learning with dynamic instance selection was compared to that of without it. Comparison criterion was the number of iterations elapsed until termination of the learning. Table 1 displays that BP with dynamic instance selection was from 1.14 to 2.12 times faster than the standard BP technique.

Table 1. *Convergence speed increase of learning with dynamic instance selection compared to the standard neural network learning for various values of learning rate. I-FP ratio of the task was 15. IRIS data set was used.*

Learning Rate	0.5	0.6	0.7	0.8	0.9	**Average Increase Rate**
Convergence Speed Increase	1.91	1.72	2.12	1.3	1.14	**1.64**

5 Conclusions

The purpose of dynamic instance selection is to improve quality of adaptation, mainly in terms of convergence speed, and not to induce additional excessive computational load. Presented dynamic instance selection satisfies both criteria. Computational complexity of the dynamic instance selection algorithm is linear. The algorithm, when applied to training techniques for neural networks (e.g. back-propagation), improves the convergence speed of learning. This quality has been demonstrated on the task with I-FP ratio 15. Average convergence speed increase for varying learning rate parameter has indicated value of 1.64. Proposed dynamic instance selection algorithm has been established on the solid theoretical ground and is widely applicable to first order line search techniques.

References

1. Géczy, P., Usui, S. (1998) Dynamic Sample Selection: Theory. *IEICE Transactions on Fundamentals*, **E81-A(9)**, 1931–1939
2. Géczy, P., Usui, S. (1998) Dynamic Sample Selection: Implementation. *IEICE Transactions on Fundamentals*, **E81-A(9)**, 1940–1947
3. Géczy, P., Usui, S. (1998) Deterministic Approach to Dynamic Sample Selection. In *Proceedings of ICONIP'98*, Kitakyushu, 1612–1615
4. Géczy, P., Usui, S. (1997) A Novel Dynamic Sample Selection Algorithm for Accelerated Learning. Technical Report NC97-03, **IEICE**, 189–196
5. Géczy, P., Usui, S. (1997) Sample Selection Algorithm Utilizing Lipschitz Continuity Condition. In *Proceedings of JNNS'97*, Kanazawa, 190–191
6. Baum, E. B. (1991) Neural Net Algorithm that Learn in Polynomial Time for Examples and Queries. *IEEE Trans. on Neural Networks*, **2(1)**, 5–19
7. Battiti, R. (1994) Using Mutual Information for Selecting Features in Supervised Neural Net Learning. *IEEE Trans. on Neural Networks*, **5(4)**, 537–550
8. Cachin, C. (1994) Pedagogical Pattern Selection Strategies. *Neural Networks*, **7(1)**, 175–181
9. Fisher, R. A. (1936) The Use of Multiple Measurements in Taxonomic Problems. *Annual Eugenics*, **7(II)**, 179–188

Part 2

Fuzzy Systems

Toward an Enlargement of the Role of Natural Languages in Information Processing, Decision and Control[1]

Lotfi A. Zadeh

Computer Science Division and the Electronics Research
Laboratory, Department of EECS, University of California, Berkeley,
CA 94720-1776;

Abstract: It is a deep-seated tradition in science to view the use of natural languages in scientific theories as a manifestation of mathematical immaturity. The rationale for this tradition is that natural languages are lacking in precision. However, what is not recognized to the extent that it should, is that adherence to this tradition carries a steep price. In particular, a direct consequence is that existing scientific theories do not have the capability to operate on perception-based information exemplified by "Most Finns are honest." Such information is usually described in a natural language and is intrinsically imprecise, reflecting a fundamental limitation on the cognitive ability of humans to resolve detail and store information. Because of their imprecision, perceptions do not lend themselves to meaning-representation through the use of precise methods based on predicate logic. This is the principal reason why existing scientific theories do not have the capability to operate on perception-based information.

In a related way, the restricted expressive power of predicate-logic-based languages rules out the possibility of defining many basic concepts such as causality, resemblance, smoothness and relevance in realistic terms. In this instance, as in many others, the price of precision is over-idealization and lack of robustness.

In a significant departure from existing methods, in the approach which is described in this talk the high expressive power of natural languages is harnessed by constructing what is called a precisiated natural language (PNL). In essence, PNL is a subset of a natural language (NL) -- a subset which is equipped with constraint-centered semantics (CSNL) and is translatable into what is called the

---

[1] Research supported in part by NASA Grant NAC2-1177, ONR Grant N00014-96-1-0556, ONR Grant FDN0014991035, ARO Grant DAAH 04-961-0341 and the BISC Program of UC Berkeley.

Generalized Constraint Language (GCL). A concept which has a position of centrality in GCL is that of a generalized constraint expressed as X isr R, where X is the constrained variable, R is the constraining relation, and isr (pronounced as ezar) is a variable copula in which r is a discrete-valued variable whose value defines the way in which R constrains X. Among the principal types of constraints possibilistic, veristic, probabilistic, random-set, usuality, and fuzzy-graph constraints.

With these constraints serving as basic building blocks, more complex (composite) constraints may be constructed through the use of a grammar. The collection of composite constraints forms the Generalized Constraint Language (GCL). The semantics of GCL is defined by the rules that govern combination and propagation of generalized constraints. These rules coincide with the rules of inference in fuzzy logic (FL).

A key idea in PNL is that the meaning of a proposition, p, in PNL may be represented as a generalized constraint which is an element of GCL. Thus, translation of p into GCL is viewed as an explicitation of X, R and r. In this sense, translation is equivalent to explicitation.

The concept of a precisiated natural language and the associated methodologies of computing with words and the computational theory of perceptions open the door to a wide-ranging generalization and restructuring of existing theories, especially in the realms of information processing, decision and control. In this perspective, what is very likely is that in coming years a number of basic concepts and techniques drawn from linguistics will be playing a much more important role in scientific theories than they do today.

Notes on Fusion of Uncertain Information

Mourad Oussalah

A K. U. of Leuven, Department of Mechanical Engineering, PMA, Celestjnenlaan 300B, B-3001 Heverlee, Belgium

Abstract: *Data fusion palys a central role in many relevant applications in industry as well in social sciences and economical fields. However, the inputs of the system are often less reliable and pervaded with imprecision. This uncertainty is obviousely propagated into the final result. This paper, deals with the manipulation of uncertain datum in the sense they are assigned some degree of certainty in the framework of possibiliy theory. Particularly, some certainty qualification reasoning in terms of Implicators and Co-implicators as well the propagation of this certainty in special cases of conjunction and disjunction combinations are investigated. This kind of methodology may be very useful for predictibility purpose, when the user may predict the certainty of the result for a given operation before performing this operation.*

Keywords: data fusion, Residual operators, α-certain information, conjunction, disjunction.

1 Basic concepts

These preliminary definitions may be found in [3,4].

Definition 1

A t-norm T is a mapping $[0,1]^2 \to [0,1]$, which is increasing in both arguments, commutative, associative and fulfilling the boundary case $\forall x \in [0,1], T(x,1) = x$

A t-conorm S is a mapping from $[0,1]^2$ to $[0,1]$, which is increasing in both arguments, commutative, associative and satisfying the boundary condition

$$\forall x \in [0,1], S(x,0) = x .$$

T-norms and t-conorms [10] correspond to a set-theoretic extension of fuzzy set intersection and union operators, and entail as special cases the min and the max operators. T and S are related by the duality relation $T(a,b)=1-S(1-a,1-b)$

Definition 2

An implicator I is a mapping:

[0,1] x [0,1] → [0,1], such that- I is non-increasing with respect to its first argument- I is non-decreasing with respect to its second argument.- $I(0,0)=I(1,1)=1$, $I(1,0)=0$

Among implication operators, one may mention the residual implicators based on the idea that implication reflects partial ordering on proposition, i.e., $I(a,b)=1$ if and only if a ### b. Using a t-norm T, one has

$$I(a,b) = \sup\{c \in [0,1], T(a,c) \le b\}.$$ Example of such case is Gödel implication corresponding to T=min: $I(a,b)=1$ if $a \le b$ and $I(a,b)=b$ id a<b.

Definition 3

A co-implicator cI is a mapping [0,1] x [0,1] → [0,1] such that cI is decreasing in its first argument and increasing in its second argument, with $cI(0,0)=cI(1,1)=0$ and $cI(0,1)=1$. It fulfills $cI(a,b)=\inf \{c \in [0,1]: S(a,c) \ge b \}$

Co-implicators are extension of the Boolean co-implicators $p \not\Rightarrow q$ -meaning that q is not necessary for p-. The implicators and the co-implicators are related by the duality relation $I(p,q)=1-cI(1-p,1-q)$.

Definition 4

Considering a t-norm T, and a possibility distribution π, the possibility of a fuzzy event A is given as

$$\Pi(A) = \sup_{x \in U} T(\pi(x), \mu_A(x)) \tag{1}$$

and its counterpart in terms of necessity measure is

$$N(A) = \inf_{x \in U} I(\pi(x), \mu_A(x)) \tag{2}$$

where I stands for an implication operator.

2 α-certainty qualification and application to fusion of uncertain inputs

In the α-certainty qualification problem, the aim of this section is to characterize the fuzzy set μ_B supporting the sure statement "x is B", given the statement "x is A is α-certain". This comes down to solve for μ_B the functional equation

$$N(A) = \inf_{u \notin A} [1 - \mu_B(u)] = \alpha. \tag{3}$$

The principle of minimum specificity leads to the solution, which coincides with the solution pertaining to the statement "x is A is at least α-certain", i.e., $N(A) \geq \alpha$ such that

$$\mu_B(u) = \max(\mu_A(u), 1-\alpha). \tag{4}$$

In the case where the certainty is represented by means of implication operator, the statement "x is A is at least α-certain" can be translated into

$$\inf_u I(\mu_B, \mu_A) \geq \alpha. \tag{5}$$

It was already proven by Magrez and Smets [6] that the solution of (5), which is in agreement with the duality relation between possibility and necessity measures is given by

$$\mu_B(u) = \min(\mu_A(u) - \alpha + 1, 1), \tag{6}$$

which corresponds to the use of Lukasiewciz t-norm

However, if the duality relation is omitted, the general solution of (5) is provided by Di Nola et al. [2] using R-implication or a reciprocal thereof. That is,

$$I_R(\mu_B(u), \mu_A(u)) \geq \alpha \iff \mu_B(u) * \alpha \leq \mu_A(u). \tag{7}$$

where $*$ is the t-norm inducing the R-implication I_R. This leads to two solutions for the certainty qualification (let S be the t-conorm dual of t-norm T):

$$\mu_B(u) = I_R(\alpha, \mu_A(u)), \tag{8}$$

and,

$$\mu_B(u) = S(1-\alpha, \mu_A(u)). \tag{9}$$

Now using the definition of co-implicators, the following holds

Proposition 1

i) $N(A) \geq \alpha \iff \sup_u cI(1-\mu_B(u), 1-\mu_A(u)) \leq 1-\alpha$

ii) $cI(\mu_B(u), \mu_A(u)) \leq \alpha \iff S(\mu_B(u), \alpha) \geq \mu_A(u)$

Proof

i) Using (5), and the definition of cI, we have

$$N(A) \geq \alpha \iff \inf_u I(\mu_B(u), \mu_A(u)) \geq \alpha \iff 1 - \inf_u I(\mu_B(u), \mu_A(u)) \leq 1-\alpha$$

$$\iff \sup_u [1 - I(\mu_B(u), \mu_A(u))] \leq 1-\alpha \iff \sup_u cI(1-\mu_B(u), 1-\mu_A(u)) \leq 1-\alpha$$

ii) $cI(\mu_B(u), \mu_A(u)) = \inf \{z \in [0,1] : S(\mu_B(u), z) \geq \mu_A(u)\}. \tag{10}$

$cI(\mu_B(u), \mu_A(u)) \leq \alpha$ is equivalent to add a constraint $z \leq \alpha$ in (10). While due to the monotony of t-conorm S, it follows, $S(\alpha, \mu_B(u)) \geq S(z, \mu_B(u) \geq \mu_A(u)$.

The development of the above inequalities and solving for μ_B the inequality $S(\mu_B(u), \alpha) \geq \mu_A(u)$ leads to the following.

Proposition 2

Implicators and co-implicators lead to the same quantification of the α-certainty information as in (8).

The proof follows straightforwardly from Proposition 1 and is then omitted.

Conjunction and disjunction of uncertain inputs

Now let us consider the basic combination modes: conjunction and disjunction provided in the context of α-certainty qualification.

Let π_1 and π_2 be two α-qualified certainty distributions with a degree of certainty equals respectively α_1 and α_2. The aim is to determine the qualification of the distributions $\min(\pi_1, \pi_2)$ and $\max(\pi_1, \pi_2)$.

First, let us consider the case when (4) is used as α-certainty qualification. Hence, the information supported by π_1 and π_2 can be translated into respectively π'_1 and π'_2 such that for all s, $\quad \pi'_i(s) = \max(1 - \alpha_i, \pi_i(s)) \quad (i=1,2).$ (11)

Proposition 3

Using the qualification (11), the conjunction and the disjunction of π'_1 and π'_2 are such that

i) $\min(\pi'_1, \pi'_2) \geq \min(\pi_1, \pi_2)$ and $\max(\pi'_1, \pi'_2) \geq \max(\pi_1, \pi_2)$,

ii) the degree of certainty ascribed to the disjunction is $\alpha_\vee = \min(\alpha_1, \alpha_2)$,

iii) the degree of certainty ascribed to the conjunction is

$$\alpha_\wedge = \min(\max(\alpha_1, \alpha_2), \max(1 - \pi_2(s), \alpha_1), \max(1 - \pi_1(s), \alpha_2)),$$

which fulfills $\min(\alpha_1, \alpha_2) \leq \alpha_\wedge \leq \max(\alpha_1, \alpha_2)$.

Proof

i) It follows immediately from the monotony of max operator in (11), so $\pi'_i \geq \pi_i$ (i=1,2), then use again the monotony of min and max to prove i).

ii) The key idea here is to identify $\alpha_\vee$ such that

$$\max(\pi'_1(s), \pi'_2(s)) = \max(\max(\pi_1(s), \pi_2(s)), 1 - \alpha_\vee).$$

$$\max(\pi'_1(s), \pi'_2(s)) = \max(\max(\pi_1(s), 1 - \alpha_1), \max(\pi_2(s), 1 - \alpha_2))$$

$$= \max(\max(\pi_1(s), \pi_2(s)), 1 - \min(\alpha_1, \alpha_2)).$$

Idem for $\alpha_\wedge$. The detail is omitted here.

An example showing the level $\alpha_\wedge$ for two given distributions is illustrated in Fig.1

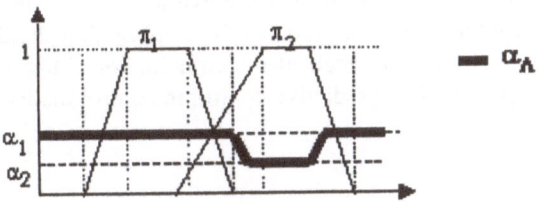

Fig. 1 Example of determination of $\alpha_\wedge$

Now let assume a qualification provided via us turn residual implicators (or equivalently co-implicators). That is, $\quad \pi_i^1(s) = I_R(\alpha_i, \pi_i(s))$, $\quad$ (i=1,2) $\qquad$ (12)

Proposition 4

If the α-certainty qualification is carried out by (12), then, using Gödel implicator, the certainty level attached to the conjunction and the disjunction of π_1 and π_2, supposed being at least certain to respectively α_1 and α_2, are given respectively by

$$\alpha_\vee(s) = \max(1 - \mu_{(\pi_1)_{\alpha_1} \cup (\pi_2)_{\alpha_2}}(s), \min(\alpha_1, \mu_{(\pi_1)_{\alpha_1}}(s)), \min(\alpha_2, \mu_{(\pi_2)_{\alpha_2}}(s))), \quad (13)$$

$$\alpha_\wedge(s) = \max(1 - \mu_{(\pi_1)_{\alpha_1} \cap (\pi_2)_{\alpha_2}}(s), \min(\min(\alpha_1, \mu_{(\pi_1)_{\alpha_1}}(s)), \min(\alpha_2, \mu_{(\pi_2)_{\alpha_2}}(s)))). \quad (14)$$

Proof

The outline of the proof is to First note that using (12),

$$\max(\pi_1^1(s), \pi_2^1(s)) = \begin{cases} 1 & \text{if } \alpha_1 \leq \pi_1(s) \text{ or } \alpha_2 \leq \pi_2(s) \\ \max(\pi_1(s), \pi_2(s)) & \text{otherwise.} \end{cases} \qquad (15)$$

To prove (13), it suffices to show that

$$H(s) = \begin{cases} 1 & \text{if } \alpha_\vee \leq \max(\pi_1(s), \pi_2(s)) \\ \max(\pi_1(s), \pi_2(s)) & \text{if } \alpha_\vee > \max(\pi_1(s), \pi_2(s)) \end{cases}$$

coincides with (15).

This comes down to showing that

$$\alpha_\vee \leq \max(\pi_1(s), \pi_2(s)) \iff (\alpha_1 \leq \pi_1(s) \text{ or } \alpha_2 \leq \pi_2(s))$$

since otherwise both formulations lead to $\max(\pi_1(s), \pi_2(s))$.

The same reasoning can be performed for $\alpha_\wedge$.

Furthermore, notice the above appraoch can be extended to compute the certainty level, which is not necessary a constant value, ascribed to any kind of hybrid combinations. This corresponds in somewhat to a predictive approach where the user knows beforehand the extend to which the result of the combination should be certain even without any computing of the result of the combination. This role is more or less similar to the one provided by predictive control in control theory

References

[1] M. A. Abidi and R. Gonzalez, *Data Fusion in Robotics and Machine Intelligence*, Acedemic Press, 1992

[2] A. Di Nola, W. Pedrycz and S. Sessa, An aspect of discrepancy in the implementation of modus ponens in the presence of fuzzy quantities, Int. J. of Approximate Reasoning **3**, (1989), 259-265.

[3] D. Dubois and H. Prade, A review of fuzzy set aggregation conectives, *Informations Sciences*, **36** (1985), 5-121.

[4] D. Dubois and H. Prade, *Théorie des possibilities. Application à la représentation des connaissances en Informatique*. Edition Masson, 1985

[5] D. Dubois and H. Prade, Fuzzy sets in approximate reasoning: Part 1 : Inference with possibility distributions, *Fuzzy Sets and Systems 25th anniversary memorial volume*, **40** (1991), 143-202.

[6] P. Magrez and P. Smets, Epestimic possibility, necessity and truth - Tools for dealing with imprecision and ncertainty in knowledge-based systems, Int. J. of Approximate Reasoning, 3 (1989), 181-198.

[7] L.A.Zadeh, Fuzzy sets as a basis for a theory of possibility theory, *Fuzzy sets and systems*, **1**, (1978), 3-28.

Fix-Mundis for Fuzzy IF-THEN Rule Bases with T-Norm Based Compositional Rule of Inference Interpretation *

Karl-Heinz Temme, Madjid Fathi

LS Informatik I, Dept. of Computer Science, University of Dortmund, Germany
Tel. +49 231 755 6373, Fax: +49 231 755 6555
e-mail: temme@ls1.informatik.uni-dortmund.de

Abstract: In [TeFa00] we have presented fixpoints and fix-mundis when interpreting fuzzy IF-THEN rules and rule bases by the simplest (standard) form of the Compositional Rule of Inference (CRI) [Zade73]. In this paper we extend our investigation to the t-norm based form of the CRI. We give solutions for fixpoints of single rules and, when using the standard aggregation operator maximum, we show, that the solution for a fixpoint of a single rule can be canonically extended to fix-mundis of rule bases. For dedicated t-norms we give examples and for a small rule base an application possibility.

Keywords: fuzzy IF-THEN rule bases, functional operators, fixpoints, fix-mundis

1 Motivation

For this paper the same motivation holds as in [TeFa00]. In classical functional analysis fixpoints are an interesting topic due to their importance in physical theories and experiments. In fuzzy control there is no need to look for fixpoints as the fuzzy sets on the right and left side of the rules are in general defined over distinct universa. Nevertheless there are applications in fuzzy logic for which fixpoints can be of great interest, an example is given at the end of this paper.

Our main interest is to interpret the semantics of fuzzy IF-THEN rules and rule bases by functional operators [LRTT98, Temm99]. After definition of inference mechanisms by those operators we are going to apply classical methods of functional analysis adapted for fuzzy logic. Some work has already been done [Thie97] but now we are interested in Eigenvalues and fixpoints. After having done the first step (see [TeFa00]) our interest focusses now on the t-norm based *Compositional Rule of Inference*, and to investigate the existence and shape of fixpoints for a single rule and a rule bases.

* This research was supported by the Deutsche Forschungsgemeinschaft as part of the Collaborative Research Center „Computational Intelligence" (SFB 531).

2   Interpretation of fuzzy IF-THEN rules

A lot of work has been done to interpret fuzzy IF-THEN rules. In our previous paper [TeFa00] we concentrated on an interpretation by the CRI in it's very standard form (introduced by Zadeh [Zade73]). In [LRTT98] we have already investigated and generalized this inference mechanism. In this paper we consider an extended version of the CRI. We look upon the interpretation of a fuzzy IF-THEN rule as the application of a functional operator $\Phi : FP(U) \rightarrow FP(U)$, whereby $FP(U)$ is the set of all fuzzy sets over U, on an input fuzzy set F'.

We expect that the reader is familiar with fuzzy sets (mappings $F: U \rightarrow [0,1]$ from a universe U into the real unit interval) and t-norms (mappings $\tau: [0,1] \times [0,1] \rightarrow [0,1]$ which fulfill the four axioms $\tau(x,0)=0 \wedge \tau(x,1)=x$; $x \leq x' \wedge y \leq y' \Rightarrow \tau(x,y) \leq \tau(x',y')$; $\tau(x,y)=\tau(y,x)$ and $\tau(x,\tau(y,z))=\tau(\tau(x,y),z)$.

Definition 1: (t-norm based fuzzy relation)
Let F and G be fixed fuzzy sets on U, τ be a t-norm:
1. $R =_{def}$ IF F THEN G is called a <u>fuzzy IF-THEN rule</u>.
2. S: $U \times U \rightarrow [0,1]$ with $S(x,y) =_{def} \tau(F(x),G(y))$ is called a <u>t-norm based fuzzy relation</u>.

Definition 2: (CRI, t-norm based form)
Let R be a fuzzy IF-THEN rule and S be a t-norm based fuzzy relation with F and G of R:
1. For an arbitrary fuzzy set F' on U we define the inferred fuzzy set G': $U \rightarrow [0,1]$ by $G'(y) =_{def} Sup\{min(F'(x),S(x,y)) | x \in U\}$.
2. The functional operator $\Phi^R: FP(U) \rightarrow FP(U)$ with $\Phi^R (F') =_{def} G'$ interprets rule R by the <u>CRI, t-norm based form</u>, for a given input set F'.

3   Examples of fixpoints for a single rule

Various papers have tackled the problem of fixpoints for fuzzy rules, e.g. [JaRe95], but most of them investigate underlying algebraic structures to get abstract results. Only a few consider concrete inference mechanisms, e.g. [Sanc78]. In the paper presented here it is assumed, that the underlying universe and the fuzzy sets are well-formed so that properties like Birkhoff's fixpoint theorem or Zorn's lemma, for example investigated [Thie97], need not be considered. In our approach a fixpoint exists, if $\forall H : \Phi^R (H) = H$.

Theorem 1: (Fixpoint for one rule)
Let R be a fuzzy IF-THEN rule.
If   R is interpreted by Φ^R (CRI for a single rule, t-norm based form),
then   the fuzzy set H: $U \rightarrow [0,1]$ with $H(x) =_{def} Sup(min(S(z,z),S(z,x)) | z \in U\}$

is a fixpoint of Φ^R, i.e. $\Phi^R(H) = H$.

Remark: It still has to be investigated, whether this is the only fixpoint for a rule.

4 Existence of fix-mundis (fixpoints for rule bases)

Let us now consider a fuzzy rule base with n IF-THEN rules and look for fix-mundis (we call fixpoints for rule bases fix-mundis). Again, we want to apply the CRI in t-norm based form, but first we have to decide how and by which operators the rules should be aggregated. When we proceed to rule bases, we have to decide whether to use the *First Aggregation Then Inference* (FATI) or the *First Inference Then Aggregation* (FITA) principle. For the t-norm based version CRI used here (see LRTT98, pages 42ff) these principles are equivalent, so we will use the FITA principle only in this paper.

Definition 3: (Fuzzy IF-THEN rule base)
Let F_i and G_i, i=1..n, n≥2, be fixed fuzzy sets on U:

IF F_1 THEN G_1

$RB =_{def}$ ...   is called a fuzzy IF-THEN rule base.

IF F_n THEN G_n

Definition 4: (CRI for rule bases, t-norm based form, *FATI* principle)
Let RB be a fuzzy IF-THEN rule base with rules R_1 to R_n and S_i t-norm based fuzzy relations.
1. For each rule IF F_i THEN G_i of RB define $S_i(x,y) =_{def} \tau(F_i(x), G_i(y))$.
2. The functional operator $FATI^{RB}$ (F'): FP(U)→FP(U) with
   $FATI^{RB}$ (F')(y) $=_{def}$ Sup{min(F'(x),max($S_1(x,y)$, ... , $S_n(x,y)$))|x∈ U}
   interprets the rule base RB by the CRI, t-norm based form, *FATI* principle, for a given input set F'.

Definition 5: (CRI for rule bases, t-norm based form, *FITA* principle)
Let RB be a fuzzy IF-THEN rule base with rules R_1 to R_n .
1. For each rule the CRI ist defined as Φ^{R_i} (F') $=_{def}$ G_i' according to Def. 2.
2. The functional operator $FITA^{RB}$ (F'): FP(U)→FP(U) with
   $FITA^{RB}$ (F')(y) $=_{def}$ max($G_1'(y)$, ... , $G_n'(y)$) interprets the rule base RB by the CRI, t-norm based form, *FITA* principle, for a given input set F'.

Theorem 2: (Fix-Mundis (fixpoints) for rule bases, *FITA* principle)
If   1. RB is a fuzzy IF-THEN rule base with rules R_1 to R_n
      2. for each rule IF F_i THEN G_i of RB holds $S_i(x,y) = \tau(F_i(x), G_i(y))$
      3. $S(x,y) =_{def}$ max($S_1(x,y)$, ... , $S_n(x,y)$)

4. RB is interpreted by FITA^{RB}

then   the fuzzy set H: $U \to [0,1]$ with $H(x) =_{\text{def}} \text{Sup}\{\min(S(z,z),S(z,x)) | z \in U\}$

is a fixpoint of FITA^{RB}, i.e. $\text{FITA}^{\text{RB}}(H) = H$.

5 Application possibility for fix-mundis

In the appendix we present an application possiblity from the technical area, which can be described as follows.

Assume, there is an engine with several temperature sensors at different spots. When operating, the engine produces heat, therefore a cooler is installed. Assume furthermore, you have an expert who classifies different temperature stati of the engine due to the sensor values into cold, warm, hot and very hot, and is able to express this knowlegde in form of appropriate fuzzy sets. To illustrate this, consider the following fuzzy sets with F1=cool, F2=very_hot, G1=hot and G2=warm; see appendix, first figure.

Of course the fuzzy sets are not selected by chance. They are suited to express the following two behaviour rules:

R1:   If the engine runs (without considering the cooler) and is cold,
      then it becomes hot
R2:   If the cooler runs (without considering the engine running) and the engine is
      very hot, then the engine is cooled down to warm

Now you are interested in how these rules mutually influence when you consider the whole system. For this you formelize both rules, put them together and create a (simple) rule base.

RB: IF F1 THEN G1
        IF F2 THEN G2

Furthermore you have to fix how to interpret this rule base. The overall goal is to determine the "operating point" of the engine where the cooler removes as much heat as the engine produces. This question can be answered by asking for the fix-mundis of the rule base. Those do not only depend on the fuzzy sets you have selected but also on the inference mechanism you have chosen. In the appendix two different solutions for the above rule base are shown, both use the CRI, t-norm based form, but they differ in $\tau = \text{prod}$ for the first one and $\tau = \text{bold-and}$ for the second.

6 Conclusions

When interpreting fuzzy IF-THEN rules and rule bases by the *Compositional Rule of Inference*, there exist fixpoints (for one rule) and fix-mundis (for rule bases) not only in the standard case [TeFa00] but also for arbitray t-norms if the CRI is based on them. We have proved their existence and have shown examples. We have presented an example from technical area to give hints how to use fix-mundis in practical applications.

7 References

[JaRe95] J. Jacas and J. Recasens. Fuzzy T-transitive Relations: Eigenvectors and Generators. Fuzzy Sets & Systems 72(2), 147-154, 1995.

[LRTT98] S. Lehmke, B. Reusch, K.-H. Temme and H. Thiele. On Interpreting Fuzzy IF-THEN Rule Bases by Concepts of Functional Analysis. Reihe CI 19/98, SFB 531, University of Dortmund, Germany, Technical Report, ISSN 1433-3325, April 1998.

[Sanc78] E. Sanchez. Resolution of Eigen Fuzzy Sets Equations. Fuzzy Sets & Systems 1, 69-74, 1978.

[TeFa00] K.-H. Temme, M. Fathi. Fix-Mundis for Fuzzy IF-THEN Rules Bases with Standard *Compositional Rule of Inference* Interpretation. Proceedings of the ACM Symposium on Applied Computing (SAC 2000), Como, Italy, 19-21 March 2000.

[Temm99] K.-H. Temme. Fuzzy Inference Methods as Functional Operator Definitions. Proceedings of the Third International ICSC Symposium on Intelligent Industrial Automation and Soft Computing, Genua, Italy, 1.-4. June, 1999.

[TeTh96] K.-H. Temme and H. Thiele. On the Chaining of IF-THEN Rule Bases interpreted by the principle FITA. Proceedings of the Fourth European Congress on Intelligent Techniques and Soft Computing (EUFIT '96), Band 2, 939-945, Aachen, Germany, 2.-5. Sept., 1996.

[Thie97] H. Thiele. Investigating Approximate Reasoning and Fuzzy Control by Concepts of Functional Analysis. In Proc. First International Conference on Conventional and Knowledge-Based Intelligent Electronic Systems, vol. 2, p. 493-500, Adelaide, Australia, 21.-23. May, 1997.

[Zade73] L. A. Zadeh. Outline of a New Approach to the Analysis of Complex Systems and Decision Process. IEEE Trans. on Systems, Man and Cybernetics, 3(1): 28-44, 1973.

94

Appendix

Application possibility example (see text) for fix-mundis in combination with the CRI, t-norm based form. The first figure shows the linguistic terms of the rule base, the next two fix-mundis for $\tau(x,y) = x*y$ and $\tau(x,y) = \max(0,x+y-1)$.

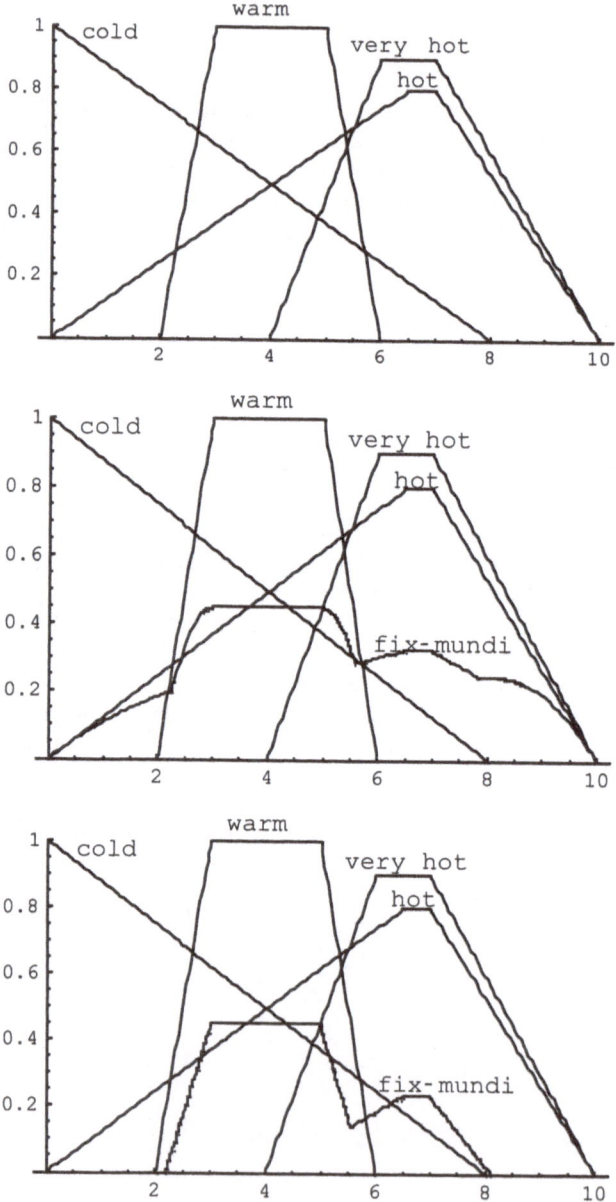

Computational Problems of Constrained Fuzzy Arithmetic

Mirko Navara and Zdeněk Žabokrtský

Center for Machine Perception, Faculty of Electrical Engineering,
Czech Technical University, Technická 2, 166 27 Praha, Czech Republic
navara@cmp.felk.cvut.cz, zabokrtz@cs.felk.cvut.cz

Abstract: In the standard fuzzy arithmetic, the vagueness of fuzzy quantities always increases. Klir [1,2] suggests an alternative—constrained fuzzy arithmetic—which reduces this effect. Little attention was paid to the problems of implementation of constrained fuzzy arithmetic, especially to its computational efficiency. We point out the related problems and outline the ways of their solution.

1 Basic Notions

We deal here with fuzzy subsets of the real line, R, i.e., with mappings from R to the unit interval $[0, 1] \subseteq$ R. By a *fuzzy quantity* (*fuzzy interval*) we mean a mapping $A: \text{R} \rightarrow [0, 1]$ satisfying the following three conditions:

1. convexity and closedness: for each $\alpha \in (0, 1]$, the α-*cut* $^{\alpha}A = \{x \in \text{R} : A(x) \geq \alpha\}$ is a closed interval,
2. boundedness: $\exists m \in \text{R} : \{x \in \text{R} : A(x) > 0\} \subseteq [-m, m]$,
3. normality: $\exists x \in \text{R} : A(x) = 1$.

If, moreover, the third condition is satisfied for exactly one x, we call A a *fuzzy number*. As a consequence of this definition, for each fuzzy quantity A there are numbers $a, b, c, d \in \text{R}$, $a \leq b \leq c \leq d$, such that

$$(a, d) \subseteq \{x \in \text{R} : A(x) > 0\} \subseteq [a, d] ,$$

$$\{x \in \text{R} : A(x) = 1\} = [b, c] ,$$

$$A \text{ is nondecreasing on } [a, b] ,$$

$$A \text{ is nonincreasing on } [c, d] .$$

The mapping $h_A: (0, 1] \rightarrow \exp \text{R}$, defined by $h_A(\alpha) = {}^{\alpha}A$, determines A uniquely, giving the *horizontal representation* of A. (To emphasize the difference, we speak of the representation of a fuzzy set by the mapping $A: \text{R} \rightarrow [0, 1]$ as the *vertical representation*.)

The horizontal representation is advantageous for the computer implementation. While we usually have to distinguish a finite, but very large number of real values, say u, it is usually sufficient to restrict attention to a much smaller number of membership degrees α; let us denote this number by t. For a fuzzy quantity A, each α-cut is a closed interval, so its horizontal representation requires to record only $2t$ real numbers (bounds of α-cuts). For general shapes of membership functions, the vertical representation would require u real numbers (membership degrees).

2   Standard Fuzzy Arithmetic

The basic aim of fuzzy arithmetic is to extend the operations $+, -, \cdot, /$ to fuzzy quantities. Let $\Box \in \{+, -, \cdot, /\}$. In the standard fuzzy arithmetic (SFA), the operation $\Box$ is extended to fuzzy quantities A, B by the following rule[1]:

$$(A \,\Box\, B)(z) = \sup\{\min(A(x), B(y)) : x, y \in \mathrm{R}, \ x \,\Box\, y = z\} .$$

Evaluation of the latter expression in the vertical representation would require two cycles over u values; the complexity of order u^2 is usually inacceptable. The horizontal representation requires only a simple interval calculation (with crisp intervals) for each α-cut:

$$^{\alpha}(A \,\Box\, B) = \ ^{\alpha}A \,\Box\, {}^{\alpha}B .$$

E.g., if $^{\alpha}A = [a, b]$, $^{\alpha}B = [c, d]$, then

$$^{\alpha}A \cdot {}^{\alpha}B = [\min(ac, ad, bc, bd), \max(ac, ad, bc, bd)] .$$

The maximal order of complexity for a binary operation is $4t$. Sometimes it can be reduced due to monotonicity. E.g., with the preceding notations,

$$^{\alpha}A + {}^{\alpha}B = [a + c, b + d]$$

and the complexity of addition is of order t.

Many usual laws for operations on real numbers do not extend to standard fuzzy arithmetic.

Example 1. If A is the (characteristic function of) the interval $[1, 2]$, $A = \chi_{[1,2]}$, then $A - A = \chi_{[-1,1]}$, so $A - A \neq 0$. Similarly, $A \cdot A / A \neq A$, etc.

3   Constrained Fuzzy Arithmetic

In [1,2], Klir suggested the constrained fuzzy arithmetic as an alternative which allows to satisfy more of the classical laws of arithmetic. Although he considered a larger collection of constraints in the form of inequalities, fuzzy relations, etc., we shall restrict here to the simplest case of *equality constraints*.

---

[1] Some problems may arise with division by zero. This case should be avoided. We do not deal with these questions here.

The constrained fuzzy arithmetic coincides with the standard fuzzy arithmetic if all fuzzy quantities are distinct. It differs if some of them appear repeatedly in the expression. E.g., the binary expression $(A \, \square \, A)_{\mathrm{CFA}}$, evaluated in the constrained fuzzy arithmetic, is defined by

$$(A \, \square \, A)_{\mathrm{CFA}}(z) = \sup\{A(x) : x \in \mathrm{R}, \ x \, \square \, x = z\} \, .$$

Its distinction becomes apparent when we write the formula for the same expression in the standard fuzzy arithmetic:

$$(A \, \square \, A)(z) = \sup\{\min(A(x), A(y)) : x, y \in \mathrm{R}, \ x \, \square \, y = z\} \, .$$

Thus $(A \cdot A)_{\mathrm{CFA}}$ is always nonnegative; this does not hold in the standard fuzzy arithmetic as the following example shows.

Example 2. Let $A = \chi_{[-1,2]}$. Then $A \cdot A = \chi_{[-2,4]}$, while $(A \cdot A)_{\mathrm{CFA}} = \chi_{[0,4]}$. In this particular case, standard fuzzy arithmetic offers a solution, too: If we consider a unary real function sqr: $x \mapsto x^2$ and extend it to fuzzy sets by the standard extension principle, then $\mathrm{sqr}(A) = (A \cdot A)_{\mathrm{CFA}}$.

In the horizontal representation, we obtain

$$^{\alpha}(A \, \square \, A)_{\mathrm{CFA}} = \{x \, \square \, x : x \in \, ^{\alpha}A\} \, ,$$

$$^{\alpha}(A \, \square \, A) = \{x \, \square \, y : x, y \in \, ^{\alpha}A\} \, .$$

In constrained fuzzy arithmetic, we have to find extremes of functions. Discontinuity can be avoided (it appears only when we divide by "fuzzy zero"), but steep continuous functions are obtained, e.g., as high order polynomials. Finding their extremes is a task that is not algoritmizable in general. The blind search would lead to the complexity of order $v \cdot u^v$, where v is the number of distinct variables in the formula. This situation is unsatisfactory. Therefore we have to use tools that allow to simplify the calculation at least in some cases. We suggest the following steps:

1. Use standard fuzzy arithmetic whenever possible. E.g.,

$$((A \cdot A + A + 1) \cdot (B + C))_{\mathrm{CFA}} = ((A \cdot A + A)_{\mathrm{CFA}} + 1) \cdot (B + C) \, .$$

We can decompose the expression (and apply the standard fuzzy arithmetic) whenever its subexpressions have disjoint sets of variables. Advanced applications of this principle should make use also of associativity and distributivity of the operations to find possible decompositions of this type even if they are not possible in the original form.

2. Use monotonicity whenever possible. E.g., the expression

$$(A \cdot A + B) \cdot (A + B \cdot B)$$

is monotonic in both variables provided that they are nonnegative. In this case the extreme values are quite easy to find.

3. **For some nonmonotonic expressions the extreme values can be found on the vertices of the multidimensional intervals determined by α-cuts.** E.g., for the expression $(A \cdot A \cdot B \cdot B)_{\text{CFA}}$, the extremes over each α-cut are found among the values in the vertices of the two-dimensional intervals representing the cartesian products of β-cuts for any $\beta \geq \alpha$. This case still admits an effective calculation by a method which we call the *vertex algorithm* [3]. The only problem remains with the 1-cuts; here the global search has to be performed. (For fuzzy numbers, the 1-cuts are singletons.)

4. **When we need to evaluate constrained fuzzy arithmetic in its full power, we start from 1-cuts and proceed to lower cuts, using the extremes already calculated.** For each α-cut, $\alpha < 1$, we search for new extremes only on the boundary of the respective multidimensional interval and compare them to the extremes already calculated. The complexity can be of order u^v.

5. In the search for local extremes on the boundary of each α-cut, we can **use the local extremes from the next higher α-cut as initial values.** Only after several α-cuts an extensive search for global extremes could be performed. If new local extremes are found for this α-cut, we return to the preceding α-cuts for verification, otherwise we take the preceding results as definite and proceed to the next lower α-cut.

4 Conclusion

The performance of constrained fuzzy arithmetic with an acceptable efficiency is a highly nontrivial task. We suggested several hints that simplify the calculations for some classes of expressions. An efficient implementation would require special procedures for various types of expressions like in symbolic integration. The whole task could lead to programs using an approach similar to that of computer algebra systems.

Acknowledgements. The authors gratefully acknowledge the support of the project VS96049 of the Czech Ministry of Education and of the grant 23p16 of Aktion Österreich-Tschechien.

References

1. Klir, G.J. (1997) Uncertainty Analysis in Engineering and Sciences. Kluwer
2. Klir, G.J., Pan, Y. (1998) Soft Computing 2. Springer
3. Žabokrtský, Z. (2000) Constrained Fuzzy Arithmetic: Engineer's View. Research Report CTU–CMP–2000–03, Center for Machine Perception, Czech Technical University, Prague

Linear Regression with Fuzzy Variables

Štefan Varga, Michal Šabo

Department of Mathematics, Faculty of Chemical Technology, Slovak Technical University, Radlinského 9, 812 34 Bratislava, Slovakia

Abstract : A method of estimation of unknown crisp parameters in a linear regression model with fuzzy variables and crisp parameters is suggested by minimizing the sum of the squares of the Diamond distances between the values from the model and the values from the observed data. The method is a generalization of the least squares estimation method from the classical linear regression model onto the fuzzy regression model.

Keywords : *Fuzzy numbers, Fuzzy statistics and data analysis, Fuzzy regression, Estimation, Observed data, Fitted data*

1   Introduction

In the paper [8] was studied the linear regression model

$$Y = A_1 f_1(x) + A_2 f_2(x) + \ldots + A_m f_m(x) \qquad (1)$$

with the unknown fuzzy parameters A_1, A_2, ... , A_m which estimations were obtained on the basis of crisp observed data (x_1, y_1), (x_2, y_2), ... , (x_n, y_n) by means minimizing the sum of the squares of the distances between the observed values of the variable Y and the estimated values of the same variable Y. This method is used in this paper for estimations of unknown crisp parameters in the model with fuzzy variables.

2   Regression model with fuzzy variables

Assume the linear regression model

$$Y = a_1 X_1 + a_2 X_2 + \ldots + a_m X_m \qquad (2)$$

where X_i (i = 1, 2, ... , m) and Y are fuzzy variables which values are symmetric triangular fuzzy numbers and a_1, a_2, ... , a_m are unknown crisp parameters. The observed values of the input variable X_i $(i = 1, 2, \ldots, m)$ are assuming in the form

$$X_{ij} = <x_{ij}, s_{ij}> \; ; \; j = 1, 2, \ldots, n \tag{3}$$

where x_{ij} is the center and s_{ij} is the spread of the symmetric triangular fuzzy number X_{ij}. Like as in (3) the observed values of the output variable Y is

$$Y_j = <y_j, s_j> \; ; \; j = 1, 2, \ldots, n \tag{4}$$

where y_j is the center and s_j the spread of the symmetric triangular fuzzy number Y_j. It is not hard to see that the fuzzy estimated value

$$Y^{(j)} = a_1 X_{1j} + a_2 X_{2j} + \ldots + a_m X_{mj}$$

based on the minimum t - norm [5], [6], [7] is the symmetric triangular fuzzy number $(j = 1, 2, \ldots, n)$

$$Y^{(j)} = <x_j^T a, s_j^T |a|> \tag{5}$$

with the center $x_j^T a$ and the spread $s_j^T |a|$, where $x_j^T = (x_{1j}, x_{2j}, \ldots, x_{mj})$, $s_j^T = (s_{1j}, s_{2j}, \ldots, s_{mj})$, $a = (a_1, a_2, \ldots, a_m)^T$, $|a| = (|a_1|, |a_2|, \ldots, |a_m|)^T$.

The main problem is to find (estimate) the vector of unknown crisp parameters $a = (a_1, a_2, \ldots, a_m)^T$ such that the estimated values $Y^{(j)}$ (5) fit the observed data Y_j (4) as well as possible ($j = 1, 2, \ldots, n$). This problem was solved by many authors (for example [1], [3], [4], [9]) but for generalization of the classical least squares method we will use, same as in [8], the Diamond distance [2] of two symmetric triangular fuzzy numbers $A = <a, s_1>$, $B = <b, s_2>$

$$d^2(A, B) = (a - b)^2 + \frac{2}{3}(s_1 - s_2)^2$$

for estimations the unknown crisp parameters $a = (a_1, a_2, \ldots, a_m)^T$. The distance of the fuzzy number $Y^{(j)}$ (5) and the fuzzy number Y_j (4) $(j = 1, 2, \ldots, n)$ is

$$d^2\left(Y^{(j)}, Y_j\right) = \left(x_j^T a - y_j\right)^2 + \frac{2}{3}\left(s_j^T |a| - s_j\right)^2 \tag{6}$$

and the estimation of the vector of unknown parameters $a = (a_1, a_2, \ldots, a_m)^T$ is in the outcome 1.

Outcome 1. Generalized least squares estimation of the vector of the unknown crisp parameters $\mathbf{a} = (a_1, a_2, \ldots, a_m)^T$ in the linear regression model with fuzzy variables and crisp parameters (2) is

$$\hat{\mathbf{a}} = \underset{\mathbf{a} \in \Theta}{\arg\min} \sum_{j=1}^{n} \left[\left(\mathbf{x}_j^T \mathbf{a} - y_j \right)^2 + \frac{2}{3} \left(\mathbf{s}_j^T |\mathbf{a}| - s_j \right)^2 \right] \qquad (7)$$

Remark 1. If the observed data

$$X_{ij} = \langle x_{ij}, s_{ij} \rangle, \quad Y_j = \langle y_j, s_j \rangle$$

$i = 1, 2, \ldots, m$; $j = 1, 2, \ldots, n$ are crisp numbers ($s_{ij} = 0$, $s_j = 0$) the estimation of the vector of unknown parameters $\mathbf{a} = (a_1, a_2, \ldots, a_m)^T$ obtained by minimizing of (7) are equal to the least squares estimations in the crisp linear regression model.

Example 1. Let triangular symmetric fuzzy numbers

$$\langle 1, 0.5 \rangle, \quad \langle 1, 0.5 \rangle, \quad \langle 3, 1 \rangle$$
$$\langle 2, 0.5 \rangle, \quad \langle 1, 0.5 \rangle, \quad \langle 4, 1 \rangle$$
$$\langle 1, 0.5 \rangle, \quad \langle 2, 0.5 \rangle, \quad \langle 5, 1 \rangle$$
$$\langle 2, 0.5 \rangle, \quad \langle 2, 0.5 \rangle, \quad \langle 6, 1 \rangle$$

are the observed data for the triple of the variables (X_1, X_2, Y). Estimate the crisp parameters a_1, a_2 of the dependence $Y = a_1 X_1 + a_2 X_2$.

Solution. In this example $n = 4$, $\mathbf{x}_j^T = (x_{1j}, x_{2j})$, $\mathbf{s}_j^T = (s_{1j}, s_{2j})$; $j = 1, 2, 3, 4$ $\mathbf{a} = (a_1, a_2)^T$, $|\mathbf{a}| = (|a_1|, |a_2|)^T$ and therefore we will minimize (7) in the form

$$\sum_{j=1}^{n} \left[\left(\mathbf{x}_j^T \mathbf{a} - y_j \right)^2 + \frac{2}{3} \left(\mathbf{s}_j^T |\mathbf{a}| - s_j \right)^2 \right] =$$

$$(a_1 + a_2 - 3)^2 + 2/3 \, (0.5a_1 + 0.5a_2 - 1)^2 + \ldots + (2a_1 + 2a_2 - 6)^2 + 2/3 \, (0.5a_1 + 0.5a_2 - 1)^2$$

$$= \boxed{32/3\, a_1^2 + 32/3\, a_2^2 + 58/3\, a_1 a_2 - 176/3\, a_1 - 182/3\, a_2 + 266/3}$$

The minimum 32.19 was obtained for a_1, a_2 which are the solution of the linear system

$$32\, a_1 + 29\, a_2 = 88$$

$$29\, a_1 + 32\, a_2 = 91$$

Generalized least squares estimations of the crisp parameters a_1, a_2 of the dependence $Y = a_1 X_1 + a_2 X_2$ are

$$a_1 = 0.967, \quad a_2 = 1.967$$

The observed values and the estimated values are in the table 1.

Table 1

X_{1j}	X_{2j}	Observed value Y_j	Estimated value $Y^{(j)}$
(0.5 ; 1 ; 1.5)	(0.5 ; 1 ; 1.5)	(2 ; 3 ; 4)	(1.47 ; 2.93 ; 4.40)
(1.5 ; 2 ; 2.5)	(0.5 ; 1 ; 1.5)	(3 ; 4 ; 5)	(2.43 ; 3.90 ; 5.37)
(0.5 ; 1 ; 1.5)	(1.5 ; 2 ; 2.5)	(4 ; 5 ; 6)	(3.43 ; 4.90 ; 6.37)
(1.5 ; 2 ; 2.5)	(1.5 ; 2 ; 2.5)	(5 ; 6 ; 7)	(4.40 ; 5.87 ; 7.34)

In this paper we proposed the method of estimations of the unknown crisp parameters in the linear regression model (2) by minimizing the sum of the squares of the distances between the observed values and the estimated values of the output variable Y. The estimations obtained by this method are the generalization of the least squares estimations in the classical (crisp) linear regression model. We used the Diamond distance of fuzzy numbers and the arithmetic of fuzzy numbers based on the minimum t-norm. It is obvious that other distances [2] and other arithmetic [5], [6], [7] can be used in this method.

References

[1] A. Bárdossy, Note on fuzzy regression, Fuzzy Sets and Systems 37 (1990), 65 – 76.

[2] A. Bárdossy, L. Duckstein, Fuzzy Rule – Based Modeling with Applications to Geophysical, Biological and Eng. Systems, CRC Press, Boca Raton, 1995.

[3] Kacprzyk, Fedrizzi, Fuzzy Regression Analysis, Omnitech Press, Warsaw, 1992.

[4] G. J. Klir, B. Yuan, Fuzzy Sets and Fuzzy Logic - Theory and Applications, Prentice – Hall PTR, Upper Saddle River, NJ, USA, 1995.

[5] A. Kolesárová, Triangular norm - based addition preserving linearity of T - sums of linear fuzzy intervals, Mathware & Soft Computing, Vol. 5, No.1 (1998) 91- 98.

[6] M. Mareš, Computation Over Fuzzy Quantities, CRC Press, Boca Raton, Florida, 1994.

[7] R. Mesiar, Shape preserving additions of fuzzy intervals, Fuzzy Sets and Systems 86 (1997), 73 – 78.

[8] Š. Varga, M. Šabo, Linear regression with fuzzy parameters, Fuzzy Sets and Systems (In print, 2000).

[9] Z. Wang, S. Li, Fuzzy linear regression analysis of fuzzy valued variables, Fuzzy Sets and Systems 36 (1990), 125 – 136.

Fuzzy-Petri Net Reasoning System and Transfering of Knowledge to the Markov Chain

Zoran M.Gacovski[1], Georgi M.Dimirovski[2], Stojce Deskovski[3]

[1]Information Technology Dept. at Ministry of Defense, Skopje, Rep. of Macedonia
[2] Institute of Automation & Systems Engineering (ASE) at Faculty of Electrical Engineering
St.Cyril and St.Methodius University, Karpos 2 BB, PO box 574, 91000 Skopje, R. of Macedonia
[3] Military Academy "Gen. Mihailo Apostolski", Skopje, Rep. of Macedonia
e-mails: zorang@morm.gov.mk, dimir@cerera.etf.ukim.edu.mk, stodes@mpt.com.mk

Abstract: This work presents an overview of a reasoning expert system we have developed and implemented in C++. It is based on fuzzified Petri nets, with rule-based decision-making and appropriate knowledge base (KB). The reasoning algorithm is consisting of calculating the degrees of fulfillment (DOFs) for all rules of the KB and their assigning to the places of the Petri net. After this, it follows reasoning process with firing of active transitions and calculating of DOFs for output places (propositions of KB) and determining of fuzzy-distribution for output variables, as well as their defuzzified values. As final step, we are transferring these values to the states of a Markov chain in order to perform different command and control tasks. Markov chains are efficient tool for simulation and modeling of stochastic discrete event processes, especially those in military operations, like command and control activities.

Keywords: Fuzzy-rule base expert system, Fuzzy-Petri net, Knowledge base, Decision and Control, Markov chains, stochastic discrete event processes.

1 Introduction

In this work we have researched possibilities for two-level control-system architecture with high-level organization and low-level coordinate layer in the supreme level and for reformulation of the Saridis organizing controller [7,8] as a fuzzy-Petri net production system. Petri net (PN) formalism when used in hybrid systems gives us a lot of advantages because of its great power for representation and modeling of parallel and concurrent processes. The formalism of Petri nets can be used for modeling fuzzy-rule based systems directly, by simply identifying some of the elements (marking function) and features (basically places and transitions) of Petri's formalism with the basic elements of a fuzzy knowledge base (KB) (propositions, degree of truth and implication relationships) [4]. The formalism is achieved with more specific aspects such as the association of propositions of the KB and places in fuzzy PN (FPN), through the definition of a bijective function, and the association of transitions and the degrees of truth that make up the KB [11]. Furthermore, a formal separation between the representational scheme (the FPN itself) and the associated dynamic process (data driven evaluation algorithm) is established using elements defined in the formalism but not included as a part of the FPN. Finally, a more adequate handling of multi-propositional rules is proposed in this work. Despite all of this, the degree of truth of the rules is still a numerical value, and the chaining is still done at the value level and thus the drawbacks are still present. Our model includes the handling of true FPS (fuzzy production system) by taking degree of truth of implication rules.

A Markov chain is a sequence of random values whose probabilities at a time interval depend upon the value of the number at the previous time. The controlling factor in a Markov chain is the transition probability; it is a conditional probability for the system to go to a particular new state, given the current state of the system. We can assign the obtained values from the reasoning system to probabilities of the states, or to transition probabilities, so we can control the events in the Markov chains.

2 Petri Net Model of FPS

We will consider the most generic representation of the rules, which make up the KB in a FPS:

R^r:IF X_1^r IS A_1^r AND.. AND X_{Mr}^r IS A_{Mr}^r THEN X_{Mr+1}^r IS B_1^r AND

...AND X_{Mr+Nr}^r IS B_{Nr}^r

where the bold parts are fuzzy propositions and τ are linguistic values of the truth-variable which qualify the rules. We are going to approach the projection of a KB onto a PN and we start by identifying the places of the PN with the propositions of the KB by means of bijective function:

$$\alpha: P \rightarrow PR, \ p_k \rightarrow \alpha(p_k)=pr_k, \ k=1,...,K, \ (1)$$

where $PR=\{ pr_k \}$ is the set of propositions in the KB and K is the number of propositions in the KB. In the case where a proposition is found several times in different rules of the KB, a different place will be assigned to it for each of these appearances in the KB.

The description of the meaning of the transitions is more complex, because of the linking rules. In our representation $T=T^R \cup T^C = \{t^1,...,t^R,t^{R+1},...,t^{R+C}\}$. Subset T^R includes the transitions associated with each one of the rules that make up the KB, whereas subset T^C includes the transitions that are associated with the existence of links between propositions. We define the input and the output functions over set T

$$I: T \dashrightarrow \phi(P) \tag{2}$$

$$O: T \dashrightarrow \phi (P) \qquad\qquad (3)$$

which associate to each transition the set of places which constitute its input and output, respectively. These functions have a different interpretation depending on the subset of T in which they are considered.

$$\text{If } t^j \in T^R, \; \forall p_i \in P, \; p_i \in I(t^j) <=> a(p_i) \in \text{Antecedent part of } R^j \qquad (4)$$

$$\text{If } t^j \in T^R, \; \forall p_i \in P, \; p_i \in O(t^j) <=> a(p_i) \in \text{Consequent part of } R^j (5)$$

$$\text{If } t^j \in T^C, \; p_i \in I(t^j), \; p_k \in O(t^j) <=> a(p_i) \text{ is linked with } \alpha(p_k) \qquad (6)$$

Therefore a single transition $t^j \in T^C$ will exist for each of the intermediate variables X_j of the KB.

The graphic representation of the PN is defined with:

$$A = U \{ \, t^j \times O(t^j) \, \} \cup \{ \, I(t^j) \times t^j \, \} \qquad\qquad (7)$$

We will define a truth function f that assigns to each $t^j \in T^R$ the linguistic truth value associated with rule R^j :

$$f : T^R \dashrightarrow V, \; t^j \dashrightarrow f(\, t^j) = \tau^j \qquad\qquad (8)$$

where V represents the set of linguistic values of the linguistic truth variable. We say that place p_l is immediately reachable from place p_k if:

$$\exists \, t^j \in T / p_k \in I(t^j) \text{ and } \; p_l \in O(t^j) \qquad\qquad (9)$$

The adjacent transitions associated with chains will represent the multiple link situations: several rules establish inferences over the same variable and one or more later rules make use of this variable in its (their) antecedent part. In this case, a transition will be associated with each chain.

3 Fuzzy-Petri Reasoning

The fundamental notion for execution of a KB is marked PN. Marking indicates that the degree of fulfillment (DOF) of the associated proposition is known, so this proposition can be used in the process of obtaining new references. It will be necessary for the DOF's of the different propositions to be available all the time. So we define the fulfillment function:

$$g : P \dashrightarrow [0,1] \qquad\qquad (10)$$

which assigns to each place a real value:

$$g(p) = DOF(\alpha(p)) \qquad\qquad (11)$$

In our representation tokens are transferred from some places to others by means of the activation of transitions, following a basic rule: A transition $t^j \in T$ is active (and will fire) if every $p_i \in I(P)$ has a token. When during the process of firing a transition the token of the input places is removed, the information obtained about the DOF of that propositions are preserved in the fulfillment function. The firing of an active transition $t^j \in T^R$ is equivalent to the application of a rule in the process of evaluating the KB. The activation of $t^j \in T^C$ is equivalent to knowing, whether it be through previously performed inferences or through observation, the DOF of propositions $\alpha(p_i)$, $\forall p_i \in I(t^j)$. In this case, the DOF for propositions $\alpha(p_k)$, $\forall p_k \in O(tj)$ is determined not by the application of rules of the KB, but by essentially the same method as the one used to determine the DOF of a proposition with observed input distribution values. Most of the operations participating in this calculation can be carried out a priori, leading to a significant simplification of the execution process. When all DOF's of the antecedent part of a rule are known and it is executed, the marking function will have placed tokens in all of the input places of the corresponding transition, activating it and causing it to fire, which will produce a new marking function.

The definition of the initial marking function M in the PN representation of the KB of a FPS can be established as:

$$M : p \dashrightarrow \{ 0,1 \}, \ p_i \dashrightarrow M(p_i) = \{ 0, \text{ if } g(p_i) \text{ is unknown}$$
$$1, \text{ otherwise} \quad (12)$$

The marking function thus makes explicit the requirement that the DOF of a set of propositions must be known before an evaluation of the KB can be carried out. From a given marking function M, the firing of a transition t^j will produce a new marking function M'. The evolution of the marking functions of a PN is described by the transition function tf:

$$tf: M \times T \dashrightarrow M, \ (M, t^j) \dashrightarrow M' \quad (13)$$

where:

$$M'(p_i) = \{ 0, \text{ if } p_i \in I(t^j)$$
$$1, \text{ if } p_i \in O(t^j)$$
$$M(p_i), \text{ otherwise} \quad (14)$$

and M represents the set of all possible marking functions of the PN. The process of executing a KB can be understood as the "propagation" of possibility distributions through the KB, via implication operations (which permit "propagating" distributions from the antecedent part of a rule to the consequent part of the same rule) and via links (which "connect" the consequent part of one or several rules to the antecedent part of other(s)). This evaluation process is carried out following a certain order, which determines at any moment in time the rule(s) that may be applied. The process finishes with the operation of aggregating all the possibility distributions inferred for each output variable into a single final possibility distribution.

Without loss of generality, we analyze a KB which consist of only two chained rules:

R^S: IF $X1^S$ IS $A1^S$ AND ... AND X_{Ms}^S IS A_{Ms}^S THEN X_{Ms+1}^S IS B_1^S AND

...AND X_{Ms+Ns}^S IS B_{Ns}^S (τ^S)

R^T: IF $X1^T$ IS $A1^T$ AND...AND X_{MT}^T IS A_{MT}^T THEN X_{MT+1}^T IS B_1^T AND...AND

X_{MT+NT}^T IS B_{NT}^T (τ^T) (15)

which are linked by :

$$X_{Ms+1}^S = X_1^T \quad (16)$$

In order to represent the rule pair in the formalism we have described, we must first define the bijective function α, which relates places and propositions to this end, we define the following set of places:

$$P = \{\, p^r_{mr} \mid m_r = 1, \dots, Mr+Nr, \; r=S,T \,\} \qquad (17)$$

and the set of propositions:

$$PR = pr^r_{mr} = \{\, "X^r_{mr} \text{ IS } A^r_{mr}", \; mr \leq Mr; \; "X^r_{mr} \text{ IS } B^r_{mr-Mr}", \; mr>Mr \,\} \quad (18)$$

Furthermore, given the simplicity of our KB, the transition for the rules and links are:

$$T^R = \{\, t^s, t^T \,\} \qquad (19)$$
$$T^C = \{\, t^3 \,\} \qquad (20)$$

The graphic representation of rules considered is shown on fig. 1:

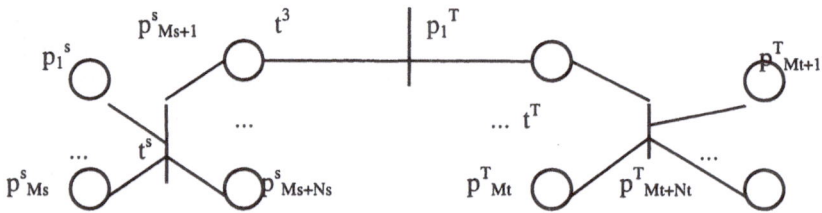

Fig.1. Representation of the chaining of two rules in the PN formalism.

We will focus on the process of obtaining the DOF corresponding to proposition $\alpha(p_1^T)$ from the DOF of $\alpha(p_{Ms+1}{}^S)$, i.e. $g(p_1^T)$ from $g(p_{Ms+1}{}^S)$. We can write:

$$\underline{b}^s_{1,i} = \tau^s(g(p_{Ms+1}{}^S) \wedge b^s_{1,i}), \quad i=1,\dots,I \qquad (21)$$

where $B^S_1 = \{\, b^s_{1,i} \}$ is the possibility distribution associated with linguistic value B^S_1 in proposition $\alpha(p_{Ms+1}{}^S)$. The DOF will be:

$$g(p_1^T) = V[\, \tau^s(g(p_{Ms+1}{}^S) \wedge b^s_{1,i}) \wedge a^T_{1,i} \,] \qquad (22)$$

where $a^T_{1,i}$ is possibility distribution of linguistic value A in propositions.

We will show now the more general case in which several rules $R^1,\dots,R^S$ perform inference over a variable, and the same variable is in the antecedent part of at least one later rule R^T. A typical example is as follows:

$$R^1: \text{IF } X_1^1 \text{ IS } A_1^1 \text{ AND} \dots \text{THEN } X^1_{M1+1} \text{ IS } B_1^1 \text{ AND} \dots \quad (\tau^1)$$
$$R^2: \text{IF } X_1^2 \text{ IS } A_1^2 \text{ AND} \dots \text{THEN } X^2_{M2+1} \text{ IS } B_1^2 \text{ AND} \dots \quad (\tau^2)$$
$$R^S: \text{IF } X_1^S \text{ IS } A_1^S \text{ AND} \dots \text{THEN } X^S_{MS+1} \text{ IS } B_1^S \text{ AND} \dots \quad (\tau^S)$$
$$R^T: \text{IF } X_1^T \text{ IS } A_1^T \text{ AND} \dots \text{THEN } X^T_{MT+1} \text{ IS } B_1^T \text{ AND} \dots \quad (\tau^T)$$

$$(23)$$

with:

$$X^1{}_{M1+1} = X^2{}_{M2+1} = \dots = X^S{}_{Ms+1} = X^T{}_1 \quad (24)$$

Following a procedure that is analogous to the previous one we will obtain the DOF for proposition $pr_1{}^T$:

$$g\,(p_1{}^T) = V\,[\ \ V[\tau^S(g(p_{Ms+1}{}^S)\ \Lambda\ b^S{}_{1,i})]\ \Lambda\ a^T{}_{1,i}\,] \quad (25)$$

4 Reasoning Algorithm

The algorithm will basically consist of two stages: definition of the marking function and production of the DOF's of the corresponding propositions and firing of the active transitions. These stages are sequentially repeated until there are no more active transitions, at in which time the inference process will have ended. Finally, we perform aggregation - assignment of a single possibility distribution to each output variable. Let IP and OP be the sets that group input and output places respectively.

Step 1- Initially we assume we know only the DOF's of the propositions that operate on input variables, that is, those associated with input places. Therefore, the initial marking function will be:

$$M(p_i) = \{\ 0,\ \text{if } p_i \notin IP;\ 1,\ \text{if } p_i \in IP\ \} \quad (26)$$

Step 2- We fire the active transitions. Let t^j be any active transition; that is,

$$t^j \in T \mid \forall p_k \in I(t^j),\ M(p_k)=1 \quad (27)$$

The transition function *tf*, which defines the successive marking functions will be as defined with *(13)*. Also, the corresponding DOF's are obtained as follows:

$$\text{If } t^j \in T^R,\ g(p_i) = \Lambda\ g(p_k)\,,\ \forall p_i \in O(t^j) \quad (28)$$

$$\text{If } t^j \in T^C,\ g(p_i) = V\,[\tau^{rk}(\ g(p_k))\ o^{rk}\ \mu_{pk,pi}]\,,\ \forall p_i \in O(t^j) \quad (29)$$

Step 3- Go back to step 2, while:

$$\exists\,t^j \in T \mid M(p_i) = 1,\ \forall p_i \in I(t^j) \quad (30)$$

Step 4- For each output variable X, its associated possibility distribution $\underline{B}=\{\underline{b}_i\}$, $i=1,\dots,I$, will be:

$$\underline{b}_i = V\ \tau^r(g(p_n{}^r))\ o^r\ \tau^r(b^r{}_{n,i}) \quad (31)$$

where the set P_x of places associated with propositions in which inferences over X are carried out is defined by:

$$Px = \{\ p_n{}^r \in P \mid \alpha(p_n{}^r) = \text{"X IS } Bn^r\text{"}\} \quad (32)$$

5 Markov Chain Assignment

In the category of discrete-event processes, there are some processes that cause different types of changes, and usually cause leap changes. The processes of planning, foresee and control are discrete-event processes, which examine structural connections between state transitions and their probability. With analysis we can obtain the schedule of transitions and the basic units of time, which are needed for each transition. For solving of these problems, we must apply transition matrices, probability matrices and Markov chains.

A Markov chain is a stochastic process that has:
- A finite number of states;
- Markovian transitions;
- Stationary transition probabilities;
- A set of initial probabilities $P(X_0=i)=q_i$, $\forall i$, $i \in [0, N]$.

A Markov chain is a sequence of random values whose probabilities at a time interval depend upon the value of the number at the previous time. A simple example is the non-returning random walk, where the walkers are restricted to not go back to the location just previously visited. The controlling factor in a Markov chain is the transition probability; it is a conditional probability for the system to go to a particular new state, given the current state of the system. For many problems, such as simulated annealing, the Markov chain obtains the much-desired importance sampling. This means that we get fairly efficient estimates if we can determine the proper transition probabilities.

Markov chains can be used to solve a very useful class of problems in a rather remarkable way. Lets suppose we have an $n \times n$ matrix of probabilities, P, such that,

$$P_{ij} \geq 0, \ \textstyle\sum_j p_{ij} \leq 1 \tag{33}$$

and we have an array:

$$g_i = 1 - \textstyle\sum_j p_{ij} \tag{34}$$

P can describe a Markov chain where the states of the chain are n integers. The element p_{ij} gives the transition probability for the random walk from state i to state j. As long as g is not zero the walk will eventually terminate. The probability that the walk will terminate after state i is given by g_i.

As an extension of our reasoning algorithm with FPS, we can assign the final obtained values for output variables, as initial probabilities of the states (or as transition probabilities) of the Markov chain. So we are creating Markov chain with obligatory state probabilities, obtained from an expert system with different purpose, after its evaluation process. On that way we can control the events in the Markov chains.

6 Conclusion

In this work we showed that by using of Petri net formalism we can develop a model of FPS as a model for inference and conclusion chaining, which is compatible with well-structured algorithms for data-driven execution of a fuzzified KB. This process, based on a KB execution approach through the compositional rule of inference, transfers most of the computational load to the design, and not execution stage. This allows the complexity of the execution algorithms to remain independent of the discretization of the discourse universes over which the linguistic variables to be manipulated in the fuzzy production systems are defined.

Despite the fact that the analysis of the whole process and the description of the algorithms is carried out for a sup-min compositional rule of inference, the same results are valid for the sup-prod rule, although with less flexibility in the definition of the linguistic truth values that qualify the rules. We have also used the Petri net formalism in order to obtain a formal structure that permits the definition of algorithms for carrying out inferences in different situations.

The controlling factor in a Markov chain is the transition probability; it is a conditional probability for the system to go to a particular new state, given the current state of the system. We can assign the obtained values from the reasoning system to probabilities of the states, or to transition probabilities, so we can control the events in the Markov chains.

7 Simulation Results

The rule base that is considered is:

0. IF X1=LP\0.12 & X6=SP\0.10 THEN X2=ZO, => dof(A00)=0.64; dof(A01)=0.70;

1. IF X1=LN\0.06 & X3=SN\0.12 THEN X2=ZO, => dof(A10)=0.82; dof(A11)=0.64;

2. IF X2=SN\0.07 & X5=LN\0.20 THEN X7=ZO, => dof(A20)=0.79; dof(A21)=0.40;

3. IF X2=SN\0.15 & X5=SN\0.25 THEN X4=ZO, => dof(A30)=0.55; dof(A31)=0.25;

4. IF X4=SP\0.05 & X3=SN\0.20 THEN X7=ZO, => dof(A40)=0.85; dof(A41)=0.40;

The Petri net with calculated DOF-s of propositions (places) is:

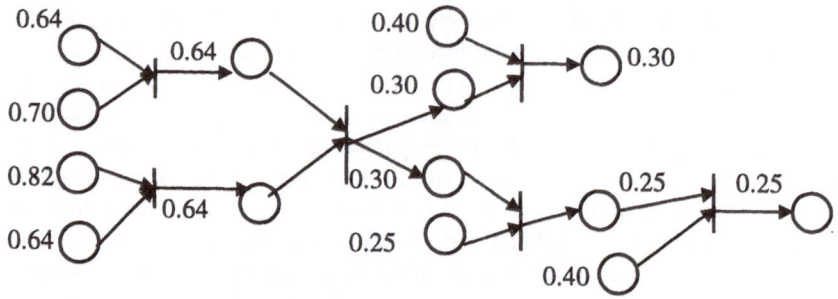

Graphic representation of the output variable:

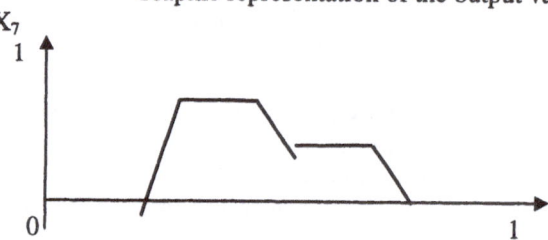

With defuzzyfication we obtain 0.415- with weight method;
0.34- with height method.

REFERENCES

[1] R. Zurawski, M.C.Zhou, "Petri Nets and Industrial Application: A Tutorial", *IEEE Trans.on Industr. Elect.*, vol.41, pp. 567-583, 1994.
[2] C.G. Moore, C.J. Harris, "Aspects of fuzzy control and estimation", Depart.of Aeronautics and Astronautics, Southampton Universety,U.K.,1994.
[3] G.V. S. Raju, J. Zhou, R.A. Kisner, " Hierarchial fuzzy control", *Department of Elec.and Comp. Eng.*, Ohio Universety, USA, 1994.
[4] A.J. Bugarin, S. Barro, " Fuzzy Reasoning Supported by Petri Nets", *IEEE Trans.on Fuzzy Systems*, vol. 2, pp. 135 - 150, 1994.
[5] L.A. Zadeh, " Outline of a new approach to the analysis of complex systems and decision processes", *IEEE Trans. Syst., Man. Cyber*, vol.3, pp.28-44, 1973.
[6] S.M.Chen, J.S.Ke and J.F.Chang, " Knowledge representation using Fuzzy Petri Nets", *IEEE Trans. Syst., Man. Cyber*, vol. 20, pp.311-319, 1990.
[7] G. N. Saridis, "Analytic formulation of the Principle of Increasing Precision with Decreasing Intelligence for Intelligent Machines", *Automatica*, vol.25, No.3, pp.461-467, 1989.
[8] G. N. Saridis, and K.P. Valavanis, "Analytical design of Intelligent Machines", *Automatica*, vol.24, No. 2, pp.123-133, 1988.

[9] H. N. Stellakis and K.P. Valavanis ," Fuzzy-logic based Formulation of the Organizer of Intelligent Robotic Systems", *Jour. of Int. and Rob.Sys.*, vol.4, No.1, p.3, 1991.

[10] G. M. Dimirovski, O. Kaynak, A. T. Dinibutin and R. Hanus, "Contributions to two-level intelligent nonlinear control systems", *Recent Advances in Mechatronics*, Bogazici Univ., Istanbul, vol. II, pp. 874-881, 1995.

[11] Z. M. Gacovski, G. M. Dimirovski, O. Kaynak, A. T. Dinibutin and R. Hanus"A contribution to fuzzy Petri reformulation of intelligent organizing controller", In *Proc. of 40th Conference of ETRAN*, Budva, Yugoslavia, 1996.

Fuzzy Conceptual Graphs: A Language for Computational Intelligence Approaching Human Expression and Reasoning

T.H. Cao

Artificial Intelligence Group
Department of Engineering Mathematics
University of Bristol
United Kingdom BS8 1TR
Tru.Cao@bristol.ac.uk

Abstract: Conceptual graphs and fuzzy logic are two logical formalisms that emphasize the target of natural language, where conceptual graphs provide a structure of formulas close to that of natural language sentences while fuzzy logic provides a methodology for computing with words. This paper proposes fuzzy conceptual graphs as a knowledge representation language that combines the advantages of both the two formalisms for computational intelligence approaching human expression and reasoning. Firstly, simple fuzzy conceptual graphs are defined as bipartite graphs of concepts alternate with conceptual relations. Fuzzy types are introduced to represent uncertainty and/or partial truth about concept or relation types. For representing complex information, simple fuzzy conceptual graphs are extended to nested fuzzy conceptual graphs. Then, as a basic operation for inference, the projection operation that matches a (nested) fuzzy conceptual graph to another one and measures the relative necessity degree of the former given the latter is defined.

1 Introduction

Natural language is a principal and important means of human communication. It is used to express information as inputs to be processed by human brains then, very often, outputs are also expressed in natural language. How humans process information represented in natural language is still a challenge to science, in general, and to Computational Intelligence, in particular. However, it is clear that, for a computer with the conventional processing paradigm to process natural language, a formalism is required. For reasoning, it is desirable that such a formalism be a logical one.

A logic for handling natural language should have not only a structure of formulas close to that of natural language sentences, but also a capability to deal with the semantics of vague linguistic terms pervasive in natural language expressions. Currently, conceptual graphs (Sowa 1984) and fuzzy logic (Zadeh 1975) are two logical formalisms that emphasize the target of natural language, each of which is focused on one of the two mentioned desired features of a logic for handling natural language. Indeed, while a smooth mapping between logic and natural language has been regarded as the main motivation of conceptual graphs (Sowa 1991, 1997), a methodology for computing with words has been regarded as the main contribution of fuzzy logic (Zadeh 1978, 1996).

Interestingly, for example, while quantifying words in natural language such as *many*, *few* or *most*, which are intrinsically vague, can be represented in conceptual graphs but not in predicate logic (Sowa 1991), the vagueness and imprecision of these words can be handled by fuzzy logic (Zadeh 1978, 1983). However, although these two logic systems have the common target of natural language, they have been studied and developed quite separately so far. Only a few researchers have recognised the great advantage of their combination towards a knowledge representation language that can approach human expression and reasoning. At this juncture, conceptual graphs provide a syntactic structure for a smooth mapping to and from natural language, while fuzzy logic provides a semantic processor for approximate reasoning with words having vague meanings. This paper proposes fuzzy conceptual graphs (FCGs) as such a language for computational intelligence.

2 Simple Fuzzy Conceptual Graphs

Firstly, a *simple FCG* is defined as a bipartite graph of *concept* vertices alternate with (conceptual) *relation* vertices, where edges connect relation vertices to concept vertices. Each concept vertex, drawn as a box and labelled by a pair of a *concept type* and a *concept referent*, represents an entity whose type and referent are respectively defined by the concept type and the concept referent in the pair. Each relation vertex, drawn as a circle and labelled by a *relation type*, represents a relation of the entities represented by the concept vertices connected to it. Each edge is labelled by a positive integer and, in practice, may be directed just for readability.

A concept referent is either a *single referent* or a *set referent* consisting of single referents. A single referent is either an *individual marker* referring to a specific entity, or a *generic marker* * referring to an unspecified entity. For example, in Fig. 1, the simple FCG G expresses "*Most* Swedes are *tall*", where *most* and *tall* are linguistic labels of fuzzy sets. The contracted form of G is G^*, where the concepts [SWEDE: {*}@*most*] and [HEIGHT: *@*tall*] are called *fuzzy entity concept* and *fuzzy attribute concept*, respectively.

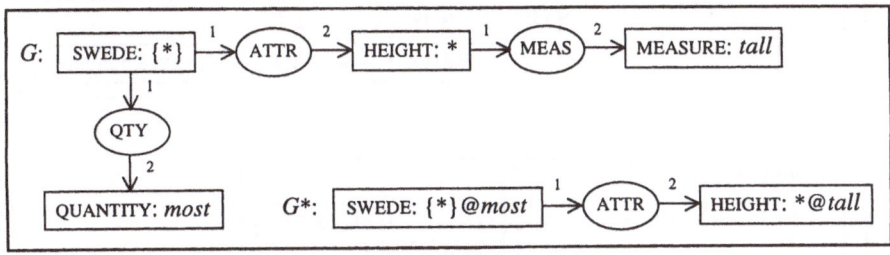

Fig. 1. Simple FCGs

A concept type or a relation type can be a *fuzzy type* to represent uncertainty and/or partial truth about the type of the entity referred by a concept or the type of a relation, where a fuzzy type is defined as a pair of a *basic type* and an uncertainty and/or truth degree. This notion of fuzzy types was first introduced in Cao et al. (1997), where an uncertainty and/or truth degree was a *fuzzy truth value*, i.e., a fuzzy set on [0, 1] whose values are interpreted as truth degrees. Here, we extend that definition so that an uncertainty and/or truth degree can be a *fuzzy probability value*, which is also defined by a fuzzy set on [0, 1] whose values are however interpreted as probability degrees.

Examples of linguistic labels of a fuzzy truth value are *more or less true* and *not very false*, while ones of a fuzzy probability value are *quite likely* and *very unlikely*. An example of a simple FCG with fuzzy types is shown in Fig. 2, which says "It is *very true* that John is an American man, who is *young*, and it is *more or less true* that he likes a car, whose colour is *blue*", where *very true*, *more or less true*, *young* and *blue* are linguistic labels of fuzzy sets.

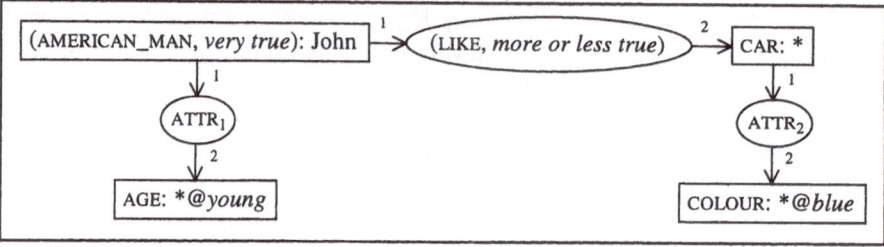

Fig. 2. A simple FCG with fuzzy types

3 Nested Fuzzy Conceptual Graphs

For representing complex information, we introduce *nested FCGs*. A nested FCG is recursively defined as a simple FCG extended by adding a *descriptor* field to each of its concepts, where a descriptor is either empty or a nested FCG, which describes the referent of a concept. For example, the nested FCG in Fig. 3 expresses "Tom shows a picture of a monster which is *about 20 feet* in length, and tells about a *very unlikely* situation that it exists in Lake Loch Ness". Here, the dotted line is a *coreference link* denoting that the two concepts [MONSTER: *] refer to the same entity. Meanwhile, representation of such nested pieces of information in linear notations, e.g. predicate logic, would be difficult to follow.

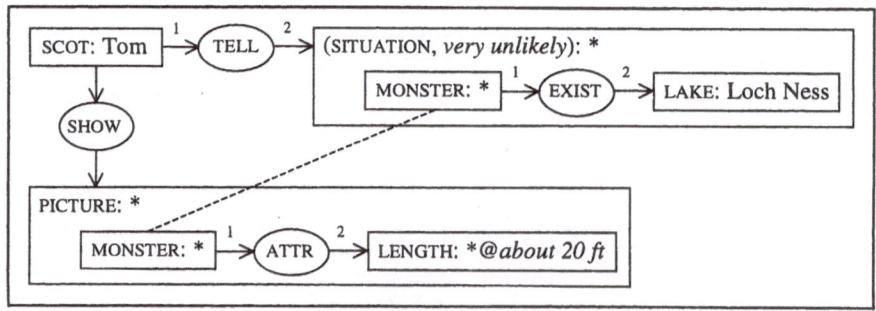

Fig. 3. A nested FCG

We now present formal definitions of the basic notions of (nested) FCGs introduced above. We especially use $\leq_t$ as the common symbol for all orders used in this paper, under the same umbrella of *information ordering*, whereby $A \leq_t B$

means B is more informative, or more specific, than A. In particular, we write $A \leq_t B$ if B is a subtype of A, or B is a fuzzy subset of A. It will be clear in a specific context which order this common symbol denotes. Also, we will write $A <_t B$ to indicate that $A \leq_t B$ and $A \neq B$.

Definition 3.1 An *FCG signature* is a sextuple $(\mathbf{T_C}, \mathbf{T_R}, \mathbf{M}, \mathbf{V}, \mathbf{A}, \mathbf{Q})$ where:
1. $(\mathbf{T_C}, \leq_t)$ is a partially ordered set of concept types.
2. $(\mathbf{T_R}, \leq_t)$ is a partially ordered set of relation types.
3. $(\mathbf{M}, \leq_t)$ is a partially ordered set of single referents consisting of pairwise incomparable individual markers and the generic marker * as the least element.
4. $\mathbf{V}$ is a set of fuzzy truth values/fuzzy probability values.
5. $\mathbf{A}$ is a set of fuzzy attribute values.
6. $\mathbf{Q}$ is a set of fuzzy quantifiers.

We note that the default quantifiers for set referents $\{i_1, i_2,..., i_k\}$ and $\{i_1, i_2,..., i_k, *\}$ are k and *at least* $k+1$, respectively. Meanwhile, by set coercion, fuzzy entity concepts [T: i] and [T: *], with single referents, can be converted to [T: $\{i\}@1$] and [T: $\{*\}@1$]. Thus, one can assume a fuzzy entity concept to be always with a set referent, which is an element in $2^\mathbf{M}$, and a quantifier. A partial order $\leq_t$ is then defined on $2^\mathbf{M}$ so that $\forall S_1, S_2 \in 2^\mathbf{M}$: $S_1 \leq_t S_2$ iff $|S_1| \leq_t |S_2|$ and $\forall m \in S_1$: $m = *$ or $m \in S_2$. For example, one has $\{i_1, *\} \leq_t \{i_1, i_2\}$, but not $\{i_1, *\} \leq_t \{i_1\}$.

Definition 3.2 A *simple FCG G* with respect to an FCG signature $(\mathbf{T_C}, \mathbf{T_R}, \mathbf{M}, \mathbf{V}, \mathbf{A}, \mathbf{Q})$ is a bipartite graph defined by a triple $(\mathbf{V_{C_G}}, \mathbf{V_{R_G}}, \mathbf{E_G})$ where:
1. $\mathbf{V_{C_G}}$ is a set of concept vertices, each of which is labelled by either:
    (i) A fuzzy concept type in $\mathbf{T_C} \times \mathbf{V}$, a concept referent in $2^\mathbf{M}$, and a fuzzy quantifier in $\mathbf{Q}$, for a fuzzy entity concept, or
    (ii) A fuzzy concept type in $\mathbf{T_C} \times \mathbf{V}$, a concept referent in $\mathbf{M}$, and a fuzzy attribute value in $\mathbf{A}$, for a fuzzy attribute concept.
    The type and the referent of each concept $c \in \mathbf{V_{C_G}}$ are denoted by *type(c)* and *referent(c)*, respectively. If c is a fuzzy entity concept, its quantifier is denoted by *quantifier(c)*. If c is a fuzzy attribute concept, its attribute value is denoted by *value(c)*.
2. $\mathbf{V_{R_G}}$ is a set of relation vertices, each of which is labelled by a fuzzy relation type in $\mathbf{T_R} \times \mathbf{V}$. The type of each relation $r \in \mathbf{V_{R_G}}$ is denoted by *type(r)*.
3. $\mathbf{E_G}$ is a set of edges, each of which connects a relation vertex to a concept vertex. The number of edges incident to a relation r is equal to the arity of *type(r)*, denoted by *arity(type(r))*, and the edges are labelled from 1 to *arity(type(r))*. For every i from 1 to *arity(type(r))*, the concept connected to r by the edge labelled i is denoted by *neighbour(r, i)*.

Definition 3.3 A *nested FCG* is a simple FCG extended with a *descriptor* for each of its concepts, which is either empty or a nested FCG. The descriptor of a concept c is denoted by *descriptor(c)*.

4 Fuzzy Conceptual Graph Projection

We now define an operation, called *FCG projection*, which matches a (nested) FCG to another one and measures the relative necessity degree (i.e., certainty degree) of the former given the latter. This relative necessity degree is defined as the infimum of those of the matched pairs of fuzzy sets and fuzzy types in the two FCGs.

Firstly, given two fuzzy sets A and A^* on a domain U, the *mismatching degree* of A to A^* is defined as in Cao (1999) as follows:

$$\Delta(A \mid A^*) = sup_{u \in U}\{max\{0, \mu_{A^*}(u) - \mu_A(u)\}\}$$

where μ_A and μ_{A^*} are the membership functions of A and A^*, respectively. The relation between $\Delta(A \mid A^*)$ and $N(A \mid A^*)$, the relative necessity degree of A given A^*, is $\Delta(A \mid A^*) = 1 - N(A \mid A^*)$.

The following definition of fuzzy type mismatching degrees is adapted from Cao (1999), where uncertainty and/or truth degrees of fuzzy types were only fuzzy truth values. In the definition, $\mathbf{V}^+$ and $\mathbf{V}^-$ are respectively the POSITIVE-characteristic and the NEGATIVE-characteristic subsets of a set $\mathbf{V}$ of fuzzy truth values/fuzzy probability values. Examples of POSITIVE-characteristic values are *more or less true* and *very likely*, while ones of NEGATIVE-characteristic values are *very false* and *quite unlikely*. Also, *lub* is the least upper bound function (with respect to $\leq_t$) on fuzzy sets.

Definition 4.1 Let $\tau_1 = (t_1, v_1)$ and $\tau_2 = (t_2, v_2)$ be two fuzzy types. The *mismatching degree* of τ_1 to τ_2, denoted by $\Delta(\tau_1 \mid \tau_2)$, is:

1. $\Delta(v_1 \mid v_2)$ if $t_1 = t_2$, or
2. $\Delta(v_1 \mid lub\{v \in \mathbf{V}^+ \mid v \leq_t v_2\})$ if $t_1 <_t t_2$ and $\exists v \in \mathbf{V}^+ : v \leq_t v_2$, or
3. $\Delta(v_1 \mid lub\{v \in \mathbf{V}^- \mid v \leq_t v_2\})$ if $t_1 >_t t_2$ and $\exists v \in \mathbf{V}^- : v \leq_t v_2$, or

undefined, otherwise.

For a definition of fuzzy quantifier mismatching degrees, *absolute quantifiers* and *relative quantifiers* on a set have to be distinguished, where the quantities expressed by the latter are relative to the cardinality of the set. Examples of absolute quantifiers are *at least 1* and *about 27*, while ones of relative quantifiers are *most* and *about 90%*. The definition of FCG projection is then as follows.

Definition 4.2 Let G and H be two FCGs. An *FCG projection* from G to H is a mapping $\pi: G \rightarrow H$ such that:

1. $\forall c \in \mathbf{V}_{C_G}$: there is an FCG projection π^* from *descriptor(c)* to *descriptor(πc)* with mismatching degree ε_{π^*}, and

   (i)   If c is a fuzzy entity concept and *quantifier(c)* is an absolute quantifier, then *referent(c)* $\leq_t$ *referent(πc)*.
   The mismatching degree of c to πc is $max\{\Delta(type(c) \mid type(\pi c)),$ $\Delta(quantifier(c) \mid quantifier(\pi c)), \varepsilon_{\pi^*}\}$.

   (ii) If c is a fuzzy entity concept and *quantifier(c)* is a relative quantifier, then *referent(c)* $\leq_t$ *referent(πc)* and *type(c)* = *type(πc)*.
   The mismatching degree of c to πc is $max\{\Delta(quantifier(c) \mid quantifier(\pi c)), \varepsilon_{\pi^*}\}$.

(iii) If c is a fuzzy attribute concept, then $referent(c) \leq_t referent(\pi c)$. The mismatching degree of c to πc is $max\{\Delta(type(c) \mid type(\pi c)),$ $\Delta(value(c) \mid value(\pi c)), \varepsilon_{\pi*}\}$.

2. $\forall r \in \mathbf{V}_{R_G}$: $neighbour(\pi r, i) = \pi neighbour(r, i)$ for every $i \in \{1,...,$ $arity(type(r))\}$.

The mismatching degree of r to πr is $\Delta(type(r) \mid type(\pi r))$.

Then the mismatching degree ε_π of π is the supremum of the mismatching degrees of all fuzzy concept pairs and fuzzy relation pairs in π.

The significance of ε_π is that $1 - \varepsilon_\pi$ measures the relative necessity degree of G given H; when $\varepsilon_\pi = 0$, H fully entails G. As such, FCG projection can be used for inference based on certainty degree qualification, propagation and modification.

5 Conclusion

We have presented a significant fact that conceptual graphs and fuzzy logic actually have the common target of natural language. Continuing Cao (1999) on combining the advantages of both the two logical formalisms for computational intelligence approaching human expression and reasoning, we have then formulated nested FCGs, with set referents and fuzzy quantifiers, and defined FCG projection as a basic inference operation on them.

FCGs can be used as a knowledge representation language at both the human-computer interface level and the storage and manipulation level. The graphical notation and the smooth mapping to and from natural language of conceptual graphs are significant to knowledge visualisation and human-computer interaction. The structure for abstracting knowledge into nested concepts is an advantage of conceptual graphs for knowledge organisation and storage. Meanwhile fuzzy logic can deal with the pervasive vagueness and imprecision of the real world as reflected in natural language.

In Cao and Creasy (1998), FCG programs were introduced and a graph-based proof procedure was developed, which was sound and complete with respect to the declarative semantics of annotated fuzzy logic programs (Cao 2000). An FCG program was defined as a finite set of Horn-like clauses whose heads and bodies were simple FCGs without set referents and fuzzy quantifiers. We are extending it to allow nested FCGs to be the heads and the bodies of program clauses. For more complex forms of reasoning with FCGs, we are studying and applying other computing-with-words methodologies (e.g. Lawry 2000), besides the one based on relative necessity degrees between fuzzy sets. Implementation of a system for editing, storing and manipulating FCGs is also among the topics that are currently investigated.

References

1. Cao, T.H. (2000), Annotated fuzzy logic programs. *International Journal for Fuzzy Sets and Systems*, 113 (2), 277-298.
2. Cao, T.H. (1999), Foundations of order-sorted fuzzy set logic programming in predicate logic and conceptual graphs. PhD Thesis, University of Queensland.

3. Cao, T.H. and Creasy, P.N. (1998), Fuzzy order-sorted logic programming in conceptual graphs with a sound and complete proof procedure. In Mugnier, M.L. and Chein, M. (eds), *Conceptual Structures: Theory, Tools and Applications*, LNAI 1453, Springer-Verlag, pp. 270-284.

4. Cao, T.H., Creasy, P.N. and Wuwongse, V. (1997), Fuzzy types and their lattices. In Proceedings of the 6th IEEE International Conference on Fuzzy Systems, pp. 805-812.

5. Lawry, J. (2000). An alternative interpretation of linguistic variables and computing with words. In Proceedings of the 8th International Conference on Information Processing and Management of Uncertainty in Knowledge-Based Systems. To appear.

6. Sowa, J.F. (1984), *Conceptual Structures - Information Processing in Mind and Machine*. Addison-Wesley Publishing Company.

7. Sowa, J.F. (1991), Towards the expressive power of natural language. In Sowa, J.F. (ed.), *Principles of Semantic Networks - Explorations in the Representation of Knowledge*, Morgan Kaufmann Publishers, pp. 157-189.

8. Sowa, J.F. (1997), Matching logical structure to linguistic structure. In Houser, N. and Roberts, D.D. and Van Evra, J. (eds), *Studies in the Logic of Charles Sanders Peirce*, Indiana University Press, pp. 418-444.

9. Zadeh, L.A. (1975), Fuzzy logic and approximate reasoning (In memory of Grigore Moisil). *Synthese*, 30, 407-428.

10. Zadeh, L.A. (1978), PRUF - a meaning representation language for natural languages. *International Journal of Man-Machine Studies*, 10, 395-460.

11. Zadeh, L.A. (1983), A fuzzy-set-theoretic approach to fuzzy quantifiers in natural languages. *Computers and Mathematics with Applications*, 9, 149-184.

12. Zadeh, L.A. (1996), Fuzzy logic = computing with words. *IEEE Transactions on Fuzzy Systems*, 4, 103-111.

A New Heuristic Measure for Learning Rules from Fuzzy Data

Francisco Botana[1], José Ranilla[2], Ricardo Mones[2], and Antonio Bahamonde[2]

[1] Universidad de Vigo, EUETF, Campus A Xunqueira, 36005 Pontevedra, Spain
[2] Universidad de Oviedo en Gijón, Centro de Inteligencia Artificial, Campus de Viesques, 33271 Gijón, Spain

Abstract: Decision tree induction and rule production methods have been proven as efficient tools in concept learning or data mining tasks. These approaches exhibit a good performance even when there are cognitive uncertainties in the data. Most systems in this paradigm use the information gain criterion in selecting attributes when learning. This paper presents an alternative approach. A heuristic measure of the impurity level of rules when dealing with fuzzy data is described and used in a classification algorithm. Results on the Sports classification problem are reported and compared with those of other learning algorithms.

1 Introduction

Learning to classify objects is a central problem in artificial intelligence. ID3 [1] and PRISM [2] are, respectively, keystones for decision tree and modular rule induction. Even when fuzzy data, various versions of ID3 and PRISM have been reported [3] [4].

These fuzzy systems share with their parents an information theoretic approach to the learning process. The learning set can be seen as a discrete information system where attribute values give information about the classification. The strategy of ID3 and its fuzzy versions is simple: after measuring the entropy of the learning set, this set is divided according to the values of each attribute, the entropy of subsets is measured, and the attribute that, *in average*, produces the greatest amount of entropy reduction is selected as the first test in the tree. The process is iterated on every subset until no further reduction is possible or some heuristic criterion decides to stop the tree growing.

PRISM and its fuzzy version rely in selecting the attribute–value pair that maximizes the information gain, instead of using the conditional entropy as a guide in the search for attributes.

This paper addresses the problem of generating learning rules with a PRISM–like algorithm, using as guide a heuristic measure of rule quality. In Section 2, this measure and its application to fuzzy data are defined. Section 3 presents the learning algorithm and Section 4 reports the experimental results.

2 The impurity level of a rule

The most elementary criterion is the accuracy of classifying known examples, when developing a rule quality measure. However, a consideration about the rule completeness must be made: a rule with accuracy $12/13 = .923$ seems to be preferable to another with accuracy $3/3 = 1$. In order to take into account this point we define the impurity level of a rule as follows [5]:

Given a rule R which is n–times applicable and has #hits success, its confidence interval [left_point,right_point] of the probability of success is given by

$$\frac{p + \frac{z^2}{2n} \pm \sqrt{\frac{p(1-p)}{n} + \frac{z^2}{4n^2}}}{1 + \frac{z^2}{n}}$$

where

- n is the number of times the rule has been used,
- p is the success proportion ($p =$#hits$/n$), and
- z is a normal value that depends of the significance level α (here $\alpha = 99$ and $z = 2.576$).

For each classification c, let $c \leftarrow$ be the random canonic rule, that is, a rule with no antecedent, and [random_left_point,random_right_point] its confidence interval. The impurity level of a rule R that concludes the classification c summarizes the R quality in a single number by measuring the interval confidence overlapping

$$\text{impurity\_level}(R) = \text{overlapping\_level}(R, c \leftarrow),$$
$$= 100 * \frac{\text{random\_right\_point} - \text{left\_point}}{\text{right\_point} - \text{left\_point}}.$$

The notion of impurity level allows us to define a preference relation between rules: rules with lesser impurity level are preferred. Furthermore, it provides a criterion when specializing a rule: augment the antecedent of a rule only if the impurity level of the new rule is less than 100.

All the classifications and the attribute values are to certain extent present in every example when dealing with fuzzy data. A fuzzy example is described by a fixed–length vector

$$(\dots, ([A_j : v_{j_1}], \mu_{ji_1}), \dots, ([A_j : v_{j_{m_j}}], \mu_{ji_{m_j}}), \dots, (c_k, \mu_{c_k}), \dots),$$

where j is the attribute index, m_j is the cardinality of the values of attribute A_j, and k is the classification index. We say a rule

$$c_k \leftarrow [A_{l_1} : v_{l_1}], \dots, [A_{l_r} : v_{l_r}]$$

can be used for an example e if

$$min(\mu_{[A_{l_1}:v_{l_1}]}(e), \dots, \mu_{[A_{l_r}:v_{l_r}]}(e)) > \beta,$$

being $0 < \beta \leq 1$ (here, $\beta = 0.5$).

In order to classify an object or an example from a set of rules, we proceed as follows: for each rule, we calculate the membership of the antecedent. The membership of the consequent will be set equal to that one. If there is more than one rule that predicts a classification, take the highest membership. So, in general, a ruleset will classify an object in all classes with different membership. An object will be correctly classified if its known class with the highest membership equals the predicted class with the highest membership.

Table 1. The Sports learning set

Ex.	Attributes										Class		
	Outlook			Temperature			Humidity		Wind				
	Sunny	Cloudy	Rain	Hot	Mild	Cool	High	Normal	True	False	Voll	Swim	Wlif
1	0.9	0.1	0.0	1.0	0.0	0.0	0.8	0.2	0.4	0.6	0.0	0.8	0.2
2	0.8	0.2	0.0	0.6	0.4	0.0	0.0	1.0	0.0	1.0	1.0	0.7	0.0
3	0.0	0.7	0.3	0.8	0.2	0.0	0.1	0.9	0.2	0.8	0.3	0.6	0.1
4	0.2	0.7	0.1	0.3	0.7	0.0	0.2	0.8	0.3	0.7	0.9	0.1	0.0
5	0.0	0.1	0.9	0.7	0.3	0.0	0.5	0.5	0.5	0.5	0.0	0.0	1.0
6	0.0	0.7	0.3	0.0	0.3	0.7	0.7	0.3	0.4	0.6	0.2	0.0	0.8
7	0.0	0.3	0.7	0.0	0.0	1.0	0.0	1.0	0.1	0.9	0.0	0.0	1.0
8	0.0	1.0	0.0	0.0	0.2	0.8	0.2	0.8	0.0	1.0	0.7	0.0	0.3
9	1.0	0.0	0.0	1.0	0.0	0.0	0.6	0.4	0.7	0.3	0.2	0.8	0.0
10	0.9	0.1	0.0	0.0	0.3	0.7	0.0	1.0	0.9	0.1	0.0	0.3	0.7
11	0.7	0.3	0.0	1.0	0.0	0.0	1.0	0.0	0.2	0.8	0.4	0.7	0.0
12	0.2	0.6	0.2	0.0	1.0	0.0	0.3	0.7	0.3	0.7	0.7	0.2	0.1
13	0.9	0.1	0.0	0.2	0.8	0.0	0.1	0.9	1.0	0.0	0.0	0.0	1.0
14	0.0	0.9	0.1	0.0	0.9	0.1	0.1	0.9	0.7	0.3	0.0	0.0	1.0
15	0.0	0.0	1.0	0.0	0.0	1.0	1.0	0.0	0.8	0.2	0.0	0.0	1.0
16	1.0	0.0	0.0	0.5	0.5	0.0	0.0	1.0	0.0	1.0	0.8	0.6	0.0

3 The classification algorithm

The rule induction process consists of the following steps: If there is more than one classification in the training set, then for each classification c_k, in turn:

```
examples <- learning set;rules <- nil;
1;antec <- nil;
2;for each possible attribute--value pair [A:v]
```

```
      ip <- impurity level(c_k <- union(antec,[A:v]));
      choose the pair with lessest level ip;
if ip<100
   then antec <- append([A:v],antec);
      examples <- examples with antec membership > beta;
if there are examples with classification different of c_k
   then goto 2
   else rules <- append (c_k <- antec,rules);
examples <- learning set - examples covered by rules;
if examples with classification c_k <> nil
   then goto 1
   else return(rules)
```

4 Experiments

The classification problem proposed in [1] and reformulated in [3] will be used to illustrate our approach. The classification task consists of deciding which sport to play on a Saturday morning knowing a bit of information about the weather. There are three classes {Swimming, Volleyball, Weight_lifting} and mornings are characterized by four attributes with values Outlook={Sunny, Cloudy, Rain}, Temperature={Cool, Mild, Hot}, Humidity={High, Normal} and Wind= {True, False}. The fuzzy membership of each attribute-value pair and each class for 16 examples is shown in Table 1. For this learning set, the algorithm returns a list of seven rules and fifteen terms with an accuracy of 100%. Table 2 shows the classification results for the training data.

- volleyball ← temperature=mild, wind=false.
- volleyball ← outlook=cloudy, temperature=cool, humidity=normal.
- swimming ← temperature=hot, outlook=sunny, humidity=high.
- swimming ← temperature=hot, outlook=cloudy.
- weight_lifting ← wind=true, humidity=normal.
- weight_lifting ← outlook=rain.
- weight_lifting ← temperature=cool, humidity=high.

In [3] a fuzzy ID3 algorithm obtains six rules and eleven terms, with an accuracy of 81%.

- swimming ← temperature=hot, outlook=sunny.
- swimming ← temperature=hot, outlook=cloudy.
- weight_lifting ← temperature=hot, outlook=rain.
- weight_lifting ← temperature=mild, wind=true.
- volleyball ← temperature=mild, wind=false.
- weight_lifting ← temperature=cool.

A fuzzy version of PRISM [4] also obtains six rules and nine terms with the same accuracy.

- swimming ← temperature=hot, outlook=cloudy.
- swimming ← temperature=hot, outlook=sunny.
- volleyball ← temperature=mild, wind=false.
- weight_lifting ← outlook=rain.
- weight_lifting ← temperature=cool.
- weight_lifting ← wind=true.

Table 2. The Sports learning set results

Ex.	Classification known in training data			Classification with learned rules		
	Volleyball	Swimming	Weight_lifting	Volleyball	Swimming	Weight_lifting
1	0.0	0.8	0.2	0.0	0.8	0.2
2	1.0	0.7	0.0	0.4	0.2	0.0
3	0.3	0.6	0.1	0.2	0.7	0.3
4	0.9	0.1	0.0	0.7	0.3	0.3
5	0.0	0.0	1.0	0.3	0.1	0.9
6	0.2	0.0	0.8	0.3	0.0	0.7
7	0.0	0.0	1.0	0.3	0.0	0.7
8	0.7	0.0	0.3	0.8	0.0	0.2
9	0.2	0.8	0.0	0.0	0.6	0.4
10	0.0	0.3	0.7	0.1	0.0	0.9
11	0.4	0.7	0.0	0.0	0.7	0.0
12	0.7	0.2	0.1	0.7	0.0	0.3
13	0.0	0.0	1.0	0.0	0.1	0.9
14	0.0	0.0	1.0	0.3	0.0	0.7
15	0.0	0.0	1.0	0.0	0.0	1.0
16	0.8	0.6	0.0	0.5	0.0	0.0

5 Conclusion

We have proposed a new heuristic measure for decision rules quality when dealing with fuzzy data. The impurity level can be used in a variety of tasks in machine learning environments. As an illustration, it is used in a rule induction algorithm, with results that outperform those of information–based approaches.

References

1. Quinlan, J. R. (1986) Induction of decision trees. Mach. Learning **1**, 81–106

2. Cendrowska, J. (1988) PRISM: an algorithm for inducing modular rules. Int. J. Man-Mach. Stud. **27**, 349–370
3. Yuan, Y., Shaw, M. J. (1995) Induction of fuzzy decision trees. Fuzzy Sets Syst. **69**, 125–139
4. Wang, C. H., Liu, J. F. et al. (1999) A fuzzy inductive learning strategy for modular rules. Fuzzy Sets Syst. **103**, 91–105
5. Ranilla, J., Mones, R. et al. (1997) El nivel de impureza de una regla de clasificación aprendida a partir de ejemplos. Proc. VII Conf. Asoc. Esp. Int. Art. AEPIA, Torremolinos, Spain, 479–488

On the Role of Transitivity in Fuzzy Relational Calculus

Bernard De Baets

Department of Applied Mathematics, Biometrics and Process Control
Ghent University, Coupure Links 653, B-9000 Gent, Belgium

Abstract: The formulation of the transitivity property of a fuzzy relation usually depends on the choice of a particular triangular norm T. Applications of this notion of T-transitivity in various fields such as clustering, control and preference modelling are identified. A fuzzy counterpart of the classical one-to-one correspondence between equivalence relations and partitions is discussed, shedding a light on the relationships between fuzzy rule-based systems and fuzzy controllers. The non-triviality of the mathematical study of additive fuzzy preference structures is illustrated by means of some transitivity-related properties of fuzzy preference relations.

1 Introduction

We trace various occurences of the notion of transitivity in fuzzy set theory. Transitivity is one of the most basic potential properties of a mathematical relation. Prototypical symmetric examples of transitive relations are equivalence relations, while partial orders are typical anti-symmetric examples. Despite its importance, transitivity is an often debated issue. Recall for instance the paradox of Poincaré concerning the indistinguishability of real numbers and the famous sugar-coffee example of Luce concerning the intransitivity of the indifference relation in preference modelling. The latter has led to the introduction of fundamental preference structures such as semi-orders and interval orders. Another direction is to consider graded relationships, leading to fuzzy relational calculus. In the case of fuzzy relations, the transitivity notion is not uniquely determined. The most popular proposals depend on the choice of a t-norm T [12], the main ones being M (minimum), P (algebraic product) and W (Łukasiewicz, $W(x,y) = \max(x + y - 1, 0)$). T-transitivity of a binary fuzzy relation R in a universe X states that $T(R(a,b), R(b,c)) \leq R(a,c)$, for any $(a,b,c) \in X^3$, and can be written as $R \circ_T R \subseteq R$, where $\circ_T$ denotes the sup-T composition.

In the symmetric case, we will explore the concept of a T-equivalence (or fuzzy equivalence relation), the corresponding notion of a T-partition (fuzzy partition), and their relationship with pseudo-metrics. Next, we will discuss the construction of T-equivalences on the fuzzy power set of a given universe X. We will focus on local approaches, i.e. approaches based on the extension of T-equivalences on $[0, 1]$. Some related insights into the connection between fuzzy rule-based systems and Mamdani controllers will be shared.

In the non-symmetric case, we will enter the framework of characterizable additive fuzzy preference structures (which is based on yet another approach to the concept of a fuzzy partition) and show how transitivity is propagated from the large preference relation to the strict preference, indifference and incomparability components of the corresponding fuzzy preference structure and vice versa. Particular attention will be given to fuzzy versions of the interval order structure, in particular to the underlying Ferrers property.

2   Transitivity in clustering and control

The concept of a T-equivalence (indistinguishability operator) is one of the most basic ones in fuzzy set theory. A T-equivalence E on a universe X is a reflexive, symmetric and T-transitive binary fuzzy relation on X; if reflexivity is replaced by the stronger condition $E(x, y) = 1 \Leftrightarrow x = y$ then we talk about T-equalities. M-equivalences enjoy the following interesting characterization: a binary fuzzy relation E is an M-equivalence on X if and only if all of its α-cuts E_α are classical equivalence relations on X. The fact that the equivalence classes of E_α become smaller for increasing α has led to the concept of a partition tree. On the other hand, W-equivalences and P-equivalences are interesting because of their one-to-one correspondence with $[0, 1]$-valued pseudo-metrics. A binary fuzzy relation E is a W-equivalence on X if and only if $d = 1 - E$ is a pseudo-metric on X [1]; it is a P-equivalence on X if and only if $d = \log E$ is a pseudo-metric on X. Consequently, E is a W-equivalence on X if and only $E' = e^{1-E}$ is a P-equivalence on X. More general, if f is an additive generator of T, then $d = f \circ E$ is a pseudo-metric for any T-equivalence E [5].

T-equalities on $[0, 1]$ can be extended to T-equalities on the class $\mathcal{F}(X)$ of fuzzy sets on it in a very natural way. Indeed, a binary fuzzy relation E on $[0, 1]$ is a T-equality on $[0, 1]$ if and only if the binary fuzzy relation E' on $\mathcal{F}(X)$ defined by

$$E'(A, B) = \inf_{x \in X} E(A(x), B(x))$$

is a T-equality on $\mathcal{F}(X)$. Let us therefore consider an interesting T-equality on $[0, 1]$. Recall that the residual implicator I_T and biresidual operator $\mathcal{E}_T$ of a t-norm T are defined by

$$I_T(x, y) = \sup\{z \in [0, 1] \mid T(x, z) \le y\}$$

and

$$\mathcal{E}_T(x, y) = \min(I_T(x, y), I_T(y, x)).$$

The latter operator $\mathcal{E}_T$ is a T-equality on $[0, 1]$ for a left-continuous t-norm T only. For such a t-norm T, we can then construct two interesting T-equalities on $\mathcal{F}(X)$ [7] (note that $E_T \subseteq E^T$ and $E_M = E^M$):

$$E^T(A, B) = \inf_{x \in X} \mathcal{E}_T(A(x), B(x))$$
$$E_T(A, B) = T(\inf_{x \in X} I_T(A(x), B(x)), \inf_{x \in X} I_T(B(x), A(x))).$$

For a continuous t-norm T with additive generator f, the former one leads to the metric

$$d(A, B) = \sup_{x \in X} |f(A(x)) - f(B(x))|.$$

For a left-continuous t-norm T such that $W \leq T$, the latter one leads to the metric $d = 1 - E_T$ on $\mathcal{F}(X)$. The above observations are important in view of their exploitation in fuzzy clustering techniques.

Similar to the one-to-one correspondence between equivalence relations and partitions (through the intermediate notion of a quotient set), there exists a one-to-one correspondence between T-equivalences and T-partitions [6]. A set $\mathcal{A}$ of modal fuzzy sets in X is called a T-semi-partition of X if

$$(\forall (A, B) \in \mathcal{A}^2)(C^T(A, B) \leq E^T(A, B)),$$

with degree of compatibility C^T defined by

$$C^T(A, B) = \sup_{x \in X} T(A(x), B(x))$$

A T-partition of X is a T-semi-partition of X such that $\{\ker A \mid A \in \mathcal{A}\}$ forms a partition of X.

We now explain briefly how the above concepts help us in understanding Mamdani's approach to fuzzy control [2,3]. A fuzzy rule "IF X is A THEN Y is B" can be modelled in (at least) two ways. Logical arguments suggest to model such a rule by means of a binary fuzzy relation L defined by $L(u, v) = I_T(A(u), B(v))$, while Mamdani suggests to model it by means of a binary fuzzy relation M defined by $M(u, v) = T(A(u), B(v))$ [11]. In both cases, given an observation "X is A'" the output "Y is B'" is defined as the direct image (based on the t-norm T) of A' under the fuzzy relation modelling the rule. In the case of inference with multiple rules, several approaches are possible. We can either model the set of fuzzy rules by means of a single fuzzy relation (either as the intersection of the individual models in the optimistic case, or as their union in the pessimistic case), or we treat them separately and combine the conclusions (by means of intersection in the optimistic case, or union in the pessimistic case). Mamdani's fuzzy graph approach can then be classified as pessimistic. We are now able to compare optimistic logical modelling with Mamdani's approach. The basic behaviour we study is the mapping of the antecedents of the fuzzy rules to their consequents. In case these antecedents are modal, then Mamdani's model is inferior to the optimistic logical model, while in case these antecedents form a T-semi-partition of the input space, the required behaviour of both approaches is equivalent.

This observation leads to the following modelling advice: for any two fuzzy rules the condition $C^T(A_i, A_j) \leq E^T(B_i, B_j)$ should be fulfilled, requiring that the degree of equality of any two antecedents should not be greater than the degree of equality of the corresponding consequents. In the case of a T-semi-partitioned input space, we can restate this requirement as follows: the degree of equality of any two antecedents should not be greater than the degree of equality of the corresponding consequents. In the case of a semi-partitioned input space this condition is trivially fulfilled, while in the (theoretical) case of a crisply partitioned input space and a set of crisp rules, both approaches coincide.

3 Transitivity in preference modelling

An important field of applications of fuzzy set theory is that of preference modelling and decision making [4]. A fundamental classical concept is that of a preference structure: a triplet (P, I, J) (strict preference, indifference and incomparability) of binary relations expressing the results of a pairwise comparison of a set of alternatives A by a decision maker. A preference structure is characterized by its large preference relation $R = P \cup I$. Of particular importance are preference structures without incomparability, i.e. for which $J = \emptyset$, or equivalently, for which R is complete. It is well known that the transitivity of R (hence, the fact that it represents a total preorder), i.e. $R \circ R \subseteq R$, is equivalent to $P \circ P \subseteq P$, $I \circ I \subseteq I$, $P \circ I \subseteq P$ and $I \circ P \subseteq P$. An important and interesting structure is the interval order, characterized by a large preference relation R which is Ferrers, i.e. $aRb \wedge cRd$ implies $aRd \vee cRb$. The latter can also be written equivalently as $R \circ \mathrm{co}\, R^t \circ R \subseteq R$ and even as $P \circ I \circ P \subseteq P$.

The study of the fuzzy counterparts of the above structures is quite instructive: it learns us that in contrast to several other fuzzifications of mathematical theories, the field of fuzzy preference modelling is not a trivial one. Based on long and tedious arguments (related to yet another approach to the concept of a fuzzy partition), the concept of a fuzzy preference structure can be defined as follows: an additive fuzzy preference structure (AFPS) (P, I, J) on A is a triplet of binary fuzzy relations on A such that I is reflexive and symmetric and $P(a,b) + P(b,a) + I(a,b) + J(a,b) = 1$ [8,14]. An AFPS $(P, I, \emptyset)$ is called an AFPS without incomparability and can be reconstructed from its large preference relation $R(a,b) = P(a,b) + I(a,b)$, and is characterized by a weakly complete R: $R(a,b) + R(b,a) \geq 1$. Note that R is called strongly complete if $\max(R(a,b), R(b,a)) = 1$.

From here on, we consider AFPS without incomparability and with a strongly complete large preference relation R. The T-transitivity of R, with $T \geq \mathrm{W}$, can be characterized by $P \circ_{\mathrm{M}} P \subseteq P$, $I \circ_T I \subseteq I$, $P \circ_{\mathrm{W}} I \subseteq P$ and $I \circ_{\mathrm{W}} P \subseteq P$ [10]. Interesting here is the observation that the t-norms M and

W come about naturally. This is a typical characteristic of fuzzy preference modelling: the use of a single t-norm does not suffice.

As an example of the mathematical intricacies of fuzzy preference modelling, we will briefly discuss fuzzy interval orders. For this purpose, a binary fuzzy relation R on A is called W-Ferrers if

$$W(R(a,b), R(c,d)) \leq W^*(R(a,d), R(c,b)) = \min(R(a,d) + R(c,b), 1)$$

and M-Ferrers if

$$\min(R(a,b), R(c,d)) \leq \max(R(a,d), R(c,b)).$$

Obviously, M-Ferrers is a stronger property than W-Ferrers. These properties enjoy nice characterizations [8]: R is W-Ferrers if and only if $R \circ_W \mathrm{co}\, R^t \circ_W R \subseteq R$, and R is M-Ferrers if and only if all of its α-cuts are Ferrers.

We introduce the following final definitions: an AFPS $(P, I, \emptyset)$ is called a W-fuzzy interval order (W-FIO) on A if $P \circ_W I \circ_W P \subseteq P$ and it is called an M-fuzzy interval order (M-FIO) on A if $P \circ_M I \circ_M P \subseteq P$. The following relationships can be proven among these concepts [8]:

$$\Pi \text{ is an M-FIO} \Rightarrow R \text{ is W-Ferrers} \Rightarrow \Pi \text{ is a W-FIO}.$$

On the other hand, the conditions $P \circ_W (I \circ_M P) \subseteq P$ and $(P \circ_M I) \circ_W P \subseteq P$ both imply that R is W-Ferrers.

References

1. J. Bezdek and J. Harris, *Fuzzy partitions and relations: an axiomatic basis for clustering*, Fuzzy Sets and Systems **1** (1978), 111–127.
2. B. De Baets, *A note on Mamdani controllers*, Intelligent Systems and Soft Computing for Nuclear Science and Industry (D. Ruan, P. D'hondt, P. Govaerts and E. Kerre, eds.), Proc. Second Internat. FLINS Workshop (Mol, Belgium, Sep 1996), World Scientific Publishing, Singapore, 1996, pp. 22-28.
3. B. De Baets, G. De Cooman and E. Kerre, *The construction of possibility measures from samples on $\mathcal{T}$-semi-partitions*, Inform. Sci. **106** (1998), 3–24.
4. B. De Baets and J. Fodor, *Twenty years of fuzzy preference structures (1978–1997)*, Riv. Mat. Sci. Econom. Social. **20** (1997), 45–66.
5. B. De Baets and R. Mesiar, *Pseudo-metrics and $\mathcal{T}$-equivalences*, J. Fuzzy Math. **5** (1997), 471–481.
6. B. De Baets and R. Mesiar, *$\mathcal{T}$-partitions*, Fuzzy Sets and Systems **97** (1998), 211–223.
7. B. De Baets and R. Mesiar, *Metrics and $\mathcal{T}$-equalities*, J. Math. Anal. Appl., submitted.
8. B. De Baets and B. Van de Walle, *Weak and strong fuzzy interval orders*, Fuzzy Sets and Systems **79** (1996), 213–225.
9. B. De Baets and B. Van de Walle, *Minimal definitions of classical and fuzzy preference structures*, Proc. Annual Meeting of the North American Fuzzy Information Processing Society (Syracuse, New York, USA, Sep 1997), 1997, pp. 299–304.

10. B. De Baets, B. Van de Walle and E. Kerre, *Fuzzy preference structures without incomparability*, Fuzzy Sets and Systems **76** (1995), 333–348.
11. E. Mamdani and B. Sembi, *Process control using fuzzy logic*, in: Fuzzy Sets: Theory and Application to Policy Analysis and Information Systems (P. Wang and S. Chang, eds.), Plenum Press, New York, 1980, pp. 249–265.
12. B. Schweizer and A. Sklar, *Probabilistic metric spaces*, Elsevier, New York, 1983.
13. E. Trillas and L. Valverde, *An inquiry into indistinguishability operators*, in: Aspects of vagueness (H. Skala, S. Termini and E. Trillas, eds.), Reidel, Dordrecht, 1994, pp. 231–256.
14. B. Van de Walle, B. De Baets and E. Kerre, *Characterizable fuzzy preference structures*, Ann. Oper. Res. **80** (1998), 105–136.

Project Network Planning on the Basis of Generalized Fuzzy Critical Path Method

Anatoliy Slyeptsov[1] and Tatyana Tyshchuk[2]

[1] Donetsk Institute of Economics and Law, 77, Universitetskaya str.,
Donetsk 340048, Ukraine,
e-mail - Slyeptsov@diec.dgtu.donetsk.ua
[2] Donetsk State University, Donetsk, Ukraine

Abstract: Project network planning problem with fuzzy durations of operations has been investigated. Two approaches to criticality analysis of operations classified as a path criticality and a float criticality ones are distinguished. It has been ascertained that both methods do not provide an efficient solution of the fuzzy network planning problem to full extent. A generalized fuzzy critical path method (FCPM) based on aggregation of the path and the float ones has been proposed. Advantages of generalized criticality degree using are demonstrated by numerical experiments.

1 Introduction

To make decisions in a project planning problems it is necessary to use information about terms of start and completion of operations, their criticality degrees, project time span, etc. The classical tool of these problems solution in case of crisp durations of operations is the critical path method (CPM). In real word problems durations of operations can be partially uncontrollable and imprecise known at the moment when calculations are carried out. In such cases to solve project network planning problems the PERT method, the Monte-Carlo simulation and the FCPM can be used. Within the framework of the PERT method probability distributions, for example beta or gamma distributions, are used to model durations of operations. The main shortcoming of the PERT method is simplifying assumption about normal distribution of the results. The Monte-Carlo simulation method has not this imperfection, but it presupposes multiple recalculations of project characteristics. In the FCPM constraints are not imposed on distributions of parameters in comparison with PERT method and a great number of recalculations can be avoided versus Monte-Carlo simulation.

Within the framework of fuzzy network planning approach, stated in the papers of Chanas [1] and Prade [2] and developed in papers of Buckley [3], Chanas [4]-[5], Kamburovski [6], Lootsma [7], Mares [8], Slyeptsov and Tyshchuk [9], durations of operations are represented by fuzzy values. Depending on available information and desired precision of results any amount of α-cuts can be used. To calculate fuzzy values of the earliest start and completion times of operations known in the classical CPM formulas, where ordinal arithmetic operations are replaced with proper extended ones, are used. Evaluation of fuzzy project time span is carried out in the same way. To solve the problem of criticality analysis of paths and operations of a project network model different approaches [4]-[5], [8], [9] were proposed. This paper is devoted to the investigation of the existing approaches to solution of this problem, nature of conflicts between them and synthesis of generalized FCPM on the basis of aggregation of the existing ones.

2 Approaches to criticality analysis in fuzzy project network models

Let a project be represented by means of a network model $G = \langle R, A, \tau \rangle$, where $R = r$ is the set of edges corresponding to the set of project operations; $A : R \times R$ is the set of arcs of G representing precedence relations for operations; $\tau : R \to \{\tilde{T}_r\}$, where r is a fuzzy duration of r; $P = \{p\}$ is the set of paths of G.

According to FCPM to calculate fuzzy values of the earliest start and completion times of operations it is necessary to use formulae which known in classical CPM, where ordinary arithmetic operations replaced by proper extended ones:

$$\widetilde{ES}_r = \begin{cases} 0, \text{if } r = st \\ \widetilde{max}_{s \in PRE(r)} \widetilde{EC}_s, \text{else}; \end{cases} \qquad (1)$$

$$\widetilde{EC}_r = \widetilde{ES}_r \oplus \tilde{T}_r \qquad (2)$$

where $\oplus, \widetilde{max}$ denote extended addition and maximum operations, $\widetilde{ES}_r$ and $\widetilde{EC}_r$ are fuzzy values of the earliest start and completion of r, $PRE(r) = \{pre(r)\}$ is the set of immediate predecessors of r, st is the unique initial operation of the project.

Fuzzy value of project critical duration can be calculated similarly. Calculation of fuzzy values of the latest start and completion times of operations in such way leads to inadequate results due to specific character of extended arithmetic operations and hence can not be used. This fact complicates the problems of floats calculation and critical path analysis which in a crisp case are solved by means of earliest and latest terms comparison.

To carry out critical path analysis within the framework of the fuzzy network planning (FNP) problem a number of methods were proposed [5,6,8,9] which can be classified in two main approaches. Both approaches imply the presence of a fuzzy set of critical paths $PC = \langle P, \mu_{PC} \rangle$ and a fuzzy set of critical operations $RC = \langle R, \mu_{RC} \rangle$ in a network model with fuzzy durations of operations. A path $p \in P$ has a possibility of criticality degree $\mu_{PC}(p) \in [0, 1]$ and an operation $r \in R$ has a possibility of criticality degree $\mu_{RC}(r) \in [0, 1]$. A zero possibility of criticality of a path indicates that it is non-critical for all possible situations, a non-zero one indicates that situations when the path is critical exist. The more $\mu_{PC}(p)$ the more quantity of possible situations when

p is critical. Similarly, a zero possibility of criticality of an operation denotes that this operation is non-critical and has a float for all possible situations. The more $\mu_{RC}(r)$ the more quantity of possible situations when r has not a float and, so, is critical.

It is necessary to accentuate that the existence of non-unique critical path in network model is the basic feature of FCPM versus CPM and PERT.

The ways of possibility of criticality degrees of paths and operations definitions are various. They are based on extensions of different properties of a critical path which take a place in a crisp case. According to the first one the length of a critical path l_p is equal to the critical duration of a project PD

$$l_p = PD. \tag{3}$$

By the second property each operation r contained in a critical path p have not a float F_r, i.e. the earliest start ES_r of each critical operation r is equal to the earliest completion $EC_{pre(r)}$ of its critical predecessor $pre(r)$

$$F_r = 0, \quad i.e. \quad EC_{pre(r)} = ES_r, \quad \forall r, pre(r) \in p. \tag{4}$$

It is necessary to point out, that these properties are equal, i.e. in a crisp case a path possesses the property (3) if and only if it possesses the property (4). A conclusion about criticality of a path or an operation can be drawn on the basis of anyone of considered properties.

In a fuzzy case to define fuzzy sets PC and RC an extension of the considered properties are used. According to the methods classified as path criticality ones developed by Chanas [5], Kamburovski [6] and Mares [8] definitions of μ_{PC} and μ_{RC} are based on the extension of (3). That is, the degree of criticality of a path p is defined by comparison of fuzzy length of the path with fuzzy critical duration of the project:

$$\mu'_{PC}(p) = Poss(\tilde{l}_p \text{ is } \widetilde{PD}) \tag{5}$$

$$\mu'_{RC}(r) = max_{p|r \in p}(Poss(\tilde{l}_p \text{ is } \widetilde{PD})) \tag{6}$$

where $\mu'_{PC}(p)$, $\mu'_{RC}(r)$ are path criticality degrees of $p \in P$ and of $r \in R$ respectively, $\tilde{l}_p$ is a fuzzy length of p, $\tilde{l}_p = \oplus_{r \in p}\tilde{T}_r$; $\widetilde{PD}$ is a fuzzy project critical duration, it is equal to the fuzzy value of the earliest complete of the final operation. According to the method of float criticality developed by Slyeptsov and Tyshchuk [9] μ_{PC} and μ_{RC} should be calculated by means of the extension of (4). Thus, the definitions of PC and RC consist in floats analysis of operations by means of fuzzy values of the earliest start and completion times of operations comparison:

$$\mu''_{PC}(p) = Poss \bigvee_{r \in p} (\widetilde{EC}_{pre(r)} \text{ is } \widetilde{ES}_r) = \tag{7}$$

$$= min_{r \in p} Poss(\widetilde{EC}_{pre(r)} \text{ is } \widetilde{ES}_r), \quad pre(r) \in p$$

$$\mu''_{RC}(r) = max_{p|r\epsilon p}\ \mu''_{PC}(p) \qquad (8)$$

where $\mu''_{PC}(p)$, $\mu''_{RC}(r)$ are called as float criticality degrees of $p \in P$ and $r \in R$; $\widetilde{ES}_r$, $\widetilde{EC}_{pre(r)}$ are fuzzy values of the earliest start (1) and completion (2) times of an operation r and its immediate predecessor $pre(r)$ respectively.

3   Development of generalized FCPM

The possibility of criticality degrees obtained on the basis both of the first (5)-(6) and the second (7)-(8) approach are not equal and can lead to non-correct conclusions about criticality degrees of operations. In particular, a non-critical operation with a non-zero float for all possible situations can have a non-zero criticality degree according to one of the approaches. During a project implementation a performance of critical operations can require additional resources. It can be reflected in speed or quality of a project as a whole and cause, for instance, a rise of its cost. When operation with a float is considered as critical (because it has non-zero criticality degree according to one of approaches) such measures are unjustified. The nature of this inconsistency is non-equivalence of the extensions of the property (3) and the property (4) in a fuzzy case versus they equivalence in a crisp case.

To avoid this inconsistency it is offered to combine the considered approaches in a generalized FCPM, where definitions of μ_{PC} and μ_{RC} should be based on both the extension of (3) and the extension of (4):

$$\mu_{PC}(p) = Poss\left(\bigvee_{r \in p} (\widetilde{EC}_{pre(r)}\ is\ \widetilde{ES}_r) \vee (\tilde{l}_p\ is\ \widetilde{PD})\right) = \qquad (9)$$

$$= min\left(\mu'_{PC}(p), \mu''_{PC}(p)\right)$$

$$\mu_{RC}(r) = min(\mu''_{RC}(r), \mu'_{RC}(r)) \qquad (10)$$

where $\mu_{PC}(p)$, $\mu_{RC}(r)$ are generalized possibility of criticality degrees of path $p \in P$ and operation $r \in R$ respectively.

The generalized possibility of criticality degrees of paths and operations reflect not only ratios between fuzzy values of lengths of the paths of a network model and project critical duration as the path criticality degrees (5)-(6) but also ratios between fuzzy terms of start and completion of operations as float criticality ones (7)-(8).

4   Numerical experiments

Example. There exists a project represented by the network model fig.1. The durations of operations are trapezoidal fuzzy numbers with a support $s(\widetilde{T_r})$

and a core $c(\widetilde{T}_r)$ (tab.1). The fuzzy earliest start and completion times of the operations are calculated according to (1)–(2) and represented in tab.1. The fuzzy critical duration of the project is equal to the earliest completion time of the operation L. The possibility of criticality degrees of operations obtained according to the considered conceptions are represented in tab.1.

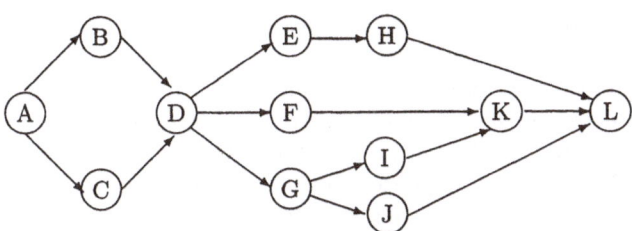

Fig. 1. Project network model (example)

Table 1. Fuzzy durations, the earliest start and completion times, possibility of criticality degrees (example)

Operation	Predecessor	$s(\widetilde{T}_r)$	$c(\widetilde{T}_r)$	$s(\widetilde{ES}_r)$	$c(\widetilde{ES}_r)$	$s(\widetilde{EC}_r)$	$c(\widetilde{EC}_r)$	$\mu'_{RC}(r)$	$\mu''_{RC}(r)$	$\mu_{RC}(r)$
A	—	7 9	7 8	0 0	0 0	7 9	7 8	1	1	1
B	A	11 12	11 11	7 9	7 8	17 21	18 19	1	1	1
C	A	2 4	3 4	7 9	7 8	9 13	10 12	0,9	0	0
D	B,C	9 11	9 11	17 21	18 19	26 32	27 30	1	1	1
E	D	3 4	3 3	26 32	27 30	29 36	30 33	0	0	0
F	D	18 24	19 22	26 32	27 30	44 56	46 52	1	0,9	0,9
G	D	9 11	10 10	26 32	27 30	35 43	37 40	1	1	1
H	E	1 3	2 3	29 36	30 33	30 39	32 36	0	0	0
I	G	2 2	2 2	35 43	37 40	37 45	39 42	0	0,25	0
J	G	17 21	18 20	35 43	37 40	52 64	55 60	1	1	1
K	F,I	1 3	1 2	44 56	46 52	45 59	47 54	1	0,9	0,9
L	H,J,K	12 15	13 14	52 64	55 60	64 79	68 74	1	1	1

The float and the path criticality degrees of the operations do not coincide. In particularly, the operation C has the path criticality degree of $0,9$ and the float one of 0. The operation C can be completed up to thirteenth week. Its unique successor is D, which can not be started before seventeenth week. So, C has a float of at least four weeks. Therefore, this operation is non-critical for all possible situations and should have a zero criticality degree. So, the path criticality degree of 0,9 do not reflect that operation C always has a float of at least four weeks. Similarly conclusions take a place for the operation I which has the path criticality degree of 0 and the float one of 0, 25.

Accordingly generalized FCPM the operations A, B, D, G, J, L have the generalized criticality degree equal to 1. The operations A, B, D, L are critical for all possible situations as they are contained in all the paths with a non-zero generalized criticality degree. These operations should be paid a special attention, as any delay of their performing will cause a delay of performing of the project as a whole. Depending on situation operations G and J or F and K can be critical. A delay of this operations performing also can cause a delay of the completion of the project as a whole. The operations C, E, F and H have the generalized criticality degree of 0 therefore they are non-critical for all possible situations and have a float.

5 Conclusions

Having investigated the FNP problem two main approaches to the extension of the notion of criticality have been distinguished. It has been shown that both the path criticality approach based on the comparison of fuzzy values of paths lengths with the fuzzy value of the project critical duration and the float criticality one based on the floats analysis by means of fuzzy earliest start and completion times of operations comparison do not reflect the notion of criticality to full extent. For effective criticality analysis in project network planning problems it has been proposed to aggregate possibility of criticality degrees of paths (5),(7) and operations (6),(8) into the generalized possibility of criticality degrees (9) and (10) and use they in a project decision making.

References

1. Chanas, S., Radosinski, E. (1976) Time pattern of activities performance in the light of fuzzy sets theory, Problemy organizacji 2, 68-76.
2. Prade, H. (1979) Using fuzzy set theory in a scheduling problem: a case study, Fuzzy Sets and Systems 2, 153-165.
3. Buckley, J.J. (1989) Fuzzy PERT. In: Evans, G., Karwowski, W., Wilhelm, M. (Eds.), Applications of fuzzy set methodologies in industrial engineering. Elsevier, 103-114.
4. Chanas, S., Kamburovski, J. (1981) The use of fuzzy variables in PERT, Fuzzy sets and systems 5, 11-19.
5. Chanas, S., Kuchta, D. (1998) Discrete fuzzy optimization. In: Slowinski, R. (Eds.), Fuzzy Sets in Decision Analysis, Operations Research and Statistics. Kluwer Academic Publishers, Boston Dordrecht London, 249-280

6. Kamburowski, J. (1983) Fuzzy activity duration times in critical path analysis, Inter. Symp. On Project Management, New Delphi, 194-199.
7. Lootsma, F.A. (1989) Stochastic and fuzzy PERT, European Journal of Operational Research 43, 174-183.
8. Mares,M. (1991) Some remarks to fuzzy critical path method, Ekonomicko-matematicky Obzor 4, 358-370
9. Slyeptsov, A. I. , Tyshchuk, T. A. (1999) Fuzzy critical path method for project network planning and control, Cybernetics and System Analysis 3, 158-170

Flexible Querying - Data Structures Unification*

Peter Marcinčák, Marcel Matula

Šafárik University, Department of Computer Science,

Jesenná 5, 041 54 Košice,

Slovak Republic

{marincak,matula}@duro.science.upjs.sk

Abstract: In our previous papers we proposed architecture of the flexible querying system and outlined main processes of uncertain query evaluation. In this paper we describe the process of fuzzy unification of the user query with the data structures in data source. We propose algorithms for such unification. In proposed algorithms metadata describing given data source play the most important role. We describe how models of the information systems (UML, ERD, etc.) and other standard metadada sources can be used in the process of fuzzy unification at metadata level.

Keywords: metadata, UML, fuzzy unification

1 Introduction

Current information retrieval a querying systems can be classified upon several criteria. From the data querying point of view it is important how the data are stored and organized. Based on this criteria querying systems can be divided into two main groups:

> - systems working with unstructured (or semistructured) data – to this category we can assign various Internet search engines and other different full text systems based on scanning and indexing of text documents.

> - systems working with structured data – relational and object-oriented database management systems and also applications running over these systems, datalog and prolog systems etc.

---

* This work was supported by the grant VEGA 1/7557/20

In present, it is the first group of systems, which dominates, but despite that fact it can be seen trend towards transformation of unstructured data to structured (semistructured) data and therefore increased need for systems working with structured data can be expected soon.

In information retrieval and querying systems, it is important not only to handle structured data, but much more important is to introduce imprecision and uncertainty into the process of information handling. This uncertainty results from different reasons:

    - syntactical errors in query formulation and/or stored data

    - semantic differencies – users and data storage designers have different views of the same data

Both types of differencies can occur at either data level (domains of attributes) or metadata level (data structures). Same algorithms and techniques can be used at both these levels [2][4].

With introduction of uncertainty into the process of querying, new requirements for the (flexible) querying systems can be defined:

    - declarative querying language close to human language

    - ability of system to order and filter results according to user requirements

    - interactive communication with user to minimize network traffic

    - ability of the system to learn

    - open interfaces to enable the enhancement of the system – interfaces to dictionaries, learning modules, metadata, etc.

    - ability to support distributed searching over several information sources

Based on requirements above we proposed architecture of the flexible querying system and outlined main processes of uncertain query evaluation [1][3][6]. In this paper we describe the core of the query evaluation - the process of fuzzy unification of the user query with the data structures in data source.

2 Data structures unification

There exist two subjects working with the data in system - an user querying the system and an analyst/developer of the system. Both actors have their own view of the system (model). While the developer's model is detailed and complex, the user's model is much simplier because the user does not think in terms like redundancy, decomposition, generalization etc. He/she only describes objects of his/her interest with their properties, relations and constraints. The next example present these two different models of the same system:

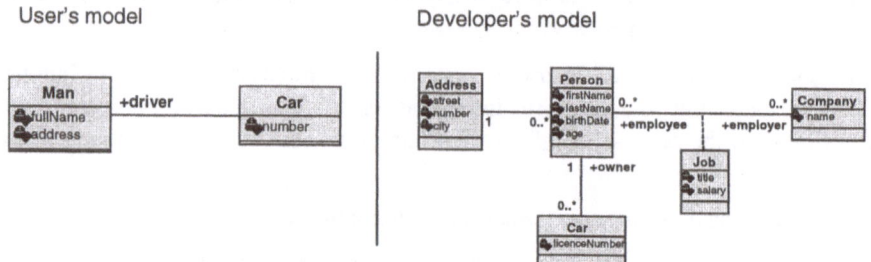

As can be seen from the previous example these two models may be very different and the main problem of the query processing is to unify these models. To make the process of unification of user's model (query) with actual model easier it is suitable to introduce some intermediary which hides the complexity of the actual model and provides several simplified views of the system which can be unified with the user's query easier. In next we will call the proposal of such intermediary the metadata engine.

3 Metadata Engine

The metadata engine represents intelligent interface to given data source. Its role in query processing is not only to provide uniform interface to different data sources but mainly to handle meta-information about the data source. The following figure presents simplified proposal of an API of the engine:

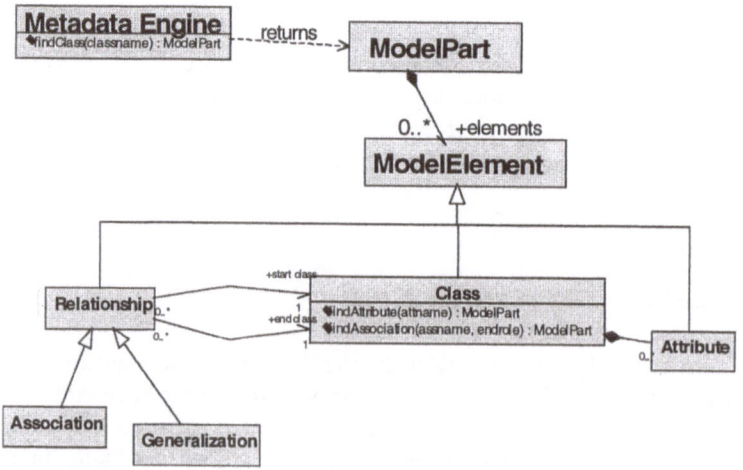

The core of proposed API represents class *MetadataEngine* with its method *findClass* returning instance of the class *ModelPart* representing part of (the model of) the datasource. This model part consists of collection of model elements like *Class*, *Attribute* or *Relationship*.

In the context of the given class one can similarly look for its attributes or associations to related classes using methods *findAttribute* and *findAssociation*.

It is important to emphasize that the return value of all *findXXX* methods is always *ModelPart* and not only a single instance of class *XXX*. For example return value of the call *Person.findAttribute('salary')* may be model part containing class *Person*, association to class *Job* and attribute *Job.salary*. On the other hand the return value is (almost) always not only a single model part but some collection of model parts ordered by some measure of relevance. For example return value of the call *Person.findAttribute('namme')* may be the following collection {([*Person.firstName*], 0.95), ([*Person.lastName*], 0.96)}.

3.1 Metadata Engine requirements

As mentioned above the main aim of the metadata engine is to manage metadata (models) describing given data source and to search for unprecisely specified submodels. This searching must be based not only on crisp matching – i.e. *findClass('Person')* would return only class *Person* and nothing else, but it must be 'smart' – i.e. *findClass('Woman')* may return class *Woman* (if such class exists in the data source), but it can also return for example class *Person* with its attribute *Person.sex* and substitution *Person.sex='F'*.

In order to provide this intelligent behavior, the metadata engine must have access to as much metainformation relating to the given data source as it is possible. This extended metadata should therefore contain not only standard metadata like UML (ERD, IDL) models but also some additional information like dictionaries of synonyms, additional descriptions of domains of attributes, etc. We would like to emphasize that these additional metadata can be divided into two groups – additional metadata independent of the data source (general dictionaries for different languages, for synonyms, opposites, etc.) and additional metadata tightly connected to the given data source (descriptions of the domains of attributes, alternative names for model elements used in the context of the data source, etc.).

The implementation of the metadata engine should also contain some algorithms for learning from previously processed requests. Such algorithms can modify and add metadata to improve performance and reliability of subsequent results.

3.2 Data Structures Unification Algorithm

The main task of the data structures unification algorithm is to transform user's model to the models which are the crisp submodels of the real data object model. During this trasformation the algorithm uses the metadata engine interface.

Object Models Unification – Algorithm

INPUTS:

- Real Data Engine - advanced Metadata Engine (for real data model)

- User Query Engine - basic Metadata Engine (for user's model)

- threshold - real number from (0,1]

OUTPUT:

- set of the crisp submodels of real data model with relevance measures greater than given threshold

The next figure expresses the basic idea of the algorithm. Firstly algorithm calls *findClass* with one parameter - name of the user's model class. The engine will return some real class – counterpart. In the next step, algorithm scans for all attributes in class of the user's model. After attribute scanning, algorithm searches for all associations. When algorithm obtains *"end class"* from association, it uses the same principle on this class and checks attributes, associations and so on. The algorithm creates a tree of the models during scanning. Each node is a representation of the model and holds relevance measure with respect to the real model. Each parent node is "crisp" submodel of child node.

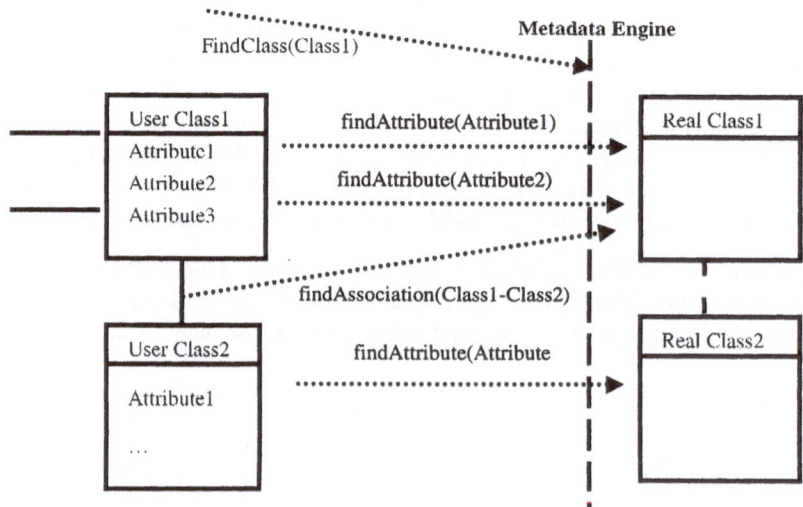

4 Conclusion

We have presented ideas which can be used in flexible querying. We have focused on introduction of uncertainty to the unification not only at data level but mainly at the metadata level. The main advantage of such approach is that the user does not need to know exact data representation. In our future work we would like to implement proposed interfaces and algorithms and to perform tests on real information systems.

References

[1] KRIŠKO, P. - MARCINČÁK, P. - MIHÓK, P. – SABOL, J. – VOJTÁŠ, P.: Low retrieval remote querying dialogue with fuzzy conceptual, syntactical and linguistical unification. In Proc. FQAS'98 Flexible Querying Answering Systems 98, Roskilde, Denmark, T. Andreasen et al eds. Lecture Notes in Computer Science 1495, Springer Berlin 1998, 215-226

[2] MARCINČÁK, P. – MATULA, M.: Fuzzy String Unification Using Logic Programming, ELITECH 99, Bratislava, 1999

[3] MARCINČÁK, P. – MATULA, M.: Flexibilný dotazovací systém – architektúra a návrh, DATASEM 99, Brno, 1999

[4] MARCINČÁK, P. – MATULA, M. - SEMANIŠIN, G.: Detekcia "podobných" záznamov v databázových systémoch, UNINFOS'99, Bratislava,1999, s. 85-90

[5] PETRY, F.: Fuzzy Databases Principles and Applications, Springer Verlag Berlin, 1996

[6] VOJTÁŠ, P.: Fuzzy reasoning with tunable t-operators. J.Advanced Comp. Intelligence (Fuji Technology Press) 2, (1998) 121-127

New Connectives for (Full) Fuzzy Resolution

Dana Smutná[1] and Peter Vojtáš[2]

[1] Department of Mathematics, Faculty of Natural Sciences, Matej Bel University, Tajovského 40, 974 01 Banská Bystrica, Slovakia
Email: smutna@fpv.umb.sk
[2] Department of Computer Science, Faculty of Science, P. J. Šafárik University, Jesenná 5, 041 54 Košice, Slovakia
Email: vojtas@kosice.upjs.sk

Abstract: In this paper we study resolution truth functions for sound and complete evaluation of many valued resolution. For modus ponens we give a formula for generation of this truth function using additive generator of underlying conjunctor. In the case of full resolution we give a construction of resolution truth function and study its properties

1 Introduction

The aim of this paper is to have a sound and complete resolution in many valued logic with arbitrary connectives.[1]

In the Pavelka's language of evaluated expresions (see [3]), we would like from $(C \vee A, x)$ and $(B \vee \neg A, y)$ infer $(C \vee B, f_\vee(x,y))$ where $f_\vee(x,y)$ should be the best promise we can give based on D the truth function of disjunction $\vee$ and x and y.

The case of resolution known as modus ponens when C is void, that is from (A, x) and $(B \vee \neg A, y)$ infer $(B, f_\vee(x,y))$ was studied in [9]. Based on a former result of P. Vojtáš, see in [11] we have a sound and complete semantics with $f_\vee(x,y) = C_{I_C}(x,y)$, the residual of material implication. Moreover we have characterized those C_{I_C} connectives for which $C \neq C_{I_C}$ but still both remain left continuous (the assumption of left-continuity we need for completeness result).

In this paper we would like to extend these results by characterizing generators of such C_{I_C}'s and by stronger soundes and completeness results for full resolution (i.e. the case when C is non-void).

---

[1] Research supported by grants VEGA 1/7557/20, 1/7146/20.

2 Different operators and their residuals

We assume our language consists of set of propositional variables and connectives: conjunction ∧, disjunction ∨ and the negation ¬ (our language does not contain implications).

In this contribution the truth function for negation is $n(x) = 1 - x$. Conjunctors in MV-logic with truth values range $[0, 1]$ are monotone extensions of the classical conjunction.

Note, that the dual operator to the conjunctor C defined by a non-decreasing mapping $D : [0,1]^2 \to [0,1]$, such that $D(a, b) = 1$ whenever $a = 1$ or $b = 1$ and $D(0,0) = 0$ is called the *disjunctor D*.

A function $I : [0,1]^2 \to [0,1]$ is said to be an *implicator* if $I(1,0) = 0$, $I(0,0) = I(0,1) = I(1,1) = 1$, I is non-increasing in its first component and non-decreasing in its second component.

In this paper truth function for conjunction is arbitrary conjunctor C and for truth function of disjunction we have $D(x, y) = 1 - C(1 - x, 1 - y)$.

Therefore starting with the conjunctor C, we can introduce the basic logic operators in $[0, 1]$-valued logic as follows:

disjunctor $\qquad\qquad\qquad D(x, y) = 1 - C(1 - x, 1 - y)$,

material implication $\qquad I_C(x, y) = D(1 - x, y) = 1 - C(x, 1 - y)$.

Commonly used conjunctors in MV-logic are the triangular norms (t-norms, in short), see [5], [4].

The following are the logical operators of material implication which are corresponding to basic t-norms Gödel T_M, product T_P, and Łukasiewicz T_L.

$$I_{T_M}(x, y) = \max(1 - x, y),$$

$$I_{T_P}(x, y) = 1 - x + x \cdot y,$$

$$I_{T_L}(x, y) = \min(1 - x + y, 1),$$

Another way of extending the classical binary implication operator to the unit interval $[0, 1]$ uses the *residuation R_C* with respect to a left-continuous conjunctor C

$$R_C(x, y) = \sup\{z \in [0, 1]; C(x, z) \leq y\}.$$

For the left continuous t-norms T_M, T_P and T_L we obtain the following residuations:

$$R_{T_M}(x, y) = \begin{cases} 1 \text{ if } x \leq y, \\ y \text{ otherwise,} \end{cases}$$

$$R_{T_P}(x, y) = \min\left(\frac{x}{y}, 1\right),$$

$$R_{T_L}(x, y) = \min(1 - x + y, 1).$$

Note, that $R_{T_L}(x,y) = I_{T_L}(x,y)$, but this equality is satisfied neither for Product t-norm nor for Minimum t-norm.

For our next considerations we try to generalize the axioms which define the well-known Φ-operator. Let C be a conjunctor and I an implicator. Define the following properties:

$$\Phi 2(C,I) \quad \text{if } C(x, I(x,y)) \leq y \quad \text{for all } x, y \in [0,1],$$

$$\Phi 3(C,I) \quad \text{if } I(x, C(x,y)) \geq y \quad \text{for all } x, y \in [0,1].$$

Now we can define the conjunctor C_I, which is generated by given implicator I

$$C_I(x,y) = \inf\{z \in [0,1]; I(x,z) \geq y\}.$$

3 More on modus ponens resolution connectives

In [9] we formulated the problem of finding connectives for sound and complete modus ponens resolution and gave some partial results. In this chapter we repeat the problem and give a strengthening of these results.

In order to apply results of [11] and in order to strengthen previous results on fuzzy resolution ([8]) we look for conjunctors C such that

    1) C and C_{I_C} are left continuous

    2) $\Phi 2(C_{I_C}, I_C)$ and $\Phi 3(C_{I_C}, I_C)$ holds

    3) C does not equal to C_{I_C}.

Now we will turn our attention to the properties 1)–3). It was shown that properties $\Phi 2$ and $\Phi 3$ are satisfied for residual operator with respect to a left continuous conjunctor C, see [5], [2]. Therefore we will look for the left-continuous conjunctors C, such that C does not equal to the left-continuous conjunctor C_{I_C}. Note that if the conjunctors C, C_{I_C} are left-continuous then $C \neq C_{I_C}$ if and only if $R_C \neq I_C$, where R_C is residual operator, see [5], [7].

First we will investigate t-norms, which satisfy properties 1) $-$ 3).

Remark 1 *Note that the properties* 1)–3) *are satisfied for the t-norms* T_P, T_M, *which are continuous. The Lukasiewicz t-norm* T_L *is continuous too, but property* 3) *is violated.*

Let T be a continuous t-norm. The properties 1) and 2) are satisfied. Property 3) is violated for each nilpotent t-norm T with additive generator, which is symmetric with respect to point $(\frac{1}{2}, \frac{f(0)}{2})$. For the rest of continuous t-norms properties 1)–3) hold true (compare also [10]).

Now we will discuss conjunctors which are generated by additive left-continuous generator. Let $f : [0,1] \to [0, \infty]$ be a strictly decreasing function, such that $f(1) = 0$, then we can define conjunctor $C : [0,1]^2 \to [0,1]$ by

$$C(x,y) = f^{(-1)}(f(x) + f(y)),$$

where the pseudo-inverse $f^{(-1)}$ is given by

$$f^{(-1)} = \sup\{t \in [0, 1]; f(t) > x\},$$

f is called an additive generator of C, see [6]. Note that the strict monotonicity of f ensures the continuity of the pseudo-inverse $f^{(-1)}$. Consequently, the continuity (left-, right-) of a generated conjunctor C is directly related to the continuity (left-, right-) of its generator f.

Now we can characterize the conjunctors which fulfill properties 1)-3).

Proposition 1 *Let $f : [0, 1] \to [0, \infty]$ be a left-continuous additive generator of a conjunctor C. Let $f(0) = \infty$ and the function f be right-continuous in the point 0 or $f(0) < \infty$ and there exists $x \in [0, 1]$ such that $f(x) + f(1-x) \neq f(0)$ and function f be continuous in the point x. Then the conjunctor C fulfills properties $1) - 3$). Moreover the conjunctor $C_{I_C} : [0, 1]^2 \to [0, 1]$ can be expressed by*

$$C_{I_C}(x, y) = l(g(x) + h(y)),$$

where

$$l(x) = 1 - f^{(-1)}(x), \ g(x) = -f(x), \ h(x) = f(1 - x),$$

and

$$C_{I_C}(x, y) = 0 \text{ holds whenever } x + y \leq 1.$$

4   Connectives for full resolution

First we translate the requirement of full resolution: from $(C \vee A, x)$ and $(B \vee \neg A, y)$ infer $(C \vee B, f(x, y))$ into the language of truth functions.

We introduce a new operator, let us call it *agregation deficit R_D*, which is based on disjunctor D. The motivation is following. Assume the truth value $TV(A) = a$. We would like to know conditions on truth values $TV(B) = b$ and $TV(C) = c$ such that it aggregates together with a or $1 - a$ to have $D(c, a) \geq x$ and $D(b, 1 - a) \geq y$. In order to acheave this agregation deficit R_D is defined by next inequalities

$$c \geq R_D(a, x) \quad \text{and} \quad b \geq R_D(1 - a, y).$$

It is easy to see that these inequalities are equivalent and the aggregation deficit we can define by

$$R_D(x, y) = \inf(z \in [0, 1]; D(z, x) \geq y).$$

Note that R_D coincides with residual coimplicator of [1].

Example 1 *For the basic t-conorms S_M, S_P and S_L we obtain the following agregation deficites:*

$$R_{S_M}(x,y) = \begin{cases} 0 \text{ if } x \geq y, \\ y \text{ otherwise,} \end{cases}$$

$$R_{S_P}(x,y) = \begin{cases} 0 & \text{if } x \geq y, \\ \frac{y-x}{1-x} & \text{otherwise,} \end{cases}$$

$$R_{S_L}(x,y) = \begin{cases} 0 & \text{if } x \geq y, \\ y - x & \text{otherwise,} \end{cases}$$

Remark 2 *Note, that $R_D(x,y) \leq y$ for $(x,y) \in [0,1]^2$ and if $x \geq y$, then $R_D(x,y) = 0$.*

Remark 3 *Note, that there is a one-to-one correspondence between agregation deficit and right-continuous t-conorm S, which is given by*

$$S(x,y) = \sup\{z \in [0,1]; R_S(x,z) \leq y\}.$$

For formulation of a result on sound and complete full resolution we will investigate the *resolution truth function* $f : [0,1]^2 \to [0,1]$, which is defined by

$$f_{R_D}(x,y) = \min_{a \in [0,1]} (D(R_D(a,x), R_D(1-a,y))).$$

Remark 4 *Note, that arbitrary resolution truth function $f_{R_D}(x,y)$ holds*

$$\text{if } x + y \leq 1 \text{ then } f_{R_D}(x,y) = 0.$$

Example 2 *For the agregation deficits R_{S_M}, R_{S_P} and R_{S_L} which are corresponded with the basic t-conorms we obtain the following functions:*

$$f_{R_{S_M}}(x,y) = \begin{cases} 0 & \text{if } x + y \leq 1, \\ \min(x,y) & \text{otherwise,} \end{cases}$$

Calculations. *Let $x + y > 1$ then*
$$f_{R_{S_M}}(x,y) = \min_{a \in [0,1]} (S_M(R_{S_M}(a,x), R_{S_M}(1-a,y))) =$$
$$= \min(\min_{a \in [0,1-y]} (\max(x,0)), \min_{a \in [1-y,x]} (\max(x,y)), \min_{a \in [x,1]} (\max(0,y))) =$$
$$= \min(x,y).$$

$$f_{R_{S_P}}(x,y) = \begin{cases} 0 & \text{if } x + y \leq 1, \\ \frac{x+y-1}{\max(x,y)} & \text{otherwise,} \end{cases}$$

Calculations. *Let* $x + y > 1$ *then*

$$f_{R_{S_P}}(x, y) = \min_{a \in [0,1]} (S_P(R_{S_P}(a, x), R_{S_P}(1 - a, y))) =$$

$$= \min \left(\min_{a \in [0, 1-y]} \left(\frac{x - a}{1 - a} \right), \min_{a \in [x, 1]} \left(\frac{y + a - 1}{a} \right), \min_{a \in [1-y, x]} \left(1 + \frac{(1 - x)(1 - y)}{a - a^2} \right) \right) =$$

$$= \min \left(\frac{x + y - 1}{y}, \frac{x + y - 1}{x} \right) = \frac{x + y - 1}{\max(x, y)}$$

$$f_{R_{S_L}}(x, y) = \begin{cases} 0 & \text{if } x + y \leq 1, \\ x + y - 1 & \text{otherwise,} \end{cases}$$

Calculations. *Let* $x + y > 1$ *then*

$$f_{R_{S_L}}(x, y) = \min_{a \in [0,1]} (S_L(R_{S_L}(a, x), R_{S_L}(1 - a, y))) =$$

$$= \min(\min_{a \in [0, 1-y]} (x - a), \min_{a \in [1-y, x]} ((x - a) + (y + a - 1)), \min_{a \in [x, 1]} (y + a - 1)) =$$

$$= x + y - 1.$$

Remark 5 *Note that if the partial mappings of disjunctor D are infimum-morfisms* ($\inf_{a \in M} D(x, a) = D(x, \inf_{a \in M} a)$, *where M is subset of interval* $[0, 1]$) *then $x \geq y$ if and only if $R_D(x, y) = 0$. Therefore the function f_{R_D} which is based on disjunctor D with this property is positive if and only if $x + y > 1$.*

Theorem 1 *Assume the truth evaluation of propositions is a model of $(C \vee A, x)$ and $(B \vee \neg A, y)$. Then*

$$TV(C \vee B) \geq f_{R_D}(x, y).$$

References

[1] De Baets, B. (1997) Coimplicators, the forgotten connectives. Tatra Mt. Math. Publ. **12**, 229–240

[2] Gottwald, S. (1993) Fuzzy Sets and Fuzzy Logic. Vieweg, Braunschweig

[3] Hájek, P. (1999) Metamathematics of fuzzy logic. Kluwer

[4] Klement, E.P., Mesiar, R. (1998) Triangular norms. Tatra Mountains Math. Publ. **14**, 161–167

[5] Klement, E.P.,Mesiar, R., Pap, E. (1999) Triangular norms. monograph, to appear

[6] Klement, E.P., Mesiar, R., Pap, E. Quasi- and pseudo- inverses of monotone functions, and the construction of t-norms. Fuzzy Sets and Systems, in press

[7] Mesiar, R. (1998) Generated conjunctors and related operators in MV-logic as a basis for AI applications. ECAI'98 Workshop 17, Brighton, 1–5

[8] Mundici, D., Olivetti, N. (1998) Resolution and model building in the infinite valued calculus of Łukasiewicz. Theoretical Comp. Sci. **200**, 335–366

[9] Smutná, D., Vojtáš, P. (1999) Fuzzy resolution with residuation of material implication. EUROFUSE-SIC '99, Budapest, 472–476

[10] Šabo, M. (1998) On many valued implications. Tatra Mountains Math. Publ. **14**, 161–167

[11] Vojtáš, P. (1998) Fuzzy reasoning with tunable t-operators. J. Advanced Comp. Intelligence **2**, 121–127

Learn the Ranking of Precedence Cases

István Borgulya

University of Pécs, Faculty of Business and Economics, H-7621 Pécs, Rákóczi út 80, Hungary

Abstract: A modification of a fuzzy classification algorithm is shown in this paper. This algorithm classifies multiple-criteria fuzzy or crisp elements and the task of the classification is traced back to ranking of elements, as well as to learning weight numbers similarly to neural networks. Two new particular versions of the algorithm can be utilized in the multiple-criteria decision-making. If we have precedence alternatives (cases), the algorithm is able to learn the ranking of alternatives when the criteria and the sequence of alternatives are known. The ready classifiers may be used as evaluating programs and further alternatives can be listed among the precedence alternatives with their help.

1 Introduction

There are many projects and practical tasks where decision-making occurs that more aims and criteria, i.e. alternatives have to be evaluated on the basis of multiple criteria. For the process of decision making by means of multiple criteria numerous models have been constructed and these models approach differently the individual steps of the decision processes. Many of models can be applied even in fuzzy environment. (see e.g. [10],[15],[16],[8],[11],[14]) The main steps of problem-handling are the same as in the case of fuzzy data: the methods for crisp data have to be substituted in a few steps only.

The fuzzy methods offer new possibilities in some steps of the decision process. Fuzzy methods can be chosen for the definition of relations between alternatives and criteria, and for the determination of the weight of criteria. For example, Yager's method [13] determines the weight numbers of the criteria by evaluating experts' opinions. When choosing aggregation processes and ranking there are even more fuzzy methods. It is possible to aggregate fuzzy variables by the Belmann-Zadech model [1], and our choices among different, discrete methods results in various ranking processes.

These methods were not developed to process precedence cases. Diverse methods are offered for the estimation of weight numbers, for the aggregation of criteria, and for ranking or choosing alternatives. Another possibility of supporting the decision process is by using precedence cases. The substance of this case-based problem-solving is finding one (or more) already solved case(s) similar to the new case, and adapting it to the new situation where its solution is developed. With a case-based system the edification of the earlier, similar cases can be reviewed and on the strength of these, the new case can be analyzed, interpreted, explained, judged etc.

The two variants of the fuzzy classification algorithm (FCR) to be demonstrated support the decision process with precedence cases also. Unlike the case-based systems, the two variants select the appropriate precedence case on the grounds of classification and the relative sequence of the cases; the solution has to be adapted to the new case by the decision-maker. The new versions of the FCR do this by learning the order of precedence alternatives. When the criteria are known and precedence alternatives with a given relative sequence are at our disposal, the ranking of alternatives can be learned by means of the new versions of the FCR. A classifier, when ready, can evaluate further alternatives on the strength of the precedence alternatives. This "evaluating program" enables the determination of the order of the new alternatives relative to the precedence alternatives.

Such a task can be set in various areas in practice. For example, in the majority of insurance cases the algorithm is applicable, because the already known compensations make the choice of suitable and evaluated alternatives possible. The actual case can be compared with earlier cases after learning. However this method can also be applied in various fields of law: it can be a very useful piece of information for legal decision-making to know what place the presented case takes when compared to previous cases already decided.

Let us now examine the variants of the fuzzy classification algorithm and the examples.

2 Learn the ranking of alternatives

2.1 The FCR algorithm

The steps of the heuristic FCR algorithm (This is a modified version of the earlier algorithm [4], [5]). Let us look at the heuristic algorithm in more detail. Denote a_1, ..., a_n the elements to be classified and the serial numbers ho_1, ho_2... ., ho_n their known classes. Let us consider each crisp, or fuzzy criterion K_j ($1 \leq j \leq m$) as a fuzzy linguistic variable and let $K_j = \{L_{j1}, \ldots, L_{jpj})$, where $L_{j1}, \ldots, L_{jpj}$ are the values of the linguistic variable, with the membership functions μ_{Lj1}, μ_{Lj2} μ_{Lpi} .

Furthermore, let w_i be the weight number of criterion K_j with a maximum value of 1. An a_i element is characterized by the $k_{i1}, k_{i2}, \ldots, k_{im}$ and ho_i input data. The chosen fuzzy ranking method (FRM) orders a real number, y_i ($i=1, \ldots, n$) to each elements a_i. (The max-min method of Yager [12] and the "mark-based method" [2] were chosen as FRM when testing the algorithm.).

Let

$$H(a_i,a_j)=1/(1+d(a_i,a_j))$$

be a similarity measure, where $d(a_i,a_j)$ represent the distance measures of the elements.(We use the "semantic distance" of Munda [9]. There is a generalization of the Minkowski p-metric with given R crisp criteria and S stochastic and/or fuzzy criteria ($m=R+S$)).

Let the number of classes be s and the number of prototypes $s+t$ (t may even be zero). Let ε be a threshold number when checking the stability of centres and γ the allowed maximal value of the false classifications. Let itt be a threshold number of the local search procedure.

1. Setting the initial values.
    Let us define the initial empty clusters (sets) of classes (or groups) as $C = \{C_i\}$, $i = 1,2,\ldots s+t$, and $c_1, c_2, \ldots, c_s$ and $p_1, p_2, \ldots p_{s+t}$ denote the centres and prototypes of classes, respectively. The centre, prototype and serial number of the cluster C_i are then c_i, p_i, o_i. Let us choose $c_i := p_i := o_i := 0$ for $i = 1, 2, \ldots$, $s+t$ at the beginning. Let us take a randomly chosen series of weight numbers $w_1, \ldots, w_m$. and an index i randomly. $i \in \{1,2,\ldots,n\}$. Let $a_j \rightarrow y_j$ from FRM.

2. A new element. Let us choose a new a_j element randomly. Let $a_j \rightarrow y_j$ from FRM.

3. Checking of analogies. If $H(a_j, p_z) = \max H(a_j, p_q)$; $q, z \in \{1,2, \ldots, s+t\}$ then the class o_z is ordered to element a_j. Let $p_z \rightarrow y$ from FRM.

4. Modification of prototypes. Let $ij:=0$
    4.1 If $(ho_j = o_z) \wedge ((c_z - y_j) < (c_z - y))$, then $p_z := a_j$ and if $(\exists x) (a_j = p_x)$

    $(x \in \{1,2, \ldots, z-1, z+1, \ldots, s+t\}$, then $c_x := o_x := 0$, $ij:=1$.
    4.2 If $(ho_j \neq o_z) \wedge (ij = 0) \wedge (c_{ii} = 0) \wedge (ii = ho_i)$ then $p_{ii} := a_j$, $c_{ii} := y$, $o_{ii} := ho_j$.

    and if $(\exists x) (a_j = p_x)$ $x \in \{s+1,s+2, \ldots, s+t\}$, then $c_x := o_x := 0$, $ij:=1$.
    4.3 If $(ho_j \neq o_z) \wedge (ij = 0) \wedge (\exists ii) (c_{ii} = 0)$, $ii = s+1,s+2, \ldots s+t$, then $p_{ii} := a_j$,

    $c_{ii} := y$, $o_{ii} := ho_j$. and if $(\exists x) (a_j = p_x)$ $(x \in \{1,2, \ldots, ii-1, ii+1, \ldots, s+t\}$, then $c_x := o_x := 0$.

5. Modification of weights.

    5.1 If $(ho_j = o_z) \wedge ((c_i < c_j) \wedge (y_i > y_j)) \vee ((c_i > c_j) \wedge (y_i < y_j))$, then

$$w_l = w_l - \eta * sign\ (y_i - y_j) * (k_{li} - k_{lj}) * (c_i - c_j) * H(a_j, a_i) * \mu_{Lli}\ (k_{li}) * \mu_{Llj}(\ k_{lj})$$

    $l=1,2,\ldots,m$

5.2 The normalization of weights.

6. Checking the stability of centres and the result.
    Let $i := j$, $it:=it+1$. If $mod(it,\ kn) \neq 0$ the iteration is continued at point 2, otherwise:

    6.1 Classification of the a_{ii} elements ($ii=1,2,\ldots,n$):

        Let $C_l=\varnothing$, $l=1,2,\ldots,s+t$. If $H(a_{ii}, p_z) = max\ H(a_{ii}, p_q)$; q,

        $z \in \{1,2, \ldots, s+t\}$ then $a_{ii}. \in C_z$

    6.2 Recomputed the values of centers: $uc_1, uc_2, \ldots uc_{s+t}$,

$$uc_l = (\sum_{q=1}^{db_l} y_q) / db_l$$

    where db_l is the number of the elements of C_l and FRM: $a_q \rightarrow y_q.\ ,a_q. \in C_l$

    6.3 Stopping condition. If

$$((\sum_{l=1}^{s+t} |c_l - uc_l| < \varepsilon\ ) \wedge (\ err\ < \gamma\ )) \vee (\ itt\ < \ it\ )$$

    is true, where *err* is the number of the fault classifications, then the iteration is continued at point 7,

    otherwise $c_l := uc_l$ for $l = 1,2, \ldots, s+t$ and the iteration is continued at point 2.

7. Weight optimization with a local search procedure

    7.1 Let $ow_{ii}=w_{ii}$ ($ii=1,2\ldots,m$), *oerr=err*, $ij=0$.

    7.2 Let $ij=ij+1$. Let us generate w_{ii} numbers randomly in the

        $[ow_{ii} -0.1,\ ow_{ii}+0.1]$ interval ($ii=1,2,\ldots,m$)

    7.3 Classification of the a_{ii} elements ($ii=1,2,\ldots,n$), and recomputed the value

        $c_1,c_2,\ldots,c_{s+t}$, and err.

    If *(oerr>err)* then $ow_{ii}=w_{ii}$ ($ii=1,2,..,m$), *oerr=err*.

7.4 If (*oerr*< γ) v (ij>100) is true, then the process is finished,

otherwise   continued at step 7.2

2.2 Special versions of the FCR

Given that a series of precedence alternatives is given and the alternatives can be ranked into the required sequence by means of the class numbers of the alternatives. We want to create such an algorithm with the special versions of the FCR that does more than merely classifying the precedence alternatives: it keeps the order of the alternatives in an incremental sequence – namely, it learns the ranking of the alternatives in addition to their classification.

The classification of alternatives requires different approaches in the case of alternatives, which are ranked into a monotone and a strictly monotone incremental sequence, respectively. If

- the alternatives are given in a monotone incremental sequence, there are classes where more than one alternative belongs to a class and their order inside the class is indifferent regarding the ranking. The ranking can be learned by a „directed" classification which keeps the monotone incremental sequence of the alternatives. To realize this, the algorithm has to ensure the monotone incremental values of the class centers in accordance with the sequence. The application of more prototypes than the number of the classes is not effective in this case (t=0).

- the alternatives are given in a strictly monotone incremental sequence, then each alternative forms a class itself. The ranking can be learned by „directed" classification again. In opposite to the previous version, the centers are connected to a single element only and a definition of prototypes loses its sense, because the prototype of the class is identical with the alternative itself. It follows that it is unnecessary to inspect the stability and so the classifying algorithm can be simplified further.

From the above it follows that two special versions of the FCR are needed for the learning of the ranking. Let us now look at the two special versions of the algorithm.

Version A: The formation of a monotone incremental sequence

To add the capability of learning the ranking, the FCR algorithm has to be modified at three points: Firstly, we have to facilitate the monotone increase in the values of the centers. Secondly, the sequence of the centers has to be tested, since one of the conditions of stopping is a monotone incremental sequence of centers. The monotone incremental sequence has to be preserved during the local search procedure as well, and so this test is also applied in step 7.
The following steps are modified:

5.1 If $(ho_j = o_z) \wedge [(o_i < o_j)\wedge((y_i \geq y_j) \vee (c_i > c_j)) \vee (o_i > o_j)\wedge((y_i \leq y_j) \vee (c_i < c_j))]$, then

$$w_l = w_l - \eta * \text{sign}\, (y_i - y_j)*(k_{li} - k_{lj})*(c_i - c_j) * H(a_j, a_i)* \mu_{Lli}\, (k_{li})* \mu_{Llj}(\, k_{lj})$$
$$l = 1,2,\ldots,m$$

6.3 Stopping condition. Let the value of *err1* logical variable be true, if the $c_1, c_2, \ldots, c_s$ sequence monotone increases, otherwise false.
If $(30000 < it) \wedge (err1 = \text{false})$ then "The learning did not succeed." is printed and the process is finished. If

$$\left(\sum_{l=1}^{s+t} |c_l - uc_l| < \varepsilon \right) \wedge (err < \gamma) \wedge err\, 1 \vee (30000\ < it)$$

is true, where *err* is the number of the fault classifications, then the iteration is continued at point 7,

otherwise $c_l := uc_l$ for $l = 1,2, \ldots , s+t$ and the iteration is continued

at point 2.

7.3 Classification of the a_{ii} elements (ii=1,2,…,n), and recomputed the

value $c_1, c_2, \ldots, c_s$, *err1* and *err*. If *err1* $\wedge$ (*oerr* > *err*) then $ow_{ii} = w_{ii}$

(ii=1,2,..,m), *oerr* = *err*.

Version B: The formation of a strictly monotone incremental sequence
This algorithm can be created from the version A of the algorithm. The main difference is that we do not need prototypes, stability checks and local learning procedures for the learning of the strictly monotone incremental sequence. Let us treat the *err* classification error rather liberally: let it mean the number of pairs (c_i, c_{i+1}) of the same value.

With respect to the fact that the algorithm may be considerably simplified in this case, the steps have to be reformulated.

Let the number of classes be identical with the number of alternatives ($s = n$),

1. Setting the initial values.

   Let the centers of classes $c_1, c_2, \ldots, c_s$. Let us choose $c_i := 0$ for $i = 1, 2, \ldots, s$ at the beginning. Let us take a randomly generated series of weight numbers $w_1, \ldots, w_m$. and an induce i randomly generated from the interval $[1,n]$. Let $a_i \rightarrow c_i$ from FRM.

2. A new element. Let us choose a new a_j element randomly. Let $a_j \rightarrow c_j$ from FRM.

3. Modification of weights.

   3.1 If $(i < j)^{\wedge}(c_i \geq c_j) \vee (i>j)^{\wedge}(c_i \leq c_j)$, then

   $$w_l = w_l - \eta * \text{sign} \, (c_i - c_j) * (k_{li} - k_{lj}) * |i - j| * H(a_j, a_i) * \mu_{Lli} (k_{li}) * \mu_{Llj}(k_{lj})$$
   $l=1,2,\ldots,m$

   3.2 The normalization of weights.

4. Checking the result. Let $i := j$, $it:=it+1$. If $\text{mod}(it, kn) \neq 0$ the iteration is continued at point 2, otherwise:

   4.1 Recomputed the values of centers: FRM: $a_{ii} \rightarrow c_{ii}$ $ii=1,2,\ldots,n$

   4.2 Stopping condition. Let the value of the *err1* logical variable true if the $c_1,c_2,\ldots,c_s$ sequence monotone increases, otherwise false. Let the number of (c_i, c_{i+1}) pairs of the same value be *err*.

   If $(30000<it)^{\wedge}(err1=\text{false})$ then "The learning did not succeed." is printed and the process is finished.
   If $(err1^{\wedge}(err<\gamma))$ is true then "The process is finished", otherwise continued at point 2.

(Because, there are no prototypes to determine, the task can be formulated even in another way in this version: those weights of criteria are looked for which lead to the correct sequence of the alternatives [3]. This reformulating means differences only in the application of the result.)

At the end of the learning process the information necessary for classification and ranking are stored in the characteristics of the classes (prototypes, centers, class numbers) and in the weights of the criteria. The ready classifiers use these vectors and matrices.

The ready classifier (in other words, the evaluating program) differs for the two versions. The root of their functioning is as follows:

> The version A in view of the prototypes and their classes, and of the criterion weights determines the place of a new alternative among the precedence alternatives by right of similarity. (corresponding to step 6.1 of the algorithm)

The version B knows the criterion weights and the class and FRM function values of the precedence cases. It determines the place of a new alternative among the precedence alternatives using the FRM: $a_j \rightarrow y$ value (corresponding to step 4.1 of the algorithm)

Regardless of the version and as a result, we always obtain x class of the "nearest" precedence alternative and the place of the new alternative in the relative series (the ($[x-1,x]$ or $[x,x+1]$ intervals).

3 Ranking of alternatives

Let us look at 3 examples of the learning of the ranking of precedence alternatives using the versions A and B. Although only the second example of the three contains genuine, really evaluated precedence cases, all of them are suitable for the demonstration of the capabilities of the versions. Naturally, the further successful applications of them prerequisites appropriate really rankle precedence alternatives.

The application of versions is demonstrated the following examples:

> IRIS data-series (version A): 150 cases (alternatives) are given, that can be classified into 3 ordered categories. Each individual alternative is characterized by 4 criteria [7]. Although, as a matter of fact, this example does not list alternatives of a decision problem, it is suitable to demonstrate how to handle a "decision problem of multiple precedence alternatives". The alternatives can be graded as long as their classification can also reflect their importance. (If we assign the 1, 2, 3 classes in an other way, they can no longer be sorted.

> Traffic cases (version B): a sequence of alternatives of 12 traffic cases, a_1, . . . , a_{12} is given and each individual alternative is characterized by 14 criteria [6].

> Land use problem in the Netherlands (version B): a series of 7 alternatives given by 13 fuzzy criteria [9].

The results of the examples can be seen in Fig. 1. Fig. 1 demonstrates the best, the worst and the average values of the *it* number of iterations and the *err* number of classification errors. By version B the problem was solved in two ways: first we ordered a learning of strictly monotone sequence (case $\gamma=1$), and second a monotone sequence (e.g. $\gamma=5$). 20 learning processes were considered where the algorithm has successfully learnt the ranking (Unsuccessful learning occurs in about 5% of cases.)

	Traffic cases		Land use pr.		IRIS data-series		
	it $(\gamma=1)$	*it* $(\gamma=5)$	*it* $(\gamma=1)$	*it* $(\gamma=5)$	*it*	Err (training set)	Err (test set)
best	4200	1043	20	20	49	0	2
average	10455	3292	21	21	2549	5	6
worst	13560	5639	22	27	3024	14	11

Fig. 1. Results of the examples ($\eta = 0.0005$, $\varepsilon = 0.01$ and *itt*=3024)

4 Conclusion

The basic idea of the demonstrated FCR algorithm and the two particular versions is that it determines the information fundamental to the classification with a neural-type learning algorithm from the alternatives to be ordered i.e. the samples. The two particular versions of the FCR can be utilized in multiple-criteria decision-making, the algorithms are able to learn the ranking of precedence alternatives when the criteria and the sequence of alternatives are known. A classifier, when ready, can evaluate further alternatives on the strength of the precedence alternatives.

The FCR and its particular versions are stochastic methods, solving the problem in about 95% of cases. The algorithm carries out the classification at a precision of 95-100%.

Acknowledgement

The study was supported by the Hungarian Research Program OTKA T 030861 and FKFP 0233/1999.

References

[1] Belman R. E., Zadeh L.A.,1970, Decision-Making in a Fuzzy Environment *Management Science* 17 (4) 140-164.

[2] Borgulya I., 1997a, A Ranking Method for Multiple Criteria Decision Making. *International Journal of Systems Science* 28, pp. 905-912.

[3] Borgulya I., 1997b, Generalization weight numbers of criteria by fuzzy systems. In: Proceeding of the 19th Int. Conf. Information Technology Interfaces, Pula, pp. 99-104.

[4] Borgulya I.,1998, Két fuzzy osztályozó módszer. *SZIGMA* XXIX. 1998/1-2. p. 7-28.

[5] Borgulya I., 1999, Fuzzy Controller Generation with a Fuzzy Classification Method. In: Reusch B. (ed): *Computational Intelligence* Springer Verlag Heidelberg, pp. 62-74.

[6] Borgulya I., 1999a, Two examples of decision support in the law. *Artificial Intelligence and Law* 7, pp. 303-321

[7] Fischer R.A.,1936, The use of multiple measurements in taxonomic problems. *Annual Eugenics*, **7**. (PartII). pp. 179-188.

[8] Fodor J. C., Rubens M. 1994, *Fuzzy Preference Modelling and Multicriteria Decision Support*. (Dordrecht, Kluwer Academic Publishers).

[9] Munda. G., 1995, *Multicriteria Evaluation in a Fuzzy Environment*. (Heidelberg, Physica-Verlag).

[10] Rommelfanger H., 1993, *Fuzzy Decision-Support-Systeme. Entscheidung bei Unschärfe*. (Berlin, Germany: Springer-Verlag).

[11] Rubens M., 1997, Fuzzy Sets and decision analysis . *Fuzzy Sets and Systems* 90, 199-206.

[12] Yager R. R., 1978, Fuzzy Decision Making Including Unequal Objectives. *Fuzzy Sets and Systems*. **1**, 87-95.

[13] Yager R. R., 1993, Non numeric multi-criteria multi-person decision making. *Group Decision and Negotiation*

[14] Yeh C. H.,Willis R. J., Deng H., Pan H. 1999, Task oriented weighting in multi-criteria analysis. *European Journal of Operational Research* 119. 130-146.

[15] Zimmermann H. J., Gutsche L. 1991, *Multi-Criteria Analyses* (Berlin, Germany:Springer-Verlag).

[16] Zimmermann H. J 1996, *Fuzzy Sets and Its Applications 3rd ed.* (Amsterdam Kluwer-Nijhoff).

Sugeno-Type Fuzzy Predictor of the MPEG Video Stream

Agnieszka Chodorek

Department of Electronics and Telecommunications, Kielce University of Technology, 25-314 Kielce, Al. Tysiąclecia Państwa Polskiego 7, POLAND, tel. +48 41 3424232, email: eweach@tu.kielce.pl.

Abstract: There is growing interest in telecommunication applications using video information, as for example real-time full-motion video or VoD systems. Most of them use MPEG standard for compression of video signal. The MPEG video traffic stream is very bursty, so in many technical problems classical modeling methods fail or are inefficient. In the paper we present an analysis of MPEG video stream and its properties which led to form fuzzy rules. The Takagi-Sugeno fuzzy inference system for prediction of MPEG video traffic is proposed.

Keywords: fuzzy systems, real-world applications, multimedia, MPEG, Quality of Service

1 Introduction

Recent advances in technology have resulted in rapid growth of high performance transmission of multimedia data. Performance of today computers and hardware devices for image and audio processing can allow design new 21st century applications, as teleconferencing systems, VoD, VDB.

Methods of video and audio signal compression are defined, among others, by MPEG (*Moving Picture Expert Group*) standard (ISO 13818). Nowadays, the standard becomes the most frequently used compression method for storing (DVD, CD-Video, etc.) and transmitting multimedia data.

The MPEG video traffic stream is very burst, so in many technical problems conventional modeling approaches, based on the classical queuing theory, Erlang formulation or Markov processes, fail or are inefficient. The aim of the paper is to propose a fuzzy logic based tool for prediction of the MPEG video traffic. Section two of this paper contains a brief overview of MPEG video encoding and discusses some design problems specified for prediction and modeling such type of data. In the third section Sugeno-type fuzzy predictor of the MPEG video stream is described, while section four summarizes our experiences

2 Properties of MPEG video stream and its impact on structure of the fuzzy system

The MPEG encoder input sequence consists of a series of frames, each containing a two-dimensional array of picture elements storing both luminance and chrominance information. The compression algorithm is used to reduce the data rate before transmitting the video stream over communication networks. The spatial redundancies of the video stream are reduced by transforms and entropy coding and the temporal redundancies are reduced by prediction of future frames based on motion vectors. It results in usage three types of frames: I (*Intra-coding*) frames, P (*Predictive*) frames, B (*Bi-directional*) frames (Table 1).

Table 1. Compression method and typical size of MPEG-2 video frames.

Frame type	Size (KB)	Compression method
I – frames	100 – 600	DCT
P – frames	50 – 300	motion prediction and DCT
B – frames	30 –200	motion prediction and DCT

After coding, the frames are formed in a deterministic periodic sequence, called Group of Pictures (GOP). The MPEG specification does not define GOP pattern, only that the first frame should be intra-coding (I frame). For professional applications, Group of Pictures typically consists of 12 (sequence: *I-B-B-P-B-B-P-B-B-P-B-B*) or 15 frames (sequence: *I-B-B-P-B-B-P-B-B-P-B-B-P-B-B*).

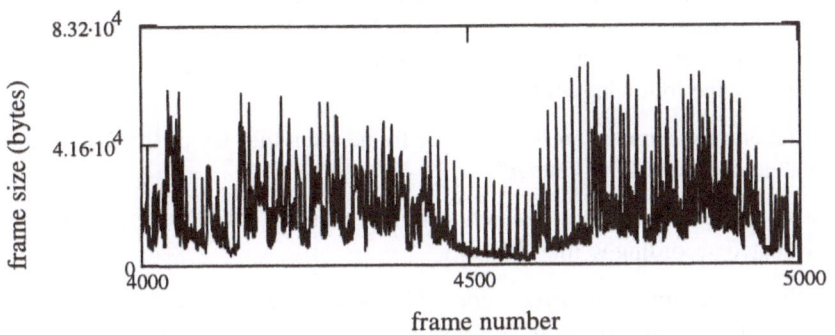

Fig.1. An example of the MPEG video traces

MPEG video traces are superposition of three various traces, corresponding with three types of frames and repeated by the GOP pattern. The multiplexed stream, and three component streams, presents a strong pseudo-periodic property.

The MPEG video stream is very bursty (Fig.1.). As reported in the literature (e.g. Heyman *et al.* 1994, Rose 1995, Mellaney *et al.* 1997, Natkaniec *et al.* 1999), it is difficult to consider any correlation aspects of MPEG streams, when methods of analysis based on descriptive statistics are used.

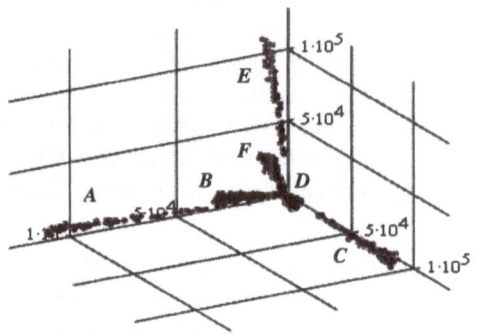

Fig.2. The first 60 seconds of the MPEG-encoded *Star Wars* video traces into the three-dimensional Cartesian space (x_k, x_{k-1}, x_{k+1}).

In our work, we insert MPEG traces into the three-dimensional Cartesian space (x_1, x_2, y), where:

☐ x_1 – the current frame size,

☐ x_2 – the previous frame size,

☐ y – the next frame size.

Results depicted on Fig.2. do not show a typical function of two variables. Points symbolizing the dependent variable do not arrange a continuous surface, but shows tendency to group into 6 collections of data. Due to the pseudo-linear character of the graph, properties of the MPEG stream can be defined by set of five rules, described by the following sentences:

1. If the current frame is an *Intra-coding* frame, then the size of the next frame is evaluated according to "line *A*".

2. If the current frame is a *Prediction* frame, then the size of the next frame is evaluated according to line "line *B*".

3. If the current frame is a *Bi-directional* frame and the previous frame is an *Intra* frame, then the size of the next frame is evaluated according to "*C*".

4. If the current frame is a *Bi-directional* frame and the previous frame is a *Predicted* frame, then the size of the next frame is evaluated according to "*D*".

5. If the current frame is a *Bi-directional* frame and the previous frame is a *Bi-directional* frame, then the size of the next frame is evaluated according to "line *E*" or "line *F*".

Lines "*E*" and "*F*" are situated on the same plane, orthogonal to the XY plane, so it is impossible to define one-to-one assignment $(x+1) = f(x, x-1)$. It is caused by the method of encoding - a *Bi-directional* frame contains reference both to the previous and to the next frame. According to the applied GOP, the rule No. 5 can be replaced by two following rules (sentences):

5. If the current frame is a *Bi-directional* frame and the previous frame is a *Bi-directional* frame and the next frame is *Intra-coding* frame, then the size of the next frame is evaluated according to "line *E*".

6. If the current frame is a *Bi-directional* frame and the previous frame is a *Bi-directional* frame and the next frame is *Predicted* frame, then the size of the next frame is evaluated according to "line *F*".

Described phenomena led to define a structure of a fuzzy predictor of the MPEG encoded video stream.

3. Fuzzy prediction of the MPEG video stream

Fuzzy inference systems for modeling and predicting the MPEG video stream has been proposed by several authors (e.g. Scheffer *et al.* 1995; Genco and Lombardo 1998; Chodorek 1999b). They were two- or three-input Mamdani-type systems, usually designed as a part of large fuzzy decision systems for telecommunication network management (Chodorek 1999b).

The proposed predictor of the MPEG video stream has been developed as a MISO (Multiple-Input Single Output) fuzzy system with singleton fuzzifier and center-average defuzzifier. Number of outputs is determined by requirements of admission control system[1]. The output quantity y represents the predicted size (in bytes) of the next frame[2]. Due to quasi-linear dependence of the output quantity on inputs, we decide to apply a Takagi-Sugeno model (Takagi and Sugeno, 1985) of fuzzy inference system. Output membership functions are the linear dependence of the linguistic variable "current frame". Six fuzzy rules (Fig.3.) are defined according to properties of MPEG video stream, described in Section 2.

---

[1] admission control system is a part of telecommunication network management system;

[2] the predictor forecast frame size which arrive to system in 40 milliseconds – it is enough time horizon for efficient network management

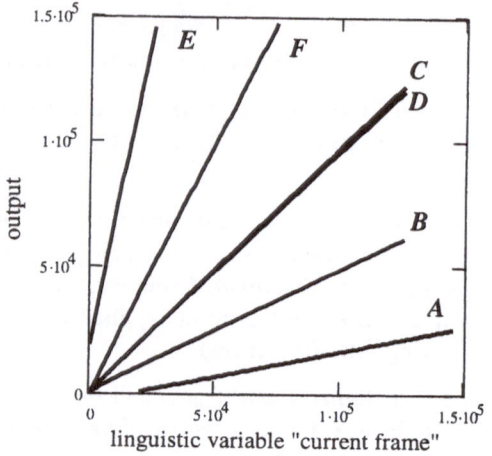

Fig.3. Linear functions in the consequents of the fuzzy rules.

The input vector consists of three components x_1 ... x_3, where: x_1 is corresponding to linguistic variable "current frame" and represents the size (in bytes) of the current frame, whereas x_2 ("previous frame") and x_3 ("next frame") represent the frame type (I, B, P). Fuzzy sets corresponding to x_1 are defined by Gaussian membership functions and corresponding to x_2, x_3 are defined by triangular membership functions. Initial values of linguistic variables x_1, x_2, x_3 were obtained using fuzzy c-means method.

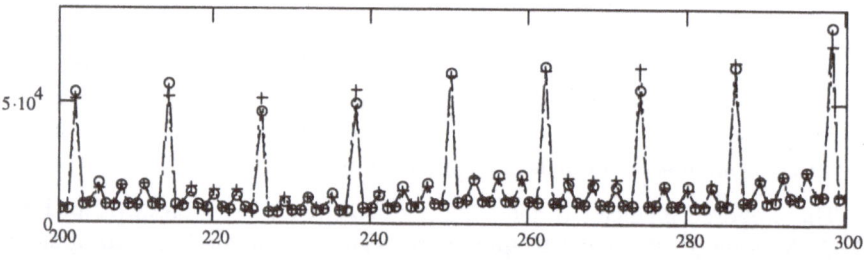

Fig. 4. The real (o's) vs. predicted (+'s) value of the frame size (*Star Wars*).

The described system has been successfully implemented. Typical results, obtained for *Star Wars* film sequence, are depicted on Fig.4. Mean Squared Error (MSE) is used as an indicator of prediction accuracy. Prediction accuracy of the Sugeno-type predictor (MSE = 57,36) is better than obtained for Markov Modulated Poisson Process (MMPS) model (MSE = 207,47) and better than described in (Scheffer *et al.* 1995) Mamdani-type fuzzy predictor (MSE = 136,51).

Results of forecasting were presented, among others, on Telecommunication Workshop PWT'99 (Chodorek, 1999a).

4. Conclusions

In the paper fuzzy predictor of the MPEG video stream was presented. Due to pseudo-linear dependence of the output quantity on inputs, we decide to apply a Takagi-Sugeno model of fuzzy inference system.

The described system has been successfully implemented. The obtained results were better than estimated by the conventional Markovian methods and better than, mentioned in the literature, Mamdani-type prediction systems.

References

1. Chodorek A., 1999a: Fuzzy modeling of the MPEG-encoded video stream. Proc. of PWT'99, Poznań, Poland (in Polish)

2. Chodorek A., 1999b: Fuzzy inference systems in telecommunication networks, Digital Communication - Technologies & Services, vol.2, No.2 (in Polish)

3. Genco A., Lombardo G., 1998: MPEG Video Frame Discard by Fuzzy Control. Proc. of Global Telecommunications Conference GLOBECOM'98. vol. 2

4. Heyman D. P., Tabatabai A., Lakshman T. V., 1994: Statistical Analysis of MPEG-2 Coded VBR VideoTraffic. Proc. of 6th Int. Workshop on Packet Video.

5. ISO 13818/H.222, Information Technology - Generic Coding of Moving Pictures and Associated Audio - Part 3: Systems.

6. Natkaniec M., Wajda K., 1999, Statistical properties of MPEG streams and issues for transmission of video information in high speed networks, Proc. of ATM Technology Users Symposium, Kosice, Slovakia

7. Rose O., 1995, Statistical properties of MPEG video traffic and their impact on traffic modeling in ATM systems, University of Wuerzburg Institute of Computer Science Research Report Series, Report No. 101.

8. Scheffer M.F., Wajda K., Kunicki J.S., 1995: Fuzzy Logic Adaptive Traffic Enforcement Mechanisms for ATM Networks. Proc. of International Teletraffic Conference, Pretoria, South Africa.

9. Takagi T., Sugeno M., 1985: Fuzzy Identyfication of System and Its Applications to Modeling and Control. IEEE Transactions on Systems, Man and Cybernetics, vol. 15.

Part 3

Miscellaneous CI Techniques

Biological Inspiration for Multiple Memories Implementation and Cooperation

Frédéric Alexandre

LORIA/INRIA-Lorraine, BP 239, F-54506 Vandoeuvre, France

Abstract: Biological inspiration has led to the design of many connectionist models and mechanisms. Among them, memorization mechanisms are of particular importance to endow biologically inspired systems with efficient and consistent adaptive abilities. In this paper, we report recent modelling works of this kind, implementing procedural, episodic and working memories and making them cooperate for autonomous agent navigation.

Introduction

Classical connectionist modelling has explored a variety of adaptive mechanisms [8] and has allowed many impressive results in the domain of pattern matching, control, prediction, etc. Coming back to biological inspiration for the design of new models or mechanisms can be justified by at least three reasons. First, original and robust adaptative properties can be extracted from the observation of animal behavior. Second, designing adaptive mechanisms in relation to their neuronal substratum can give a framework to make these mechanisms cooperate in integrated tasks and not act alone on artificial problems. Third, the reference to animal behavior favors the implementation of ecological tasks that are too rarely investigated. In this paper, this kind of researches is illustrated through the design of three different kinds of memories (namely, procedural, episodic and working memories) and their interaction in a cerebral framework for endowing an autonomous agent with navigation and environment exploration capacities.

1 Procedural memory

Procedural learning is the ability to learn functions or procedures. This ability is reported as a property of the associative posterior cortex which can learn for example sensorimotor coordination. This learning is very slow and many trials are necessary for example to learn how to guide one's hand with one's eye. This kind of learning can be somehow related to the slow statistical learning performed by feed-forward networks like multi-layer perceptrons. Indeed, a pattern matching can be learned between an input space and an output space and can correspond to learn the transformations necessary to go from one reference frame (for example retinal) to another (for example muscular).

From this basic property, illustrated by classical connectionist models, biologically inspired models of the associative posterior cortex can bring additional structural and adaptive properties. Concerning structure, an important improvement can be brought to information representation with the implementation of cortically inspired areas [1]. Such areas, close to Kohonen self-organizing maps [10], implement batteries of filters and can accordingly be learned with Kohonen-like competitive mechanisms. Receiving information from sensors or actuators, such monomodal areas can build a mapping representing basic prototypes of perceptive or motor events, which is a first step in the internal representation of the external world.

Procedural learning will be performed in associative areas, combining monomodal or other associative maps. Basically, this learning lies on hebbian associative mechanisms, computing correlations between events in associated areas. Thus, for example, an association can be learned between the image of the arm, represented in retinal coordinates into a visual area and its sensation, represented in muscular coordinates into a sensory area [3]. Additional biologically inspired mechanisms have been proposed (see for example [4]) and can lead to such interesting properties as generalization, robustness to noise, transfer of learning and association of sequences of events. This latter property is very important, for example to learn the consequences of one's actions on the environment. Such a learning has been used to build a reactive architecture allowing an autonomous agent to move, in order to reach a goal it could see [4].

2   Episodic memory

In addition to this slow procedural learning, humans and animals are obviously able to memorize after just one or two experiences, episodes of events they have just lived. The hippocampus has been reported [14] as the neuronal structure able to perform episodic learning. Basically, this learning can be described as follows[12] : As explained above, the posterior cortex includes many associative areas representing multimodal information. All these associative areas project in the entorhinal cortex which thus gives a snapshot of the current state of the associative posterior cortex. Thanks to its recurrent connectivity, the CA3 structure in the hippocampus is then able to store a prototype of this activity. Similarly, Hopfield-like recurrent neural networks [9] are reported as able to store prototypes of activity as stable states and act as auto-associative memory to converge from a close initial state toward this stable state. In the same way, the hippocampus can detect that the current state of the associative posterior cortex is novel or that a close state has been recently experienced. In the former case, the state can be memorized in a distributed way in the hippocampal structure. In the latter case, the memorized event, including its spatial and temporal context, can be retrieved and sent back to the cortex [13]. Such a short term, rapid memorization can allow an autonomous agent to reach a goal that was seen before, even it is no longer viewed [7]. It was also tested, in cooperation with a model of posterior cortex, as a supervisor of this latter structure [11], thus allowing for an internal cooperation between episodic and procedural memories.

3 Working memory

Both episodic and procedural memories can reveal insufficient to guide an autonomous agent if obstacles or other problems prevent it from directly reaching a goal. In this case, a working memory is necessary to manipulate goals and subgoals and perform planning. The prefrontal cortex is known as the neuronal structure responsible for this kind of reasoning [6]. Basically, a mechanism has been proposed in [2] to explain how sensorimotor goals and subgoals, detected in the posterior cortex, can be controlled over time to organize behavior. Neurons in the prefrontal cortex are known to have lasting activities during such planning behavior. It is then proposed that they act like stacks, memorizing current and past states of the posterior cortex, together with the corresponding transitions. This knowledge can then be exploited to organize these states with regard to a goal and to trigger them when necessary. It was also proposed [6] that the same system could be used as a memory of the future and thus anticipate consequences of its actions. Such a model of prefrontal cortex, cooperating with a model of posterior cortex was implemented [5] to organize the behavior of an autonomous agent with regard to several motivations.

Discussion

The purpose of this paper was to propose a rapid overview of some recent biologically inspired models that exploit current knowledge about memory systems in the brain. We wish to underline here that these models are not only theoretical but that they were really implemented and used for the navigation of simulated or real robots. Even if it was not possible to gather all these data in this paper, the reader is invited to refer to the references to get more details about underlying equations or performances. Beyond these important data, the goal of this paper was to show that neurosciences accumulate more and more knowledge about brain functioning that can be more and more easily integrated in operational softwares. From this partial overview, it also appears that modelling the brain necessarily consists in designing cooperating modules, each performing a specific kind of information processing and memorization, as a result of phylogenesis. Thus, the cerebral framework prevents from only focusing on specific local mechanisms and underlines a distributed view of cooperating systems, from which new robust mechanisms can emerge. What we have proposed here is that wondering about memorization capabilities can be a fruitful way to build such an artificial cerebral system.

References

1. D. H. Ballard. Cortical connections and parallel processing: Structure and function. *The Behavioral and Brain Sciences*, 9:67–129, 1986.
2. Y. Burnod. *An adaptive neural network the cerebral cortex*. Masson, 1989.
3. R. Caminiti, P. Johnson, C. Galli, S. Ferraina, and Y. Burnod. Making arm movements within different parts of space: the premotor and motor cortical representation of a coordinate system for reaching to visual targets. In *J. Neurosci.*, volume 11, pages 1182–1197, 1991.
4. H. Frezza-Buet and F. Alexandre. Selection of action with a cortically-inspired model. In *Seventh European Workshop on Learning Robots*, pages 13–21, 1998.
5. H. Frezza-Buet and F. Alexandre. Modeling prefrontal functions for robot navigation. In *International Joint Conference on Artificial Neural Networks*, 1999.
6. J. M. Fuster. Frontal lobe and the cognitive foundation of behavioral action. In A.R. Damasio, H. Damasio, and Y. Christen, editors, *Neurobiology of Decision-Making*. Springer, 1996.
7. P. Gaussier, C. Joulain, J. P. Banquet, S. Lepêtre, and A. Revel. The visual homing problem: an example of robotics/biology cross fertilization. In *Robotics and Autonomous Systems*, 1999.
8. J. Hertz, A. Krogh, and R. Palmer. Introduction to the theory of neural computation. Addison Wesley, 1991.
9. J. J. Hopfield. Neural networks and physical systems with emergent collective computational abilities. In *Proceedings of the National Academy of Sciences, USA*, pages 2554–2558, 1982.
10. T. Kohonen. *Self-Organization and Associative Memory*. Springer-Verlag, 1988.
11. J. Murre. *Hippocampus*, volume 6, chapter 6, TraceLink : A model of Amnesia and Consolidation of Memory, pages 675–684. David G. Amaral and Menno P. Witter, 1996.
12. R. O'Reilly and J. W. Rudy. Conjunctive representations in learning and memory : principles of cortical and hippocampal function. Technical report, Department of Psychology, University of Colorado, 1999.
13. N. Rougier and F. Alexandre. Spatial knowledge transfer between models of hippocampus and associative cortex. In *International Joint Conference on Neural Networtks*. IJCNN, July 1999.
14. L. R. Squire. Memory and the hippocampus: A synthesis from findings with rats, monkeys and humans. *Psychological Review*, 99(2):195–231, 1992.

Optimization as a Multistage Decision Making

Jiří Pospíchal

Department of Mathematics, Slovak Technical University, 812 37 Bratislava, Slovakia

pospich@cvt.stuba.sk

Abstract: An optimization approach is investigated, which uses an iterated two-stage process. The first stage is based on information from the past history of the search, while the second stage is based on a step-vise build-up of a solution using a heuristic. The approach is exemplified on a traveling salesman problem with the first stage using simulated annealing and hill climbing, while the second stage is using tour construction heuristics like nearest neighbor addition, cheapest insertion, and a newly designed "second nearest neighbor". The results suggest, that for the TSP the approach might be viable for more regular graphs.

Keywords: optimization, construction heuristic, simulated annealing, hillclimbing, TSP

1 Introduction

Every optimization, which is not equivalent to a blind search (where any feasible solution is selected for evaluation with the same probability), must employ some additional information to produce a new promising solution. There are two kinds of such an information. One kind can be obtained from some sort of a heuristic, which can be regarded as an optimization of a function related in some way to the target optimized function. Such a related function is normally not perfect for finding a globally optimal solution of our target function, but since it is usually much easier to evaluate, it might be at least useful for finding a local optimum of our target function. The other kind of information can be obtained from the past history of the search, that is from some kind of information processing of the already investigated solutions and their quality.

Both these kinds of information can be used in an optimization method, where a general structure of each prospective solution can be broken down to its components. In a case of a problem with a solution represented by a suitable permutation, the components are natural numbers. The investigated approach will build up a prospective solutions stepwise. Each step would be chosen quasirandomly, taking into account already filled in components of the solution and combining this information with either a heuristic function, or with an information extracted from the already investigated solutions. Quasirandom selection means, that several prospective possibilities will be evaluated by a fitness for each future step and the resulting step would be chosen with a probability proportional to its currently calculated fitness. Similar approach was already used in [6,8].

2 TSP and construction heuristics

The above described approach is tested on the traveling salesperson problem. The data consist of a finite complete graph composed of N vertices (cities) and $N(N-1)/2$ edges (connections). Each edge $e=[i,j]$, connecting the vertices – cities i and j, is evaluated by a positive number $d_{i,j}$ (called a weight or distance between cities i and j). The objective is to find a hamiltonian cycle (that is, a cycle passing through all the vertices) of the minimum total weight. This is determined by a permutation P of N objects $P=(p_1,p_2,...,p_N)$ that minimizes the quantity

$$D(P) = \sum_{i=1}^{N-1} d(p_i, p_{i+1}) + d(p_N, p_1) \tag{1}$$

Only the symmetric TSP was considered, where traveling from city p_i to city p_j has the same distance as traveling from p_j to p_i, $d(p_i,p_j)=d(p_j,p_i)$ for $1\leq i,j\leq N$. There exist many popular tour construction heuristics that can find near-optimal solutions in a short time. The most popular are nearest neighbor [3,4], nearest insertion, nearest merger, cheapest insertion, farthest insertion [4], Christofides algorithm, greedy algorithm [3], Clarke and Wright approach [2,3], most of which running times range from $O(N^2)$ to $O(N^3)$. We shall use only the nearest neighbor, the cheapest isertion and a new second nearest neighbor.

A sequence of vertices $p_1,p_2,...,p_N$ is called a *nearest neighbor* heuristic tour starting at randomly chosen vertex p_1 when a distance between p_i and p_{i+1} is equal to $\min\{d(p_i,p_j) \mid i\leq j\leq N\}$ for each $1\leq i<N$. It can be found by the following heuristic: 1. Start at vertex p_1. 2. Among all vertices not yet visited, choose as a vertex which is nearest to the current vertex. Repeat this step until all vertices have been visited.

A *cheapest insertion* heuristic tour starting at p_1 is obtained by the following heuristic: 1. Start with a tour consisting of p_1 with a self-loop. 2. Find a vertex p_k not on the tour which can be inserted between two neighboring vertices p_i and p_j on the tour in the cheapest possible way, so that $\min\{ d(p_i,p_k) + d(p_j,p_k) - d(p_i,p_j) \mid i\leq j\leq tour\_length$ and $k>tour\_length\}$. Insert this vertex between two neighboring vertices on the tour in the cheapest possible way. Repeat until the tour is complete.

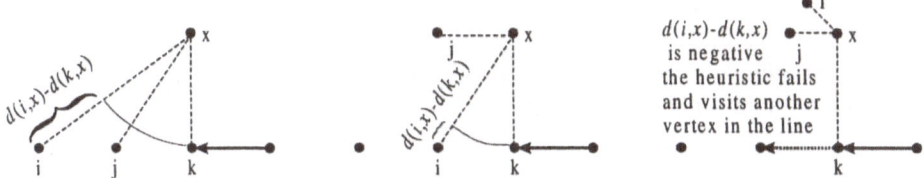

Figure 1. A scheme explaining a second nearest neighbor heuristic. The considered city is x and its nearest neighbours are j and i. Suppose, that there are cities in line and one or two cities like x farther outside the line. The nearest neighbor heuristic would fail to visit the aside cities first. The second nearest neighbor fails, only when a cluster of aside cities is greater than 2.

A *second nearest neighbor* heuristic tour designed here by the author is obtained by the following process: start with a tour consisting of p_1. Find a vertex p_k not on the tour so that the difference between its second nearest non-visited neighbor and the last vertex on the tour is maximal, and join it to the last vertex of the tour. Accounting for this second distance should prevent leaving a single city or a couple of non-visited cities in an enclosure of visited cities, so that the distance of the single step to and from that city would become too large, when it would have to be visited at the end (see Fig. 1).

3 Stochastic extension of heuristics

Each of the heuristics evaluates all the possibilities of the next step. The first simple extension of this process is a decision, where to go next, taken not deterministically, but by a roulette wheel known from the genetic algorithms [1]. Each prospective next step i would be given a fitness $f(i)$ based on its evaluation, and a decision would be taken pseudorandomly, with steps selected with a probability based on their fitness, so that

$$Pr\,obability\_of\_next\_step(i) = \frac{f(i)}{\sum_{j=1}^{all\ feasible\ next\ steps} f(j)} \qquad (2)$$

The recalculation of the evaluation of the steps into their fitness can be done in various ways [1]. In our calculations we ordered the evaluations decreasingly, resp. increasingly, depending whether we looked for a maximum (in the second nearest neighbor) or for minimum (nearest neighbor, cheapest insertion), and then we give each step (i.e. a vertex) a fitness starting with 1.0, which was multiplied by a decreasing factor (for a square grid we used a steep factor $s=0.01$) if the previous step was better than the current one. The approach actually uses a greater dispersion of result values for a multiple start. The average results for pseudorandom decisions are worse, but the best results, which we are after, are better, so that for a single run of a heuristic it is not preferable to use pseudorandom decision, while it is preferable for multiple runs with a selection of the best solution. The recalculation of evaluations of steps into fitness must be fitted to a type of problem. For a square grid positions of cities it is suitable to choose just the best values, but for a randomly distributed cities the pseudorandom decision is more suitable, see Fig. 2.

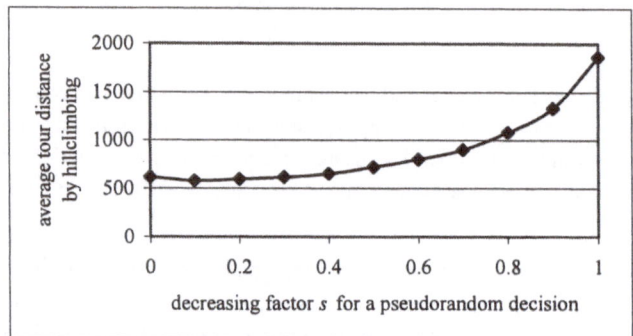

Figure 2. Results for a hillclimbing combined with a nearest neighbor heuristic and applied to 49 cities randomly distributed on a 100*100 square. The results are averages from 100 runs, where each run lasted 1000 "perturbations". On the horizontal axis are values of a factor controlling randomness of the city selection. Factor 0 means strict nearest neighbor acceptance, while factor 1 means a totally random choice. The best results for the current settings were achieved for decreasing factor equal to 0.1.

The other adaptation of a heuristic will be the same one as was already used in [6], that is a perturbation or mutation used for simulated annealing approach and hillclimbing. This adaptation uses a first part of the previous solution for a starting point, that is, we generate random integer k smaller than the maximum length of the previous path, and the part of permutation - path $p_1, p_2, ..., p_k$ is copied into a current path, so that with the current path we do not have to start from the scratch, but we can build up on a part of the previous good solution, starting from the kth vertex.

4 Simulated annealing and hillclimbing

The above described approaches outline methods of obtaining a totally new solution, or a new solution from an old one. Whether such a new solution would be accepted as a valid solution and in which way, that will be decided by another optimization algorithm, which will include the described stepwise build-up of the solutions as a perturbation or mutation. Hillclimbing and simulated annealing will be used for this purpose [5,7]. Hillclimbing is implemented simply as an iterated procedure, which applies a perturbation to a current solution, and when the new solution is better, it replaces the current solution. The simulated annealing algorithm [5,7] is based on an analogy between annealing of solids and optimization problems. Metropolis designed the Monte Carlo Method [7], in which a small random perturbation of a state (or provisional solution of optimization) is generated, and its energy $E_{perturbed}$ (value) is compared with an energy $E_{current}$ (value) of current state (solution). The probability of acceptance is calculated by a formula

$$Pr(perturbed \leftarrow current) = \min(1, exp(-(E_{perturbed} - E_{current})/T) \qquad (3)$$

In order to achieve an equivalent of a thermal equilibrium for a given temperature T, this algorithm is repeated k_{max} times. Simulated annealing method is a sequence of Metropolis algorithms performed for a sequence of decreasing values of temperature. In the present examples there was used quite a primitive method of decreasing of a temperature $T:=\alpha*T$, with parameter α equal to 0.95. The initial temperature T_{max} was set to a value, where about a half of perturbed states would be accepted at the beginning, and the minimum temperature T_{min} was set low, so that termination was decided by a maximum value of 30 000 evaluations of total path distance during a single run. The only difference in comparison with a regular SA method is the perturbation algorithm, which changes from some randomly chosen point the whole "tail" of the permutation - solution.

5 Numerical results on a square grid

Simulated annealing and hillclimbing procedures were compared with a multiple start, when a solution is repeatedly constructed by a heuristic from afresh randomly chosen first vertex, and the iterations are stopped, when the known minimum is achieved. The numerical results are shown in tables 1 and 2. For testing purposes a city distribution on grids 5×5 to 10×10 was used, where the ideal minimum tour length is known. The slight discrepancy between odd and even number of cities, where for odd number of cities one edge must be crossways, shows also in the computational demands, which for odd number of vertices are only slightly greater than for the previous even number of grid vertices. Even though it may appear, that the multiple start is sometimes superior to the hillclimbing and simulated annealing, it is not so. Since the generation of a new path in hill climbing or simulated annealing in the average starts from an already half-constructed part of a solution, the computational requirements to finish it are also reduced to a half. To compare their computational demands with a multiple start procedure, their number of total path length evaluation must be divided by a half. For example, for 100 cities on a square grid the hillclimbing procedure helps to reduce the computational cost in comparison to multiple start to 746,69/(2*1248,73)=0.3. The fact, that a simulated annealing did not prove substantially better than a simple hillclimbing can be explained by the fact, that mostly only a few hundred perturbations were performed, which is a too small number for the simulated annealing to show its advantages. The newly designed "second nearest neighbor" heuristic might be of use for more regular graphs of a larger size, comparing with the cheapest insertion heuristic.

Table 1. Results for N cities on a square grid for cheapest insertion and a second neighbor heuristics (results are average no. of total path evaluations needed to achieve the ideal minimum length from 100 runs)

N	Cheapest insertion heuristic			Second neighbor heuristic		
	Sim. Ann.	Mult.	Hillclimb.	Sim. Ann.	Mult.	Hillclimb.
25	2,86	2,09	3,24	3,14	3,78	3,25
36	20,92	15,8	18,44	27,17	19,32	31,97
49	23,73	13,19	27,05	40,77	50,41	52,79
64	227,64	133,63	116,97	150,38	182,88	153,85
81	202,03	166,46	281,73	154,36	197,97	235,77
100	1657,46	1587,9	1655,54	920,85	1248,73	746,69

Table 2. Results for N cities on a square grid for nearest neighbor heuristics (iter. = average no. of total path evaluations from 100 runs; when the number exceeded 30000, the number of failures flr. was recorded and an average best achieved distance dist. from 10 calculations is given)

N	Nearest neighbor heuristic								
	Simul. Anneal.			Multiple start			Hillclimbing		
	iter.	flr.	dist.	iter.	flr.	dist.	iter.	flr.	dist.
25	248,09			358,47			185,37		
36	1129,55			3860,89			901,88		
49	4751,83			>30000	7	49,82	5120,3		
64	18753	4	64,52	>30000	9	65,92	20993	5	64,6
81	>30000	9	82,93	>30000	10	85,27	>30000	10	83,13
100	>30000	10	103,05	>30000	10	106,15	>30000	10	103,64

6 Conclusions

The results show, that if there is available a step-by-step constructive heuristic for a solution and the optimum for a more complicated case is wanted, it should be advisable to do two things: (1) Instead of a multiple start of the heuristic combine the heuristic with an evolutionary algorithm, for simpler cases the hillclimbing should do, for the more complicated cases it should be a simulated annealing or possibly a genetic algorithm, where the mutation or perturbation means copying a first part of a solution (of random length) and construction of the rest by a heuristic. (2) If the solution is not a regular one like cities on a square grid, where a construction heuristic may be perfectly compatible with a local optimization, but it is more difficult, like randomly distributed cities, the heuristic should be given more of a stochastic nature too, so that it finds worse average solutions, but better "best achieved" solutions. The newly designed "second nearest neighbor heuristic" proved to be better than cheapest insertion heuristic for a more complicated studied case. The paper does not pretend to describe an ideal approach to traveling salesman problem without other restrictions, for that purpose it would be probably more advisable to use memetic genetic algorithms, which combine global optimization with local search [10]. It is difficult to compare fairly the described approach with other algorithms, because the used constructions of solutions are much more demanding than those for a simple genetic algorithm. However, in comparison with the standard genetic algorithm from [9], the above described approach required several orders of magnitude more evaluations of a total path distance to achieve results of similar quality.

Acknowledgements: This work was supported by the grants # 1/7336/20 and # 1/5229/98 of the Slovak Republic Scientific Grant Agency

References

(1) Baeck, T., Fogel, D.B., Michalewicz, Z. (Eds.) (1997): Handbook of evolutionary computation. IOP Publishing, Bristol

(2) Clarke, G., Wright, J.W. (1964): Scheduling of vehicles from a central depot to a number of delivery points. Operations Res. 12, 568-581

(3) Johnson, D.S., McGeoch, L.A. (1997): The Traveling Salesman Problem: A Case Study in Local Optimization. In: Aarts, E.H.L., Lenstra, J.K. (Eds.): Local Search in Combinatorial Optimization. John Wiley, London, 215-310

(4) Kindervater, G.A.P., Lenstra, J.K., Shmoys D.B. (1989): The parallel complexity of TSP heuristics. Journal of Algorithms 10(2), 249-270

(5) Kvasnička, V., Pospíchal, J. (1996): Simulated annealing. Communications in Mathematical Chemistry (MATCH) 34, 7-49

(6) Kvasnička, V., Pospíchal, J. (2000): Simulated annealing construction of shortest path on incomplete graphs. Intended for Journal of Intelligent Manufacturing

(7) Otten, R.H.J.M., Van Ginneken, L.P.P.P. (1989): The annealing algorithm. Kluwer, Boston, MA

(8) Pospíchal, J. (2000): Multistage decision making for an automaton by simulated annealing. In: Proceedings of Abstracts from The Fifth International Conference FSTA 2000 On Fuzzy Sets Theory And Its Applications, Liptovský Ján 31.1.-4.2.2000, Slovakia, 148, a revised version sent for publication to J. Soft Computing

(9) Wall, M. (1996): GAlib: A C++ Genetic Algorithm Library, program ex26.C. Available at the internet address http://lancet.mit.edu/galib-2.4/, adapted from T. Grueninger, (c) 1994-1996 Massachusetts Institute of Technology

(10) Watson, J. P., Ross, C., Eisele, V., Denton, J., Bins, J., Guerra, C., Whitley, D., Howe, A. (1998): The Traveling Salesrep Problem, Edge Assembly Crossover, and 2-opt. In: Eiben, A.E., Bäck, T., Schoenauer, M., Schwefel, H.-P. (Eds.): Parallel Problem Solving from Nature V, LNCS 1498, Springer Verlag, 823-832

Can Computers Be Conscious?
Methodological Considerations from the Standpoint of the Humanities

Marek Dobeš

Institute for Social Sciences, Slovak Academy of Sciences, Karpatská 5, 04001
Košice, Slovak Republic
e-mail: dobes@saske.sk

Abstract: Computer science and psychology can come together by resolving the problem of consciousness. We can think of functional models which attempt to copy the properties of the human consciousness or evolutionary models that try to formulate the basic concepts and let more complex qualities emerge from them. Basically, there are no fundamental obstacles hindering us from modelling consciousness in silico.

1 Introduction

Consciousness is a phenomena that is very familiar to any of us, one that we regularly experience, yet it is one of the greatest mysteries today's science is faced with.

Consciousness became a centre of focus especially of cognitive science – science that encompasses psychology, computer science, philosophy, neurophysiology, linguistics in an attempt to explain cognitive processes.

Myself, being a psychologist interested in computer science, I speculate in this article about the ways psychology and computer science can together accelerate the research of this phenomena.

I consider basically two approaches towards modelling (and in this way explaining) consciousness in silico: Functional approach which focuses on modelling the features that are known about human consciousness regardless of its real structure and Evolutionary approach which attempts to model the workings of consciousness by modelling the basic parts that are hypothesized about as being fundamental for consciousness.

In this paper I will provide more views of consciousness. However, if not stated differently, I use term consciousness as the ability of the system to be aware of itself and its impact on the environment, all of which allows it to behave more effectively and flexibly.

2 Functional approach

Much has been written on the subject of consciousness in the past few years. It is possible to sort the views on what is consciousness into several levels of complexity:

At the basic level consciousness is a state where subject is able to react to the environment in any way. Such a reaction can be either a change in its internal state – memory, learning, emotional arousal or production of any behaviour. Subject is thus aware of the environment, however, it is neither aware of itself being aware, or aware of its own existence.

Harvey (1997) uses the term consciousness in four different contexts, from which two are applicable at this basic stage. We also consider the ability of computers to exhibit the consciousness in any of them:

consciousness1 as a state of functioning of the system, when it is able to process and react to the given stimuli. In general, computers have no problems exhibiting this kind of consciousness.

consciousness2 as capability of the inner state of the system to be influenced by the incoming information and adapt to it. Neural networks (which care for the change in the inner state of the system) combined with tools of evolutionary programming (taking care of the adaptation of the structure of the system) can exhibit this quality.

At the next stage, we may define conscious entities as those who are capable of being aware of their own actions. That is, independently from whether they see themselves as specific entity or just a part of the environment, they are capable of taking the output of their activity (mental or physical) as an input for their further information processing. This also forms base for a very important feature of conscious systems – making internal models of their possible actions and deciding among them. As soon as I learn about the relation between my actions and impact they have upon the environment (which, in turn, has impact upon me), I become capable of more than reflexive behaviour.

It is possible to design a computer programme that will exhibit such a feature. First, it should know the function through which environment determines its effectiveness and function via which its action influences its environment. Upon deciding about its future action, system tests various alternatives of its action – how such action affects the key aspects of the environment that affect the system. In this way system develops an internal or "mental" model of itself and environment which is one of basic characteristics as well as functions of consciousness (Velmans, 1998). Rules that govern relation between the system and its environment should not necessarily be perfectly known to the system. However, using feedback on its actions, system can learn from the feedback and modify the knowledge of the rules and consequently its further action. Such a learning can be achieved on the analogy of the way genetic algorithms work – several alternatives for rules are presented and the population of rules that leads to the best results is used. Such a process can be observed with humans going from implicitly learned rules to the explicit ones. People start designing implicit theories of how the world around them works and continually test those theories against the reality. Successful theories then form a framework for explicit knowledge about the world.

At this level of complexity we may mention Harvey's (1997) further classification of the views of consciousness:

consciousness3 means the ability to restructure the information into the meaningful output, e.g. resume a past experience. Here, the word „meaningful" is tricky as the meaning is dependent from the culture the subject dwells in. Thus, in principle, computers can be conscious also in this third context as they are able to abstract some information from the data (using factor analysis, neural networks etc.). The problem is they are not equipped with the culture dependent information and this does not often does not allow them to produce a „meaningful" output, leaving it up to the native humans.

consciousness 4 as the ability to „feel", subjectively experience the outer stimuli. Explanation of such a conscious experience or "qualia" represents for the philosophers of the mind (e.g. Chalmers, 1996) a „hard" problem, as until recently no neural correlates of this quality were known in the human brain. Velmans (1998) notices that such feelings can be results of the goodness-of-fit of currently focused on material with prior material stored in long-term memory. He mentions the resemblance with Hopfield's computation in which the goodness-of-fit of number of mutually interacting nodes is condensed into a single index.

We may mention one more view of consciousness:

consciousness 5 as the capability of the subject to be aware of its own existence. This level of consciousness is so far found only in humans and to some extent in higher primates. The last two kinds of consciousness are the challenge for the computer science. Attempts to model them can shed new light on understanding of the human brain.

3 Evolutionary approach

Consciousness surely emerged as a new phenomena with higher primates. However, its emergence can be traced down to several smaller steps, the fact that gives us new clues on how to model it in silico.

In the psychological studies of how human consciousness emerges Piaget's findings play a key role. Piaget postulates that innate motoric activity transforms into mental activity. Minds of children are being built on the basis of so called schemas – aspects or objects of the environment. Such schemas gradually generalize and incorporate more and more of novel situations (Harter, 1973).

To teach computer form concepts is not really a difficult task. Relatively simple neural network can be made to distinguish among basic geometrical shapes or even between small and big objects. Thus a concept or schema of a "triangle" or of anything "small" can exist in the computer. At higher level, such schemas combine into more complex entities – a network can be created associating networks for shapes and qualities and we can move towards working with "small square" or "quickly moving circle". Neural networks are able to generalize, i.e. select the most important characteristics of the incoming pattern and suppress the others, and categorize, i.e. form groups of objects that differ one from another. These are qualities observed also in cognitive development of children (Vasta, Haith, Miller, 1992).

By joining together partial networks or functional nodes a way can be made free to start the emergence of new qualities.

4 How should an artificial model of consciousness look like?

Self-modifying structure is necessary, enabling the model to optimize its workings. System can thus modify not only its contents (within the framework of the neural networks this can be a set of weights) but also its structure (network architecture, learning algorithm, etc.). Interesting research has been made combining various programming techniques (neural networks, genetic programming) to allow a neural network to adapt to the problem it is solving.

Changing basic structure of the model makes it possible for new qualities to arise. It is still a problem to actually understand how characteristics of a neural network influence its effectiveness. System that could produce populations of various networks suited for various problems, can form a base for categorisation (again, a neural network can be used to filter the parameters of population of neural networks) of neural networks extending their application in technical and natural sciences towards the humanities.

As for the model to be „human like" it is necessary to develop an interface that allows computer to acquire the part of data relevant for humans (develop kind of meta-language which supplies the computer system with the knowledge that humans naturally know). Such an interface would enable computers to learn from the cultural sources like electronic books and newspapers.

5 Software models of consciousness

There are attempts to develop software capable of modelling some levels of consciousness. Sun (1996) reports about CLARION, a system consisting of encoder of explicit declarative knowledge, encoder of implicit procedural knowledge and episodic memory.

Other systems have been development for visual consciousness, Yehouda (1994) provides a model explaining phenomena like free will.

One interesting model, based upon the Baars's Global Workspace Theory is presented by Franklin and Graesser (1999). They understand consciousness as a cognitive process that is necessary to solve complex tasks. When subconscious information processing in brain is not able to solve a task, more subconscious modules activate simultaneously and thus reach the critical threshold necessary for activation of consciousness. Consciousness thus enables a person to perform tasks which involve various areas in the brain and acts as a global workspace. It simply interconnects more resources and thus a more complex tasks can be dealt with.

6 Conclusion

The function of consciousness in humans is still not fully understood. Clear evolutionary advantage of consciousness is in the ability to plan actions and behave above the level of a mere reflex. Also if we accept the thesis of consciousness as a way to allocate more cognitive resources, it enables conscious beings to carry out more demanding tasks. The ability of conscious experience (or qualia) still does not bring any apparent advantage. It may be just a by-product of evolution of higher cognitive processes or a kind of emotional arousal that accompanies perception.

No fundamental obstacles seem to prevent us from making artificial systems conscious in the future. If we were capable of modelling consciousness in computers, it would help the mankind in several ways. Understanding of ourselves would increase. Computers would be capable of more complex tasks than before, they would be able to pursue programmed goals independently – a quality which is indispensable everywhere where people can not be directly present to make decisions. Exploration of our inner universe can thus in turn help us to explore more of the universe around us, exploration that is so far limited by the fragile biological structure of humans.

References

Chalmers, D. J. (1996) Das Rätsel des bewussten Erlebens. Spektrum der Wissenschaft, 40-47.

Franklin, S., Graesser, A. (1999) A Software Agent Model of Consciousness. Consciousness and Cognition, 8, 285-301.

Harter, S. (1973) Piaget's Theory of Intellectual Development: The Changing World of the Child. In: Zigler, E.F., Child, I.L. (eds) Socialization and Personality Development, Addison-Wesley, London.

Harvey, I. (1997) Evolving Robot Consciousness: The Easy Problems and the Rest. (University of Sussex Working Paper).

Sun, R. (1996) Learning, Action and Consciousness: A Hybrid Approach toward Modelling Consciousness. (The University of Alabama Working Paper).

Vasta, R., Haith, M. M., Miller, S. A. (1992) Child Psychology: The Modern Science. John Wiley and Sons, New York.

Velmans, M. (1998) Introduction to the Science of Consciousness. In: Velmans, M. (ed.) The Science of Consciousness, Routledge, London.

Yehouda, H. (1994) The Way Human Cognition is Implemented in the Human Brain. http://www.yehouda.com/

Part 4

Hybrid Systems

GA-FIS for Dynamic Environment

Radek Matoušek, Pavel Ošmera and Jan Roupec

Institute of Automation and Computer Science, Brno University of Technology, Technická 2, 616 69 Brno, Czech Republic

{matousek, osmera, roupec} @ uai.fme.vutbr.cz

Abstract - Applications of Genetic Algorithms (GAs) for optimization problems are widely known as well as their advantages and disadvantages in comparison with classical numerical methods. This article discusses GA possibilities for search of the time variously optimum. The classical haploid GA versus new designed GA-FIS (GA with Fuzzy Inference System) was tested. A balance between the utilization of the whole space and the detailed searching of some parts can be adapted to pressure of selection and recombination operators. This balance is critical for a GA behavior, because the operators have a direct influence on the GA convergence. The GA-FIS uses the adaptive change of GA operators during the run of a GA. Statistic methods are used for appraisal of affectivity of GA-FIS.

Keywords: Genetic Algorithms, GA-FIS, Fuzzy Setting of GA Parameters, Statistic methods

1 Introduction

The setting of GA parameters is often a seriously complicated procedure because it must meet two contradictory requirements:

- to search up the whole space
- to search some parts of the space in detail

A balance between the utilization of the whole space and the detailed searching of some parts can be adapted to pressure of selection and recombination operators. This balance is critical for a GA behavior. For this reason, it is very important to understand the influence of the selection and recombination operators on the GA efficiency. The operators have a direct influence on the GA convergence.

In our research we tested the GA with fuzzy inference system, denoted as GA-FIS, versus classical haploid GA. Artificial dynamic environment was used. GA-FIS is original developed method for dynamic setting of the GA parameters. GA-FIS represents a part of our present work in the area of genetic algorithms and heuristic optimization methods. The full description of this algorithm is in

192

references [1,3]. We were also inspired by the article [4]. In [4] the original diploid GA for optimization in dynamic environment was used. In this paper we compared the classical GA behavior versus GA-FIS. The statistical approach was used for analyzing the results obtained.

2 Genetic Algorithms with FIS

The GAs was used a generation model of GA [2]. The short formal description of the GA is:

$$P_{n+1} = f(P_n, \xi_n), \quad \xi \in (S, C, M) \tag{1}$$

Where: P...population; ξ ...a set of GA operators (S ...selection, C ...crossover and M...mutation); n ...number of generation (iteration)

Fuzzy Inference System – FIS is used for the fuzzy control of the GA parameters. The following properties must be determined for applications of FIS to control the GA:

- input values
- model of FIS

This extended GA (so called GA-FIS) is shown in Figure 1. The setting of FIS depends on the expert and represents a subjective point of view.

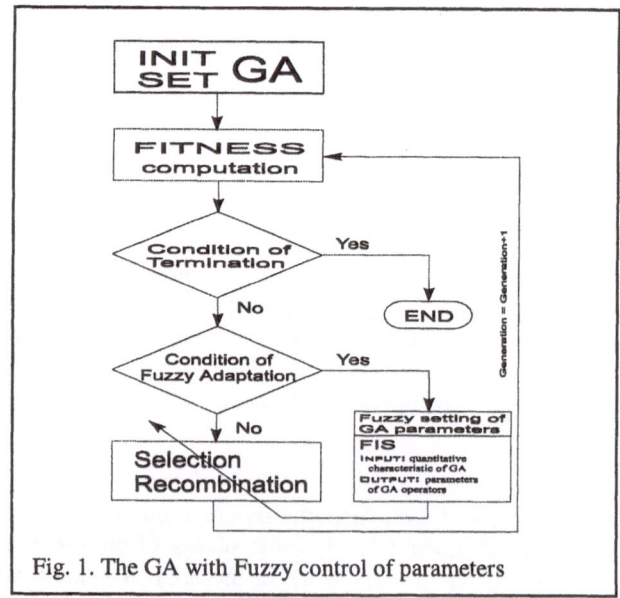

Fig. 1. The GA with Fuzzy control of parameters

3 Dynamic Environment

In order to demonstrate the effectiveness and robustness of the GA-FIS, we used a simple dynamic objective function (2) shown in picture 2:

$$f(x, p) = -e^{-m(x-p)^2} \cdot \cos(\omega(x - p))$$

(2)

Where: x ... independent variable, p ... "time" dependent parameter show shift on the x-axes with size of step $sStep$, $m>0$, ω ... a constant parameter

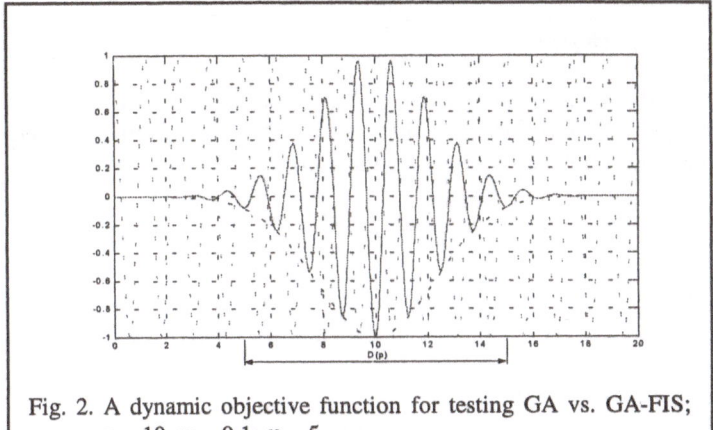

Fig. 2. A dynamic objective function for testing GA vs. GA-FIS; p = 10, m = 0.1; ω = 5

The objective function $f(x,p)$ has one global minimum for each value of p, $f(x_{opt},p) = -1$ and many local minimum determined by parameters m, ω. Parameter p represents the x-shift of the function and responds on the periodic change in the given range $D(p)$. The values of parameters used for the testing are shown in tab.1:

Global parameters for test function $f(x,p)$			
t, $t{\equiv}n$	independent discrete value interpret a time		
$p{\in}D(p)$	$D(p){\equiv}$ [5 15], k...number division of interval $D(p)/2$; k={1,2...10}		
$sStep$	$sStep{=}D(p)/(2k){=}\{5;2.5;1.66;1;25;1;0.83;0.71;0;625;0.55;0.5\}$		
ω, $\omega{=}5$	frequency of cosine part of function $f(x,p)$		
m, $m{=}0.1;1$	coefficient of exponential part of function $f(x,p)$		
Global parameters for haploid GA and GA-FIS			
S,C,M	Expert setting	S,C,M	Fuzzy setting
Size of population	50	Size of population	50
encoding	binary, gray; 16 bit/p.	encoding	binary, gray; 16bit/p.
max#Iter	400	max#Iter	400

Table 1. Values of given parameters

4. Statistic Analysis

If you want to say any results about process with random behavior, then you must use any statistic. Several statistical methods were used for interpreting of our results. 10 runs of the GA and the GA-FIS were repeated 30 times for all values of the k parameter shown in Figure 3. In this figure the o-dot points represent the MSE (Mean Square Error) of the GA and the x-dot points represent the MSE of the GA-FIS.

$$MSE = \frac{1}{max\#Iter} \sum_{i=1}^{max\#Iter} (y_i - \hat{y})^2 \qquad (3)$$

Where: max#Iter...maximum number of generation; the termination condition of one run of GA resp. GA-FIS, y_i... the vector of the best results of an algorithm in the i-th generation (iteration), $\hat{y} = -1$...the value of the global extreme

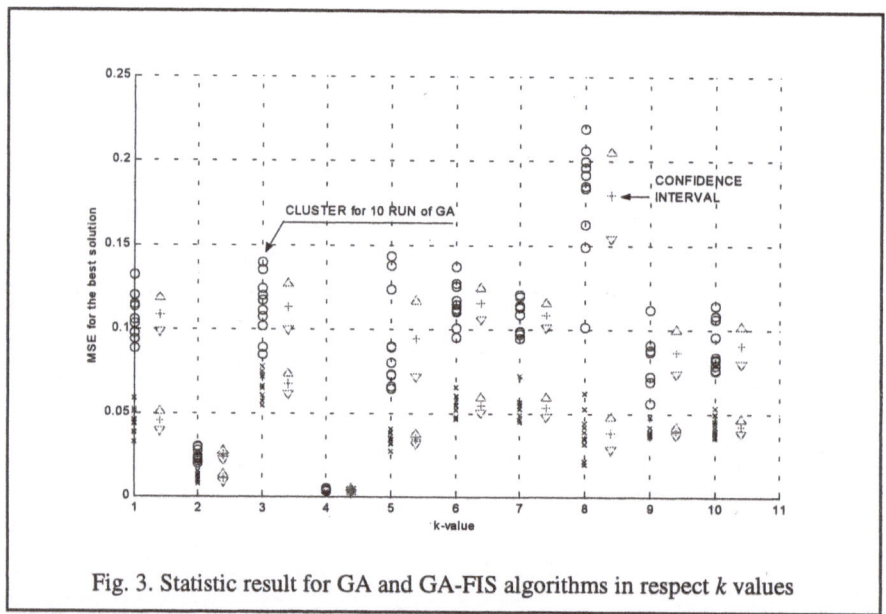

Fig. 3. Statistic result for GA and GA-FIS algorithms in respect k values

The result of the statistic computations shows the essentially better quality of the solution for GA-FIS for our case. The 1-sample t-confidence interval (CI) was used for the statistic interpretation. A confidence interval is a range (interval) that includes the population mean value.

The confidence interval is:

$$Left = \bar{x} - t_{n-1}(\alpha/2)\frac{x\sigma_{n-1}}{\sqrt{n}}, \qquad Right = \bar{x} + t_{n-1}(\alpha/2)\frac{x\sigma_{n-1}}{\sqrt{n}} \qquad (4)$$

The Normal distribution of data sample is a precondition for t-CI test. The Kolmogorov test can be used to verify of this precondition.

5. Conclusion

In the first step we tested a normal distribution of data sample for both algorithms. Samples of data for this part of the test represent 50 runs of algorithms and present kind of the cluster as you can see in figure 3. The Kolmogorov test was used to test the null hypothesis that the population distribution of the data sample is drawn is a Normal distribution. Our results were positive for each sample of cluster. The calculated value of Kolmogorov test GV=0.082 is lower than critical table value KV(50)=0.127, and so the hypothesis that population distribution is normal is acceptable.

The second part of analysis was to determine the confidence interval for each cluster by means of equation (4). Table 2 corresponds with data samples in Figure 3. The level of significance is α=0.05 and the corresponding t-test table value is $t_{n-1}(\alpha/2) = 2.262$.

k	nStep	CI for GA			CI for GA-FIS			Intersection of CI
	5/k	mean	left	right	mean	left	right	
1	5.000	0.1088	0.0988	0.1188	0.0454	0.0397	0.0512	Negative
2	2.500	0.0248	0.0221	0.0274	0.0112	0.0092	0.0133	Negative
3	1.666	0.1137	0.1001	0.1273	0.0677	0.0617	0.0738	Negative
4	1.250	0.0045	0.0040	0.0050	0.0026	0.0023	0.0029	Negative
5	1.000	0.0945	0.0720	0.1170	0.0349	0.0320	0.0378	Negative
6	0.833	0.1157	0.1063	0.1251	0.0550	0.0503	0.0598	Negative
7	0.714	0.1083	0.1010	0.1156	0.0540	0.0481	0.0598	Negative
8	0.625	0.1799	0.1542	0.2056	0.0384	0.0284	0.0483	Negative
9	0.555	0.0868	0.0736	0.1000	0.0395	0.0370	0.0421	Negative
10	0.500	0.0909	0.0800	0.1018	0.0428	0.0385	0.0470	Negative

Table 2. Confidential interval for GA and GA-FIS

Because all intersection of CI for given pair of the clusters (k has the same value for the both GAs) are negative, we can say that GA-FIS is significantly better for search of optimum better than classical GA. This statement is based on statistic analysis with a level of significance 95% (α=0.05). As one can see the position of data clusters corresponds with the test function and the size of the step. We can conclude that the shape and the position of cluster respond the difficulty of optimization for the tested algorithm.

The generalization of our result for another multimodal function in dynamic environment is questionable, because many degrees of freedom are in this exercise (dynamic environment, shape of function, freedom design of FIS or GA-FIS defined in work [1]. The analysis of these influences will be the topic of the future work.

Acknowledgement

This work has been supported by MŠMT grant No: CZ J22/98 260000013.

References

[1] Matoušek, R. (1999) "Využití vybraných metod UI pro optimalizaci regresního modelu s vazební podmínkou", Teze disertační práce, ÚAI VUT-FSI Brno, Czech Republic, (In Czech)

[2] Goldberg, D. E. (1989) "Genetic Algorithms in Search, Optimization and Machine Learning", Addison-Wesley

[3] Matoušek, R., Ošmera, P. (1999) "A Fuzzy Setting of GA Parameters", Proceeding of 7th Zittau Fuzzy Colloquium 1999, p.154-160

[4] Ošmera, P., Kvasnička, V., Pospíchal, J. (1997) "Genetic Algorithms with Diploid Chromosomes", Proceedings of MENDEL'97, p. 111-116

Genetic Method for Optimization of Fuzzy Neural Networks Structure

Vladimír Olej[1], Jiří Křupka[2]

[1] Matej Bel University, School of Finance, Department of Information Systems, Tajovského 10, 974 01 Banská Bystrica, Slovak Republic, E-mail: <u>olej@ financ. umb.sk</u>

[2] Military Academy, Faculty of Air Defence, Department of Technical Support Systems and Automation, 031 01 Liptovský Mikuláš, Slovak Republic, E-mail: krupka@valm.sk

Abstract: The paper presents a possibility of application of genetic algorithms for an optimization of fuzzy neural networks structure and its application to pattern recognition. A genetic method to generate a fuzzy neural network, which has both structure and synapse weights adequate for a given task is proposed.

Keywords: Optimization, neural networks, fuzzy neural networks, fuzzy sets, genetic algorithms, pattern recognition.

1. Introduction

Neural networks (NNs) [1] and fuzzy neural networks (FNNs) [2] can be used (in addition to other fields of artificial and computational intelligence) for analysis of decision processes of discrete systems [3] and for pattern recognition [4]. Evolution stochastic optimization algorithms (ESOAs) [1] present a set of algorithms that use evolution processes for solving problems, search and optimization in complicated systems. Choice of the best algorithm is a compromise between time of computing and correctness of result. Calculation was often stopped in a local extreme and did not achieve required global extreme during scanning of multidimensional space. Search for solutions of these problems results in usage of ESOAs, that look for optimal solution by stochastic scanning of solution space. Genetic algorithms (GAs) are robust adaptive optimization methods based on biological principles. They represent an efficient technique of learning based on dynamics of the evolution [5 to 10]. Fuzzy neural networks employing basic fuzzy logic operations are introduced in [4]. In the learning process (by GAs), they enable to shorten the time of method convergence towards the global maximum. Crisp numbers express input and output values of FNNs. Input values in the FNNs formulation can be realized as fuzzy sets [11], outputs as membership function values into the given fuzzy set.

The paper presents a possibility of exploitation of GAs for optimization FNN structure and its application to pattern recognition. Generally, there can be several approaches to generation structure of NNs (FNNs) based on GAs. Two of them are used most frequently. In the first approach, NNs (FNNs) are only generated from a genotype while in the second approach from two genotypes. These methods make use of GAs to determine [12 to 16]: synapse weights NNs (FNNs), where their structure is known in advance or structure of NNs (FNNs) and synapse weights.

2. Basic Notions

This proposal belongs to the second group of methods. These make use of GAs to determine structure and synapse weights NNs (FNNs). It is possible to characterise it in the following way [10 to 14]:

• It can work with general NNs (FNNs) [2,17,18,19]. It does not have any limitation for synapse weights between neurons. The synapse weights have one of three values (R, 0 and -R, where R is a set of real numbers) for NNs or they are from the interval [0,1] for FNNs.

• The type of each synapse is determined by its direction. The direction of synapse can be defined as forward character (the synapse goes out of the neuron and its type is 1), or as backward character (the synapse goes into the neuron and its type is -1), or cannot be defined (the synapse is not created and its type is 0). In NN (FNN) the neuron is represented by a genotype.

• The NNs and FNNs are created by an input as well as by hidden and output layers. The hidden layer can have more layers. Every layer contains some neurons that are connected by some synapses. Every synapse has its weight and every neuron has its threshold.

• The input neuron IN_i is connected to a neuron of the hidden layer (summation fuzzy neuron for FNNs [3,4]) H_j. Synapse weights between the input layer neuron IN_i and the hidden layer neuron H_j are v_{ij}. These weights obtained in the learning process by GAs acquire values from the set of real numbers R.

• Synapse weights between the hidden layer neuron H_i and the output layer (logical fuzzy neuron for FNNs [3,4]) OUT_j are w_{ij}. These weights obtained in the learning process by GAs acquire values from the interval $w_{ij} \in [0,1]$.

The idea of applying ESOAs to NNs (FNNs) is not new, and several researches have been performed in the last few years. Evolution stochastic optimization algorithms are stochastic algorithms during whole behaviour of computation, every time finding global extreme, but in independent on time. During computation using ESOAs it is important to pre-set conditions, when actual result from the algorithm is a global result of the solved problem. Therefore fitness η of a result is computed for each partial result. If fitness η satisfies the defined conditions, the algorithm is stopped and result from the algorithm is a solution of the defined problem. Difference between individual ESOAs is in the time of computing and in ability to achieve global extreme during scanning of results space. Generally, if time of computing is increased, the space of results is scanned better. According to the time of computing and ability to find the best result of configuration individual ESOAs can be the following [5 to 10]: Hill Climbing, Tabu Search, Simulated Annealing, Evolution Strategy, and Genetic Algorithms.

Distributed genetic algorithms (DGAs) [8] make use of GAs. Their task is to divide the population between defined number of independent GAs. All independent GAs work in a distributed system with the same task and with their own population. Distributed genetic algorithm provides exchange of the population parts between individual GAs. Conditions of this exchange (the number of individuals, the method of choice of individuals, etc.) are predetermined by the user. The fitness η is evaluated at every GA independently from the other GAs. It enables to decrease the time consuming of the convergence towards the global maximum.

3. Optimization of Neural Networks and Fuzzy Neural Networks Structure

Distributed genetic algorithm is used for a generation and an optimization of NNs (FNNs) structure. Its goal was an identification of input patterns and it made possible to decrease the time of computing because the generation and an optimization of NNs (FNNs) structure are time consuming. Creation of final phenotype, i.e. the NN (FNN) structure depends on a correct choice of rules. The rules are responsible for division of neurons. This formal description can be expressed in the following way [12 to 16]

$$G = \{R_1, R_2, \dots, R_i, \dots, R_n\}, \text{ where} \tag{1}$$

- R_i is i^{th} rules of genotype G;
- $R_i = \{D_1, D_2, \dots, D_j, \dots, D_m\}$ and D_j is j^{th} describe of ith rules;
- $D_j = \{g_1, g_2, \dots, g_k, \dots, g_l\}$ and g_k is k^{th} gene of jth describe.

For example, j^{th} describtion of ith rules can be defined in the following way

$$D_j = \{P_r, P_s, RP, \text{Threshold, Weight}\}, \text{ where} \tag{2}$$

- $P_r, P_s \in <0,n>$ they determine a creation of neuron according to rules. If it equals 0 then the neuron is not created;
- $RP \in <1,s>$ is a relative position and defines possible number of directions where neuron can be located;
- Threshold and Weight $\in <-R,R>$ for NNs or it is from the interval [0,1] for FNNs.

Then a maximal fitness η for input patterns can be defined in this way

$$\eta = \alpha * q + \beta * \gamma - \nu * \delta, \text{ where} \tag{3}$$

- α can be defined as (a number of output of FNN - 1) * (a number of output of FNN) * (a number of patterns);
- q is a number of correct classifications of input patterns;
- β is a number of outputs of FNN;
- γ is a number of outputs of FNN, where the deviation is smaller than the predetermined limit for all patterns;
- ν is 1/ (a number of patterns);

- δ is an error that is a sum of errors of actual value on the FNN output from the required value for all patterns and FNN output.

The algorithm of generation of FNN structure consists of three parts. The first part creates a defined number of neurons in general, the original genotype G can be divided into two new genotypes (P_r, P_s).

- If $P_r \neq 0 \wedge P_s \neq 0$, then from the genotype G two genotypes can be created;
- If $(P_r = 0 \wedge P_s \neq 0) \vee (P_r \neq 0 \wedge P_s = 0)$, then from the genotype G one genotype can be created;
- If $P_r = 0 \wedge P_s = 0$, then from the genotype G no genotype can be created.

A number of divisions are computed from the number of all neurons. It guarantees, that NN (FNN) structure can consist of any number of neurons. The new genotypes become the original genotype in the next step of algorithm. A fitness η is obtained when the division is finished. If fitness η is zero, then a genotype was not created and the generation of FNN structure finishes. If fitness η is not zero, then an arrangement of created neurons begins on an area. The second part arranges the created neurons on area d * d, where d provides that two neurons do not have the same position. The greatest problem is to determine distance v_n, where v_n is the distance between two neurons and it can be expressed as follows $v_n = (d / s_n)$, s_n is a number of really created neurons. Every neuron has information about its position according to the equation (2). An arrangement of created neurons depends on a size d. In the third part, connection of neurons is realized. It is dependent on a step of branching k. On this basis, size of neuron surrounding where the search will take place can be defined. The search will be realized around all neurons. A forward synapse has value equal 1 and a backward synapse has value equal −1. If both values are not found, then the research continues. The algorithm generates the first neuron in input layer, then in hidden or output layer, next it creates synapses, and it finishes by determining synapse weights.

A value of synapses weight is obtained from variable Weight and every neuron has this variable. If the step of branching k is small, then the size of surrounding of neuron is small, too. This neuron will be connected with a smaller quantity of neurons. It can influence fitness η (for complicated NNs (FNNs) structure) negatively. But it can influence a faster convergence of method (for simpler NNs (FNNs) structure), too. If the step of branching k increases, then the number of synapses (type 1 and −1) is bigger than the number of synapses (type 0).

4. Verification of Algorithm for Generation and Optimization of Fuzzy Neural Network Structure

The created FNN structure is going to test and evaluate after the third part of algorithm. On the basis of variable Weight and a list of synapses for each neuron is threshold for a neuron calculated. Next, the fitness η of NN (FNN) is calculated after a determination of the thresholds of individual neurons. Let the FNN structure be created according to Section 3 that it identifies input patterns O, R, C, P and noisy input patterns O', R', C', P', which are in Fig.1.

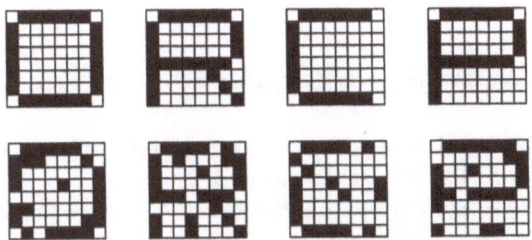

Fig.1. Input patterns for fuzzy neural network

These patterns are represented by some fuzzy sets $O, R, C, P, O', R', C', P'$. Next, let us consider the FNN which is composed of the input layer $IN = \{IN_1, IN_2, ... , IN_m\}$, the hidden layer $H = \{H_1, H_2, ... , H_n\}$ and the output layer $OUT = \{OUT_1, OUT_2, ... , OUT_b\}$ with these parameters: a full neuron number is 84 and $m = 64$, $b = 4$, $d = 50$ and $k = 7$.
From the values of a membership functions μ of outputs $OUT = \{OUT_1, OUT_2, OUT_3, OUT_4\}$ it follows, as we can see in Table 1: if input FNN is O (O'), then output OUT_1 represents degree of membership function to fuzzy sets O (O') with value $\mu_O = 0.98$ ($\mu_{O'} = 0.92$), output OUT_2 represents degree of membership function to fuzzy sets R (R') with value $\mu_R = 0.11$ ($\mu_{R'} = 0.16$) etc.

Table 1. Values of fuzzy neural network outputs for input patterns

Input Pattern	OUT_1		OUT_2		OUT_3		OUT_4	
	μ_O	$\mu_{O'}$	μ_R	$\mu_{R'}$	μ_C	$\mu_{C'}$	μ_P	$\mu_{P'}$
O (O')	**0.98**	**0.92**	0.11	0.16	0.19	0.12	0.18	0.21
R (R')	0.19	0.12	**0.96**	**0.88**	0.17	0.19	0.18	0.21
C (C')	0.12	0.19	0.21	0.22	**0.89**	**0.81**	0.19	0.28
P (P')	0.27	0.13	0.28	0.28	0.15	0.25	**0.89**	**0.85**

5. Conclusion

The paper proposes a method described in Section 3 that determines synapses by using an optimizing method DGA. The method changes the NN (FNN) structure dynamically according to DGA. A NNs (FNNs) is assumed to be a virtual living thing which has genes of genotypes representing synapse weights between its neurons. Several initial NNs (FNNs) generated randomly are removed or reproduced according to their fitness η, and one of the best NNs (FNNs) is obtained as the result of generation iterations.

References

1. Lippman, R. P. (1987) An Introduction to Computing with Neural Nets. IEEE ASSP Magazine, **4**, 4–22
2. Buckley, J. J. (1993) Numerical Relationships Between Neural Networks, Continuous Function, and Fuzzy Systems. Fuzzy Sets and Systems, **60**, 1–8
3. Olej, V., Křupka, J. (1996) Analysis of Decision Processes of Automation Control Systems with Uncertainty. [Scientific Monograph], Elfa, Košice, Slovak Republic
4. Lehotský, M., Olej, V., Chmúrny, J. (1995) Pattern Recognition Based on the Fuzzy Neural Networks and their Learning by Modified Genetic Algorithms. Neural Network World, **5**, No.1, 91–97
5. Holland, J. H. (1975) Adaptation in Natural and Artificial Systems. University of Michigan Press, Ann Arbor
6. Spiessens, P. (1988) Genetic Algorithms. AI MEMO, No. 88-19, Vrije Universitiet Brussel.
7. Hoffmeister, F., Back, T. (1990) Genetic Algorithms and Evolution Strategies. Similarities and Differences. Proc. of 1st Workshop on Parallel Problem Solving from Nature, Dortmund, Germany, 455–469
8. Olej, V. (1997) Realization of Distributed Genetic Algorithms nd Evolution Strategies. Proc. of 17th International Conference on Artificial Intelligence and Information - Control Systems of Robots, World Scientific, Printed in Singapore by Uto-Print, Smolenice, Slovak Republic, 277–285
9. Radcliffe, N. J. (1994) The Algebra of Genetic Algorithms. Annals of Mathematics and Artificial Intelligence, **10**, 339–384
10. Goldberg, D. E. (1989) Genetic Algorithms in Search, Optimization, and Machine Learning. Addison – Wesley, Reading, MA
11. Zadeh, L. A. (1965) Fuzzy Sets. Information and Control, **8**, 338–353
12. Cangelosi, A., Parisi, D., Nolfi, S. (1994) Cell Division and Migration in a 'Genotype' for Neural Networks. Network: Computation in Neural Systems, **5**, 497–515
13. Nagao, T., Agui, T., Nagahashi, H. (1993) A Genetic Method for Optimalization of Asynchronous Random Neural Networks and its Application to Action Control. Proc. of International Joint Conference on Neural Networks '93, Nagoya, Japan, 1–4
14. Whitley, D., Starkweather, T., Bogart, C. (1990) Genetic Algorithms and Neural Networks: Optimizing Connection and Connectivity. Parallel Computing, **14**, North Holland, 347–361
15. Adeli, H., Hung, S. L. (1995) Machine Learning – Neural Networks, Genetic Algorithms, and Fuzzy Systems. John Wiley and Sons, Inc., New York
16. Nikolopoulos, C., Hwang, Y. R. (1994) Evolutionary Topology Configuration of Neural Nets. Neural Network World, **5**, 553–566
17. Buckley, J. J., Hayashi, Y. (1993) Hybrid Neural Networks can be Fuzzy Controllers and Fuzzy Expert Systems. Fuzzy Sets and Systems, **60**, 135–142
18. Godjevac, J. (1994) Comparison Between Classical and Fuzzy Neurons. Proc. of 2nd European Congress on Fuzzy Intelligent Technologies, **1**, Aachen, Germany, 1326–1332
19. Uchino, E., Yamakawa, T., Kohno, M. (1994) Restoration of Saturated and/or Internittent Signal by Using a Neo-Fuzzy-Neuron. Proc. of 2nd European Congress on Fuzzy Intelligent Technologies, **1**, Aachen, Germany, 170–173

A Reverse Neural Model
of a General Planar Transmission Line

Zbyněk Raida

Brno University of Technology, Dept. of Radio Electronics
Purkyňova 118, 612 00 Brno, Czech Republic

Abstract: In the paper, an original exploration of neural networks for the design of planar microwave transmission lines is discussed. Since no analytical models of these transmission lines are at the disposal, an accurate finite-element analysis of a certain number of selected structures is performed and obtained results are used as learning patterns for training a neural network. In order to obtain a design tool, inputs of the network are associated with technical parameters of the transmission line, and outputs correspond to its physical parameters. Training of the network is based on a novel genetic algorithm, which ensures low error and good convergence of the learning process. Validity of the model is verified using previously published data.

Keywords: Back-propagation network, finite-element target, genetic learning

1 Introduction

Nowadays, radio communication channels are shifted into higher and higher frequency bands in order to win sufficient capacity for various services. This fact makes analysis and design of circuits, antennas, and transmission lines on frequencies over 10 GHz highly demanding. Unfortunately, analysis of the above systems on such high frequencies has to be performed in full-wave manner[1] exploring numerical methods (e.g., finite differences, finite elements, moment methods etc.), which is rather complicated and time-consuming.

---

[1] Description of microwave systems, i.e. systems working on frequencies over 300 MHz, is based on Maxwell's equations [1]. On frequencies below 10 GHz, this set of differential equations (or integral ones) can be converted into a closed-form description of an investigated structure assuming certain simplifications. On frequencies over 10 GHz, simplified closed-form description loses its validity which enforces us to solve unsimplified Maxwell's equations for an investigated structure (so called full-wave solution is sought). In most cases, analytical solution of Maxwell's equations is unknown, and therefore, analysis have to be performed numerically.

In order to overcome the described difficulty, neural networks can be used. In the first step, certain number of representatives of a modelled structure is numerically analysed to get learning patterns for training a neural network.

Inputs of a neural network are associated with physical parameters of the structure of interest (dimensions of the structure, permittivity and permeability of substrate, etc.). Outputs of a network are related to technical parameters of the structure (characteristic impedance, dispersion characteristics of a transmission line). Finally, the whole neural network behaves as an efficient and fast model of the investigated system. For purposes of design, such neural models have to be completed by a proper optimization algorithm.

If inputs of the network are related to technical parameters and outputs are associated with physical ones, a reverse neural model is obtained, which directly performs the design procedure, and therefore, it does not require being completed by any additional optimization routine.

In the presented paper, both direct and reverse neural model of a general microwave transmission line is going to be discussed, which can be considered as an original contribution to the exploration of neural networks and genetic algorithms in the area of microwave techniques.

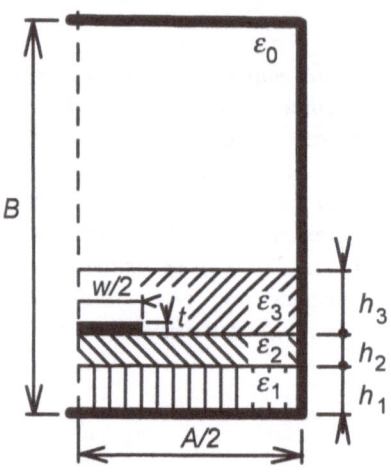

Fig. 1 A shielded microstrip line in a multi-layered dielectric substrate

In section 2 of this paper, a general planar transmission line is described and its numerical modeling using finite-element method is given. Exploring finite elements, a certain number of couples (input pattern, desired target) is produced. In section 3, rules for election of optimal number of training couples and placing input patterns in the input space, which maximises accuracy of the neural model, are presented. In section 4, a novel back-propagation neural network with original genetic training algorithm is described, and moreover, both direct and reverse neural models are presented here.

2   General planar transmission line

A general representative of planar transmission lines is proposed in Fig. 1. In this model, geometrical symmetry of the structure (see dashed line) is supposed, electrically conducting shielding waveguide of fixed dimensions $A = B = 12.7$ mm (thick solid lines) is assumed, negligible thickness of microstrip is taken for granted, and number of dielectric layers is limited to 3 (microstrip is expected being etched on the second layer). On the other hand, height of dielectric layers h_1, h_2, h_3, their permittivity ε_1, ε_2, ε_3, and width of microstrip w can vary.

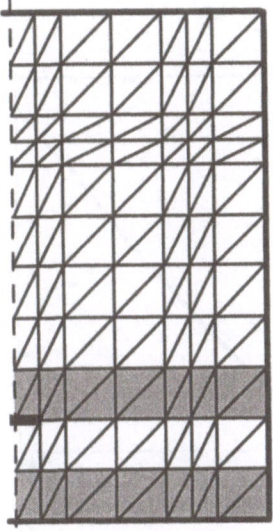

Dealing with the design of the transmission line, such values of permittivity and height of dielectric layers and such width of microstrip are going to be found so that the desired dispersion characteristics can be reached. Exploring finite-element method, the transmission line is analysed on frequencies $f_1 = 20$ GHz, $f_2 = 25$ GHz, and $f_3 = 30$ GHz), i.e. phase constants of the dominant mode of wave propagating along the transmission line $\mathbf{P} = [\beta_1\ \beta_2\ \beta_3]^{\mathrm{T}}$ is computed for the above frequencies depending on variables

$$\mathbf{T} = [h_1\ h_2\ h_3\ \varepsilon_1\ \varepsilon_2\ \varepsilon_3\ w]^{\mathrm{T}}.$$

If reverse neural model is going to be built, column vectors $\mathbf{P}$ are considered as input patterns and column vectors $\mathbf{T}$ as output ones. In the case of direct neural model, inputs and outputs are swapped.

Fig. 2 An example of a finite-element mesh consisting of rectangular bi-elements

The reverse neural model can be used as a direct design tool: introducing desired dispersion characteristics $\mathbf{P}$ to the input of the neural network causes an immediate response of the net, which contains corresponding physical parameters of the structure $\mathbf{T}$. If direct neural model is built, the neural model has to be completed by a proper optimization routine.

3 Influencing accuracy of neural model

Accuracy of neural model can be significantly influenced by proper placing input patterns into the input space of the neural network.

Rules for placing input patterns into the input space can be derived exploring the sampling theorem: if small changes of signals at the inputs of neural network cause rapid changes in the space of responses of a neural network then number of training patters has to be relatively high. Since the changes of the level of the output signal are described by its spectrum, spectrum of responses is computed using Fast Fourier Transform. If amplitudes of higher spectral components are high then sampling rate has to be increased in respective region (i.e., distance between input patters has to be reduced there). The region demanding the increase of sampling rate can be revealed exploring information hidden in the phase of the output spectra.

Assume two single-output neural networks. In the case of the net **A**, distances between responses to equidistantly spaced input patterns are relatively small and they slightly decrease in the output space. Therefore, components of amplitude spectrum of output responses reaches relatively small level and phase of components goes from negative values to zero.

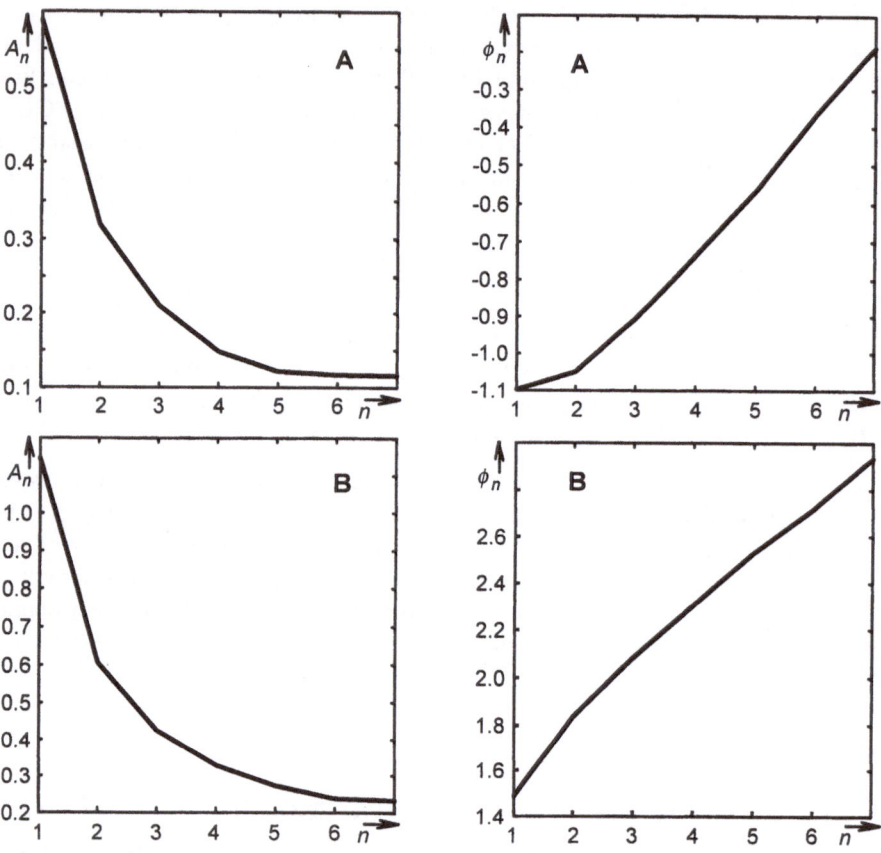

Fig. 3a Amplitude spectra of output responses when sufficiently small distances among patters are elected (A) and when distances among patterns are too long (B).

Fig. 3b Phase spectra of output responses when longer distance among patterns is at the beginning (A) of the sample set or at its end (B)

Situation of the network **B** is complementary: distances between responses are relatively large (see higher values of components of amplitude spectrum) and they are slightly increasing in the output space (see positive phase).

Therefore, computing (multi-dimensional) spectra of output patterns can revealed regions containing insufficient number of learning patters.

4 Novel genetic training

Since classical training algorithms suffer from the problem of local minima of error function, which is minimized during training process, genetic algorithms were proposed to be used in order to overcome this difficulty. Unfortunately, genetic algorithms exhibit low convergence rate and high computational requirements. Therefore, a novel genetic algorithm, which exhibits improvèd properties, was developed based on tournament selection. Novelty of this algorithm consists in varying number of individuals both in every generation and in every tournament, in varying probability of crossover, in varying number of elitists in every generation, etc. By this way, convergence properties can be improved.

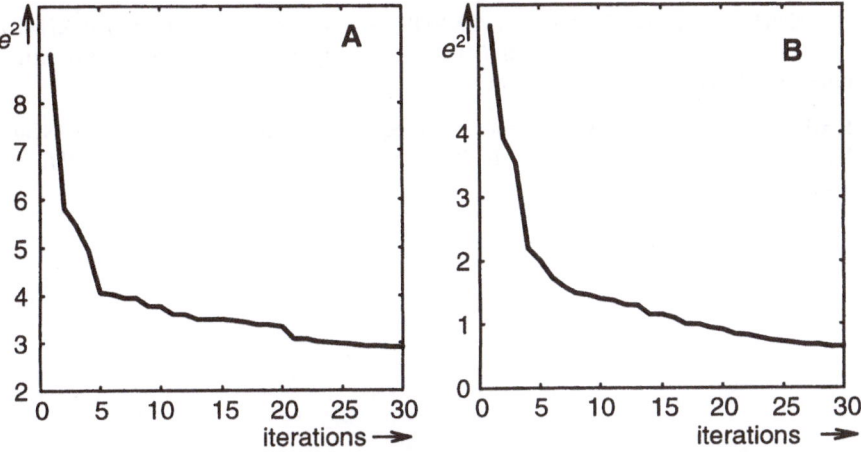

Fig. 4 Learning curve of a neural network trained using classical tournament selection (**A**) and modified one (**B**). Mean squared error computed over 30 realizations.

The novel genetic training was used for training of both direct and reverse neural model. Since the formulation of reverse neural model contains ambiguities in representation of patterns, the learning process is highly time-demanding and exhibits high level of misadjustment. Therefore, exploring direct neural model and genetic optimization for the search of proper parameters of the transmission line seems to be better solution.

5 Conclusions

The paper describes an original way of designing microstrip transmission lines of desired dispersion properties. Novelty of the presented approach consists in developing original neural model of a general microstrip transmission line, in deriving rules, which ensure high accuracy of a neural model, and in introducing a novel genetic training of the net. As a result, efficient and accurate tool for the design of planar transmission lines is obtained.

References

1   GUPTA, K. C., GARG, R., BAHL, I., BHARTIA, P. (1996) *Microstrip lines and slotlines*. 2/E. Artech House, Norwood.

2   LEE, J. F. (1994) Finite element analysis of lossy dielectric waveguides. *IEEE Transactions on Microwave Theory and Techniques*. Vol. 42, no. 6, p. 1025 - 1031.

3   ČERNOHORSKÝ, D., RAIDA, Z., ŠKVOR, Z., NOVÁČEK, Z. (1999) *Analýza a optimalizace mikrovlnných struktur* (Analysis and Optimization of Microwave Structures). Nakladatelství VUTIUM, Brno.

4   RAIDA, Z. (1999) Full-Wave Design of Frequency-Selective Surfaces Using Neural Networks and Genetic Algorithms. In *Proceedings of the URSI General Assembly '99*. Toronto (Canada), p. 60.

Fuzzy Sets and the Theory of Neuronal Group Selection for the Problem of Interpretation

Savely Girshgorn[1]

[1]The Research Centre of Training Quality Problems. Izmaylovskoe sh. 6, Moscow Russia.

Abstract:The paper is devoted to the problem of reconstruction of an incomplete pattern (image). The procedure of reconstruction is proposed to be realized with using of conventional sign. Such a sign contains missing information in generalized form estranged from the specifics of a certain pattern. The solution of this problem is supposed to be found with the utilization of the mechanism that formalizes some propositions of the Edelmen's theory of neuronal group selection. The paper contains the fuzzy descriptions as for the propositions of the theory of selection so for the mechanism of reconstruction itself. The possible way of development of such a mechanism is outlined in conclusion.

1. Introduction

In the large variety of processes concerning with interpretation we are taking up those ones connected with determining of what does a generalized characteristic mean in different situations - it makes sense when in uncertain conditions the missing information is presented in "abstract" form alienated from the actual circumstances. We assume that this process can be realized by means of a "cognitive" mechanism which eliminates uncertainty of the incomplete pattern so that the reconstructed structure agree with given generalized characteristic. We assume also that there can be an external environmental instrument - conventional sign - that indicates the characteristic and activates the proper part of the "cognitive" mechanism. Thus we talk about the sign interpretation problem and consider it as the representative of the numerous class of "mental" phenomena which provide intellectual operations with the aid of environmental means.

The general way of modeling of such a phenomenon may consist of two steps. First we create a model that describes of invariant environmental conditions - conditions which remain unchanged in various situations. Then we apply this model as an instrument that (partly) determines or aims the "cognitive" means.

2. The neuronal group selection theory and it's application for description of invariant conditions

The Edelmen's neuronal group selection theory contains the following propositions [Edelmen,1987]:

- The cerebral cortex consists of the great amount of neuronal groups; each group probably contains 50-10000 neurons and matches to the certain configuration of input signal - it responds to the matched signal with the special output activity;

- Regarding to the input signal the set of neuronal groups is superfluous - there are several groups which respond to any signal and vice versa - any two signals call the reaction of different or partly merged sets of groups;

- In response to input signal those groups are selected which more or less match to the signal or "recognize" the signal; the result of selection is the set of groups which will be picked out with increased probability when the similar input signal comes in future.

In order to provide these propositions with a formal description we'll put in force some simplifications. First of all we'll consider that the functioning of neuronal group can be simulated by neural network: the better network matches the configuration of input signal (stimulus) the bigger output value it gives.

Let $E_S=\{S_1,S_2,...,S_j,...\}$ be the set (infinite) of stimulus and $E_G=\{G_1,G_2,...,G_N\}$ be the population of neuronal groups. When stimulus S_j affects the population $E_G=\{G_1,G_2,...,G_N\}$, it makes each group $G_i \subset E_G$ give a response - an output value R_i. A multitude of possible responses can be described by a function $R_i=F\{G_i,S_j\}$.

For each stimulus $S_j \subset E_S$ we can build up a fuzzy set of neuronal groups (or neural networks) A_{Sj}, that shows how these groups respond to the stimulus. To do so we must fit the range of values of function $F\{G_i,S_j\}$ in the [0;1] interval, and thus we'll receive another function $\mu(G_i,S_j)$, that shows the degree of membership of group G_i in the set A_{Sj}. So the set A_{Sj} is a fuzzy subset of E_G:

$$A_{Sj} = \{ G_1 \mid \mu\{G_1,S_j\}, G_2 \mid \mu\{G_2,S_j\},..., G_N \mid \mu\{G_N,S_j\} \}.$$

To simulate the selection mechanism we may use a concept of α-level subset. If α gives a critical value of function $\mu(G_i,S_j)$, up to which we decide whether select the group G_i or not, the result of selection is the α-level subset:

$$A_{\alpha Sj}=\{ G_i \mid \mu(G_i,S_j) \geq \alpha \}.$$

With the stated above scheme of selection the invariant description problem - it is possible to name it here as the class description problem - can be solved by means of creating of a subset of groups where each group gives a good response for the essential (invariant) trait of the class. The general way is to produce a multitude of stimulus $E_S=\{S_1,S_2,...,S_N\}$ where alien to the class and insignificant traits are varied and the essential one (or ones) remains. Each time stimulus S_j causes the process of selection, we receive an α-level fuzzy subset: $A_{\alpha Sj} = \{G_1|\mu(G_1,S_j),\ G_2|\mu(G_2,S_j),\ ...,\ G_M|\mu(G_M,S_j)\}$. Therefore the multitude of stimulus E_S engender the set of fuzzy α-level subsets: $A_S=\{A_{\alpha S1},\ A_{\alpha S2},...,A_{\alpha SN}\}$.

Intersection of these sets $A_{\cap}=A_{\alpha S1}\cap A_{\alpha S2}\cap...\cap A_{\alpha SN}$ will contain only those groups which respond to the steadily repeating elements of the stimulus - those elements which constitute the essential trait (traits) of the class (we'll use the minimax interpretation of fuzzy logic operations given in [Zadeh,1973]). Note that along with the fuzzy subset $A_{\cap}=\{G_i|\mu(G_i,S_j)\}$ we can operate with a classic set $E_{\cap}=\{G_i\}$ which contains the same elements. In order to determine whether the groups from $E_{\cap}$ (or $A_{\cap}$) provide correct class description, we can take any two stimulus - S_j and S_k - of the concerned class. These stimulus engender two fuzzy subsets: $A_{Sj}=\{G_i|\mu(G_i,S_j)\}$ and $A_{Sk}=\{G_i|\mu(G_i,S_k)\}$, where $G_i \subset E_{\cap}$.

If the groups from $E_{\cap}$ provide effective recognition of essential trait and are insensitive to alien features, the fuzzy subsets A_{Sj} and A_{Sk} must coincide with each other. The proximity of two fuzzy subsets can be estimated with the Hamming distance:

$$\delta(A_{Sj},A_{Sk}) = (1/N_\alpha) * \Sigma_{i=[1,N\alpha]}\ |\ \mu(G_i,S_j) - \mu(G_i,S_k)\ |,$$

where N_α is the number of neuronal groups in $E_{\cap}$, G_i - groups from $E_{\cap}$, $\mu(G_i,S_j)$ and $\mu(G_i,S_k)$ -functions of membership of groups G_i in subsets A_{Sj} and A_{Sk}.

So we consider that the class description is correct if for any S_j and S_k the value of $\delta(A_{Sj},A_{Sk})$ is less than an arbitrarily prescribed criterion: $\delta(A_{Sj},A_{Sk})<\varepsilon$. In addition to this we can give another condition - for any two stimulus S_j and S_m where S_j belongs to the concerned class but S_m doesn't belong to it, the value of $\delta(A_{Sj},A_{Sk})$ must be more than an arbitrarily prescribed criterion $\delta(A_{Sj},A_{Sk})>\varepsilon$.

3. The sign interpretation modeling

The next task of this paper is to show how the description of invariant environmental conditions can determine or aim an intellectual operation, which consists in reconstruction of an incomplete pattern (image). Let us imagine a system that can receive two kind of stimulus - images and conventional signs, each sign names a certain class of images. Applying the virtual reality terminology we can give a concrete expression to this situation and consider that the system has two sensorial channels: "video"-channel and "text" one.

Let the system be able to work in two modes: learning mode and interpreting mode. In learning mode system trains to classify images. The revealed classes receive names - conventional signs, transmitted on the text channel. In interpreting mode system receives an incomplete image (stimulus) and a sign that indicates what class this image belongs to. The aim of the system is to restore the incomplete image according with the sign.

Let's take such a class of images, where each image contains two objects and the first object is arranged exactly under the second one (such a class of images can be called "one-under-another"). In order to learn the system to recognize this class of stimulus we can affect on the system with a multitude of images - representatives of the concerned class, which differ from each other with the characteristics of the objects they consist of. The result of selections is the set of fuzzy subsets: $A_S = \{A_{\alpha S1}, A_{\alpha S2}, ..., A_{\alpha SN}\}$. According to the previously discussed ideas we can receive an intersection of these subsets $A_\cap$ that will contain only those groups which are insensitive to the characteristics of objects and respond only on the certain manner of their arrangement. In conclusion of the learning mode stage the groups of fuzzy subset $A_\cap$ - let's denote these groups as $E_\cap$ - are put into accordance with a conventional sign - let's denote it as Sn.

In interpreting mode the system receives incomplete stimulus - in our example such a stimulus may consist of two isolated objects, that are not composed in one picture. The stimulus must be accompanied with a sign, transmitted on the text channel. Let's imagine that the sign, transmitted along with two random (maybe absolutely new) objects, is the Sn one and therefore the aim of the system is to arrange these objects so that the composed image belong to the class "one-under-another".

The sign Sn activates the corresponding set of groups $E_\cap$ and fuzzy subset $A_\cap$ that shows the etalon reaction to the stimulus of this class. Now if the system forms any random arrangement it will be able to analyze the degree of proximity of the formed arrangement to the required one. To do so the system has to use the formed arrangement as an external stimulus and receive the respond on it from the set of groups $E_\cap$. The response of these groups is the fuzzy set - name it A_S: $A_S = \{G_1 | \mu(G_1, S), G_2 | \mu(G_2, S), ..., G_N | \mu(G_M, S)\}$, where $G_i \subset E_\cap$, S-stimulus that represents the formed arrangement.

The proximity of a formed arrangement to the required one can be determined on the base of the estimation of proximity of two fuzzy subsets A_S and $A_\cap$, i. e. by means of Hamming distance $\delta(A_{Sj}, A_{Sk})$. Modifying the arrangement of the objects and watching after the $\delta(A_{Sj}, A_{Sk})$-criterion the system can gradually reach the desired arrangement.

The method by which the system generates control signals and thus modifies image doesn't matter in this scheme. For example we can change the direction of the vector that connects two objects with each other and according to the trend of the $\delta(A_{Sj}, A_{Sk})$ value choose the required control impact. The method stops when the $\delta(A_{Sj}, A_{Sk})$-criterion became less than arbitrarily prescribed value ε: $\delta(A_{Sj}, A_{Sk}) < \varepsilon$.

4. Conclusion

In the described scheme of interpretation, sign *Sn* is an instrument which plays an important role in the process of interpretation of it's own "meaning", aiming the internal operations of the system. This fact has something in common with how the psychological science considers the social signs as the means by which human get control over his own cognitive processes [Vygotsky,1962]. Despite this comparison is extremely delicate, the extending of this analogy in the area of simulation seems to be very perspective. Thus the possible development may consist in researching how the model of some part of environment can be used as a mean by which the system modifies an incomplete image.

Another promising way of development consists in expansion of application sphere of invariant descriptions - it seems to be possible to apply the same description to the different stimulus received from different data domains or even from different sensorial channels. On our opinion this is especially important for studying of how the natural processes of understanding and interpretation work.

References

Edelmen G.M. (1987). Neural Darwinism: the theory of neuronal group selection. New York. Basic.

Zadeh L.A. (1973). The concept of a linguistic variable and its application to approximate reasoning. N.Y.:Elsevier.

Vygotsky L.S. (1962). Thought and language. Cambridge, MA: The MTI Press.

Neuro-Fuzzy Architectures with Various Implication Operators

Danuta Rutkowska, Robert Nowicki, Leszek Rutkowski

Department of Computer Engineering, Technical University of Czestochowa

Al. Armii Krajowej 36, 42-200 Czestochowa

E-mail: {drutko, rnowicki, lrutko}@kik.pcz.czest.pl

Abstract: Neuro-fuzzy architectures of fuzzy systems based on various fuzzy implications are considered and their performance is analysed in the paper.

Keywords: neuro-fuzzy systems, fuzzy implications, fuzzy inference.

1 Introduction

Different neuro-fuzzy system architectures can be created using various types of fuzzy implications which correspond to fuzzy IF-THEN rules. Specific architectures can be found in [4]-[7], [11], [12] and [16]. However, they are confined to Mamdani and Larsen implications, most often applied in fuzzy control systems. In this paper we consider the neuro-fuzzy systems based on the following implications: Mamdani, Larsen, Boolean, Lukasiewicz, Zadeh, Willmott, Goguen, Gödel, Sharp, stochastic [1], [2]. A connectionist, multi-layer architecture of these systems is proposed. The paper extends previous results of the authors [8]-[15] and introduces a general architecture of the systems. Performance of the implication-based neuro-fuzzy systems is compared and the results are presented in section 3.

2 Implication-based architectures

A fuzzy system consists of a fuzzifier, a fuzzy inference engine with a fuzzy rule base, which is a collection of IF-THEN rules, and a defuzzifier [2], [5], [11], [12], [16]. Fig. 1 presents a general architecture of neuro-fuzzy systems composed of four layers. The first layer corresponds to the antecedent part of fuzzy IF-THEN rules

$$R^k: \quad \textbf{IF } x \text{ is } A^k \textbf{ THEN } y \text{ is } B^k \qquad (1)$$

Elements of this layer realise membership functions $\mu_{A^k}(x)$ of fuzzy sets $A^k = A_1^k \times \ldots \times A_n^k$, $k=1,\ldots,N$, in the antecedent part of rules (1). In formula (1) $\mathbf{x}=[x_1,\ldots,x_n]' \in \mathbf{X}$ and $y \in \mathbf{Y}$ are linguistic variables, where $\mathbf{X} \subset R^n$, $\mathbf{Y} \subset R$.

The first layer also performs fuzzification by employing the most often used singleton fuzzification. The fuzzifier maps crisp inputs $\bar{\mathbf{x}}=[\bar{x}_1,\ldots,\bar{x}_n]' \in \mathbf{X}$ into fuzzy set $A' \subset \mathbf{X}$ characterised by membership function $\mu_{A'}(\mathbf{x})$, which equals to 1 if $\mathbf{x}=\bar{\mathbf{x}}$ and equals to 0 if $\mathbf{x} \neq \bar{\mathbf{x}}$. The consequent part of rules (1) contains fuzzy sets B^k with membership functions $\mu_{B^k}(y)$ and centers $\bar{y}^k$, $k=1,\ldots,N$.

The second layer (inference layer) performs the inference process based on implication $A^k \rightarrow B^k$ corresponding to IF-THEN rules (1). The implication is a fuzzy relation with membership function $\mu_{A^k \rightarrow B^k}(\mathbf{x},y)$. This inference is conducted for each individual rule R^k, $k=1,\ldots,N$, according to compositional rule of inference, which for singleton fuzzifier can be expressed as follows

$$\mu_{B'^k}(y) = \mu_{A^k \rightarrow B^k}(\bar{\mathbf{x}}, y) \tag{2}$$

The fuzzy inference engine determines fuzzy sets B'^k, with membership functions $\mu_{B'^k}(y)$, inferred for each fuzzy rule (1) according to formula (2).

Fuzzy sets B'^k are then aggregated in order to obtain output fuzzy set B'. The membership function of this fuzzy set is expressed by the following formulas

$$\mu_{B'}(y) = \underset{k=1}{\overset{N}{S}} \mu_{B'^k}(y) \qquad \text{or} \qquad \mu_{B'}(y) = \underset{k=1}{\overset{N}{T}} \mu_{B'^k}(y) \tag{3}$$

where S denotes S-norm and T denotes T-norm, applied in so-called constructive [2], [11], [12], [16] and destructive [3], [17], [15], [9] approach to fuzzy inference, respectively. The aggregation layer realises this operation.

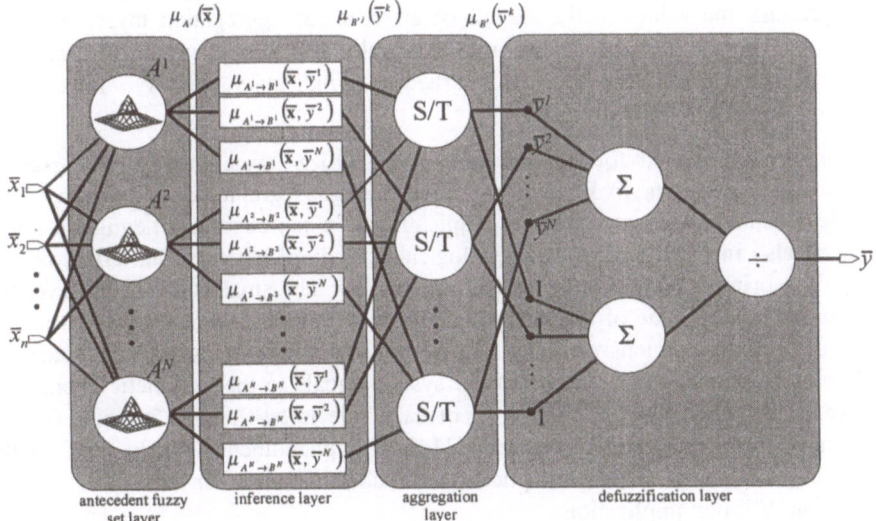

Fig. 1. General architecture of neuro-fuzzy systems

The last layer performs the defuzzification task; we use COA (center of area) defuzzification method [2], [9], [15]. The defuzzifier transforms output fuzzy sets to crisp point $\bar{y} \in Y$.

For each implication-based fuzzy system we can determine a formula which describes the crisp output of the system, $\bar{y}$, as a function of the crisp inputs $\bar{x}$. Several examples of these system descriptions, based on particular implications, are presented in [8]-[16]. Each of these formulas can be used in order to construct the particular architecture of the neuro-fuzzy system, which is a special case of the general architecture shown in Fig. 1. The difference between them fundamentally refers to the inference layer [8]-[16]. Overlapping consequent fuzzy sets (OCFS) and non-overlapping consequent fuzzy sets (NOCFS) are distinguished; see e.g. [9]. Performance of these neuro-fuzzy systems is compared in the next section.

3 System performance analysis

We have analysed the neuro-fuzzy systems which employ four rules ($N = 4$). The fuzzy sets in the antecedent and consequent parts of these rules are shown in Fig. 2 and Fig. 3, respectively. We assumed that $x \subset R$, what means that $n = 1$ and $\bar{x} = \bar{x}_1$.

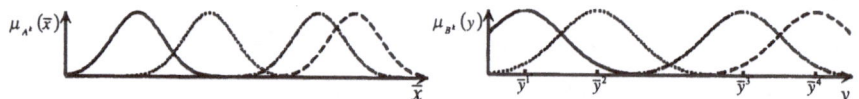

Fig. 2. Gaussian antecedent fuzzy sets   **Fig. 3. Gaussian consequent fuzzy sets**

In Fig. 4 to Fig. 7 we show two graphs for each of the neuro-fuzzy systems. The first one presents the values of the signals obtained at the aggregation layer. We used different types of the line for the individual rule. The second graph illustrates the defuzzification result. The horizontal dashed lines indicate values: $\bar{y}^1$ - lowest, $\bar{y}^2$, $\bar{y}^3$, $\bar{y}^4$ - highest, at $\bar{y}$ coordinate axis.

Fig. 4a presents results for the well known neuro-fuzzy system based on Larsen or Mamdani implication. In Fig. 4b we show analogous graph for system based on Boolean, Lukasiewicz or stochastic implication. We can observe a negligible effect noticed also in [3] for the simplified logical reasoning method. This effect occurs when the firing level $\tau_k = \mu_{A^k}(\bar{x})$ of the rules is low. The smaller the firing level the closer the output value of the system, $\bar{y}$, to the arithmetic average of universe Y. This effect is more intensive in the NOCFS neuro-fuzzy systems based on Zadeh or Willmott implication. The output of the system equals to the arithmetic average of universe Y, when the firing level τ_k of each rule is less than 0.5. This effect is shown in Fig. 4c and was discussed in [14]. This phenomenon occurs also for the OCFS system based on Zadeh implication, but does not occur for this kind of system based on Willmott implication.

The properties of the OCFS neuro-fuzzy systems are similar to that of the NOCFS systems, however the output value depends also on shape of the fuzzy sets in the consequent part of IF-THEN rules. For this reason the output of the OCFS systems based on Mamdani and Larsen implication with Gaussian consequent fuzzy sets never equals to $\max_{k=1..N} y^*$ or $\min_{k=1..N} y^*$. The OCFS systems based on Boolean, Lukasiewicz and stochastic implication have got the similar property.

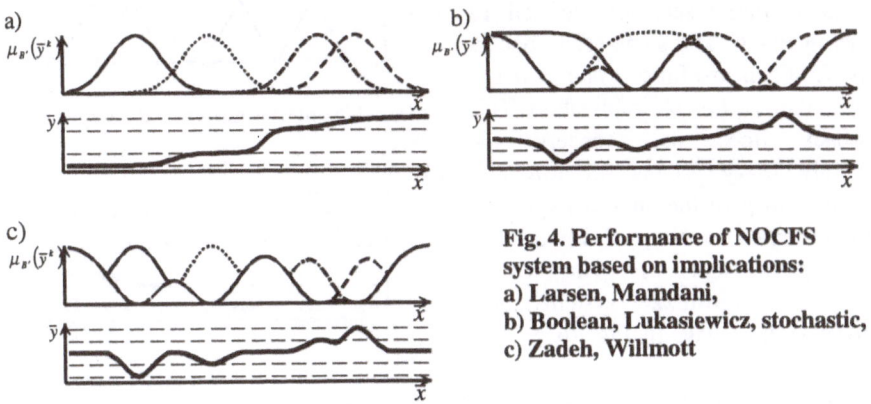

Fig. 4. Performance of NOCFS system based on implications:
a) Larsen, Mamdani,
b) Boolean, Lukasiewicz, stochastic,
c) Zadeh, Willmott

In Fig. 5 we can see the results for the OCFS architecture based on Sharp, Gödel, Goguen and Yager implication. The NOCFS neuro-fuzzy system based on these implications with Gaussian antecedent fuzzy sets does not work properly. In Fig. 5a we can see the most important disadvantage of the system based on Sharp implication. There are input values $\bar{x}$, for which the system can not work properly. The output is not specified. Note that the output value $\bar{y}$ of this system is always equal to one of $\bar{y}^k$ values or the arithmetic average of a few of them. This is a very desirable property in classification application. The system based on Gödel implication does not have this disadvantage and gives similar answer (see Fig. 5b). The systems based on Goguen and Yager implication work similarly; the results are

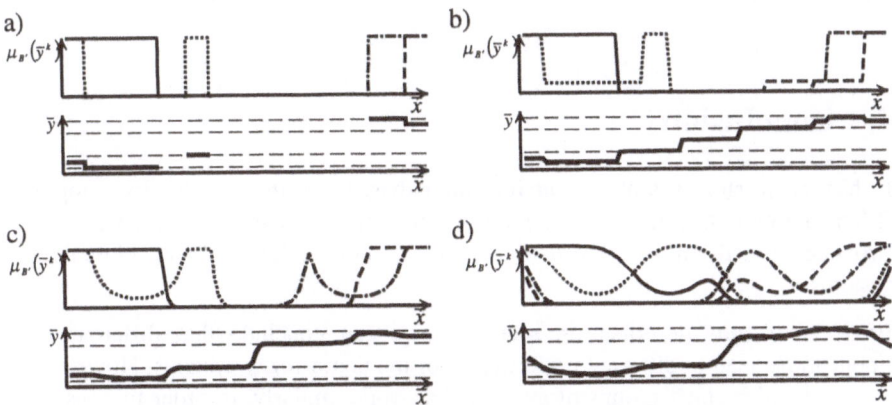

Fig. 5. Performance of OCFS system based on implications:
a) Sharp, b) Gödel, c) Goguen, d) Yager

218

presented in Fig. 5c and 5d. The last one is broadly discussed in [10].

The well known disadvantage of the constructive fuzzy systems is the fact that they can not work properly when the firing level of all rules is equal to zero. In other words, they require complete partitioning of the input space by the fuzzy sets in the antecedent part of the rules. In Fig. 7a we can see the gaps in correct reasoning in the NOCFS neuro-fuzzy system, when the antecedent fuzzy sets are defined as shown in Fig. 6. The same effect occurs in the OCFS neuro-fuzzy systems based on Mamdani or Larsen implication. This drawback does not concern the destructive fuzzy systems. All of them in this situation give the answer expressed as the arithmetic average of universe Y (see Fig. 7b and c). The OCFS destructive neuro-fuzzy systems also perform in this way. In Fig. 7b we see

Fig. 6. Triangular antecedent fuzzy sets

a)

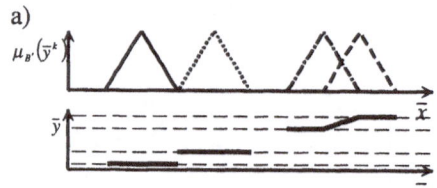

b)

c)

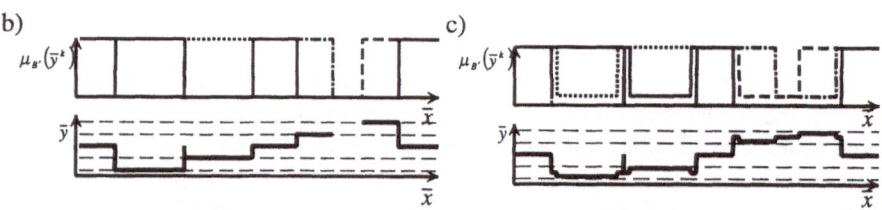

**Fig. 7. Performance of NOCFS system based on implications:
a) Larsen, Mamdani b) Sharp, Gödel, Goguen, Yager, c) Gödel (OCFS)**

the drawback of all fuzzy systems based on Sharp implication, mentioned above. The OCFS neuro-fuzzy system based on Gödel implication (the results are presented in Fig. 7c) is a good alternative for the OCFS system based on Sharp implication.

4   Conclusion

It has been shown that the architectures based on the constructive approach (Mamdani or Larsen implications) are useful as fuzzy control systems, whereas the structures based on the destructive approach are useful as fuzzy classification systems.

From the results described in section 3 we can conclude that different fuzzy implications lead to different performance of the neuro-fuzzy systems. However, we can distinguish some groups of systems that work similarly. In order to construct a system for particular application it is necessary to choose a proper implication and the final form of the rule base with proper shapes of the fuzzy sets.

References

1. O. Cordón, F. Herrera, A. Peregrín, (1997) Applicability of the fuzzy operators in the design of fuzzy logic controllers, Fuzzy Sets and Systems, pp. 15-41.

2. D. Driankov, H. Hellendoorn, M. Reinfrank, (1993) An Introduction to Fuzzy Control, Springer-Verlag Berlin Heidelberg.

3. D. Filev, R. R. Yager, (1995) Simplified methods of reasoning in fuzzy models, Proc. IEEE International Conference on Fuzzy Systems, Yokohama, Japan, pp. 123-129.

4. J. S. R. Jang, C. T. Sun, E. Mizutani, (1997) Neuro-Fuzzy and Soft Computing, Prentice Hall, Englewood Cliffs.

5. N. Kasabov, (1996) Foundations of Neural Networks, Fuzzy Systems and Knowledge Engineering, The MIT Press, Cambridge.

6. C. T. Lin, C. S. G. Lee, (1996) Neural Fuzzy Systems – A Neuro-Fuzzy Synergism to intelligent Systems, Prentice Hall, New Jersey.

7. D. Nauck, F. Klawonn, R. Kruse, (1997) Foundations of Neuro-Fuzzy Systems, John Wiley & Sons, England.

8. R. Nowicki, D. Rutkowska, (1999) Fuzzy inference neural networks based on destructive and constructive approaches and their application to classification, Proc. Fourth Conference Neural Networks and Their Applications, Czestochowa, pp. 294-301.

9. R. Nowicki, D. Rutkowska, (2000) New neuro-fuzzy architectures, Proc. ACIDCA'2000, Monastir, Tunisia, pp. 82-87.

10. R. Nowicki, D. Rutkowska, (2000) Neuro-fuzzy architectures based on Yager implication, Proc. Fifth Conference Neural Networks and Soft Computing, Zakopane.

11. D. Rutkowska, M. Pilinski, L. Rutkowski, (1997) Neural Networks, Genetic Algorithms and Fuzzy Systems, PWN, Warsaw, (in Polish).

12. D. Rutkowska, (1997) Intelligent Computational Systems, PLJ Academic Publishing House, Warsaw, (in Polish).

13. D. Rutkowska, R. Nowicki, L. Rutkowski, (1999) Singleton and non-singleton fuzzy systems with nonparametric defuzzification, in: Computational Intelligence and Applications, P. S. Szczepaniak (ed.), Springer-Verlag, pp. 292-301.

14. D. Rutkowska, R. Nowicki, L. Rutkowski, (1999) Neuro-fuzzy system with inference process based on Zadeh implication, Proc. Third International Conference on Parallel Processing & Applied Mathematics, Czestochowa, pp. 597-602.

15. D. Rutkowska, R. Nowicki, (1999) Constructive and destructive approach to neuro-fuzzy systems, Proc. EUROFUSE-SIC'99, Budapest, pp. 100-105.

16. L. X. Wang, (1994) Adaptive Fuzzy Systems and Control, PTR Prentice Hall, Englewood Cliffs.

17. R. R. Yager, D. P. Filev, (1994) Essentials of Fuzzy Modelling and Control, John Wiley & Sons.

Fuzzy Cluster Identification Using Neural Networks[1]

Peter Sinčák, Marcel Hric, Norbert Kopčo, Ján Vaščák

Computational Intelligence Group, Laboratory of AI, Department of Cybernetics and AI, Faculty of Electrical Engineering and Informatics, TU Košice, Slovakia
E-mail: cig@neuron-ai.tuke.sk, http://neuron-ai.tuke.sk/cig

Abstract: The paper deals with development of ARTMAP-like neural network to analyze feature space for classification purposes. The proposed tool is providing information about value of membership function of the unknown input vector to each class of interest. The designed ARTMAP-like system is called MF-ARTMAP based on the fact that membership functions are calculated. The functions shape is predefined as gaussian with adaptation of mean value and variance in each feature space dimension during the training procedure . The usefulness of this approach is presented on the benchmark classification problems e.g. circle in the square and spiral and on real-world data from satellite images over Slovakia. Results are similar when compared with Gaussian ARTMAP and provide additional information about membership function's values for tested input concerning classes of interest. Classification accuracy is calculated using the contingency tables approach on actual and predicted classes of interest.

Keywords: classification, neural networks, ARTMAP, MF-ARTMAP, gausian ARTMAP, membership function, fuzzy sets, fuzzy cluster, accuracy assessment, contigency tables

1 Introduction

Classification procedures are very important parts of pattern recognition problems. There are many approaches based on various methods that work on the discrimination procedure in the feature space to achieve the highest classification accuracy. Classification procedure is related to data distribution in feature space, and is represented by representative sets, which consist of training and testing subsets of data concerning each class of interest. In fact, if we have "good" type of features then discrimination hyperplane between classes is simpler and if we

---

[1] This project is supported by Slovak National Science Agency under project # 9433 "Computational Intelligence for decision procedures" , 1999-2001

have "bad" type of features then discrimination hyperplane is very non-linear and difficult to approximate. The challenge is to find a proper approximation of discrimination hyperplane based on training data analysis during learning procedures. The classification is then tested on benchmark and real-world data.

2 Motivation of the project

Classification is mapping from feature space into space of classes. It very often happens that it is very difficult to decide if a certain point in feature space belongs to a certain class. Therefore an approach based on fuzzy sets has many advantages to reduce misclassification results. Sometimes it is more convenient to have results in the form of transparent information concerning relations of the observed point in the feature space to all classes of interest. Instead of the crisp classifier output we can be more satisfied with outputs based on fuzzy sets and namely on values of membership functions of observed input to fuzzy cluster and fuzzy classes. The notions of fuzzy clusters and fuzzy class are described in the next part of this paper. The motivation is to provide for the end-user a smaller number of misclassifications and higher readability of the classification results. The output of these classification results is a vector of values describing relation of the input to each class of interest. The desire is to have a highly parallel tool with incremental learning ability similar to ARTMAP family neural network.

3 Description of the Method

The project is based on the assumption that data in feature space are organized in fuzzy cluster. Fuzzy cluster A is considered as a fuzzy set A in multidimensional feature space representing a set of the ordered couples e.g.

$$A \in \{[x_1, \mu_A(x_1)], ..., [x_n, \mu_A(x_n)]\} \qquad (1)$$

Where A is a fuzzy set and $\{x, \mu_A(x)\}$ are ordered couples, where x is a point in multidimensional feature space and $\mu_A(x)$ is a value of the membership function of x to fuzzy cluster (set) A. There are many fuzzy clusters in feature space and a certain set of fuzzy clusters create a fuzzy class. Fuzzy class is the union of fuzzy clusters belonging to a considered class defined by a training set e.g.

$$CL = \{\bigcup_{i=1}^{n} A_i\} \qquad (2)$$

Generally we can consider fuzzy class as a set of fuzzy sets A_i representing the variety of the numerical representation of the class. Relation between $\mu_{CL}(x)$ and $\mu_A(x)$ must be as follows:

$$\mu_{CL}(X) = \max_{i = 1, n}(\mu_{Ai}(X)) \qquad (3)$$

where A_i is a fuzzy cluster which belongs to class CL and n is a number of fuzzy clusters creating class CL. The MF-ARTMAP is intended to be such a tool to calculate values of membership functions of X to each class of interest in feature space.

3.1 Description of the neural network topology

Topology of MF ARTMAP is based on a similar architecture to ARTMAP. In Figure 1 can be seen two MF-ARTMAP neural networks with 4 neural layers. The input layer is mapping the input into the comparison layer where the comparison between input pattern and mean values of existing clusters are compared. In Figure 1a is a starting situation where only one cluster is identified, while in the Figure 1b, 3 clusters are already revealed so the input pattern is tested if it does not belong to one of the clusters. In this case the second layer is dynamically changing according to the number of clusters in the 3-rd layer. So the 2-nd and 3-rd layers are extending according to the number of clusters found in the feature space.

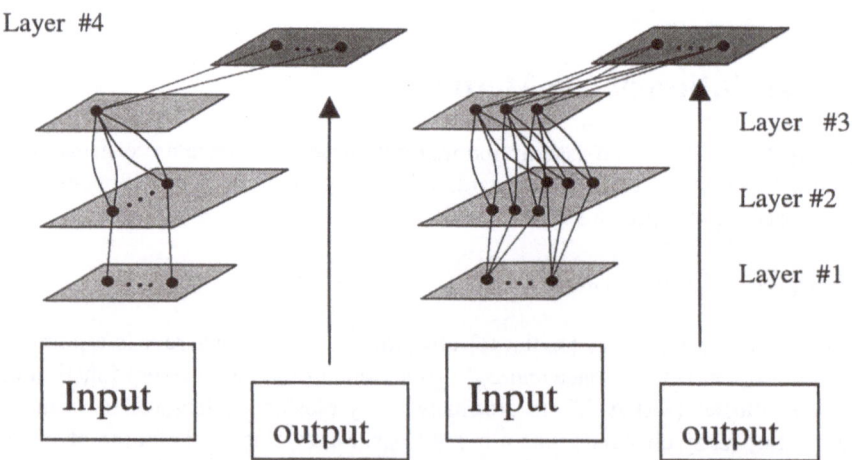

1a - MF-Artmap with one cluster   1b - MF-Artmap with three clusters

Figure 1: Basic topology for MF-Artmap neural networks

The recurrent connection between the 2-nd and 3-rd layer is the encoding of mean value and mean square deviation associated with a particular membership function based on a gaussian type of representation. The 4-th layer is representing the mapfield like part of a neural network whose role is to integrate the clusters into a resulting class. The input to the mapfield is from the 3-rd layer and also from outside of the neural network as associated output into the overall MF-Artmap neural networks. More detailed topology is in figure #2, where a situation with more clusters is represented. Basically it can be listed the number of neural layers in the MF-Artmap can be listed as follows:

☐ Layer #1 – input mapping layer, number of neurons equal to "n", where n is dimensionality of the feature space,

☐ Layer #2 – comparison layer, number of neurons equal to "n x nc", where nc is the number of clusters identified in the recognition layer,

☐ Layer #3 – recognition layer, number of neurons equal to "nc", where nc is the number of clusters,

☐ Layer #4 – mapfield layer, number of neurons equal to "M", where M is the number of classes for classification procedure.

More detailed description of the MF-Artmap is presented in the figure #2

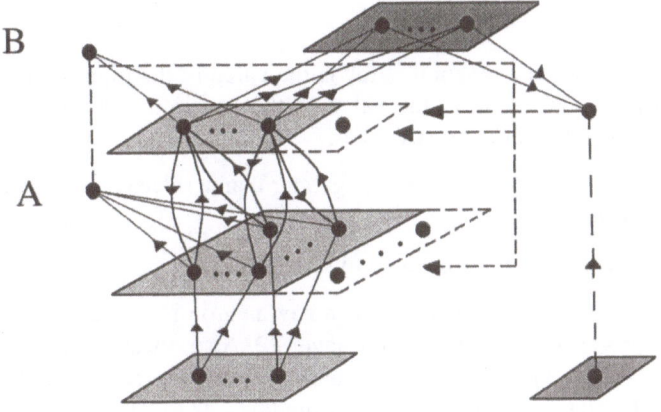

Figure 2 : General MF-ARTMAP topology with a dynamic number of neurons in the 2-nd and 3-rd neural network layer.

The important role is done by neurons A and B, which reset and freeze some of procedures during training. These neurons are fed from the comparison layer with values which represent a difference between input patterns and mean values of the membership functions. If the maximum of these differences is greater than a threshold, then a new cluster is setup immediately. If not, then there is a chance that input pattern belongs to one of the clusters identified in the past procedures. Then a training and updating of the recurrent synapses is underway to adapt the shape of the membership function. The adaptation procedure is described in the following section.

3.2 Adaptation procedure for parametric and structural learning

The overall training procedure on MF-ARTMAP is made in the following steps of procedures during one epoch:

1. If there is an input the mapping procedure of the input into the layer #2 (comparison layer) and output is set to the mapfield. If there is no input then exit this training or start training for the next epoch.

2. For each dimension the calculations are made as follows:

$$nv = (in - mc) \qquad\qquad (4)$$

Where "nv" is neuron activation, "in" is the value of the input in a particular dimension and "mc" is mean the value of the gaussian type of membership function of the input to the fuzzy cluster.

3. If at least one of the values of "nv" is greater than a selected threshold then an associated cluster is frozen.

4. If at least one cluster is not frozen go to step #6

5. A new cluster is created – that means a new neuron is added to layer #3 and also a new raw of neurons is added to layer #2. Also mean values of the new cluster are projected into the synaptic connections downwards from layer #3 to layer #2 and also synaptic connections from layer #2 to layer #3 are initialized into starting values for standard deviations related to shapes of membership functions. After this procedure jump to step #1.

6. The signal comes to recognition layer #3 and each neurons' activation values represent the membership functions values of input to the fuzzy cluster represented by this neuron. If the value of this function is lower than the selected threshold, then freeze the cluster.

7. If all clusters are frozen jump to step #5.

8. Regarding the non-frozen clusters, the values are evaluated and the max value is selected and the input is associated with the selected class which is represented with the winner neuron.

9. If the selected class is corresponding with the class associated to the input on the mapfield layer, then the adaptation procedure for recurrent connections is accomplished as follows:

$$mc(t+1) = (1-q^{-1})mc(t) + q^{-1}in \qquad (5)$$

$$\sigma^2(t+1) = (1-q^{-1})\sigma^2(t) + q^{-1}(mc(t+1)-in)^2 \qquad (6)$$

where "q" is number of inputs already associated with cluster. After adaptation jump to step #1 .

10. If there is no correspondence indicated in the previous step, then jump to step #5.

The overall procedure will map all selected membership functions into the feature space as it is illustrated in figure # 3. Some fuzzy clusters can represent a fuzzy class as it is indicated in the section before.

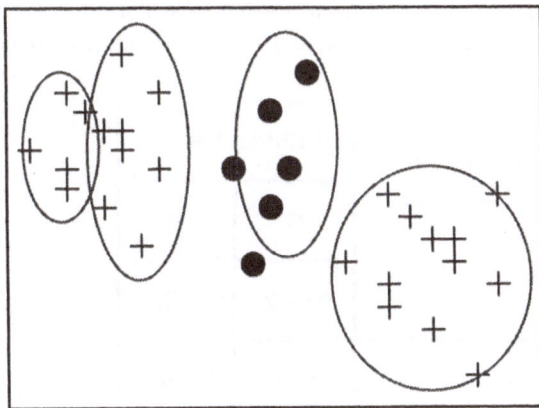

Figure 3: Illustration of membership functions in the feature space representing the fuzzy class consisting of fuzzy clusters.

4 Experimental results

Experiments using benchmark and real-world data were done during this project. The aim was comparative analysis of known CI systems with those modified or developed during the research namely MF-Artmap, GA-Artmap. Basically the same real-word data were used and so the comparison can be done assuming the same training and testing data, which means the same amount of knowledge was used for classification procedure.

4.1 Accuracy assessment

Accuracy assessment was evaluated using contingency table analysis. A contingency table was used in a basic comparison study between all methods, which were investigated and developed. Some details about contingency table analysis for accuracy assessment of classification results can be found in [8].

4.2 Experiments on benchmark data

There were 2 benchmark data used for testing classification results for comparative purposes. Circle in the rectangle and double spiral problem was used for dichotomous classification testing. These two benchmark data are used the most for estimating the classifier level of sophistication. If results on these benchmark data are good there, is a good assumption that the classifier will be successful in main applications. On the following tables are the results from the selected benchmark classification procedure. Results are on testing data.

Predicted Class	Actual Class	
	A	B
A'	97.62	2.92
B'	2.38	97.08

Table #1: Results on the "circle in the square" dichotomous classification.

Predicted Class	Actual Class	
	A	B
A'	87.54	10.76
B'	12.46	89.24

Table #2: Results on the "double spirals" dichotomous classification.

4.3 Experiments on real-world data

Experiments were done on benchmark and real-world data. Basically the behaviors of the methods were observed on multispectral image data with the aim to obtain the best classification accuracy on the test data subset. The Košice data consists of a training set of 3164 points in the feature space and of a test set of 3167 points of the feature space. A point in the feature space has 7 real-valued coordinates of the feature space normalized into the interval (0,1) and 7 binary output values. The class of a fact is determined by the output which has a value of one; the other six output values are zero. The data represents 7 attributes of the color spectrum sensed from Landsat satellite. The representation set was determined by a geographer and was supported by ground verification procedure. The main goal was landuse identification using the most precise classification procedure for achieving accurate results. The image was taken over the eastern Slovakia region particularly from the City of Kosice region. There were seven classes of interest picked up for classification procedure as it can be seen in figure 4.

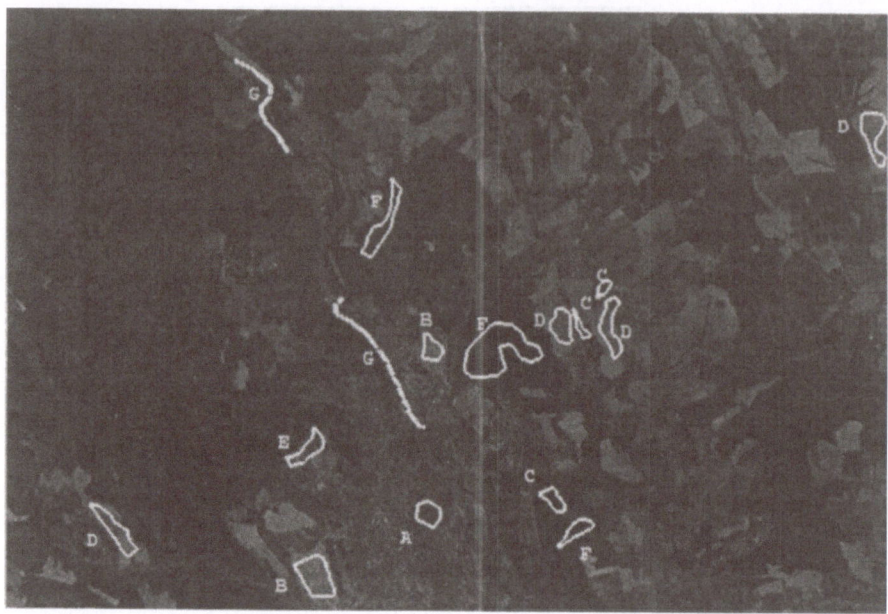

Figure 4: Original image. Highlighted areas were classified by expert (A – urban area, B – barren fields, C – bushes, D – agricultural fields, E – meadows, F – forests, G – water)

Predicted Class	Actual Class						
	A	B	C	D	E	F	G
A'	94.87	0.83	0.00	0.00	4.68	0.00	5.41
B'	0.00	84.30	0.00	3.77	6.43	0.00	0.00
C'	0.00	0.00	99.03	0.00	0.00	0.00	0.00
D'	0.64	9.71	0.00	96.01	1.17	0.00	1.35
E'	4.49	4.96	0.97	0.22	87.72	0.17	4.05
F'	0.00	0.00	0.00	0.00	0.00	99.74	0.00
G'	0.00	0.20	0.00	0.00	0.00	0.09	89.19

Table #3 Contingency table of Landsat TM classification on the test sites

Figure 5: Classification results on Landsat TM data using MF Artmap approach

5 Conclusion

The paper presents the MF-ARTMAP approach to the classification procedure. The advantage of this approach is higher readability of the neural network in providing the values of membership functions of input to fuzzy clusters or fuzzy classes identified by this approach. Results of these neural networks are comparable with GA ARTMAP [7] on benchmark and real-world data and in addition, provide more useful information about the measure of membership into all fuzzy classes and fuzzy clusters discovered in the feature space. This seems to be an interesting advantage of this approach.

References

[1] P.M. Atkinson and A.R.L. Tatnall, "Neural networks in remote sensing," *Int. J. Remote Sensing,* vol. 18, 4, 1997, 711-725.

[2] J. Richards, *Remote sensing digital image analysis: An introduction.* Springer Verlag: Berlin, 1993.

[3] B.G. Lees and K. Ritman, "Decision-tree and rule-induction approach to integration of remotely sensed and GIS data in mapping vegetation in disturbed or hilly environments," *Environmental Management*, vol. 15, 1991, pp. 823-831.

[4] C.H. Chen, "Trends on information processing for remote sensing," in *Proceedings of the International Geoscience and Remote Sensing Symposium (IGARSS)*, vol. 3, Aug. 3-8 1997, pp. 1190-1192.

[5] P. Werbos, Beyond Regression: New Tools for Prediction and Analysis in the Behavioral Sciences, Ph.D. thesis, Harvard University, 1974.

[6] G.A. Carpenter, M.N. Gjaja, S. Gopal, and C.E. Woodcock, "ART neural networks for remote sensing" Vegetation classification from Landsat TM and terrain data," *IEEE Transactions on Geoscience and Remote Sensing*, vol. 35, no. 2, 1997, pp. 308-325.

[7] N. Kopčo, P. Sinčák, and H. Veregin, "Extended Methods for Classification of Remotely Sensed Images Based on ARTMAP Neural Networks," in *Computational Intelligence – Theory and Applications (Lecture Notes in Computer Science 1625), Proceedings of International Conference "The 6-th Fuzzy days,"* Dortmund, Germany, May 1999, pp. 206-219.

[8] P. Sinčák, H. Veregin, and N. Kopčo, "Conflation techniques in multispectral image processing," *Geocarto Int*, March, pp. 11-19. 2000.

[9] S. Grossberg, "Adaptive pattern classification and universal recoding, I: Feedback, expectation, olfaction, and illusions," *Biological Cybernetics*, vol. 23, 1976, pp. 187-202.

[10] G.A. Carpenter, B.L. Milenova, and B.W. Noeske, "Distributed ARTMAP: a neural network for fast distributed supervised learning," *Neural Networks*, vol. 11, no. 5, Jul. 1998, pp. 793-813.

[11] J.R. Williamson, "Gaussian ARTMAP: A neural network for fast incremental learning of noisy multidimensional maps," *Neural Networks*, vol. 9, 1996, pp. 881-897.

[12] R.K. Cunningham, *Learning and recognizing patterns of visual motion, color, and form*, Unpublished Ph.D. thesis, Boston University, Boston, MA: 1998.

[13] R. Duda and P. Hart, *Pattern Classification and Scene Analysis*, Wiley, New York: 1973.

Part 5

Applications and Case Studies

Soft Computing Applications Developed by ECANSE

Roman Blaško

SWH Siemens Business Services, Dúbravská cesta 9, SK-842 37 Bratislava, Slovakia, E-mail: Roman.Blasko@swh.sk

Abstract: ECANSE is a software development environment for application of soft computing technologies like neural networks, fuzzy logic, and genetic algorithms. The presented applications are from power engineering, environment monitoring and telecommunication.

1. Introduction

There are several successful industrial applications developed by ECANSE system. ECANSE is a software development environment for application of soft computing technologies like neural networks, fuzzy logic, and genetic algorithms. Some applications from power engineering, environment monitoring and telecommunication are presented in the following. The applications are described by specification of requirements and achieved results, which are in all cases better than by using conventional techniques.

A soft-computing studio **ECANSE** (Environment for Computer Aided Neural Software Engineering) [1] was used for development of all mentioned applications as a very powerful and flexible tool. The ECANSE system provides a user with several types of neural networks. The MLP (Multi-Layer Perceptron) module has been used for the most of applications mentioned in this paper. The processing by the neural networks implemented in the MLP module consists of two phases: training and testing. During the *training phase,* the designed task is trained using the historical information taken over the past period. During the *testing phase,* the required data are processed depending on the current measured data.

A brief survey of industrial applications is in Ch.2. Basic features of a ground-level ozone concentration forecast project are introduced in Chap.3. Some conclusions and general perspectives for application of Ecanse for development of industrial applications are in Ch.4.

2. Industrial Applications

2.1. Load Forecast

A main concern in electric power distribution is to predict the future electrical load requirements for a given region so that the power generation can be planned optimally with minimum loss and cost. The load required by a region is affected by factors including the general trend, time dependent factors (season, holidays), weather, and special events (strike, special television program). Load forecasting systems take into account these factors and facilitate the management of energy reserves and operation of the power generators. The forecast accuracy plays an important role in the operating costs of power generation plant. This predicted power system load is the quantity for planning sufficient generation, spinning reserve and standby reserve.

The automatic neural network based method in ECANSE®, with modular system architecture, has very high prediction accuracy. Using this method, the mean absolute error of the forecast is between 1 and 2 % (including special days such as public holidays). The forecast can be done hourly, half-hourly or even quarter-hourly.

2.2. Neural Filtering in Automatic Generation Control

The principle objective of Automatic Generation Control (AGC) is to be able to alter the power output of defined generators within a prescribed area in response to changes in system frequency and/or tie line loadings as well as their reference values. The power output should be changed to meet the area obligation to contribute to system regulation and/or interchange agreements with other areas. The deviations from the area obligations are defined as the Area Control Error (ACE). The ACE has to be filtered.

The performance measure is taken as the sum of the absolute value of all control signals. The neural approach reduces this measure up to 50% compared to a conventional low-pass filter without any influence on the area's contribution to system regulation and/or interchange agreements.

2.3. Load Estimation

Power utilities are interested in the instantaneous total load on the power system. A precise estimate of instantaneous load is important for the economical and effective planning of operations as well as load following.

In real life, the instantaneous total load is not known and the total can only be determined with a delay of several hours or days. The only available information is the instantaneous load measurements from specific points in the network.

However, the deduction of total load from these measurements is not an easy task since the relationship is not known.

A precise real-time estimate of the instantaneous load is computed by the neural network based method developed in ECANSE®. A real application performs with a mean estimate error of about 1 %.

2.4. Monitoring of Water Dam

A water dam is a subject to deformation due to various influences. The most important factors are the height of the water level and the temperature. A large dam may be deformed up to several centimeters within a year. In order to assess the security of the dam, it is important to model the elastic and reversible displacement of the dam. Comparing measured data to this model can do monitoring. In addition, irreversible deformations such as shrinkage and cringing of concrete as well as deformations of the underlying boulder have to be considered in the model during the first years.

The Neural Network based method in ECANSE® offers a significant improvement in modeling. Depending on the modeling period, the mean absolute error for the ECANSE based model lies between 0.1% and 1.0%, what is much better than by other conventional methods.

2.5. Applications for Telecommunication

A very promising application of neural networks for telecommunication is their application for diagnostics of telecommunication networks and devices, and for risk management like fraud detection. Interesting results have been achieved in both of these areas.

3. Ground-level Ozone Forecast

A molecule of the **ozone** (O3), as a chemical substance, is the same molecule regardless of where it is found. We distinguish two basic types of the ozone from the environment and pollution monitoring point of view: stratospheric ozone and ground-level ozone. The **stratospheric ozone** is important for humans and all live on this planet as it shields us from harmful ultraviolet radiation coming from the Sun. The **ground-level ozone**, accumulating at the ground level, is considered as an air pollution gas which may be harmful for people, animals, crops, and materials. Only the ground-level ozone concentration is considered in the following and reffered to as an ozone cocentration.

An ozone concentration over a national standard may cause lung and respiratory disorders. A short-term exposure may result in shortness of breath, coughing, chest tightness, or irritation of nose and throat. Individuals exercising outdoors, children, the elderly, and people with pre-existing respiratory illnesses are particularly susceptible. However also materials like rubber, nylon, plastic, dyes, and paints may be damaged by ozone. The ozone pollution is mainly a daytime problem during summer months because sunlight performs a primary role in its formation. Nitrogen oxides (NOx) and carbon oxides (COx) are known as principal "precursors" of the ozone. These compounds react by sun radiation and produce ozone gas. Other influence factors are given by weather participating with all its attributes like: temperature, wind speed, wind direction, humidity, and air pressure.

One of the main concern in pollution monitoring is a prediction of the ground-level ozone concentration for the next 24 hours, for a given region. The forecast results enable to warn people if the National Ambient Air Quality Standard is exceeded. There are several conventional methods, such as multiple regression, Kalman filter, ARIMA models, etc., which are developed for prediction of behavior or processes of different types. We have developed a new automatic neural network based method by ECANSE. In comparison to conventional methods, the prediction is typically twice more accurate and adaptable on-line. The project involves measured data from several measuring stations, in different regions. We have designed a special modular configuration for every region, supplied by the specific measured data. The basic configuration created by ECANSE is about the same for every region. The configuration is hierarchical and includes also some other specific sub-configurations. The learning rate is changing dynamically as an input parameter of the module to be possible to pay a special attention to high concentration days in the forecast processing. The **dynamic adaptation of the learning rate** is processed by a special sub-configuration. The algorithm of this sub- configuration modifies the learning rate by the maximum ozone value in a day-profile, during the learning phase. After finishing the development and testing of this application task, the run-time version of the program is used, without any modification. The run-time version is used by the final user for automatic forecasting for different regions of the country. The forecast can be done hourly, half-hourly or just for the 3-hours-average maximum of the next day, depending on the quality of the measured input data.

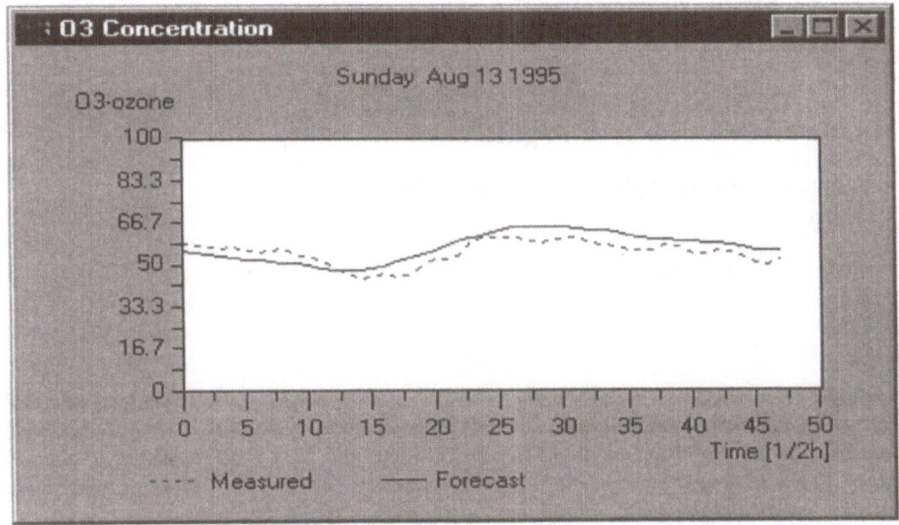

Fig.1 Measured and forecast ozone profile

An example of the final forecast results, in the form of the complete half-hour day profile, is in Fig.1. The more dynamic curve represents the measured data and the more smooth curve represents the forecast profile.

4. Conclusions

We have presented a brief survey of applications of soft computing technologies for industrial projects. All these applications have been developed by the soft-computing studio ECANSE. Both, the Ecanse system and applications are under an intensive development for their improvement and extension, to be possible to cover a large area of requirements of customers from different industrial areas.

References

1. "ECANSE: Environment for Computer Aided Neural Software Engineering", SIEMENS AG Austria, Vienna, 1999, (a set of documentation materials);

Tetris Player: Strategy Driven Algorithm

Martin Lukáč[1]**, Paul Bourgine**[2]

[1] Institute of Measurement Science, Slovak Academy of Sciences, Bratislava, Slovakia

[2] CREA, Ecole Polytechnique, Paris, France

Abstract: In this paper we explore the problem of computational artificial life. For this purpose we choose to model Tetris, a simple ruled game. We propose a simple algorithm based on the duality of exploration and exploitation as a base for a powerful prediction system. This is done by the strategy driven algorithm. We use the TD(λ) reinforcement learning in combination with a multilayer perceptron.

1   Introduction

The ability of living organisms to solve complex problems is limited by their cognitive resources. They decompose the problem. In some situations they are able to use their know-how in exploiting a situation already encountered in their experience, while in other situations they switch to an exploration of a new situation. An organism can change its behavior if it has enough energy to spend for analysis of an unexplored situation. To model a similar behavior we use a combination of a perceptron and reinforcement learning, and define a strategy that balances the exploration and exploitation. This strategy is based on the TD(λ) algorithm operating on outputs from the perceptron. It enables to choose the best positioning of the current piece-to-play. Classical learning methods such as Q-learning [4] or backpropagation have a fixed strategy and are very sensitive to local minima. Here we try to provide a deterministic learning algorithm which changes its own strategy by switching between different modes of analysis. We are not aware of any similar deterministic methods used for solving game problems. But similar nondeterministic methods using TD(λ) in playing TD-Gammon [4] have provided very good results. We base our work on successful nondeterministic methods and we use the determinism just to simplify the learning process.

2 Algorithm description

We analyze Tetris with small 4x4 matrix. Our decision is based on two criteria, the maximum length of the piece-to-play and the maximum gain earned adding a piece-to-play, i.e. 4 lines (see Fig.1). At the beginning of the game set we generate all 2^{16} possibilities of 4x4 binary matrix and we evaluate them by a 3-layer perceptron with 16 inputs, 8 hidden and 1 output units. We choose 10 best patterns $P_i(t)$ (4x4 matrices) with values $p_i(t)$ along the borderline, then we complete these 10 patterns by the piece-to-play in the best manner and we obtain another set of 10 patterns. So we obtain ten couples of patterns $\{P_i(t), P_i(t+1)\}$.

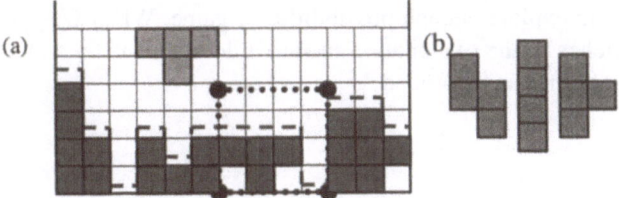

Figure 1: (a) Sketch of the Tetris game space. Piece on the top, in light gray color, is the current piece-to-play. Laid on the bottom, dark gray, are already played pieces-to-play. Current configuration of the game space is given by 4x4 matrices, one of which is illustrated by dotted line. The matrices (which serve as inputs to the perceptron) span the entire width of the game space and follow the dashed borderline. (b) Some piece-to-play examples. All of them can be rotated.

We define the situation couples $\{s_t, s_{t+1}\}$ such as the values of the complete game space before and after the completion by the piece-to-play. For each couple $\{P_i(t), P_i(t+1)\}$ we have a couple of situation $\{s_t, s_{t+1}\}$, where these patterns are set. During the evaluation of a pattern $P_i(t)$ we can define the a_t as the complete value of pattern $P_i(t)$ at time t such as $a_t = p_t + \kappa * s_t$, where κ is the factor that weights the influence of current situation s_t on the decision process. Value of s_t depends on two complementary parameters that are l, the height where the pattern $P_i(t)$ was read and h, the number of holes in the game space under the borderline. We choose the winner $i*$ from the 10 couples of patterns and we modify the winner pattern by the difference of $a_{i*}(t+1) - a_{i*}(t)$. This term enters the perceptron learning rule as the difference between the target and actual outputs.

Next we describe the TD(λ) algorithm [3] used for updating winner pattern value. TD(λ) algorithm has the form:

$$\Delta p_{i*}(t+1) = \alpha(a_{i*}(t+1) - a_i*(t)) \sum_{k=0}^{T-1} \lambda^{t-k} \partial a_{i*}(t+k) / \partial p_{i*}(t+k)$$

where $\Delta p_{i*}(t+1)$ is the error of the complete pattern value to be propagated on the perceptron for the winner $P_{i*}(t+1)$, α is the learning rate.

For all couples of winning patterns $\{P(t),P(t+1)\}$ we define the strategy $\sigma_i(t)$ defined as $\sigma^2_i(t)=E(a_i(t+1)-a_i(t))^2$ where $E(.)$ denotes the mean. Then we define the global strategy Ω of the game. It is generated at the beginning of the game such that all possible moves can be made within its range. During the game the estimation of Ω is calculated as $\Omega = \Sigma^{13}_{t=1}\sigma_{i*}(t)/13$. The convergence of Ω indicates how large a value of the step can be, i.e. how different can be the couple of winning patterns $\{P_{i*}(t),P_{i*}(t+1)\}$. So we can define the condition to play a piece is $\sigma_{i*}(t) < \Omega$. In fact we observe the estimation of the mean of the evaluation of couples of patterns to obtain a new strategy of play.

The aim is to obtain the convergence of Ω to 0. However we must avoid a too fast convergence in order to explore enough possibilities of game. When Ω approaches 0, the algorithm switches to the exploitation mode while higher is the value of Ω, the more unknown patterns can be probed.

3 Reward

Every positioning of the piece-to-play is associated with reward. Here in contradiction with classical Tetris game the reward is only given if one or more lines are completed. We are looking to learn Tetris-player to elaborate some strategy how to earn more possible reward at one time. Moreover a situation is well estimated if it was encountered frequently and if it was rewarded in the past. We are looking for an optimum equilibrium between the optimal prediction of reward $V^*(s')$ earned in the situation s' the and the average value $V(s')$. The estimation of total reward of the situation (pattern and piece-to-play) is based on dynamical programming [2]. However, in this case it is simplified in order to have a faster computational results. The reward for each step is:

$$V*(s') = max_{\Omega}\{r_{\Omega}(s')\}+R(t)$$

where $V^*(s')$ is the total accumulated reward of the current state, $max_{\Omega}\{ r_{\Omega}(s')\}$ is the optimal reward of the current situation s' (by playing a piece-to-play, in situation s and under the strategy Ω), $R(t)$ is the accumulated reward of all states of game until the last step. Here the search of a solution is made at maximum to three steps ahead. We choose this as a compromise between the time to stay in play and resolution of the current situation as fast as possible with the greatest gain. This is easier if the skill to play Tetris is high and we can frequently reach the initial position. For an optimal game the maximum height is 4 lines. This is because in this space all the useful patterns are presented. We suppose that one can first explore 4 x n large game space to learn play Tetris and after can play in a complete game space.

The complete algorithm can be written as follows :

```
Initiate_patterns()                    // set all 2^16 initial values p_t
while not (end_of_game) {
    get current_piece-to-play();       // at time t
    for (game_space_width)             // i = 1,....,10
        set borderline();              // for the pattern P_i(t)
        get best_pattern();            // finding the best P_i(t)
        add piece-to-play();           // calculation of the P_i(t+1)
    If (T>0) set current_piece-to-play to next_piece-to-play;
    play (best_pattern);
    modify (value of the best pattern);   // p_{i*}(t) = p_{i*}(t) + (a_{i*}(t+1) – a_{i*}(t))
    adapt (the strategy of the game);     // update Ω
```

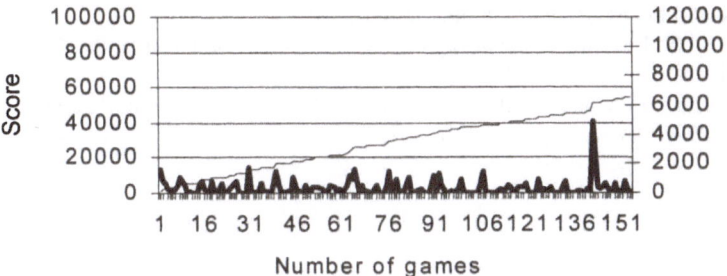

Figure 2: Results of a short game set. The important thing to note is the appearance of a good game visible after some 140 played games. In the graph the thick line represents the score for one game the thin line the total score for all previous games.

4 Simulation

First we evaluated all patterns by the perceptron. The values of the patterns were all set at the beginning of the game set based on their border line and the number of holes in the landscape. In Fig.2, we present an evolution of the score during a game set. We can see that the first interesting result of the experiment is present after 100 iterations (games). With a higher number of played games the frequency of high scored games is higher. We do not make enough experiments so our result are preliminary. We suppose that based on the learning algorithm of the TD-gammon, the number of iterations have to be at least 10 times higher to have a really significant results. The master level of play in TD-Gammon was achieved after more than 1 0000 played games.

5   Conclusion

We modeled Tetris Player switching between two modes of learning: exploration and exploitation. Preliminary results we obtained show that the strategy determined as the consequence of previous steps gave a specific plasticity to the decision process. However, as mentioned above, more simulations are required in order to reinforce our approach to modeling computational game playing.

References

[1] Tesauro G.: TD-Gammon, self teaching backgammon program, achieves master level play. IBM, 1994.

[2] Bellman R.: On application of dynamic programming to the synthesis of logical system. Journal of the ACM, 6(4):486-493, October 1959.

[3] Sutton R.S.: Learning to predict by the methods of temporal differences. Boston: Kluwer Academic Publishers, 1988.

[4] Christopher J., Watkins C.H. and Dayan P.: Q-learning. Machine Learning, 8(3):279-292, 1992.

Electrical Daily Load Forecasting Using Artificial Neural Network in the Power System of Slovak Republic

Peter Szathmáry and Michal Kolcun

Department of Electro-Power Engineering, Technical University of Košice,
Faculty of Electrical Engineering and Informatics, Vysokoškolská 4, 041 20
Košice, Slovakia, e-mail: szathmar@tuke.sk, kolcun@tuke.sk

Abstract: The presentation deals with the state of the electrical load forecasting in the Slovak Republic. We have developed artificial neural network based models for the problem of electrical daily load forecasting. Two paradigms of neural network – Backpropagation and Adaline – are used for forecasting. The prediction models were tested using the real load and meteorological data from Slovak Republic. The best model showed the forecasting error 1.84% (mean absolute percentage error) in the year 1997.

Keywords: Electrical Load Forecasting, Neural Network, Time Series Decomposition, Backpropagation, Adaline

1 Introduction

Daily electrical load forecasting plays an important role in the planning and controlling of power system. In the operation of power system, the variation in demand throughout the day and from day to day, it is necessary to plan in advance the start-up and shutdown of the power plants, especially the large steam-driven generating units. Then the prediction of electrical load are essential for load dispatching, unit commitment, reserve allocation, security assessment and short and long term scheduling of overhauling of power system electrical equipments such as generators, transformers, lines etc.

The prediction times range from a few minutes ahead for the economic loading of power plants to over forty years for the economic planning of new generating capacity and transmission networks. That is way the forecasting methods are divided into long term load forecasting - from 1 year to several years in advance, medium term load forecasting - from 1 week to 1 year in advance, short term load forecasting - from 1 day to 1 week in advance, ultra short term load forecasting - from several minutes to 1 day in advance.

The goal of this contribution is short term electrical load forecasting in power system of Slovak Republic.

Many factors influence the waveform of daily electrical load curve. The most significant factors are:

- weather factor - variables such as outdoor temperature, wind speed, visibility, illumination level, humidity and etc. can significantly effect the daily electricity demand,

- television audience behaviour – popular television programmes can cause very significant affects on the evening demand,

- holidays – national holidays (Christmas, New Year's Day etc.) cause discontinuities in the automatic operation of the load predictor,

- onset of darkness – the onset time and extend of the evening lighting load is an important factor,

- industrial load monitoring – the demand of large industries should be separately monitored for shutdowns, strikes or unusual patterns of working.

Forecasting error is effected by given factors. The quality of power system control and the economy of operation are highly sensitive to forecasting error. For example, in the United Kingdom, at the time of 1984, an increase of 1 % in forecasting error would the result in increase in operating costs of about £ 10 million per year. That is way it is important to investigate new prediction models for improving prediction error.

2 Electrical Load Forecasting in Slovak Republic

System operators in Control Centre of Slovakia perform daily electrical load forecasting based on assumed similarity of forecasted day with daily electrical load curve in previous time and by their experiences only. That is way it is essential to research forecasting on scientific base.

2.1 Prediction approaches

Two different approaches of electrical load forecasting are proposed:

- direct,

- indirect.

The first method (direct aproach) is based on the idea, that the value of hourly loads and outdoor temperatures form directly the input system of sets for neural network. The cardinal problem of this acces is to choose the convenient input sets.

The neural network alone derives the relation between input and output system of sets.

The second method (indirect method) for solving the problem of electrical load forecasting is based on the method, that hourly electrical loads are decomposed into four parts: trend, seasonal, weather sensitive and residual component.

These four components are easier analysed and that is way the results of forecasting are better than the results without decomposition.

2.2 Direct approach

The input data are hourly loads from daily load database of Slovak republic. If "D" is the forecasted day, then "first" input is hourly loads of the day "D-7", which represents the same day of previous week. There are 24 input neurones in the neural network. Further 3 neurones represent maximum, minimum and average value of the day "D-1". The code of the day is given by combination of seven neurones, where Monday is "1 0 0 0 0 0 0", Thursday is "0 1 0 0 0 0 0", etc. The given input is shown in Fig.1.

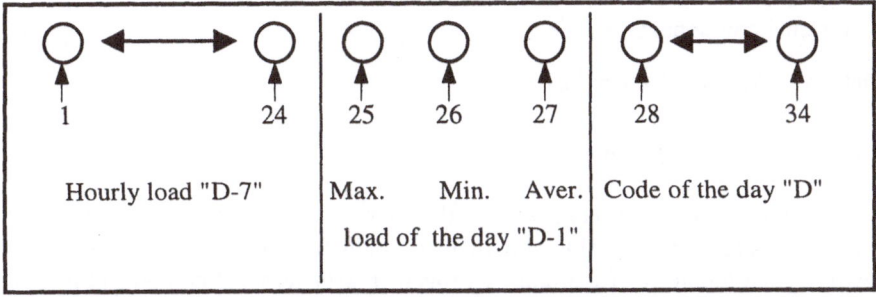

Fig.1 Topology of neural network (direct approach)

A lot of experiments with parameters of neural network were made and one of the best network topology is as follows: two hidden layers with 14 and 15 neurones respectively and two different transfer function (1st hidden layer – log sigmoid, 2nd hidden layer – tan sigmoid). The result is shown in Fig.2, where lower waveform represents the daily mean absolute percentage error (*MAPE*) and higher waveform is daily maximum absolute percentage error (*MAP*) in the year 1996 (*MAPE* = 2.29% and *MAP* = 5.71 %).

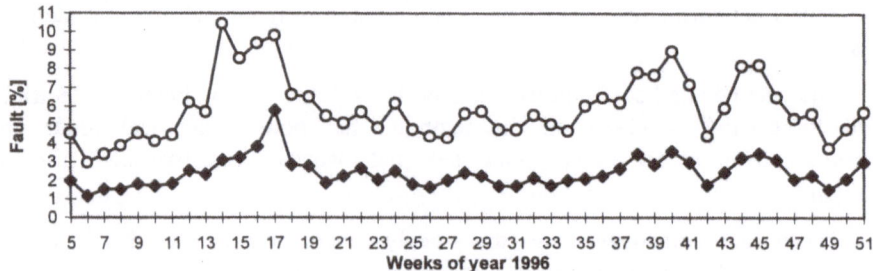

Fig.2 Prediction fault (direct approach)

2.3 Indirect approach

The indirect approach is based on the decomposition of the time series (L – *electrical load*) into fundamental components:

- trend component – L_T,
- seasonal component (short term and long term component) – L_S,
- weather sensitive component – L_W and
- residual component – L_R,

where $L = L_T + L_S + L_W + L_R$.

2.3.1 Trend component

The trend component reflects the long-term movement of the electrical load from year to year. This part of load could be detected by Adaline neural network. The topology of the input set together with seasonal component is given in Fig. 3, where trend component is obtained by means of variable $D = \{1,2,\cdots,365\}$

2.3.2 Seasonal component

Seasonal component includes short-term (weekly) and long-term (periodical) parts. Short-term component is obtained by means of dummy variable such as the code of the day in the direct approach. Long-term part is easy to express using input sets as follows:

$$Cos2 = \cos\left(\frac{2\pi D}{365}\right) \qquad\qquad Sin2 = \left(\frac{2\pi D}{365}\right)$$

$$Cos3 = \cos\left(\frac{3\pi D}{365}\right) \qquad\qquad Sin3 = \left(\frac{3\pi D}{365}\right)$$

$$\vdots \qquad\qquad\qquad\qquad \vdots$$

$$Cos8 = \cos\left(\frac{8\pi D}{365}\right) \qquad\qquad Sin8 = \left(\frac{8\pi D}{365}\right)$$

For each hour $h = \{1,2,\cdots 24\}$ and each type of the day $TD = \{Sunday, Monday, \cdots, Saturday\}$ it is necessary to compose $24\cdot7=168$ implementations of Adaline neural network. The example of the input set for detection of trend, short-term (in this example for Monday) and long-term component is shown in Fig.3.

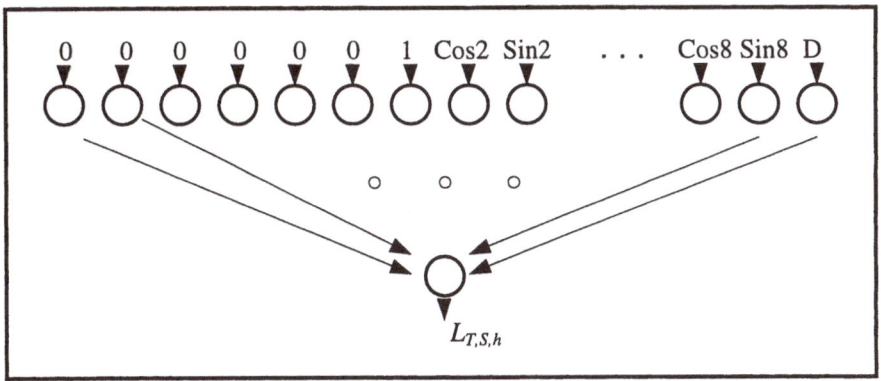

Fig.3 Topology of input set for trend and seasonal component

2.3.3 Weather sensitive component

Many factors influence the daily load. One of the most significant factors is outdoor "effective" temperature, which is calculated by numerical method – exponential smoothing:

$$T_{e,D} = \alpha T_{P,D-1} + (1 - \alpha) T_{e,D-1}$$

where $T_{e,D}$ is "effective" outdoor temperature of the day "D", α is a smoothing coefficient, $T_{P,D-1}$ is temperature of the day "$D-1$" and $T_{e,D-1}$ is "effective" outdoor temperature of the day "$D-1$". The effect of "effective" temperature on the load is calculated using backpropagation neural network with one neuron. The input set is "effective" temperature and output set is load.

2.3.4 Residual component

The residual component, which is the electrical load minus the trend, seasonal and weather sensitive components, is much more difficult to analyse.
This analysis is computed by backpropagation neural network. The input

248

set of network is given by 24 hour residual load one day before the predicted day. The output set is residual load of predicted values.

2.3.5 Results of indirect approach

The results of indirect approach are better than results of direct approach, because load is decomposed into four simpler time series, which are easier to analyse. The weekly *MAPE* error is 1.84 %.

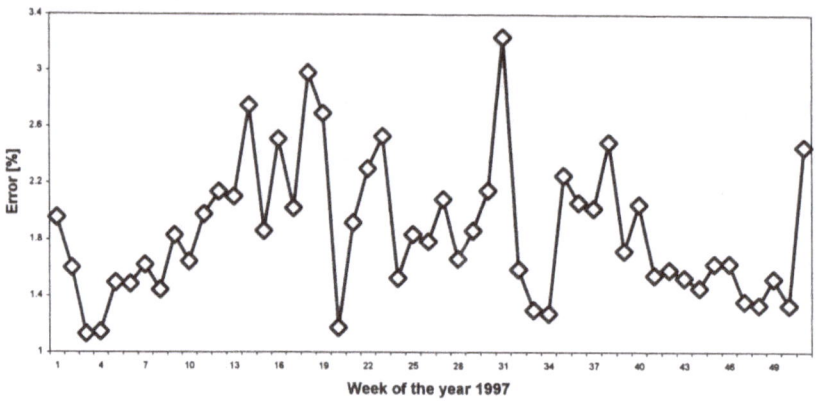

Fig.4 Prediction fault (indirect approach)

3 Conclusion

The contribution deals with daily electrical load forecasting using artificial neural network. Two different approaches are described – direct and indirect. The *MAPE* error is 2.29% for the direct approach and 1.84% for the indirect approach.

References

1. Bunn, D., W., Farmer, E., D.: Comparative Models for Electrical Load Forecasting, John Wiley & Sons Ltd., ISBN 0-471-90635-2, p. 224,

2. Piras, A.: A Multiresponse Structural Connectionist Model for Short Term Electrical Load Forecasting, Dizertačná práca, Lausanne, EPFL, 1996, p. 160,

3. McMenamin, S.: Why Not Pi? A Primer on Neural Networks for Forecasting, Regional Economic Research, Inc., April, 1997, p. 23-42,

4. Szathmáry, P.: Electrical load Forecasting Using Artificial Neural Network, Thesis, October, 1999, p. 126,

5. Kermanshahi, B., S., Poskar, C., H., Swift, G., Buhr, W., Silk, A.: Artificial Neural Network for Forecasting Daily Load of a Canadian Electric Utility, IEEE, 0-7803-2566-4, 1996, P. 268-273.

Practical Approach to Prediction of Plant Technological Parameters with Missing Data

Marián Hrehuš, Štefan Figedy

VÚJE Trnava, a.s., Okružná 5, 918 64 Trnava , Slovak Rep.

Abstract: The novel approach how to determine the past and future time horizon for prediction of plant technological parameters with missing data is described. These situations frequently happen in real life when the whole spans of time data are missing due to e.g. plant outages. For this, the mutual information analysis has been proposed to use. The hierarchical training of ANNs has been applied to reduce the error of time series forecasting.

1   Introduction

For any industrial plant the availability of machines, reduction of maintenance costs and improvement of efficiency is crucial for operating the plant effectively.

The nuclear power plant turbo-generator has been chosen to test the proposed method for the predictive maintenance. The magnitude of vibrations of one of the bearings should not cross certain limits otherwise the turbine has to be stopped. The aim is to warn the turbine operator enough time ahead in order the turbine might be fixed in the most appropriate period of time.

Monitored parameters are mutually dependent through the underlying process so the problem refers to the multivariate time series forecasting. As we deal with a technological system its operation is frequently broken by outages. The problem of missing data both in the phase of training and recall has to be overcome. This paper presents the practical approach how to train the system for forecasting the technological parameters when data is missing.

2   Data preprocessing; mutual information analysis

For a particular case of condition monitoring of a nuclear power plant turbo-generator, the amplitude of a bearing vibration had been chosen as one of the parameters critical for predictive maintenance. To do it's prediction in time the other 22 technological parameters had initially been selected for monitoring by expert judgement. Each data sample represents one-hour average so the prefiltering has been done by data acquisition system itself. Then data were conditioned for outliers and zero mean and standard deviation 1.

Due to a limited amount of process training data and for simplification of neural network the number of signals involved in further analysis has been reduced by mutual information analysis [1].

In order to compute mutual information, an event m is defined as some interval of values of the data. For each interval which the total range of values is divided into a probability $P(m)$ is computed; $P(m)$ is the probability that the data contains a value lying within the interval m. The average information content for a set of events M is computed as the Shannon entropy :

$$H(M)=-\sum_{m} P(m) \log P(m) \tag{1}$$

For the other set of events N the value of entropy is computed the same way. Next, the concept of entropy is extended to include the case of a pair of events, m and n. The joint entropy $H(M,N)$ is the amount of information available from the pair of measurements :

$$H(M,N)=-\sum_{m,n} P(m,n) \log P(m,n) \tag{2}$$

, $P(m,n)$ is the joint probability that the values fall into intervals m and n simultaneously.

Mutual information defined as

$$\tag{3}$$
$$I(M,N)=H(M)+H(N)-H(M,N)$$

represents the amount of information that can be predicted about one time series from the measurements made on a second time series.

Applying the mutual information analysis to the respective sets of measured parameters, only parameters with the highest degree of mutual information related to the predicted amplitude of a bearing vibration have been selected. As a result, only 5 of 22 most influencing parameters remained, including the predicted parameter in question.

Next, the principal component analysis has been used to eliminate the correlated variables. It did not find any linear combination among data parameters selected in the previous step so that any further reduction of input space has not been obtained.

3   Displacement analysis in time domain

The crucial moment for time series forecasting is to discover and choose the time span the series can be forecasted into future and the influence of the past input data on the prediction. Unfortunately in the case of missing data the continuous time series is broken into subsequences which make the use of classical frequency domain analysis, e.g. auto and cross correlation, applicable only with difficulties. There are practical approaches, which deal with incomplete patterns by various methods to "fill-in" the missing input values first and then train the networks [2].

We propose an alternative method based on time displacement of parameters which makes full use of the information potentially available from the incomplete time series patterns. The mutual information analysis can be applied to determine the time horizons for which signal can be forecasted into the future and also the time lags into the past which influence the current values. The procedure is as follows:

Let a table of signals be constructed in which the first column is the time evolution of the signal. First, we want to compute the time horizons of this signal itself. Then the next columns are the same signal, just shifted relatively to the first one by multiples of time step τ (see Table   1 below). These columns now represent separate signals for which the mutual information is to be computed. In case there are missing data in signals the columns will encompass the empty intervals. To compute the Shanon entropy (see Eq. 1), for each column the probabilities $P(m)$ will be evaluated. The joint probabilities $P(m,n)$ between the first and the respective columns will be evaluated for each pairs of columns. The evaluation of probabilities runs only over not empty rows. As a result we obtain the mutual information I (see Eq. 3) between the first and the respective columns and choose those with the highest one. Their time shifts reflect the time horizons when the signal starts to resemble to itself and they are taken for future forecast and past time lags.

Next, the task is to determine the influence of past values of the respective input

Table 1. Time shifts of signals

0τ - shift	1τ - shift	...	kτ - shift	...
...	...	...	...	...
$S(t_{i-1})$	$S(t_{i-1-\tau})$	...	$S(t_{i-1-k\tau})$	...
$S(t_i)$	$S(t_{i-\tau})$	...	$S(t_{i-k\tau})$	...
$S(t_{i+1})$	$S(t_{i+1-\tau})$	...	$S(t_{i+1-k\tau})$	...
...	...	...	...	...

signals on the predicted one. Again the similar approach has been applied, with the only difference that the second and the next columns in the table 1 are the time shifts of the signal the influence of which is to be determined. The first column containing the time evolution of predicted signal is kept unchanged. The columns with the highest mutual information *I* related to the first one are found. Their time shifts determine the time lags important to consider of the input signal being analyzed. This procedure is then repeated for all input signals.

In our particular case for 5 input parameters we obtained the following time horizons:

Table 2. Time horizons of parameters

vibration bearing 1	temperature bearing 1	turbo-gen. power	vibration bearing 2	rotor excentricity
-24 h	-134 h	-24 h	-10 h	-13 h
-105 h		-113 h	-51 h	-122 h
+105 h forecast				

4 Hierarchical training of ANNs

Hierarchical training has been proposed in [3] to reduce the error of the time series forecasting and speed up the training process as the smaller networks are needed. The ability to generalize is improved compared to the only larger network used in classical approach.

The input signals are fed into several networks. The first step is to train network 1 with desired signal forecasted as a target output. Next the network 1 is left unchanged and network 2 is trained with the identical inputs to correct the difference between desired target and output of the previous network. Adding more networks ideally reducing the error can successively project this scheme. The sum of all the outputs approaches the target signal.

In our particular case we trained only the networks 1 and 2 as the residual error of prediction of the first network consisted almost entirely from the stochastic unpredictable part. The second network was capable to recognize and generalize only a small constituent of it. The remaining residual was even more stochastic and there was no use to add any new network.

In the task of time series forecasting the goal is to minimize the prediction error. One way to achieve it is to use the time differences of input and target values instead of their real time values. As a matter of fact we predicted how much the amplitude of vibrations is to be changed in 105 hours (the time horizon for future as determined by mutual information analysis). The value in future will then be the sum of the current value and the predicted difference. Similarly, the inputs of the neural networks are the differences of parameters over the time lags into the past as shown in Table 2.

5   Missing data during the recall phase

When in the recall phase one encounters with just few missing values or outliers in time series this can be overcome by a "local" predictor. Its goal is to substitute the missing data, which further enter as inputs into the long-term predictor. This local predictor can be realized e.g. by recurrent neural networks, autoregressive models etc.

In case of longer plant outages the missing data cannot be replaced. After such period the predictor has to wait until enough data from history will have been collected. In our case the longest time window into the past was 134 hours. In order to shorten the time to wait another neural network with time window only up to 24 hours has been trained to give an approximate prediction in the meantime.

6 Results

Figure 1 shows the results of turbo-generator bearing vibration amplitudes

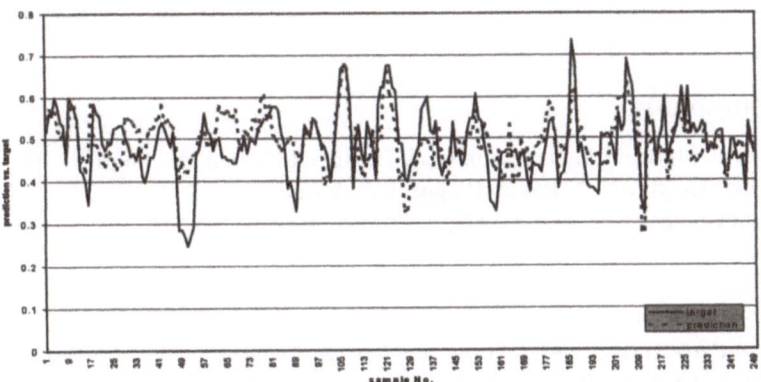

Fig. 1 . Target and predicted values on a validation set of data

prediction in 105 hours into the future on a validation set of data. The RMSE error as the measure forecast accuracy was 6.2 %.

7 Conclusions

The above mentioned results approve us to summarize that the proposed method of handling the missing data in the training phase based on time displacement of parameters is applicable to time series broken into subsequences. This can frequently happen in the plant equipment condition monitoring due to e.g. outages.

The mutual information analysis can be applied to determine the time horizons for which signal can be forecasted into the future and also the time lags into the past which influence the current values.

References

1. Gray R.M. (1990) Entropy and Information Theory. New-York: Springer-Verlag

2. Bishop Ch.M. (1997) Neural Networks for Pattern Recognition. Clarendon Press.Oxford

3. Deppisch J. et al. (1991) Hierarchical Training of Neural Networks and Prediction of Chaotic Time Series. Physics Letters A. 158, 57-62

Application of Artificial Neural Networks to Represent the Rainfall-Runoff Process for Flow Forecasting

Pavel Fosumpaur

Czech Technical University, Faculty of Civil Engineering, Department of Hydrotechnics, Thakurova 7, 166 29 Prague, Czech Republic,
fosump@fsv.cvut.cz

Abstract: There are several different approaches for modelling the rainfall-runoff process, which we can divide in two main groups: deterministic models and statistical models. This paper describes the neural rainfall-runoff model for flood forecasting in real time, and compares it with the linear ARMAX model (auto-regressive moving average with exogenous inputs). The results of this study have shown that the non-linear neural ANN model can be considered as an advanced statistical approach. The advantages of a neural operational forecasting model increase with growing lead time interval.

Keywords: rainfall-runoff process, artificial neural networks, flow forecast

1 Introduction

The rainfall-runoff process represents a very complex non-linear problem, and there are several approaches to solving it. Using physically based conceptual or component models is mathematically correct, but usually costly and time consuming. The complex process is divided into several hydrological subprocesses of the catchment, and the relevant differential equations and constraints are defined.

In order to describe hydrological subprocesses, it is essential to define a suitable schematization of the system. This simplification can cause a loss in result accuracy. In these cases we have to give close consideration to the use of simple black box or statistical methods that can bring more benefits. Deterministic physically-based models contain realistic parameters that are determined during calibration. If some parameters after calibration have reached unrealistic values, this may indicate the unsuitable schematization of the model.

Statistical methods provide a very simple and flexible tool for satisfactorily accurate real time forecasting of flows. The most commonly used statistical model for operational flow forecasting is the linear ARMAX model (auto-regressive moving average with exogenous inputs) popularized by Box and Jenkins [2]. The time series ARMAX model uses auto-regression relationships between the predicted flows and the antecedent flows and precipitation. The short lead time interval of the forecast makes the ARMAX model very useful. According to Kitanidis and Bras [7], it is better to use conceptual models for lead time intervals longer than 6 hours.

The linear ARMAX model tends to overshoot the peak flow and is inadequate in those parts of the hydrograph where the gradient is rapidly changing. In those cases, the model has a strong tendency to continue in an antecedent trend, where it is less accurate than in other parts of the hydrograph. This tendency grows as the lead time interval increases.

Artificial neural networks (ANN) provide a very flexible tool for identifying the difficult non-linear relationship between inputs and outputs and their application for real-time flow forecasting, investigated in this paper. The neural approach to studying the rainfall-runoff process is compared with the statistical linear ARMAX model.

2 Literature Background

The theory of ANN dates back to McCulloch and Pitts [9] in 1943. Recently, significant progress has been achieved in non-linear parallel computing. In 1986, Rumelhart [12] found an effective algorithm Backpropagation for learning feed forward multilayer neural networks. This discovery has led to many successful applications of ANN. ANN is now used in many fields of study.

Nachazel and Toman [11] have investigated the possibility of using ANN for optimising energy production of the hydropower plant system. Stary [13] has used the neural model for maximum flow prediction and for prediction of flood volume in the Ostravice river in the Czech Republic. Inputs to the model consist of duration of the rain event, rainfall depth in the antecedent week, and rain intensity. The author has shown that ANN was able to approximate strongly non-linear rainfall-runoff process with high accuracy.

Hsu, Gupta and Sorooshian [6] have compared solutions of the rainfall-runoff process using the conceptual SAC-SMA (Sacramento soil moisture accounting) model of the U.S. National Weather Service [3], the linear ARMAX model and the ANN model. The authors dealt with one ahead forecast with day time discretization, and they used the Linear Least Squares Simplex algorithm.

Minns has studied the use of ANN in hydrology since 1995, and has published several works on this topic. In a theoretical study [10] Minns proved that ANN is capable of solving the rainfall-runoff process. Minns used a hypothetical basin, and he showed that extrapolation of ANN for unlearned patterns is dangerous.

3 Artificial Neural Networks

Several types of ANN are known. In this paper the multilayer feed forward neural network is described. This network is used mainly for prediction and pattern recognition. Feed forward networks can approximate an arbitrary multivariable non-linear function which is continuous and sufficiently smooth. The principle of the neural network can be described as the transformation of vector X which has dimension m into vector Y with dimension n.

To simulate a neural network we used the NeuroSolve program [4], written in C++. The simulator allows us to load an unlimited net topology and unlimited data, constrained only by the amount of free disk space and by RAM size. The NeuroSolve program simulates a multilayer feed forward neural network trained by the Backpropagation algorithm. The learning rate, the gain of the sigmoidal threshold function, and the other parameters of the net can be changed by learning. By learning it is possible at any time to stop the training or restart the weights. The weights can be initialised in the interval defined by the user. The neural network topology can easily be changed by adding or removing hidden layers or hidden neurons during learning.

There are several techniques for finding an optimum neural network topology. The method of Dynamic Node Creation [1] is based on starting with a small neural topology, and further neurons are added if learning does not converge.

4 Application to the Sazava Basin

The neural model for studying the rainfall-runoff process was calibrated and tested for the basin of the Sazava river (800 km^2) in the Czech Republic [5]. The altitude varies between 401 m and 806 m and the mean annual precipitation is 712 mm. Precipitation is measured at six meteorological stations located in the basin. There were five rainfall-runoff events from 1965 to 1977. Each event presents a summer flood, and each historical data set contains the time series of six-hour rainfall depth and the time series of the river flows with one hour discretization. The first and the longest episode from 1965 was used for calibration, and the other events for evaluation. The training data set is representative, because it is the longest and contains the largest maximum flow.

In this paper we use the model ARMAX(3,5,1) where the forecast flow is determined by 3 antecedent flows, 4 antecedent six-hour rainfall depths and 1 predicted six-hour rainfall depth and 1 model error. The neural rainfall-runoff model uses the same inputs as the ARMAX model. An Antecedent Precipitation Index (API) was added to include the influence of soil moisture. The neural model consists of a three layer feed forward neural network. The use of larger networks did not bring any improvements, and overtraining occurred. Rumelhart [12] recommends the use of small robust networks which have the best generalisation during testing. According to Kurkova [8], overtraining of the net occurs when the number of model parameters is greater than or similar to the number of patterns. We will use the notation of the rainfall-runoff neural models in the shape ANN(x,s,r), where x is the number of inputs neurons (9), s is the number of hidden neurons, and r is the number of output neurons. The number of hidden neurons was optimised to a value of 9. The number of output neurons depends on the lead time of the forecast.

The time step of the rainfall depth is 6 hours. The forecast is computed every hour and the instantaneous flows are aggregated to the 3 hour discretization. The neural model computes a 3, 6, 9 and 12 hour forecast of the flows, which is equivalent to 1, 2, 3 and 4 ahead forecasts. A neural approach allows us to compute, in a single computational step, all predicted flows Q_{t+1} to Q_{t+r}. In case of the ARMAX model the recursive multi-step process is used in order to make a forecast for r time steps. Testing of the models for 4 ahead forecast (12 hours) using the evaluation data set 1977 is shown in Fig. 1.

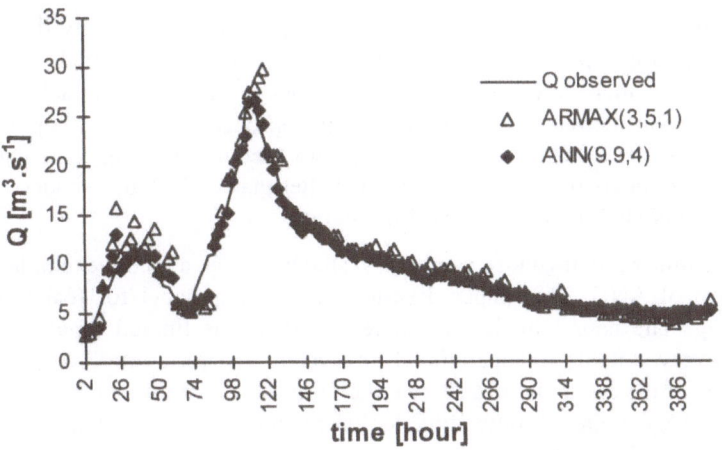

Fig. 1. Evaluation performance of the linear ARMAX model and the ANN model

The forecasting reliability was tested using four criteria: R-squared (R^2), root mean square error (RMSE), relative volume error (%VE) and relative error of maximum flow (%MF). It is generally recommended to consider more than one criterion in determining goodness of fit. Fig. 2 shows the RMSE statistics for the ANN(9,9,r) model for varied lead time intervals of the forecast r. The results of the ANN(9,9,r) model are compared with the linear ARMAX(3,5,1) model. The evaluation set in Fig. 2 is represented by all evaluation series altogether.

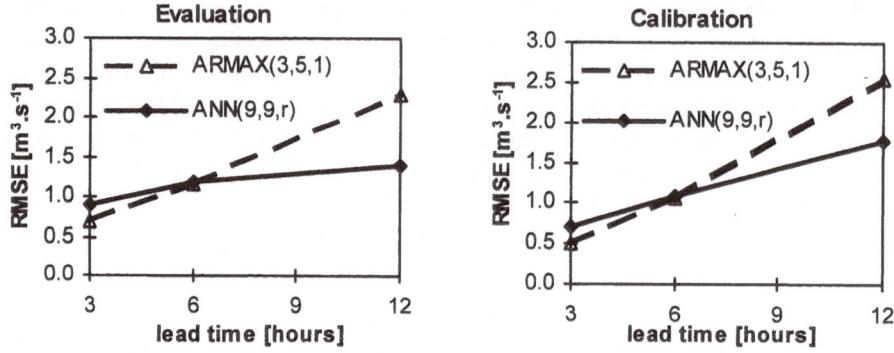

Fig. 2. The RMSE during calibration and evaluation for different lead time forecasts

5 Conclusions

ANN is mainly available for solving very complex, mathematically difficult-to-describe relationships, or relationships which can be described only after simplification which may lead to significant loss of accuracy. In each case it is necessary to consider closely which modelling approach to choose. If a physically-based approach is suitably accurate, taking into account the used schematization and all constraint conditions, then it will be better than a black box model. In other cases the ANN method offers a possible solution.

Modelling the rainfall-runoff process is shown to be a good example of the application of ANN. This paper describes the neural model for real time flow forecasting. The neural model is simple and demands limited input data. It is therefore very suitable for operational forecasting and for control of river flows. The results of the research have shown that for a short lead time of the forecast the linear ARMAX model is more suitable, but for forecasts longer than 6 hours the non-linear neural model is better.

Acknowledgements. This research has been supported by grant of the Grant Agency of the Czech Republic on EXTREME HYDROLOGICAL EVENTS IN CATCHMENTS, No. 103/99/1470 and No.103/99/D031, Prague. The author wishes to thank Robin Healey for his careful proofreading and editing of the manuscript.

6 References

[1]   Ash.T. - Dynamic node creation in back-propagation networks. Technical Report 8901, Institute for Cognitive Sciences, University of California, San Diego, 1989.

[2]   Box, G.E. - Jenkins, G.M., Time Series Analysis: Forecasting and Control, Holden-Day, Oakland, Calif., 1976.

[3]   Brazil, L.E. - Hudlow, M.D., Calibration procedures used with the National Weather Service Forecast System, In. Proc. IFAC Symposium on Water and Related Land Resource Systems, Int. Fed. of Autom. Control, Cleveland, Ohio, 1980.

[4]   Fosumpaur, P., NeuroSolve for Windows 95/NT, Software for simulation of artificial neural networks, Prague, 1998.

[5]   Fosumpaur, P., Application of artificial neural networks in water management, Ph.D. dissertation, CTU, Prague, 1998.

[6]   Hsu, K. - Gupta, H.V. - Sorooshian, S., Artificial neural network modeling of the rainfall-runoff process, *Water Resour. Res.*, 1995, 31(10), 2517-2530.

[7]   Kitanidis, P.K. - Bras, R.L., Real-time forecasting with a conceptual hydrological model, *Water Resour. Res.*, 1980, 16(6), 1025-1033.

[8]   Kurkova, V., An Incremental Architecture Algorithm for Feedforward Neural Nets. *In Proc. of IEEE Workshop Computer-Intensive Methods in Control and Signal Processing*, 1998.

[9]   McCulloch, W.S. - Pitts, W., A logical calculus of the ideas immament in nervous activity. Bull. Math. Biophys., Vol 5, 1943.

[10]   Minns, A.W., Extended rainfall-runoff modeling using artificial neural networks. Hydroinformatics'96, Muller(ed.), Balkerna, Rotterdam, 1996, 207-213.

[11]   Nachazel, K. - Toman, M., Problems of the artificial neural networks and their application to optimize energy production of hydropower plant system, *J. Hydrol. Hydromech.*, 45(3), 1997, 129-150.

[12]   Rumelhart, D. - Hinton, E.G. - Williams, R.J., Learning internal representations by error propagation. MIT Press, Cambridge, Mass., 1986.

[13]   Stary, M., Neural networks and the prediction of peak flows and flood volumes in the Ostravice river basin - profile Šance, *J. Hydrol. Hydromech.*, 46(1), 1998, 45-61.

Using Neural Network in Cryptography

Eva Volná

University of Ostrava, 30.dubna-st. 22, 70103 Ostrava 1, Czech Republic,
e-mail: eva.volna@osu.cz

Abstract: This paper deals with using neural network in cryptography, e.g. designing such neural network, that would be practically used in the area of cryptography both in cryptography and cryptoanalysis. The method should be fully independent on the frequency analyse in the text. Thus, it means: to design the topology of the neural network, to design the method of training algorithm of the neural network, to design the training set for training.

1. Introduction to cryptography

The cryptography deals with building such systems of security of news, that secure any from reading of trespasser. Systems of data privacy are called the cipher systems. The file of rules are made for encryption of every news, it is called the cipher key. Encryption is a process in which we transform the open text, e.g. news to cipher text according to rules. Cryptanalysis of the news is the inverse process, in which the receiver of the cipher transforms it to the original text. The cipher key must have several heavy attributes. The best one is the singularity of encryption and cryptanalysis. The open text is usually composed of international alphabet characters, digits and punctuation marks. The cipher text has the same composition as the open text. Very often we find only characters of international alphabet or only digits. The reason for it is the easier transport per media. The next cipher systems are the matter of the historical sequence: transposition ciphers, substitution ciphers, cipher tables and codes.

Simultaneously with secrecy of information the tendency for reading the cipher news without knowing the cipher key was evolved. Cipher keys were watched very closely. However, it was much easier to set the cipher correspondences, it means to cryptology. Its main goal is to guess the cipher news and to reconstruct the used keys with the help of good analysis of cipher news. It makes use of mathematical statistics, algebra, mathematical linguistics, etc., as well as known mistakes made by ciphers too. The legality of the open text and the applied cipher key are reflected in every cipher system. Improving the cipher key helps to decreases this legality. The safety of the cipher system (key) is in its immunity against the decipher.

2. Application of evolutionary algorithm to neural network

The paradigm makes the basic attribute for neural network. As paradigm we understand its topology, adaptation and activation. In my paper I work with feedforward neural nets with adapted backpropagation. Optimisation of neural network topology by the help of evolutionary algorithm is used for this type of neural network. The neural network topology must correspond to the complexity of task, e.g. the number of training pattern, its inputs and outputs and the structure of relations, that are described. By the adaptation of a small net (this adaptation) is stopped in local minimum and the network must be enlarged by other units. Conversely, the big network allows to find the global minimum of error function, however, the computing absorption is increased. The found configuration of network usually generalises the training pattern including its inaccuracies to a great extent and for untaught patterns, it gives false results.

Among the stochastic evolutionary algorithms, the genetic algorithms are used for optimisation of the designed neural network topology, the standard training algorithm and genetic algorithms are used for adaptation. These algorithms utilise the information from previous step. We want the sum of square of deviation of output from neural network to be the least. One of the main conditions for representation of variables is the appropriate representation of variables with chain of characters (e.g. bit chain with 0 and 1) and the speed of calculation of fitness function in the given point. The method of calculation [2]: First, we must propose maximal architecture of neural network (e.g. maximum number of hidden layers and maximum number of hidden units) before the main calculation. Every individual in the population is characterised by its representation scheme. To optimise the population is it necessary to solve the defined problems. Thereafter the process of genetic algorithms is applied. The finding of optimal population is ended when the population achieves the maximal generation or when fitness function achieves the maximal defined value. We want to find the best architecture with weights, that are adapted. Next, three digits are generated for every connection coming out from a unit. In case the connection does not exist, three zeros are attached to the given place. To every non zero weight value numerated in the following way is thus assigned:

$$w_{i,j,k,l} = \eta \cdot [e_2 (e_1 \cdot 2^1 + e_0 \cdot 2^0)],$$

where $\quad w_{i,j,k,l} = w(x_{i,j}, x_{k,l})$ is the weight value between the j-th unit in the i-th layer and the l-th unit in the k-th layer,

η is a parameter of learning (the constant equal 0.1)

e_i ($i = 0, 1$) is a randomly generated digit

e_2 is a sign bit: if $e_2=0$ resp. $e_2=1$ the expression is positive resp. negative

Every population is then described by chromosomes of individual. For every scheme the number of connections between units, number of hidden units and number of hidden layers are calculated. Error (E) between the desired and the real output is solved in a procedure which implements the forward distribution of signals in multi layer neural network. On the basis of it, these entries for every topology of the appropriate individual its fitness function is calculated as follows:

$$Fitness_i\ast = k_1 \cdot (E_i)^2 + k_2 \cdot (hidden\_units_i)^2 + k_3 \cdot (hidden\_layers_i)^2$$

The general fitness function is calculated as follows:

$$Fitness_i = \begin{cases} k - \left(Fitness_i^* + k_5\right) & \text{if } E_i > k_4 \\[2em] k - Fitness_i^* & \text{otherwise} \end{cases}$$

for $i = 1, ..., N$,

where E_i is error for the i-th network;

$hidden\_units_i$ are the number of hidden units for the i-th network;

$hidden\_layers_i$ are the number of hidden layers for the i-th network;

$k_1, k_2, k_3, k_4, k_5, k$ are constants;

N is the number of individuals in the population.

Values of constants $k_1, k_2, k_3, k_4, k_5, k$ are needed to be chosen with the dependency of solution tasks, for the fitness function values appropriate neural network to be calculate the best. For each fitness function is calculated the probability of reproduction its existing individual by standard method (see [1]). The main *crossover* runs in two following steps: we choose two suitable parents to crossover randomly. Next we generate two numbers randomly. The first of them is from the above limitation of number of biases (e.g. coded biases values). The other is from the above limitation of number of weight connections (e.g. coded weight values). The chosen individuals exchange their substrings of bias and weight connections from the places defined in substrings. If the input condition of *mutation* is fulfilled, one of the individual is randomly chosen and in its genetic representation is randomly chosen in one place. To optimise the population is it necessary to solve the problems defined in the introduction. Adaptation of the best found network architecture is finished with backpropagation.

3. Experiment

Every practical encryption system consists of four fundamental parts:

- The message that you wish to encrypt (called the *plain text*)

- The message after it is encrypted (called the *cipher text*)

- The encryption algorithm

- The key (or keys), which is used by encryption algorithm

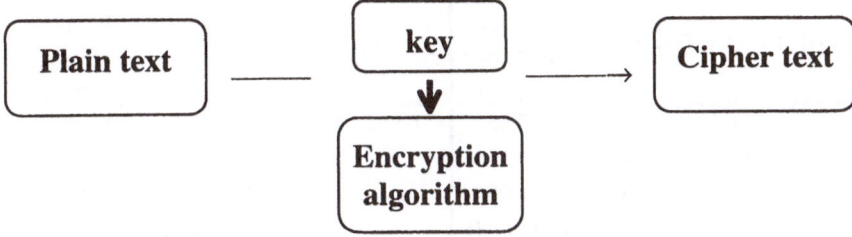

Fig. 1. A simple example of encryption

We can successfully use neural networks as an encryption algorithm in cryptography. Parameters of the adapted neural network are then included to key. We will work with a multilayer neural network that is adapted by backpropagation. Topology of this neural network is based on the training set (see table). Thus, to decrypt the message the neural network will have a topology of 5 - ? - 6, and to encrypt the message it will have a topology of 6 - ? - 5 where symbol „? " is a unknown number of hidden units. The chain of chars of the plain text in a training set is equivalent to a binary value, that is 96 less than its ASCII code. The cipher text is a random chain of bits. The number of units in the hidden layer is suggested using the above described method. The security for all encryption systems is based on a cryptographic key. The simple encryption systems use a single key for both encryption and decryption. The good encryption systems use two keys. A message encrypted with one key can be decrypted only with the other. If we use the neural network as decryption algorithm, the key will have the adapted neural network parameters; it is its topology (architecture) and its configuration (the weight values on connections). Generally, the key is written as follow:

[*Hidden, Input, N_1....N_{hidden}, Output, Biases, Weights coming from the input units, Weights coming from the hidden units*]

where   *Hidden*   is the number of hidden units;

         Input   is the number of input units;

         N_1....N_{hidden} is the number of units in the relevant hidden layer;

Output   is the number of output units;

Biases   are the values of biases;

Weights coming from the input units   are the weight values coming from the input units to hidden units and output units;

Weights coming from the hidden units   are the weight values coming from the hidden units to next hidden units and output units;

Table 1. The training set

THE PLAIN TEXT			THE CIPHER TEXT	THE PLAIN TEXT			THE CIPHER TEXT
Char	ASCII code (DEC)	The chain of bits	The chain of bits	Char	ASCII code (DEC)	The chain of bits	The chain of bits
a	97	00001	000010	n	110	01110	011100
b	982	00010	100110	o	111	01111	101000
c	99	00011	001011	p	112	10000	001010
d	100	00100	011010	q	113	10001	010011
e	101	00101	100000	r	114	10010	010111
f	102	00110	001110	s	115	10011	100111
g	103	00111	100101	t	116	10100	001111
h	104	01000	010010	u	117	10101	010100
i	105	01001	001000	v	118	10110	001100
j	106	01010	011110	w	119	10111	100100
k	107	01011	001001	x	120	11000	011011
l	108	01100	010110	y	121	11001	010001
m	109	01101	011000	z	122	11010	001101

The figure 2 shows the full-interconnected neural network topology for decryption problem and the corresponding key has the following parameters: [*1, 5, 5, 6, biases, weight values coming from the input units, weight values coming from the hidden units*]

The figure 3 shows the full-interconnected neural network topology for encryption problem and the corresponding key has the follow parameters: [*1, 6, 6, 5, biases, weight values coming from the input units, weight values coming from the hidden units*]

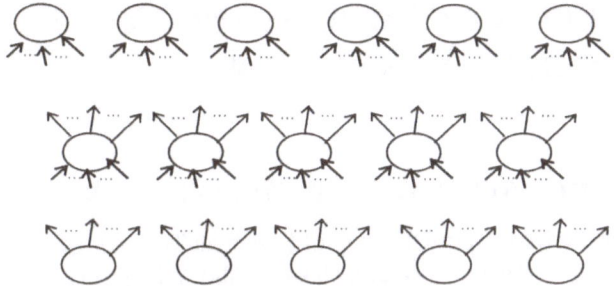

Fig. 2. The neural network topology for decryption problem

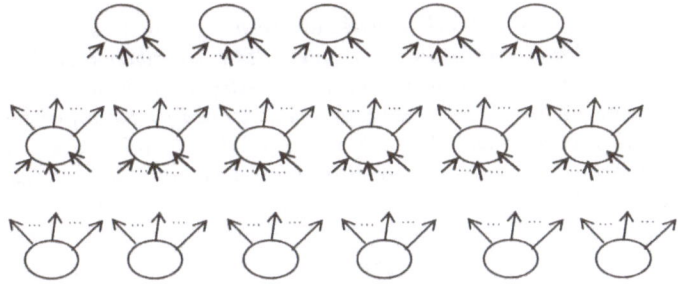

Fig. 3. The neural network topology for encryption problem

4. Conclusion

The goal of cryptography is to make it impossible to take a cipher and reproduce the original plain text without the corresponding key. With good cryptography, your messages are encrypted in such a way that brute force attacks against the algorithm or the key are all but impossible. Good cryptography gets its security by using incredibly long keys and by using encryption algorithms that are resistant to other form of attack. The neural net application represents a way of the next development in good cryptography.

References

1. Lawrence, D.: Handbook of genetic algorithms. Van Nostrand Reinhold, New York 1991.
2. Volná, E.: Learning algorithm which learns both architectures and weights of feedforward neural networks. (Neural Network World. Int. Journal on Neural & Mass-Parallel Comp. and Inf. Systems. **8(6)** (1998), 653-664.
3. Garfinger, S.: Šifrování pro každého. PGP: Pretty Good Privanci. Computer Press, Praha 1998.

Application of Artificial Neural Network Strategies in Process Control

Alojz Mészáros, Anton Andrášik, Anton Rusnák

Department of Process Control, Faculty of Chemical Technology,
Slovak University of Technology Bratislava, Radlinského 9, 812 37 Bratislava

Abstract: Artificial Neural Networks (ANN) have been enjoying an increasing attention in various fields of theory and application, lately. This contribution addresses the new concepts of introduction of the ANN approach into system identification and control. Both, ANN model based predictive control strategy and adaptive PID control are introduced. To demonstrate the feasibility and the performance of the control schemes, a continuous biochemical reactor is chosen as a realistic non-linear case study. Simulation results demonstrate the usefulness and the robustness of the proposed control algorithms.

1   Introduction

In spite of communication barriers between the disciplines (like neurobiology and control theory), the ANN approach has started to play an increasing role in process modelling and control. A possible state space estimator and feedback state controller are introduced. The inverse ANN model, in the role of a direct ANN controller is described.

To avoid the use of locally linearized models of the process to be controlled as in the classical GPC approach (Clarke *et al.* 1987), and complex optimization techniques, we present a new simple solution of deriving long-range predictive control based on ANN. The design of this solution is based on the training of a recurrent and a feedforward neural network. The recurrent and the feedforward neural networks are respectively used as a multi-step predictor and for calculating the control signal (neural controller). The multi-layer feedforward ANN is trained so as to achieve the control objective. The main idea presented in this study concerns the use of stochastic recursive approximation techniques as learning tool for the design of neural networks controllers to solve both unconstrained and constrained predictive control problems.

Further, we present a new simple solution of deriving adaptive PID control based on ANN. The design of this solution is based on the training of a recurrent and a feedforward neural networks. The recurrent and the feedforward neural networks are used as a predictor and neural feedback controller, respectively. The controller consists of a multi-layer feedforward ANN and a discrete-time PID algorithm. The network serves for adaptive tuning of the PID controller. Thus, as to the performance, the proposed controller structure corresponds to a self-tuning adaptive PID control.

2 Forward modeling

The procedure of training a neural network to represent the forward dynamics of a system is referred to as forward modelling. The system to be identified is governed by the following non-linear, discrete-time difference equation

$$y(k + 1) = f[(y(k); y(k-1); ... ; y(k-n+1); u(k); u(k-1), ... , u(k-m+1)] \quad (1)$$

The block diagram of a forward neural network model is shown in Fig. 1.

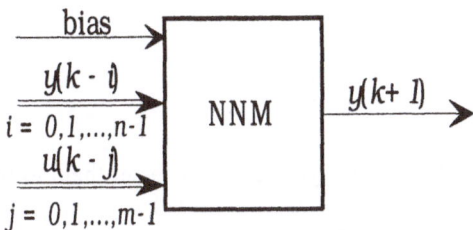

Fig. 1 Forward neural network model

3 Inverse modeling

Inverse models of dynamical systems play a crucial role in a range of control structures because an inverse ANN model may serve as a direct ANN controller in feedback. The inverse mathematical model of the plant to be controlled can be considered in the form

$$u(k) = f^{-1}[y(k); y(k-1); ...; y(k-n+1); y^*(k+1); u(k-1); u(k-2); ...; u(k-m+1)] \quad (2)$$

where $y(k + 1)$ is not known so it has been replaced by reference, $y^*(k + 1)$. The block diagram of an inverse ANN model is shown in Fig. 2.

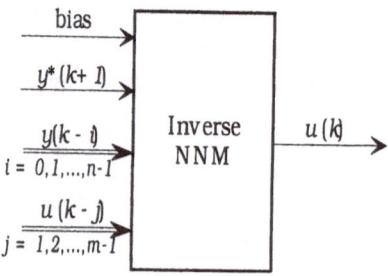

Fig. 2 Inverse neural network model

4   State space representation

Consider the state space description of the process to be identified (controlled) in the well-known form

$$x(k + 1) = A\,x(k) + B\,u(k) \tag{3}$$

$$y(k) = C\,x(k) \tag{4}$$

By a suitable choice of the state variables we can set them to be the outputs of the hidden layer of the forward ANN model without any bias at the hidden layer. An appropriate combination of the forward and the inverse plant model can result in a feedback control structure where both, state observer and state feedback controller are present. Such a scheme, in a second order system terms is presented in Fig. 3.

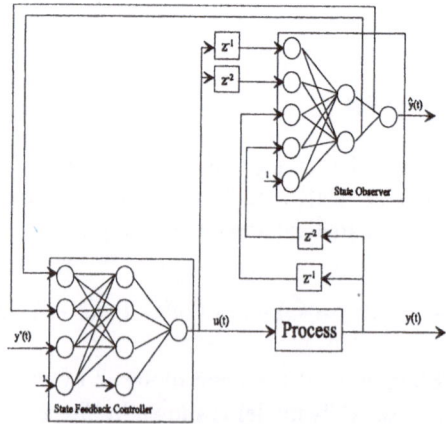

Fig. 3 ANN in state feedback control

Some new approaches to advanced process control in terms of ANN methods are shown in the following.

5 ANN predictive control

The model predictive control is based on the minimization of the objective function

$$J = \sum_{j=N_1}^{N_2} \left(y^*(t+j) - y(t+j)\right)^2 + \sum_{j=1}^{N_u} \lambda(j)\left(\Delta u(t+j-1)\right)^2 \qquad (7)$$

where $y(.)$, $u(.)$, and $y^*(.)$ are the controlled variable, future control increments, and setpoint, respectively. N_1, and N_2, are, respectively, the minimum and the maximum prediction horizon. The weighting factor, $\lambda(j)$ $(j=1,.N_2)$ serve for penalization of the future control increments, Δu. Usually $\lambda(j)$ is considered as a constant λ.

Consider the problem concerning the design of an algorithm which at time t predicts simultaneously the outcomes of the process $\{y(t)\}$ at time t, $t+1$, $t+2$, . , $t+N_2$ where N_2 is the prediction horizon. In this study we have used a time-lag recurrent ANN as a multi-step predictor. The training process of this ANN predictor is carried out using a backpropagation through the time algorithm (Werbos 1990), and the genetic algorithm is used for the initialization of the weights. A multilayer feedforward ANN is used as a controller. The controller inputs consist of the plant predictions which are provided by the recurrent neural network and the desired value of the plant output. The outputs correspond to the present and future increments of the control signal. The weights of this ANN controller are updated directly using a stochastic approximation algorithm which minimizes the control objective (7) subject to eventually some constraints. These weights are considered as the controller parameters. Since control action is based on the prediction of the plant behavior, offset can occur due to disturbances and model mismatch when the ANN is used as a dynamic model of the controlled process. Therefore, the plant output is predicted at each sampling time as follows:

$$y(t) = f(U,W) + d(t) \qquad (8)$$

where U are the ANN inputs, W is a vector of the weights to be optimized, and d is a disturbance. This disturbance (correction) d of the prediction is computed by the following equation:

$$d(t+i) = d(t) = y(t) - \hat{y}(t) \qquad (9)$$

where y is the current value of the plant output and $\hat{y}$ is the prediction of y generated by the ANN predictor. The disturbance is assumed to be constant over the prediction horizon. The general schematic diagram of the predictive controller is depicted in Fig. 4.

272

6   Adaptive neural PID control

A new simple solution of deriving adaptive PID control based on ANN policy is
introduced. The design problem consists of training of both, a recurrent and a
feedforward neural network model. The recurrent and the feedforward neural
network are respectively used as a predictor and adaptive neural feedback
controller. They are trained using the back-propagation through the time and
stochastic approximation algorithms , respectively. The multi-layer feedforward
ANN is trained so as to achieve the control objective (7). The controller consists of
a multi-layer feedforward ANN and a discrete-time PID algorithm. The network
serves for adaptive tuning of the PID controller. Thus, as to the performance, the
proposed controller structure corresponds to a self-tuning adaptive PID control.
The controller network inputs consist of the plant predictions, which are provided
by the recurrent neural network and the desired value of the plant output. The
outputs correspond to the PID controller parameters: K, T_i and T_d .The general
schematic diagram of the proposed control algorithm is depicted in Fig. 5.

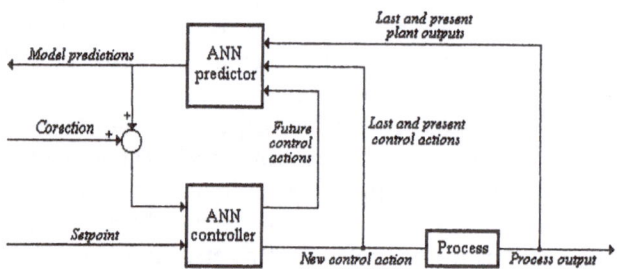

Fig. 4 The ANN predictive control structure

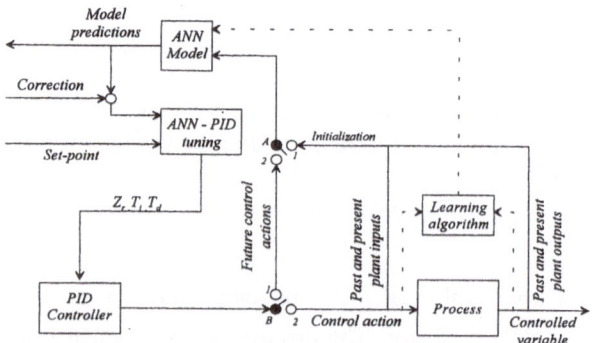

Fig. 5 The ANN-PID control system structure

7 Simulation results

To demonstrate the performance and the feasibility of the approaches described above, we have applied it to control the continuous-flow stirred biochemical reactor, in which the growth of Saccharomyces cerevisiae on glucose takes place. The dynamic model and the mathematical description of the kinetic model mechanism are adopted from [9]. The aim of the experiment was to control the dissolved oxygen concentration, c_o, using the dilution rate, D_g, as the manipulated variable. Controlled variable profiles for ANN predictive control and ANN PID control are presented in Fig. 6 and Fig. 7, respectively. Fig. 7 shows also an alternative adaptive control profile as a result of recursive (LDDIF) identification based self-tuning control.

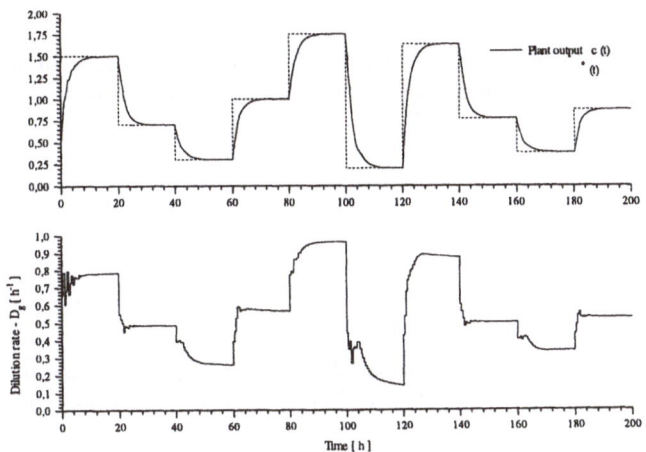

Fig. 6 Predictive ANN control responses

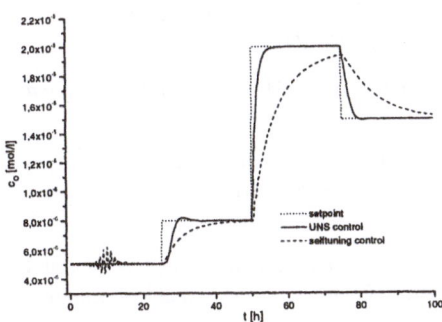

Fig. 7 Adaptive ANN-PID control responses; a comparison with recursive selftuner

8 Conclusion

In this paper, new approaches to intelligent, ANN modeling based identification and control were introduced. State space controller, predictive and adaptive PID control strategies were described. The selected simulation experiments on a continuous-flow stirred biochemical reactor model have shown good regulatory and tracking performance on the control systems proposed. However, when applied the neural controller to linear problems, no significant improvements have been proved.

Acknowledgement

The authors are pleased to acknowledge the financial support of the Scientific Grant Agency of the Slovak Republic under grant No. 1/5220/98.

References

[1] Hunt, K. J. et al.: Neural networks for control systems - A survey. *Automatica*, **28** (1992), 1083-1112.

[2] Clarke, D.W. Mohtadi, C. and Tuffs, P.S.: Generalized predictive control - Part I. The basic algorithm, Part II. Extensions and interpretations. *Automatica*, **23** (1987), 137-160.

[3] Werbos, P.: Backpropagation through time: what it does and how to do it. *Proceedings of the IEEE*, **78** (1990), 1550-1560.

[4] Kiefer, J. and Wolfowitz, J.: Stochastic estimation of the maximum of a regression. *Ann. Math. Stat.* **23** (1952), 462-466.

[5] Ljung, L. Pflug, G. and Walk, H.: *Stochastic approximation and optimization of random systems*. Berlin, Springer-Verlag, 1992.

[6] Najim, K., Rusnák, A., Mészáros, A. and Fikar, M.: Constrained long-range predictive control based on artificial neural networks. International Journal of System Science, **28** (1997), 1211-1226.

[7] Mészáros, A., Rusnák, A. and Fikar, M.: Adaptive neural PID control. Case study: tubular chemical reactor. Computers and Chemical Engineering Supplement (1999), S847-S850.

[8] Mészáros, A., Rusnák, A. and Najim, K.: Intelligent control of continuous bioprocesses using neural network models. Chem. Biochem. Eng. Q., **11** (1997), 81-88.

[9] Mészáros, A., Brdys', M. A., Tatjewski, P., Lednický, P.: Multilayer adaptive control of continuous bioprocesses using optimising control technique. Case study: Baker's yeast culture. Bioprocess Engineering, **12** (1995), 1-9

Design of a Fuzzy Adaptive Autopilot

Ján Vaščák[1], Peter Kováčik[2], František Betka[2], and Peter Sinčák[1]

[1] Technical University of Košice, Faculty of Electrical Engineering and Informatics, Department of Cybernetics and Artificial Intelligence, Computational Intelligence Group, Letná 9, 041 20 Košice, Slovakia, E-mail: vascak@tuke.sk, sincak@tuke.sk

[2] Military Aviation Academy, Rampová 7, 041 21 Košice, Slovakia, E-mail: kovacikp@topgun.vvslnet.sk, fbetka@topgun.vvslnet.sk ***

Abstract: Aircraft behaviour can be described by sets of parameters that characterize their aerodynamic properties and flight conditions. They are obtained by measuring in aerodynamic tunnels under special laboratory conditions however not fully describing all possible flight situations. Their accuracy is also limited. As considerable changes of the description occur during a flight, the use of non–adaptive autopilots, especially in a combat aircraft, is considerably limited. The removal of this obstacle is possible only by means of a continuous on–line adaptation of an aircraft model and by a consecutive adaptation of the autopilot. This paper deals with the design of a performance– adaptive fuzzy controller as an autopilot. The structure of such a contoller, as well as the adaptation principle, are described with the aim to implement it to an autopilot of a combat aircraft.

Keywords: adaptive fuzzy controller, adaptation principle, autopilot, fuzzy relation, incremental model, performance.

1 Introduction

Any system that is able to adapt its parameters depending on changes in the controlled system is by the classical definition, adaptive. As each fuzzy controller fulfils this condition, we understand the notion "adaptive fuzzy controller" (AFC) as a system which is able to self–learn or to self–tune. The basic structure of an AFC is depicted in fig. 1.

A non–adaptive (classical) fuzzy controller is supplemented by a process monitor and an adaptation mechanism changing the knowledge base by evaluations obtained from the process monitor. The process monitor observes the behaviour of the whole control circuit and tries either to evaluate the current state or to describe changes in the controlled system. We see that the adaptation depends on the principle of the process monitor and therefore there are two basic AFC:

*** This project is supported by Slovak National Science Agency under project # 9433 "Computational Intelligence for decision procedures", 1999–2001

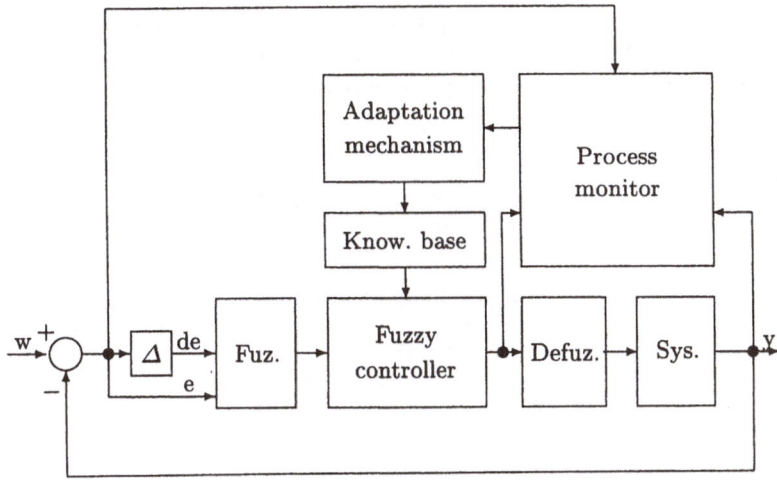

Fig. 1. Basic structure of an adaptive fuzzy controller.

1. **Parameter–adaptive systems**
2. **Performance–adaptive systems**

The first type is based on the principle of identifying the parameters of the aircraft model. The information attained is then transformed into the form of fuzzy rules of the controller. Setting up such a transformation is however difficult and problem–oriented. A performance–adaptive system does not require explicit knowledge of an aircraft model and is based on measuring the control quality, in accordance with verified control criteria. Such an approach is both more general and enables defining and grading more types of control criteria (e.g. speed of control, quantity of energy necessary for control, etc.). We concentrate our attention to the design of a performance–adaptive fuzzy autopilot as a controller connected to an aircraft model in a negative feed back as shown in fig. 2.

2   Structure of a performance–adaptive fuzzy autopilot

The basic description of an aircraft model going from motion equations by a fuzzy state model [2] consists of four state quantities:

u – total velocity of flight (a vector sum of all 3 coordinates)
w – vertical velocity (projection of u into the vertical plane)
θ – pitch angle (angle between the longitudinal aeroplane axis and earth)
q – pitch rate (derivative of θ)

The inputs to AFC are pitch angle error e_θ (difference between the desired θ_d and current pitch angle θ) and its derivative e_q, see (1) and (2). Each aeroplane is controlled by an elevator, i.e. by the elevator angle η and its change $\Delta\eta$. For the sake of simplicity we take into account only the longitudinal flight. The control circuit with a performance–adaptive AFC as the adaptive autopilot and the aeroplane model are shown in fig. 2.

$$e_\theta = \theta_d - \theta \qquad (1)$$

$$e_q = \frac{e_\theta}{dt} \qquad q = \frac{d\theta}{dt} \qquad (2)$$

Adaptive fuzzy controller

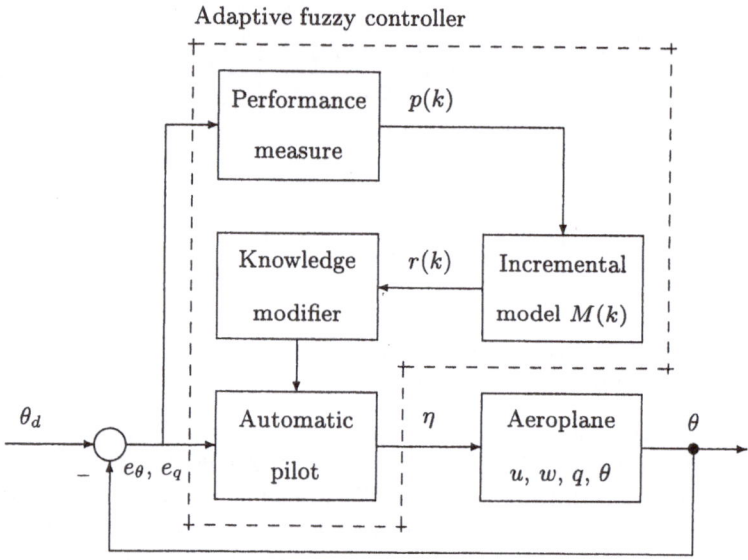

Fig. 2. Structure and connection of an adaptive autopilot into the negative feed back.

Following quantities are in this model of AFC:
T – sampling time (real time $t = k.T$, $k = 0, 1, 2, \ldots$)
$p(k)$ – performance measure corresponding to the desired changes
$M(k)$ – incremental model of the controlled process ($\theta(k) = f_M(\eta(k))$)
$r(k)$ – reinforcement value, i.e. change to the desired rule consequent
    Performance measure is determined on the base of a dumping ratio (8). In other words, $p(k)$ expresses the opposite of the control quality. Its value corresponds to the magnitude and direction of changes to be performed in the knowledge base of the controller. The basic design problem of AFC consists in the design of an incremental model M, where for each time sample $t = K.T$ ($K = 0, 1, \ldots$) a simplified incremental model $M = J.T$ (J – Jacobian) is created that is analogous to the linear approximation of the first order differential equation. It can be proved that J is equal to the determinant of the dynamics matrix, i.e. it is a numerical value. J is calculated or at least

estimated in each calculation cycle and this fact increases the robustness of the autopilot, an aspect belonging to the elementary criteria of quality at the system appraisal [1].

Now we need to transform such a description of a controlled system to the description of a controlling system, i.e. a controller. Going from the properties of the feed back connection we can see that $\theta(k) \approx e_\theta(k)$. As inputs and outputs of a controlled system change to outputs and inputs of a controller, respectively we can get the controller description like the inverse function of $\theta(k) = f_M(\eta(k))$, i.e. the model of the controller (autopilot) is $\eta(k) = f_M^{-1}(\theta(k))$. Because J is a number, then M^{-1} is the reverse value of $J.T$. The reinforcement value $r(k)$ is computed as:

$$r(k) = M^{-1}.p(k) \tag{3}$$

The knowledge base adaptation can be either relation–based or rule–based. We use the first way and utilize the compositional inference. It is true that we lose the knowledge representation in the form of IF–THEN rules but the control process is fully automatic and we need not know the content of the knowledge base. The second way causes enormous growth of the number of rules so the computational complexity rises and introduction of the so–called garbage collection mechanisms is necessary.

The adaptation is based on removing such rules that caused a "bad" control in the previous time step and including new "reinforced" rules. The relation–based adaptation principle for the next time step $k + 1$ can be described in the following form:

$$R(k + 1) = (R(k) \cap \overline{R_{bad}}(k)) \cup R_{new}(k), \tag{4}$$

where:
$R(k)$ – fuzzy relation describing the knowledge base in $t = k.T$
$R(k + 1)$ – fuzzy relation describing the knowledge base in $t = (k + 1).T$
$R_{bad}(k)$ – "bad" fuzzy relation (responsible for a "bad" control)
$R_{new}(k)$ – "reinforced" fuzzy relation (added $r(k)$)

As there are two inputs (e_θ and e_q) and one output ($\Delta\eta$) the fuzzy relations $R(k)$, $R(k + 1)$, $R_{bad}(k)$ and $R_{new}(k)$ have the same dimensions in the form of three–dimensional cubes, see fig. 3.

$$R = \int_{E_\theta \ x \ E_q \ x \ \Delta\eta} \mu_R(e_\theta, e_q, \Delta\eta)/(e_\theta, e_q, \Delta\eta) \tag{5}$$

$R_{bad}(k)$ and $R_{new}(k)$ are Cartesian products between controller inputs and outputs that are fuzzified. The simplest fuzzification is in the form of singletons but generally, other forms are possible, too. $R_{bad}(k)$ is derived from the combination of previous inputs and outputs which caused "bad" control. $R_{new}(k)$ is created by reinforcing $R_{bad}(k)$ on the base of $r(k)$ as seen in (6) and (7). We can see only the output is modified. Inputs stay unchanged.

$$R_{bad}(k) = \text{fuzz}(e_\theta^*(k)) \ x \ \text{fuzz}(e_q^*(k)) \ x \ \text{fuzz}(\Delta\eta^*(k)) \tag{6}$$

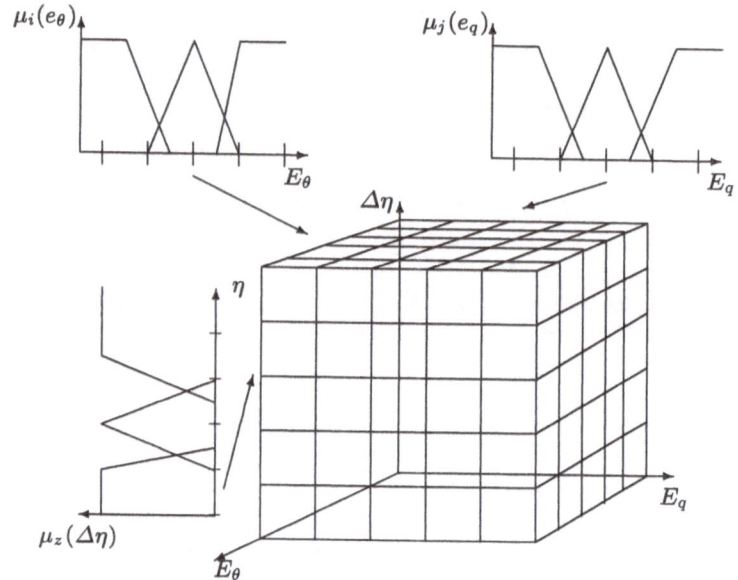

Fig. 3. Forms of fuzzy relations for $R(k)$, $R(k+1)$, $R_{bad}(k)$ and $R_{new}(k)$

$$R_{new}(k) = \text{fuzz}(e_\theta^*(k)) \; x \; \text{fuzz}(e_q^*(k)) \; x \; \text{fuzz}(\Delta\eta^*(k) + r(k)) \qquad (7)$$

3   Design procedure of an autopilot

We can divide the design procedure of such an AFC into these steps:

1. Design of the initial membership functions
2. Set up of the initial rule base
3. Design of the performance measure calculation
4. Calculation or estimation of Jacobian of the dynamics matrix

The first two steps are not necessary but adding certain initial knowledge about the controlled system can shorten the adaptation time. As this adaptation method is recursive, also the "worst" knowledge base is gradually modified until the control error is minimized.

The performance measure p has to be close to r, i.e. $p \approx r$. It is defined as the difference between the optimum dumping ratio and the current λ. If λ is big then the control is slow and with small oscillations. If λ is small then the control is fast but with big oscillations. The optimum λ seems to be the value $0,7$. Then p is $0,7 - \lambda$, see fig. 4. The goal of the control is to minimize p or $\lambda \to 0,7$ which is identical to the physical point of view, i.e. to stabilize the pitch angle θ at a certain value.

$$\lambda = \frac{0,8.t_d - t_r}{0,7.t_r + 2,5.t_d} \qquad (8)$$

where t_d and t_r are delay and rise time, respectively.

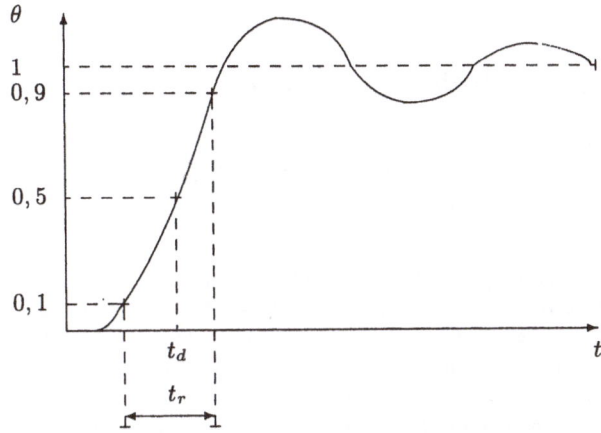

Fig. 4. Transition process of the pitch angle stabilization.

4   Conclusions

The principal advantage of this approach is the substitution of a human expert in establishing the fundamental knowledge about the fuzzy controller (autopilot) which is the most serious disadvantage of standard fuzzy systems. The design presented enables fuzzy systems to be used for the control of systems showing strong changes of parameters during their working. The most critical part seems to be the estimation of the dynamics matrix needed in each calculation cycle. This problem can be solved in many ways, e.g. by neural networks enabling parallel computation and so reducing the time pretension of the calculation [3].

References

1. Procyk, TJ. - Mamdani, E.H. (1979) A linguistic self–organising process controller. Automatica N. 15, 15–30
2. Vaščák, J. - Kováčik, P. - Betka, F. (1998) States knowledge–based filtering of a fuzzy state model. BUSEFAL N. 75, 27–32. ISSN 0296-3698
3. Žilková, J. (1996) System Identification by Neural Networks (in Slovak). SEKEL '96, Stará Lesná, 55–60

Mobile Robot Control Using BP Based Adaptive Critics

R. Jakša, M. Hudec, P. Sinčák

Computational Intelligence Group
Department of Cybernetics and Artificial Intelligence, Technical University, Košice
E-mail: jaksa@neuron-ai.tuke.sk

Abstract: The paper presents results of experimental analysis of backpropagation and adaptive critic based control architecture. A number of experiments were performed with the application of a given method for mobile robot navigation. The number of variations of actor and critic neural networks were tested, and results show the ability of algorithm to deal with as many as six layers of units in networks. Observed ability of algorithm to deal with very big learning rates and simple experimental method for stabilization of algorithm are also discussed in the paper.

1 Introduction

Adaptive critic method (AC) based on the backpropagation algorithm (BP) is virtually very powerful technique that combines advantages of adaptive critics (ability to optimize according to arbitrary cost function) with advantages of backpropagation algorithm (ability to deal with complex multilayer neural networks, robustness of the algorithm considering the training data set and generalization abilities). Backpropagation algorithm [7,1] and adaptive critic method [5] are well known techniques that are broadly and routinely used in the control area [2,8]. The combination of both, however, is not used so frequently. Backpropagation is usually used in strict supervised learning mode, whether as a learning algorithm for the whole neurocontroller, or for the training of neural networks used as parts of a complex control scheme. Adaptive critics are usually constructed using table based algorithms or single layer CMAC networks. Backpropagation is usually used in adaptive critic systems only for a critic network training, what is in fact a simple supervised learning task. Only simple actor networks are usually used in adaptive critic systems (critic networks vary in wider scale). This way, the complexity of the critic is the main parameter used for the determination of whole controller complexity. The role of the actor complexity in control tasks is an interesting question, especially when considering attempts to control complex systems. Theoretical background for application of the backpropagation algorithm in adaptive critics was done by Werbos works [2,8,6] and practical applications in recent works of Prokhorov [4]. From the backpropagation

This project is supported by Slovak National Science Agency under project #9433 "Computational Intelligence for Decision Procedures", 1999-2001 point of view, used actor-critic architecture is an extension of basic back-propagation algorithm (supervised learning) with the ability to solve more general (reinforcement learning) tasks.

Mobile robotics offer a wide range of different control tasks and even "simple" task of vehicle navigation to fixed target position can be scaled from a very simple, to a very hard problem. This flexibility makes the mobile robotics area interesting for experiments with a given control method.

2 Control task

The main goal of the control was to start robot movement from any position in an unknown environment and reach a desired position without the supervisor's intervention. Apriori knowledge was not used for the initialization of neural networks and all the control strategy was built by the learning algorithm during control.

3 Controller

In the experiments, the classical adaptive critic scheme was used, where actor network is used for direct control of the plant and adaptive critic network realizes an evaluation of the actor network behavior.

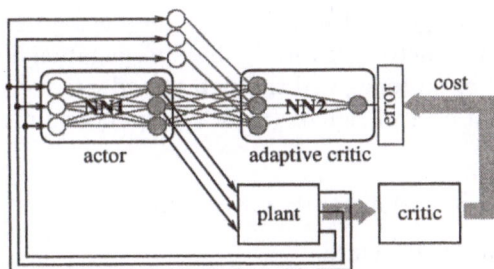

Fig. 1. Adaptive critic controller

Both, actor and adaptive critic networks are general multilayer feed-forward neural networks with complex topology. Both are trained with the backpropagation algorithm. Network NN2 (*adaptive critic*) is used for critic approximation and is trained to match critic's outputs (*error function, minimized during training, is* $J_1 = (cost_{critic} - cost_{NN2})^2$). Network NN1 (*actor*) represents the controller and is trained to produce actions minimizing the cost computed by NN2. If NN2 is working correctly and produces output corresponding to critic's output, then NN2 output minimization also minimizes critic computed cost. In this case, NN2 output or some function of this output, is an error used in the learning process.

Considering recent popularity of the temporal difference method (TD) in reinforcement learning applications, it's necessary to note that in these experiments, TD methods weren't used. TD deals with learning, which reflects time sequences in training data. This is a common situation in control tasks, however they are situations where immediate cost is adequate for evaluation of the controller's action. Example of such a situation can be the navigation of a mobile robot (simple dynamics) in an environment without obstacles, where information about the current state is sufficient for the computation of optimal action. Sequence of state informations can be used in this case too, and may result in simpler computation. Direct usage of cost signal, instead of the TD type of evaluation, brings differences in stability properties of actor training.

Algorithm:

1. initialization of weights of both networks
2. evaluation of current controller behavior (cost computation)
3. adaptation of adaptive critic network
   (a) adaptation of weights of output units by LMS rule (1)
   (b) adaptation of weights of other units by BP algorithm (2)
4. adaptation of actor network
   (a) backpropagation of error through adaptive critic network
      i. computation of proposed weights changes (error signal) for output units, using rule (3)
      ii. backpropagation through other units using BP rule (2)
   (b) adaptation of actor network by backpropagation algorithm using error signal backpropagated through the adaptive critic
5. computation of control signals (actor's output) and return to 2. or end

LMS rule used:
$$\Delta w_{ij} = -\gamma x_j f'(in_i)(d_i - x_i) \tag{1}$$

Backpropagation rule used:

$$\Delta w_{ij} = f'(in_i)\frac{x_j}{x_i} \sum_{h=1}^{N_h} \Delta w_{hi} w_{hi} \tag{2}$$

Actor adaptation rule (for output of adaptive critic):

$$\Delta w_{ij} = -\gamma x_j f'(in_i) \tag{3}$$

This rule (3) realizes simple gradient descent minimization of the cost (x_i) produced by the adaptive critic network.

If rule (3) or rule (2) is used for real adaptation of weights, then Δw_{ij} are applied to weights according to: $w_{ij}^{new} = w_{ij}^{old} + \Delta w_{ij}$. If rule (3) or (2) is used only for error backpropagation through the network, without actual adaptation of weights, then Δw_{ij} is used only in (2) for recursive computation of the next value of Δw_{jk}.

Symbols:

w_{ij} is the weight of connection from unit j to unit i; Δw_{ij} is the proposed change of the weight ij; x_i is activation of the unit i; d_i is the desired value for the unit i (from training data set); in_i is input to the unit i; $f(in_i)$ is activation function of the unit i; N_h is the number of units connected to the unit i (i is source); γ is the learning rate.

In the model of neuron: $x_i = f(in_i)$ $in_i = \sum_{j=1}^{N} w_{ij}x_j + w_{i0}$ sigmoidal and linear activation functions $f(in_i)$ were used. N is the number of inputs to the unit (neuron) i and w_{i0} is bias of this unit.

4 Experiments

Experiments were done on the mobile robot simulator. Robot, environment model and the controller were implemented in c language as independent processes interoperating in real-time mode.

Many different neural network configurations were tested in experiments. Combinations of signals: x and y position of vehicle, direction of vehicle, distance from the target position, distance in x and in y direction and all these parameters in previous time steps; were used as inputs for control. Proposed direction of the vehicle or direction change and signals for control of the vehicle acceleration/deceleration, was output(s) of actor. All these signals were transformed to appropriate form for used model of neuron[1]. Binarization[2] of signals was used too. The number of inputs of actor varied between 2 and 30 and the number of outputs between 1 and 20 according to used signals and encoding.

The number of hidden units was also scaled. In both, actor and adaptive critic networks 0, 1 or 2 hidden layers with up to 100 units were used.

The adaptive critic output was usually single valued cost, but multiple-value costs were tested too. The cost function (critic) was based on vehicle distance from target position, difference of this distance in two time steps, optimal vehicle direction or on the difference between optimal and actual direction. Weighted combination of these parameters and splitting of parameters[3] was used too.

4.1 Learning/adaptation dilemma

Experiments show sensitivity (of some configurations) of backpropagation based actor-critic architecture to learning rate value (γ). On the other side,

---

[1] values from some interval; interval range depends on activation function used

[2] transformation of analog value to multiple binary values

[3] for instance splitting of distance to target position to distance in x and distance in y direction

the ability of algorithm to deal with very big values of γ was observed. Learning rate values over 1 can very quickly destroy knowledge aggregated by network during previous learning, but they can also very quickly reconfigure network to deal with new situations. Choosing between big and small learning rate values in real time backpropagation based control, can be called learning/adaptation dilemma. Realized experiments show the possibility of using big γ values in given architecture and the ability to operate in "pure adaptation" mode. This allows, for instance, adaptation of γ in a very wide range and quick changes in actor functionality.[4]

4.2   Stability of learning algorithm

Stability of the used algorithm is not guaranteed in general case. Realized experiments show some instability of algorithm – wrong behavior of the controller in neighborhood of target position or in directions close to the optimal one. As was found later, the reason for this was instability of used architecture/algorithm in near optimal state. This was proved experimentally by the reduction of the controller and cost function to very simple form, for which it was possible to analytically derive optimal weights. These weights were used for network initialization. Observed divergence from the optimal state was a clear sign of instability. The system was analyzed and stabilized. Instead of direct usage of cost value, the second square of the cost as error function for actor adaptation was used. In this case rule (3) is changed to:

$$\Delta w_{ij} = -2\gamma x_j f'(in_i)x_i \qquad (4)$$

Rule (4) can't be considered universal in any way, it is result of an experimental study of one particular configuration of experiments. However, the used approach of the monitoring of controller behavior in optimal or near optimal state can help in some situations. For optimal state "acquisition" it can be used instead of analytical derivation, supervised control of actor network. This, of course, requires availability of some alternative functional controller for training data generation.

4.3   Complexity of networks

The main object of interest in this work, is the study of relation between complexity[5] of used neural networks and behavior of the algorithm. Variations of topologies of actor networks and adaptive critic networks were studied. Chaining of networks in actor-critic architecture can lead to a bigger number of layers (in supervised learning domain it is common to use 1 or 2 hidden layers). Experiments show ability of backpropagation algorithm to deal with as

---

[4] It's necessary to note the existence of more advanced techniques for quick real-time neural network training, however they were not tested in these experiments.

[5] the number of units and layers in used topology

many as 6 layers of units in network, this is a basic requirement for the usage of complex neural networks in "multi-network" actor-critic control schemes. Networks with multiple hidden layers can be used in actor role and trained by signal backpropagated through multi-layered adaptive critic.

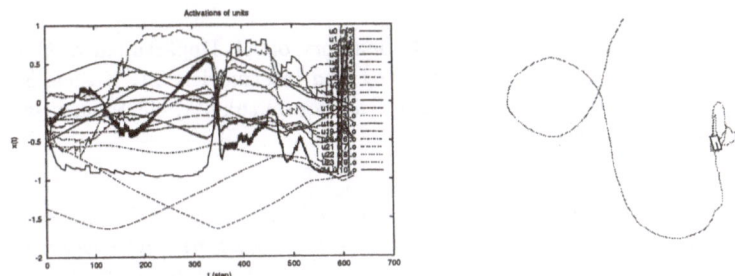

Fig. 2. Example of signals courses and example of trajectory of vehicle

5 Conclusion

Realized experiments show the possibility of using big learning rate values and complex neural networks (trained by backpropagation algorithm) in adaptive critic and in actor in the actor-critic control scheme. Also a method for simple experimental check of the stability of the used algorithm in near optimal state is proposed in this paper.

References

1. Yves Chauvin and David E. Rumelhart, editors. *Backpropagation: Theory, Architectures, and Applications.* Lawrence Erlbaum Associates, 1995.
2. W. Thomas Miller III, Richard S. Sutton, and Paul J. Werbos, editors. *Neural Networks for Control.* MIT Press, 1996.
3. Omid Omidvar and David L. Elliot. *Neural Systems for Control.* Academic Press, 1997.
4. Danil Prokhorov and Don Wunsch. Adaptive critic designs. *IEEE Transactions on Neural Networks,* 1997. http://www.acil.ttu.edu/ .
5. Richard S. Sutton and Andrew G. Barto. *Reinforcement Learning (An Introduction).* MIT Press, 1998.
6. Paul J. Werbos. Stable adaptive control using new critic designs. Technical report, National Science Foundation, Room 675, Arlington, Virginia, USA, 1998.
7. P.J. Werbos. *The Roots of Backpropagation.* Wiley, 1994.
8. David A. White and Donald A. Sofge, editors. *Handbook of Intelligent Control.* Van Nostran Reinhold, 1992.

Computational Intelligence Controllers for Lego Robots - Comparison Study

M. Gavalier, M. Hudec, R. Jakša, and P. Sinčák

Computational Intelligence Group, Laboartory of AI, Department of Cybernetics and AI, Faculty of Electrical Engineering and Informatics, TU Košice, Slovakia
E-mail: {gavalier,hudecm,sincak,jaksa}@neuron-ai.tuke.sk, cig@neuron-ai.tuke.sk, http://neuron-ai.tuke.sk/cig

Abstract: The paper deals with a comparsion of selected controllers for an intelligent parking procedure. Conventional fuzzy controller and BP neural networks were tested for Lego-mindstorm robot control. The results show that BP controller seem to be a very satisfactory approach if the control task is starting from the area of trained paths. Also BP control is smoother and fuzzy control depends on the enhancement of membership functions within the fuzzy controller. The project was done on the Lego-mindststorm conventional kit and the development of control strategies was done in C language and downloaded to RCX brick.

Keywords: fuzzy controller, neural networks, intelligent parking, lego robots

1 Introduction

Intelligent parking is an interesting task to control a vehicle from any point in the environment to a desired position. The basic idea of moving a vehicle form point A to point B can be extended to more complex problems. If for example, we want to get the vehicle to point B in a desired angle, velocity, and with avoiding obstacles. In addition with more than one vehicle, we have to control a more complex system. This specification of requests is similar for performing robosoccer, for example.

In the first step we had to select the control method. The first one was the Fuzzy system described in [1] and the second was an ANN system with BP [2]. Results of our experiments are described in the conclusion. The next step is the implementation of these control systems to a real robot, and the validation of the results of simulation.

2 The model of the robot

At first we specified input and output variables for each controller. The input variables were the robot angle θ and the x-position coordinate x. The output variable was the steering-angle ϑ. The variable ranges were set as follow:

This project is supported by Slovak National Science Agency under project #94333 "Computational Intelligence for decision procedures", 1999-2001

- $0 \leq x \leq 100$
- $-90 \leq \theta \leq 270$
- $-30 \leq \vartheta \leq 30$

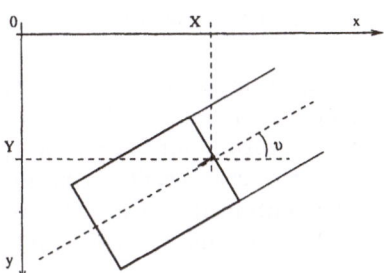

Fig. 1. Model of vehicle

Positive value of ϑ represented clockwise rotations of the steering wheel and the negative value represented counterclockwise rotation. Further we specified the fuzzy-set value of the input and output fuzzy variables. The fuzzy sets are numerically represented by linguistic terms, which describe the control's system behavior. The values of the fuzzy variables were chosen as follow:

Angle θ	**x-position x**	**Steering-angle signal ϑ**
RB: Right Bellow	LE: Left	NB: Negative Big
RU: Right Upper	LC: Left Center	NM: Negative Medium
RV: Right Vertical	CE: Center	NS: Negative Small
VE: Vertical	RC: Right Center	ZE: Zero
LV: Left vertical	RI: Right Center	PS: Positive Small
LU: Left Upper		PM: Positive Medium
LB: Left Bellow		PB: Positive Big

3   Fuzzy control

For fuzzy control, a conventional Mamdami fuzzy controller was used. Fuzzy membership functions can have different shapes depending on the designer's preference or experiences. In practic fuzzy engineers have found that the triangular and trapezoidal shapes can help to capture the modeler's sense of fuzzy numbers and simplify computation. Figure 2 shows membership-function graphs of the fuzzy subnet above.

In Figure 2 the fuzzy sets CE, VE, and ZE are closer than other fuzzy sets. These close fuzzy sets permit fine control of the robot near to the loading dock. Wider fuzzy sets were used to describe the endpoints of the range of the fuzzy variables θ, ϑ, and x. The wider fuzzy sets permitted rough control far from the loading dock.

Further, the fuzzy rulebase, or bank of *fuzzy associative memory* (FAM) rules were described. Fuzzy associations or "rules" (A, B) associate output fuzzy sets B, of control values, with input fuzzy sets A, input-variable values. Fuzzy association can be written as antecedent-consequent pairs or IF-THEN statements. The FAM bank contained 35 rules (Figure 3). For example, the FAM rule of the upper block (FAM rule 1) corresponds to the following fuzzy association:

$$IF\ x = LE\ AND\ \theta = RB\ THEN\ \vartheta = PS$$

FAM rule 18 indicates that if the robot is near the equilibrium position, then the controller should not produce a positive or negative steering-angle signal. The FAM rules in the FAM-bank matrix reflect the symmetry of the controlled system.

For the initial condition $x = 50$ and $\theta = 270$, the fuzzy controller did not perform well. The symmetry of the FAM rules and the fuzzy sets cancelled the fuzzy controller output in the rare saddle point. For example, the rule

$$IF\ x = 50\ AND\ \theta = 270\ THEN\ \vartheta = 5$$

corrects the problem. Finally, the output action given the input condition, was determined . For these results, the correlation-minimum inteface method was used. Each FAM rule produced the output fuzzy set clipped at the degree of membership determined by the input conditions and the FAM rule. Alternatively, correlation-product inference would combine FAM rules multiplicatively. Each FAM rule emitted a fit-weighted output fuzzy set O_i at each iteration. The total output O added these weighted outputs:

$$O = \sum_i min(f_i, S_i)$$

where f_i denotes the antecedent fit value and S_i represents the consequent fuzzy set of steerin-angle values in the ith FAM rule. The fuzzy set O must "defuzzify" to produce a numerical steering-angle signal. *Centroid* defuzzification is a effective procedure. This method use the *fuzzy centroid* ϑ as output:

$$\vartheta = \frac{\sum\limits_{j=1}^{p} \vartheta_j m_O(\vartheta_j)}{\sum\limits_{j=1}^{p} m_O(\vartheta_j)}$$

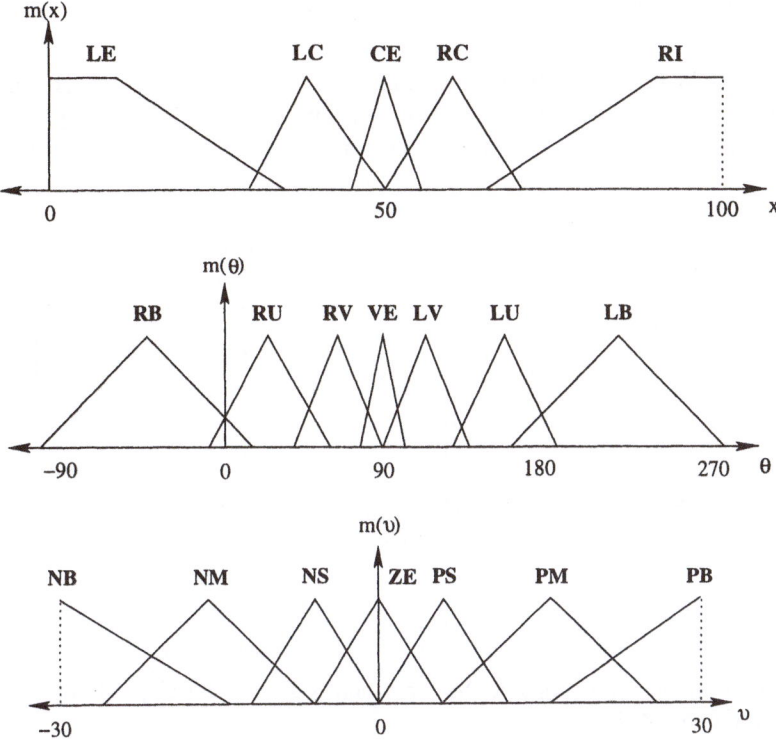

Fig. 2. Fuzzy membership functions for each linguistic fuzzy-set value.

		LE	LC	CE	RC	RI
	RB	PS[1]	PM[2]	PM[3]	PB	PB
	RU	NS	PS	PM	PB	PB
θ	RV	NM	NS	PS	PM	PB
	VE	NM	NM	ZE[18]	PM	PM
	LV	NB	NM	NS	PS	PM
	LU	NB	NB	NM	NS	PS
	LB	NB	NB	NM	NM	NS

x

Fig. 3. FAM-bank matrix for the fuzzy controller.

where O defines a fuzzy subnet of the steering-angle universe.

With 35 FAM rules, the fuzzy controller produced successful robot trajectories starting from any initial position. Figures 4 and 5 shows typical examples of the fuzzy-controlled trajectories from different initial positions.

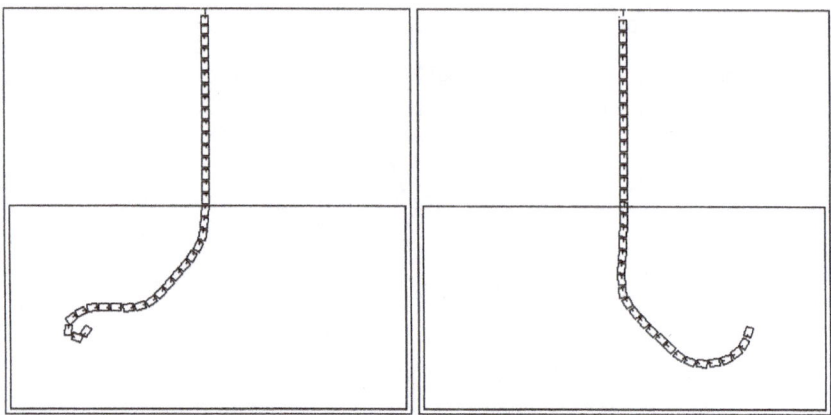

Fig. 4. Sample robot trajectories of the fuzzy controller for initial positions (20, 80, 260) and (80, 80, 260).

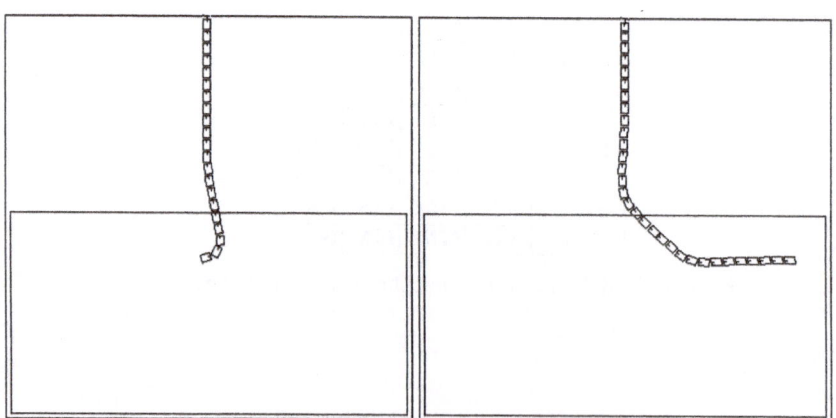

Fig. 5. Sample robot trajectories of the fuzzy controller for initial positions (50, 60, 0) and (90, 60, 180).

4 Neurocontrol

The neural controller consisted of multilayer feedforward neural networks trained with the backpropagation algorithm. The controller network produces an approximate steering-angle signal output given for any parking coordinates (x, y), and the angle θ. The robot simulator computes the next position of the robot and takes it as an input to the controller.

The Controller Network was trained with backpropagation algorithm. The controller network used 7 hidden neurons with logistic sigmoid functions. In the training of the controller, the ideal steering-angle signal at each stage before controller network were trained, was estimated. In the simulation, the trajectories produced by the fuzzy controller were as the ideal trajectories. The fuzzy controller generated each training sample $(x, y, \theta, \vartheta)$ at each iteration of the process. 3000 training-sample vectors and 600 iterations were used to train the controller network . Figures 6 and 7 show typical examples of the neural-controlled trajectories from several initial position.

Fig. 6. Sample robot trajectories of the neural controller for initial position (20, 80, 260) and (80, 80, 260).

5 LEGO Mindstorms robot

The robot has used pieces from 4 Mindstorms kits: 2 main 'Robotic Invention Kits' and 2 'Expansion Kits'. The key features of the robot include:

- 2 motorpowered wheels , used for movement and tuning.
- The RCX, processes data received from the computer and environment via the sensors, using program.
- A chassis to hold the RCX, motors and sensors

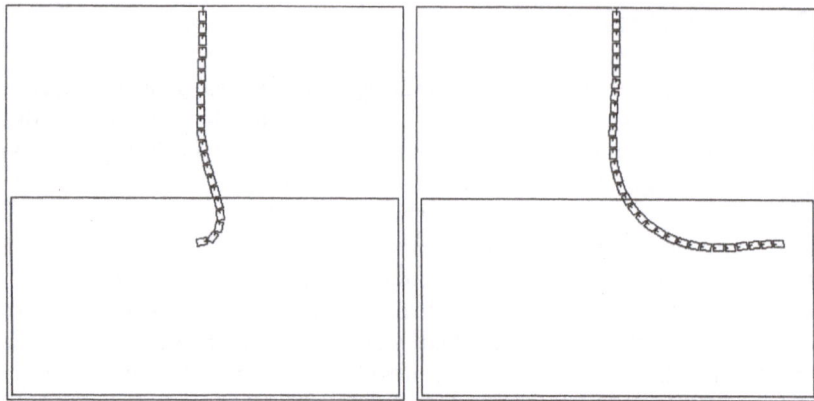

Fig. 7. Sample robot trajectories of the neural controller for initial position (50, 60, 0) and (90, 60, 180).

- A floor facing light sensors used to detect the edge of the work field and obstacles.
- Skid at the front to reduce friction with the floor.
- Dimensions: 150mm long, 105mm wide and 90mm high.

Figure 8 shows the robot.

6 Conclusion

In this paper a comparison study between fuzzy and neurocontrol and its results is presented. A comparison of control strategies was done in simulation of the robot environment. The results show that the neurocontrol of the vehicle was better than the control of the fuzzy controller. Vehicle controlled by trained neurocontroller had less wall collisions than fuzzy controlled vehicle. Error of parking (error of θ) was the same for both controllers i.e. 0. Rate of error of trajectory was better for the neurocontroller (i.e. 10% shorter trajectory of neurocontrolled vehicle). The trajectory of neurocontrolled vehicle was smoother than fuzzy controlled, where the activation of fuzzy rules can be observed. These results can't give us satisfactory results (because of similar control results) and further work is needed (ie. implementation in a real robot as it was proposed)

References

1. Kosko, B.: Neural Networks and Fuzzy Systems - A Dynamical Systems Approach to Machine Intelligence., Prentice-Hall International, pp 339-361 ,ISBN: 0-13-612334-1.

2. Sinčák P., Andrejková A.: Neurónové siete I., http://neuron-ai.tuke.sk/cig/html/m/bookshelf.html
3. Nguyen, D., Widrow, B.: The truck Backer-Upper: An Example of Self-Learning in Neural Networks, Proceedings of International Joint Conference on Neural Networks (IJCNN-89),vol. II,1989.
4. Haykin, S.: Neural Networks:A comprehesive foundation, Prentice-Hall Int., ISBN 0-02-352761-7.

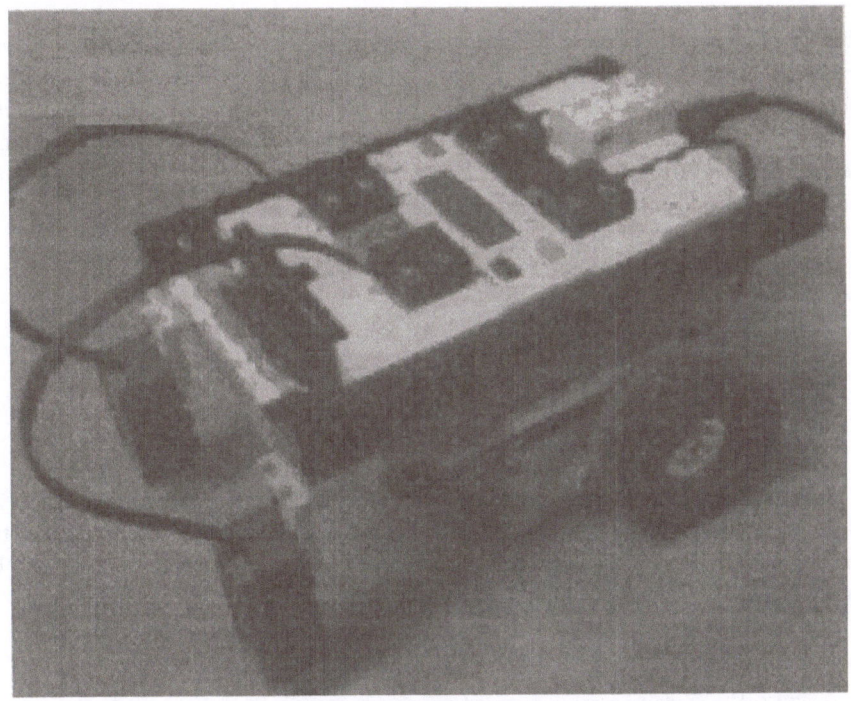

Fig. 8. The robot.

Document Clustering with Neural Networks [1]

Rastislav Lencses

Department of Computer Science, Faculty of Science, University of P. J. Safarik, Kosice, Slovakia, lencses@duro.science.upjs.sk

Abstract: Document clustering consists of creating clusters (classes) based on defined similarity measure. In the most cases, similarity is strongly based on document representation. We will present in our paper some known representations. Our contribution is presenting enriched selected representation (distributional semantics) with the notion distance between terms. We will define similarity measure based on this representation and use with Kohonen learning for our enriched approach.

Keywords: clustering, document representation, Kohonen learning, vector space, distributional semantics

1 Vector space model

Widely used document representation is vector space (or "bag of words"), see [2]. Each document d^i is represented by a vector ($w_1^i,.., w_M^i$), where w_j^i is the importance (weight) of term t_j in document d^i . Weights can be determined by one of well established method of document classification - TFIDF, as follows:

$$d^i = TF(t_i) \, \& \log(\tfrac{D}{DF(t_i)}),$$

where $TF(t_i)$ is term frequency - number of occurences of term t_i in document d^i; D is number of documents and $DF(t_i)$ is document frequency - number of documents, where term t_i is occured. Second argument of the product is also called inverse document frequency. TF IDF method gives greater weight to the terms, which more frequently appear in more documents.

Example of vector space representation (for abstract of this contribution):

---

[1] supported by grant VEGA 1/7557/20

terms	weights
document	2
representation	4
measure	2

Vector space representation can be enriched by N-grams. The main idea is based on using word sequences instead of single words.

Usual similarity of documents (or documents and query) is based on cosine of angle of two vectors :

$$sim(d^i, d^j) = \frac{d^i \exists d^j}{\cup d^i \cup \exists d^j \cup} = \left(\frac{\sum\limits_{k=1}^{M} w_k^i w_k^j}{\sqrt{\sum\limits_{k=1}^{M}(w_k^i)^2 \sum\limits_{k=1}^{M}(w_k^j)^2}} \right)$$

2 Distributional semantics

Another interesting model is distributional semantics, see [3]. This model assumes, that two terms are similar, if their contexts are similar. Following, two documents are similar, if contexts of their terms are similar.

The context of term is defined within co-ocurrence model. In this model co-ocurrence frequency of two terms is defined as number of their ocurrences in sequence of terms (sentence, paragraph or entire document). We define selected group of terms with cardinality M - so-called indexing features. For the term t_j we define co-ocurrence profile - vector of co-ocurrence frequences of this term and indexing features:

$$c^j = \left(c_1^j, .. c_M^j \right)$$

Entire document is represented by

$$d^i = \sum_{j=1}^{M} w_j^i c^j$$

where w_j^i are weights from vector space model.

Note: great number of used terms can slow down effectiveness of clustering. Therefore, there is used so-called feature selection and extraction. This is a process, which select and extract important terms (features). Very simple example is "stop-list" - list of very frequent and not important words, such "a", "and", etc. There are other technics in this area.

We will enrich co-ocurrence model by the idea that context closer to a term is more important. We define co-frequence of two terms as a pair (n, s) - number of their occurences in some textual unit and their distance in this textual unit.

$$c(t_1, t_2) = (n(t_1, t_2), s(t_1, t_2))$$

We can aggregate this pair to one number (because we want easely define similarity):

$$c(t_1, t_2) = \frac{n(t_1, t_2)}{s(t_1, t_2) + 1}$$

So, we can define document vector as follows:

$$d^i = \sum_{j=1}^{M} w_j^i c^j,$$

where w_j^i are weights (equivalent to weights in vector space). We will use cosine similarity (defined above) on comparison of this vectors. With enriched definition of document representation we can get also relevance between documents.

3 A comparison between similarities

We made a comparison between similarities of documents based on different representations. Data consists of 50 scientific abstracts (about 100 kB). They were used in LabelSOM [4]. For this abstracts we have constructed document vectors, as we have defined above (we have indexed stemming words from prunning of words from this document collection) .

We selected one document and have computed similarity of this document to another document, see Fig. 1. Results show us strong correlation between three tested similarities – the similarity based on vector space, the similarity based on the distributional semantics and our similarity based on the distributional semantics with a distance. Similarity based on the distributional semantics and especially distributional semantics with a distance will probably differs from other similarities, if abstracts would be larger and have logical parts, whose contents would differ.

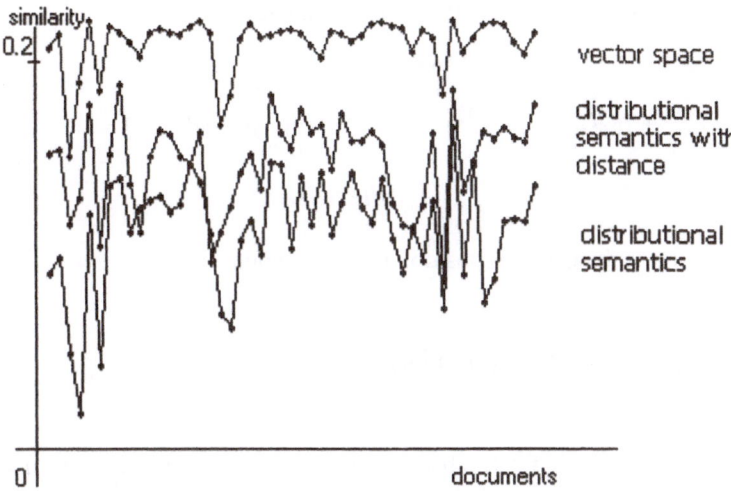

Fig. 1. Correlation between three similarities

4 Kohonen learning

Kohonen learning is widely known [1]. We will briefly show, how we can use similarity based on ditribution semantics in this algorithm.

We have a set of documents represented by vectors d^i. We want to cluster them in groups such that they are maximally similar within group and minimally similar beside group. If we have representant r_l of group T_l (number of groups is h), for every d^i we choose l such

$$l = \max_{k=1,..h} sim(r_l, d^i)$$

Error will be (k is number of documents in group T_l) :

$$E = \tfrac{1}{k} \sum_{i=1}^{k} (1 - sim(r_l, d^i)$$

The network is composed of two fully interconnected layers. Input layer consist of n neurons (n is a dimense of document vector). Inputs are documents vectors. Output layer has h neurons in meaning of representants of clusters. Weights r_l determine position of representant in space. Output neurons has value:

$$y_j^{(t)} = 1 \quad , if \ j = \max_{l=1,..h} sim(d^{(t)}, r_l)$$

$$= 0 \quad , othervise$$

There is the idea "winner take all" - only one neuron has value 1.

Weights change its value as follows:

$$r_{jm}^{(t)} = r_{jm}^{(t-1)} + \eta(d_m^{(t-1)} - r_{jm}^{(t-1)}) \ , \ \ if \ j = \max_{l=1,..h} sim(d^{(t)}, r_l)$$

$$= r_{jm} \qquad\qquad\qquad\qquad , otherwise$$

Winning neuron change your position to actual input.

5 Experimental clustering

We made clustering of 50 abstracts (described above) with using three similarities. We set number of cluster to eight (same as in LabelSOM) . Examples of ten documents with keywords :

- 1.knowledge, discovery, relation, concept, classify, data, feature, process, legal
- 2. classify, concept, database, automation, tool, database
- 3. concept, relation, analyze, document, space
- 4. classify, document, process, software, problem
- 5. analysis, classify, text,hierarchy, retrieval, document, feature
- 6. knowledge, analysis, classification, case, document, legal, archive
- 7. classify, text, document, neural, hierarchical
- 8. classification, hierarchical, neural, document
- 9. knowledge, classify,.document, process, product, software
- 10. data, knowledge, process, validation, method

Typical examples of corresponding clusters:

- 1, 2, 3 and 5, 6, 7, 12, 15 and 8, 9, 10, 13, 14 (vector space)
- 1, 2, 4, 5, 6, 7, 8 (distributional semantics)
- 1, 3, 4, 5, 8, 9, 10 (distributional semantics with distance)

First cluster (for vector space) is identical with cluster found in LabelSOM. In general, clustering with Kohonen learning with similarity based on vector space method is the most similar to results in LabelSOM (they used vector space method too, but we used Kohonen learning and they used self-organizing map). Two other methods found a little another clusters.

As we can see, different similarities produce different clusters, but we can see correlation between them. Document collection consist of abstracts from people from one department and therefore they are similar; so little difference in similarity function causes a shift in clusters. More document representations enable us create more clustering and select suitable one.

Again, our document representation would be more usefull in greater documents with more logical parts, whose content differ. In this paper we do not test such document collections, we will make it in our further research.

Summary: We have enriched distribution semantics model in information retrieval. We have shown, how to use similarity based on this model in document clustering with Kohonen learning. We made comparison between clustering based on two known methods of document representation and our representation.

References

1. Šíma J., Neruda R.: Teoretické otázky neurónových sítí, MatfyzPress, MFF UK, 1996

2. Mladenic D.,: Machine learning on non-homogeneus, distributed text data, PhD thesis, Ljubljana 1998

3. Besancon R, Rajtman M., Chappelier J.C.: Textual Similarities based on a Ditributional Approach, International Workshop on Similarity Search (IWOSS99), Firenze, Italy, Sept 1-2, 1999

4. A. Rauber. LabelSOM: On the Labeling of Self-Organizing Maps Proceedings of the International Joint Conference on Neural Networks (IJCNN'99), Washington, DC, July 10 - 16, 1999

Dual-Tone Multiple Frequency Detection Using Adaptive Filters and Neural Network Classifiers

Georgi Iliev and Nikola Kasabov

Department of Information Science, University of Otago

PO Box 56, Dunedin, New Zealand

phone: +64 3 4798319; fax: +64 3 4798311
giliev, nkasabov@infoscience.otago.ac.nz

Abstract: We use an approach for dual-tone multiple frequency (DTMF) detection based on adaptive filters and neural network classifiers. This approach is computationally efficient and reliable and meets the International Telecommunication Union (ITU) Recommendations. The talk-off tests and tests in the presence of noise show the robustness of the detection method. This method can replace the more complex realisations based on Goertzel algorithm, or those using classical filter design methods, thus minimising the time and the equipment used for the task.

Keywords: Adaptive algorithms, Neural networks, Digital signal procesing, Digital filters

1 Introduction

Dual-tone multiple frequency (DTMF) signalling is a standard in all telecommunication systems [1]. A DTMF codec incorporates an encoder that translates digit information into dual-tone signals, as well as a decoder that detects incoming DTMF tone signals. A DTMF signal consists of two superimposed sinusoidal waveforms with frequencies chosen from a set of eight standardised frequencies. These frequencies should be generated and detected according to the ITU Recommendations Q.23 and Q.24.

The task to detect DTMF tones in an incoming signal and to convert them into actual digits is certainly more complex than the encoding process. As the incoming signal is a sum of two frequencies, which uniquely determine the transmitted digit, we need a technique for extracting spectral information from the input signal.

First option is to design a set of narrow-band filters for the eight allowed frequencies and other eight for the second harmonics in order to be able to discriminate DTMF tones from possible speech and music. Here the classical method for digital filter design can be used, or alternatively the Goertzel algorithm could be applied, the latter proved to be more efficient [2]. Yet both methods need the computational power for calculating the parameters of 16 digital filters.

Here we propose a new approach for the purpose of DTMF detection. Bearing in mind that at every particular time the incoming signal is composed of two frequencies the task is to identify these frequencies. We design our DTMF detector on the basis of adaptive filters and neural network (NN) classifiers.

2 Method

Our system for extracting spectral information is shown in Fig. 1. We use a realisation based on a second order lattice circuit [3]. Using this circuit it becomes possible to implement a second order notch/bandpass section. This realisation is very efficient for the present application because it is possible to control independently the notch frequency and the bandwidth.

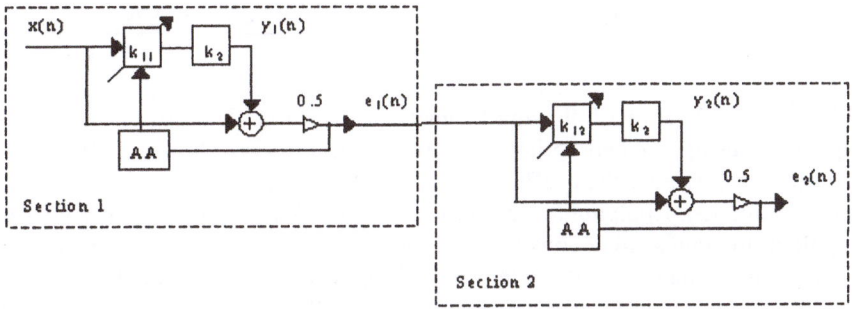

Fig. 1. Adaptive system for extracting spectral information

Thus if the all-pass function $A(z)$ is

$$A(z) = \frac{k_2 + k_1(1+k_2)z^{-1} + z^{-2}}{1 + k_1(1+k_2)z^{-1} + k_2 z^{-2}}, \quad (1)$$

then k_1 controls the notch frequency ω_0 while k_2 is related to the bandwidth (BW) via

$$k_1 = -\cos \omega_0 \quad (2)$$

$$k_2 = \frac{1 - \tan(BW/2)}{1 + \tan(BW/2)}. \quad (3)$$

Table 1. Coefficient-to-digit mapping for DTMF detector based on adaptive digital second-order notch filters according to ITU bandwidth specifications

Digit	Section 1	Section 2
0	$-0.4660 < k_{11} < -0.5297$	$-0.7215 < k_{12} < -0.7563$
1	$-0.5547 < k_{11} < -0.6087$	$-0.8437 < k_{12} < -0.8637$
2	$-0.4660 < k_{11} < -0.5297$	$-0.8437 < k_{12} < -0.8637$
3	$-0.3618 < k_{11} < -0.4362$	$-0.8437 < k_{12} < -0.8637$
4	$-0.5547 < k_{11} < -0.6087$	$-0.8104 < k_{12} < -0.8345$
5	$-0.4660 < k_{11} < -0.5297$	$-0.8104 < k_{12} < -0.8345$
6	$-0.3618 < k_{11} < -0.4362$	$-0.8104 < k_{12} < -0.8345$
7	$-0.5547 < k_{11} < -0.6087$	$-0.7696 < k_{12} < -0.7986$
8	$-0.4660 < k_{11} < -0.5297$	$-0.7696 < k_{12} < -0.7986$
9	$-0.3618 < k_{11} < -0.4362$	$-0.7696 < k_{12} < -0.7986$

The system works in the following manner: each section identifies one of the two frequencies using an appropriate adaptive algorithm. As shown in Fig. 1 we propose to update only the coefficients k_{11} and k_{12}, while k_2 is a priori determined from equation (3). Applying this constraint we fix BW and make the distance from the pole to the unity-circle constant. Thus we can reduce considerably the number of computations and can guarantee the stability of the adaptive structure. Here we introduce the normalised least mean square (NLMS) algorithm for adjusting the filter coefficients as shown below:

$$e_i(n) = 0.5[e_{i-1}(n) + y_i(n)] \qquad (4)$$

for $i = 1,2$ and $e_0(n) = x(n)$

$$k_{1i}(n+1) = k_{1i}(n) - \mu \frac{e_i(n)\, y'_i(n)}{[y'_i(n)]^2} \qquad (5)$$

$$y'_i(n) = \frac{d\, y_i(n)}{d\, k_{1i}(n)}$$

for $i=1,2$

where $e_i(n)$ is the error signal, μ is the step size and $y'_i(n)$ is the derivative of $y_i(n)$ with respect to the coefficient subject of adaptation.

The last step is to map the values of k_{11} and k_{12} to the corresponding digits in order to identify them (see Table 1). Here we round the values of coefficients with a precision of four digits after the decimal point. That turns out to be quite sufficient for the proper work of our decoder and also suggests robustness in implementations with finite precision.

There are two ways of mapping the coefficients (k_{11}, k_{12}) to the corresponding digit. Firstly, by using a combination of logic schemes (AND, OR) according to Table1. This approach has good performance for channels with low and moderate level of noise. If the channel has high level of noise then an aprroach based on fixed logic fails to yield good performance results. The basic reason is that in noisy channels the boundaries of the coefficient cannot be determined exatly and the error rate is high. To tackle this problem we use a neural network classifier (Fig. 2). In this arrangement adaptive filters are used to extract spectral information from the incoming signal followed by a NN classifier performing the mapping of the coefficcients to the relevant digit. The important requirement for continuous, on-line learning can be provided by using a NN model that allowes such mode of operation. An example is the evolving fuzzy neural network [4].

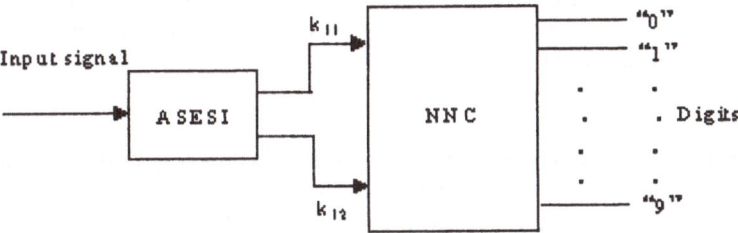

Fig. 2. DTMF detection using adaptive system for extracting spectral information (ASESI) and neural network classifier (NNC)

3 Experiments

We test here how our method addresses the basic issues related to DTMF detection namely:

☐ capability of correctly identifying different digits;

☐ robustness in a noise environment;

306

□ speech rejection.

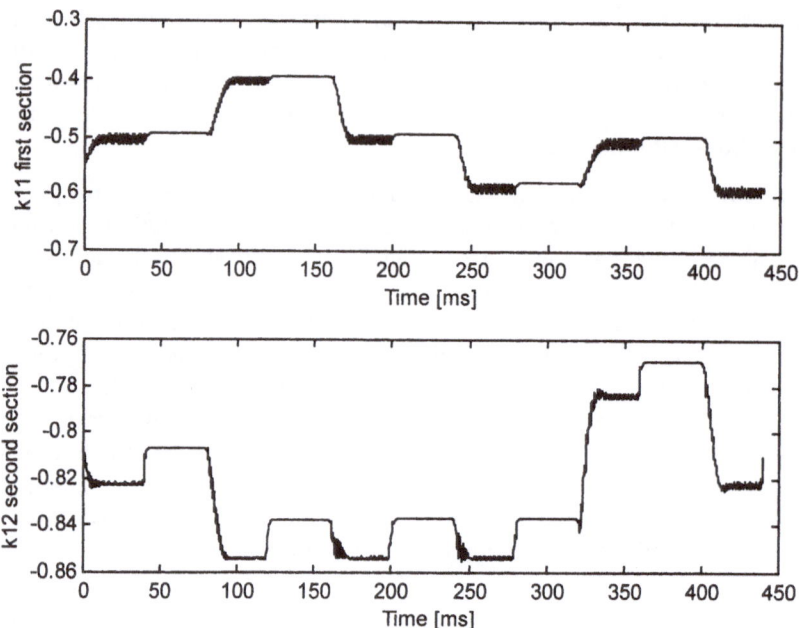

Fig. 3. Trajectories of coefficients k_{11} and k_{12} (the DTMF signal corresponds to a six-digit telephone number (532 184) composed according to the Recommendations of ITU)

The capability of identifying different digits is related closely to the tracking of the two sinusoidal waveforms presented in the incoming DTMF signal. This is illustrated with an example shown in Fig. 3. The DTMF signal corresponds to a six-digit telephone number (532 184) composed according to the Recommendations of ITU. Apparently the adaptive system as depicted in Fig. 1 is able to track the changing frequencies of the sinusoidal waveforms. Next step is to map the values of the coefficients to the relevant digit (see Table 1). We tested our method in noise environment of –24 dBV AWGN (MITEL Specification) [5]. The system was able to detect correctly all 1000 tone bursts. Finally we set an experiment where our detector was exposed to speech samples (previously recorded speech in .wav format). We tested our detector on 1000 .wav files (about 35 minutes of speech) and it did not respond a single time.

4 Conclusions

To summarise, we propose a computationally efficient and reliable method for the implementation of DTMF detector in telecommunication applications according to ITU Recommendations. This method can replace the more complex realisations based on Goertzel algorithm, or those using classical filter design methods.

References

1. Freeman, R. (1994) Reference Manual for Telecommunications Engineering. New York: John Wiley & Sons

2. Proakis, J., Manolakis, D. (1992) Digital Signal Processing: Principles, Algorithms, and Applications. New York: Macmillan

3. Regalia, P., Mitra, S., Vaidyanathan, P. (1988) "The digital all-pass filter: a versatile signal processing building block," Proc. IEEE, vol. 76, Jan., pp. 19-37

4. Kasabov, N. (1996) Foundations of Neural Networks, Fuzzy Systems, and Knowledge Engineering. Cambridge, MA: MIT Press

5. MITEL Technical Data (1980) Tone Receiver Test Cassette CM7291

An Experiment with Feed-Forward Neural Network for Speech Recognition

Bohumir Jelinek[1], Jozef Juhar[1], Anton Cizmar[1]

[1] Technical University of Košice
Faculty of Electrical Engineering and Informatics
Department of Electronics and Multimedia Communications
Park Komenského 13, 040 21 Košice

Abstract: This article deals with continuous speech recognition of Slovak digits exploiting ANN (artificial neural network) architecture. Feed-forward neural network with one hidden layer is used in experiments. We applied 5-frames wide context window of 26 mel-frequency cepstral coefficients (MFCC) with energy and deltas included (130 features) as input for neural network to categorise central speech frame (third of five frames). The hidden layer has 200 units. Neural network output units provide posterior probabilities of their corresponding phonetic categories. We used 238 context-dependent phoneme-based phonetic categories. Time matrix of these probabilities is searched by Viterbi search (constrained by pronunciations and grammar) to get the most probable digit string hypothesis. Our experiments were performed using CSLU (Center for Spoken Language Understanding - Oregon Graduate Institute of Science and Technology) speech toolkit [1].

Keywords: speech recognition, neural networks

1 Introduction

There are several new attempts to overcome certain drawbacks of traditional speech recognition approaches – Hidden Markov Models (HMM). One of the upcoming ways is to explore neural network architecture in so-called hybrid HMM/ANN systems [2]. New idea of the hybrid systems is that they use neural network to estimate emission probabilities of HMM. Their advantage is that ANN training process is based on posterior probabilities and not on maximum likelihood principle (HMM case). Neural network classifiers are discriminative in their nature and they don't need constraining assumptions as uncorrelated coefficients and special (Gaussian) modelling of feature distribution [1].

2   Speech Recognition Process

Speech recognition is a process that usually includes several basic steps. Possible structure of the speech recognition system utilising neural network is illustrated in figure 1.

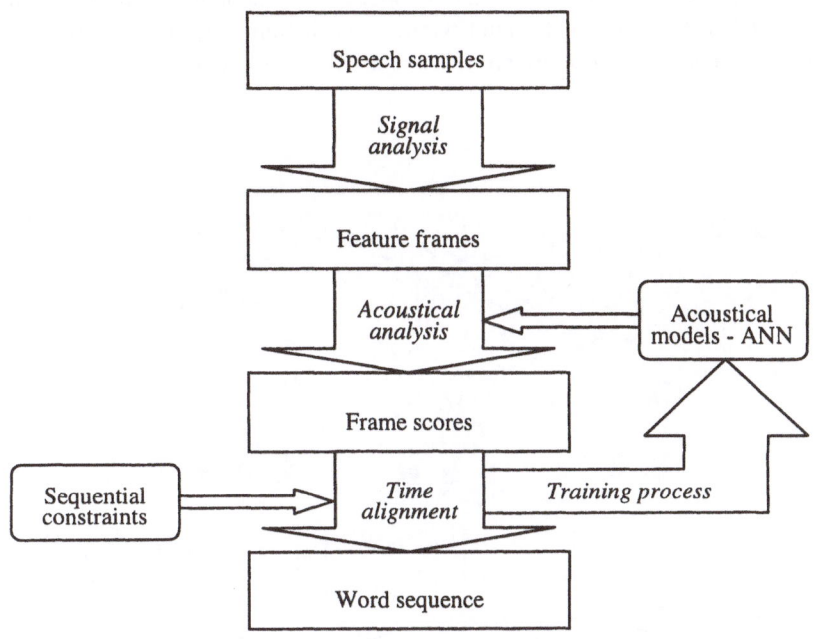

Fig. 1 Overview of the speech recognition process

First pre-processing step is digitalisation of the analogue speech signal. Next we compute spectral characteristics of the speech samples. These are called features and they are computed every 10-msec from a wider (25 ms) speech section called speech frame. A group of coefficients corresponding to one speech frame is called feature frame. Then a neural network is used to classify a central frame of five feature-frames wide context window into phoneme-based phonetic categories. Neural network outputs are scores (posterior probabilities) of the phonetic categories corresponding to each output unit. Finally a Viterbi search is used to find the most probable word's sequence (from a set of all possible sequences of phonetic categories defined by a grammar and pronunciations). Search goes through the time sequence of neural network output scores for all phonetic categories. Result of the search is the best word hypothesis.

3   System Components

3.1 Neural network

CSLU neural network has 130 input nodes, corresponding to all features (coefficients) in 5 frames wide input window (each frame consists of 26 spectral coefficients). There are 200 hidden nodes and 238 output nodes (one output node for each phonetic category).

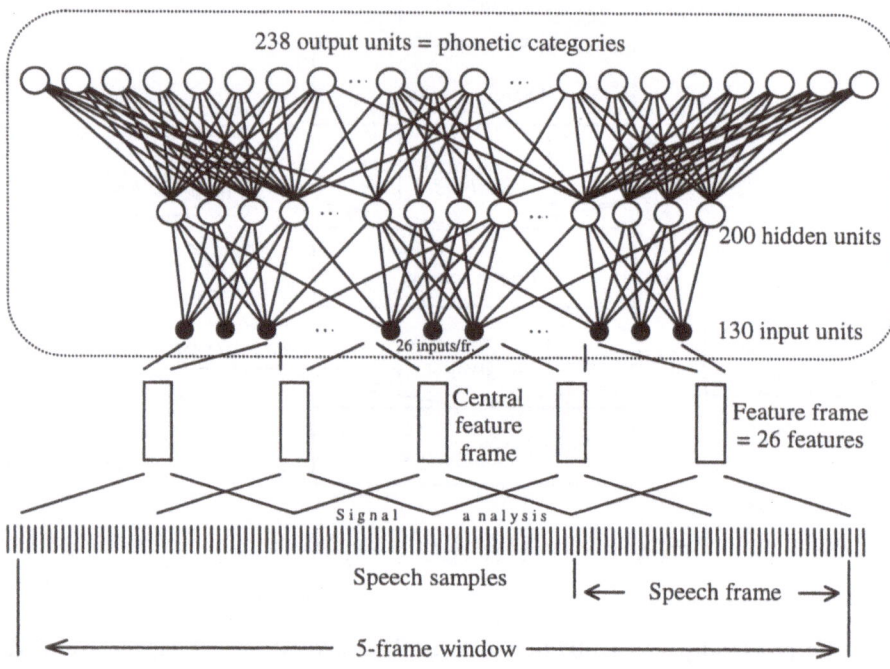

Fig 2 Neural-network architecture

3.1.1   Input units

We compute twelve mel-frequency cepstral coefficients (MFCC coefficients), twelve MFCC delta features, one energy feature and delta-energy feature – totally 26 features per frame. Cepstral-mean-subtraction (CMS) of the MFCC coefficients is performed to remove involved noise.

Central feature frame (that we want to categorise) as well as four frames surrounding this central frame are used as an input to neural network, to take dynamic nature of speech into consideration. We send features from one context window to a neural network for classification (26 features/frame times 5 frames = 130 features). Next - hidden layer has 200 units with sigmoidal transfer function.

3.1.2 Output categories

To take coarticulatory effects into account, neural network has more than one category per each phoneme. Each phoneme is divided into one, two, or three parts, depending on the influence of surrounding phonemes. For example phoneme /E/ is split into three parts and phoneme /n/ may be split into two parts, or kept as a one-part phoneme. Such decisions are made using acoustic-phonetics knowledge as well as practical experience. Similar surrounding categories are grouped into one of eight broad contexts, more detailed description can be found in [3]. For example, this broad context approach results in 576 categories for all American English phonemes. Categories that do not occur often in the training corpora are then tied to acoustically similar categories that have more training data; this can lead to reduction from of output unit's number. In the case of Slovak language we have used 238 phonetic categories. Some phonetic contexts were grouped together to form a broad-context grouping.

Tab. 1. Slovak digits lexicon

No.	Word	Pronunciation	No.	Word	Pronunciation
0	nula	[n u l a]	5	päť	[p ae tj]
1	jeden	[j e d e n]	6	šesť	[sh e s tj]
2	dva, dve	[d v a, d v e]	7	sedem	[s e d e m]
3	tri	[t r i]	8	osem	[o s e m]
4	štyri	[sh t i r i]	9	deväť	[dj e v ae tj]

Neural network was trained and tested on the DaTUKE1 corpus. Outputs of the neural network estimate posterior probability of the phonetic categories. It is shown in [1] that neural networks can classify patterns in this way given enough training data and hidden nodes.

We use ANN to build a probability matrix of the phoneme-based categories over the time by sending context windows for all feature frames to the neural network.

3.1.3 Theoretical justification

Interpretation of the ANN output activation as posterior class probabilities (Duda and Hart, Hampshireand and Pearlmutter) establishes theoretical justification for using ANN as posterior probability estimator in speech recognition system. It was shown that ANN outputs (under certain assumptions) converge to $P(c_i|x)$ - posterior probability of classification class c_i conditioned by acoustic feature vector x. In case of hybrid HMM/ANN system this probability is converted to scaled likelihood (by applying of Baye's rule), which can be used as HMM emission probability $p(x|q_i)$

$$p(\mathbf{x}\,|\,q_i)= p(\mathbf{x})\frac{p(q_i\,|\,\mathbf{x})}{P(q_i)} = const \cdot \frac{p(q_i\,|\,\mathbf{x})}{P(q_i)} \tag{1}$$

In this equation $P(q_i)$ denotes prior probability of HMM state q_i. The number of neural network output units is then equal to the total number of HMM states.

3.2 Viterbi search

Primary goal of speech recognition process is to find the most probable word sequence based on given acoustic data

$$W_1^*, W_2^* ... W_n^* = \operatorname*{arg\,max}_{all\ possible\ W_1, W_2 ... W_n} P\big(W_1, W_2 ... W_n\,|\,\mathbf{X}\big) \tag{2}$$

(W is word from finite vocabulary and $\mathbf{X}$ is observed feature vector). This formula is usually decomposed to language modelling and acoustic modelling component. Language modelling problem is avoided because all the words have the same probability in case of continuos digit task.

CSLU toolkit implements Viterbi search supported with pronunciations and grammar. It applies word duration and word transition penalties in spite of utilising HMM structure in hybrid HMM/ANN system.

Output of the neural network is a matrix of classification probabilities (first dimension is number of classification categories, second is time index of classified frame). The target-word pronunciations are then expanded into strings of phonetic-based categories, and a Viterbi search is used to find the best path through the matrix of probabilities for each legal string. The output of recognition process is the word string that corresponds to this best path.

4 Discussion

We have done several basic experiments with above described configuration of neural network and Slovak digits collected in small DaTUKE1 database. The database contains about 500 sentences spoken by 50 male and female speakers. For experimental purpose it was splitted in two parts - training parts (30 speakers) and testing part (20 speakers). Training part was fully fonetically hand-labelled. The resulting average accuracy on testing data was 87,63%. The results are not as good as for example in [4], but there is a potention to improve the recognizer by retraining it with larger speech database. Generally it confirm that ANN architectures can improve state-of-the-art speech recognition system performance. CSLU speech toolkit is a good starting point to perform experiments with ANN implementations for small vocabulary tasks.

References

1. Morgan, N., Bourlard, H.: Continuous Speech Recognition, Signal Processing Magazine, 1995

2. Bourlard, H., Wellekens, J.: Links between Markov Models and Multilayer Perceptrons, IEEE Transactions on Pattern Analysis and Machine Intelligence, vol. 12, no. 12, pp. 1167-1178, 1990

3. http://cslu.cse.ogi.edu - Center for Spoken Language Understanding, Oregon Graduate Institute of Science and Technology, USA

4. Cosi, P., Hosom, J-P.: HMM/Neural Network-Based System for Italian Continuous Digit Recognition, Proceedings of the 14th International Congress of Phonetic Sciences (ICPhS) 1999, San Francisco, August 1999.

Increase the Pattern Capability in System for Flying Object Recognition[*]

Radosław Semkło

Air Force Information Centre, 02—800 Warsaw, POLAND

Abstract: The problem of the flying object recognition is described in this paper. The neural networks used for the flying object recognition have been presented. The problems of the pattern capability in system for flying object recognition have been discussed. The issues of work have been presented. The proposition of solution (hybrid expert system) in this kind of system was shown.

Keywords: Object recognition, neural networks, pattern capability

1 Introduction

The research on the flying object recognition has been intensified last years. It takes place because the significance of air forces is still rising. Flying object recognition is the one of the most important subjects in modern Air Force and Army at all. One of the solutions to this problem is the object recognition based on radar signal. But this is not the only way to recognize the flying object and take appropriate decision. Another way of the flying object recognition is to analyze their picture. The trials for recognition using traditional (Haff transform) methods have not given satisfying results. It follows from realising time boundaries and the data size needed for military application.

The author has used the neural network for this purpose. It is able to learn. Moreover, the precise algorithm of the recognizing is not required. It is very important when we consider the object recognition in military application. For above reasons the neural networks are used in many systems where a lack of failure is required.

Author has checked a few kind of neural networks, which are more effective in picture flying object recognition than others are.

In the final analysis authors have chosen multilayer perceptron. The main advantage of this network is the simplicity (architecture) and effectiveness of the recognition. The main fault of the multilayer perceptron is necessity of the supervised learning.

---

[*]This paper is sponsored by State Committee for Scientific Research as part of work nr 0 T 00A 012 17

2 Pattern capability problem

Experiments [3] have led to the conclusion that the perceptron is the neural network, which can be used in flying object recognition. Besides supervised learning in this kind of network is a problem as far as pattern capability is considered. One kind of an object can be presented in many ways. It can be seen from up, down, left, right side and all kinds of rotation (see Fig. 3).

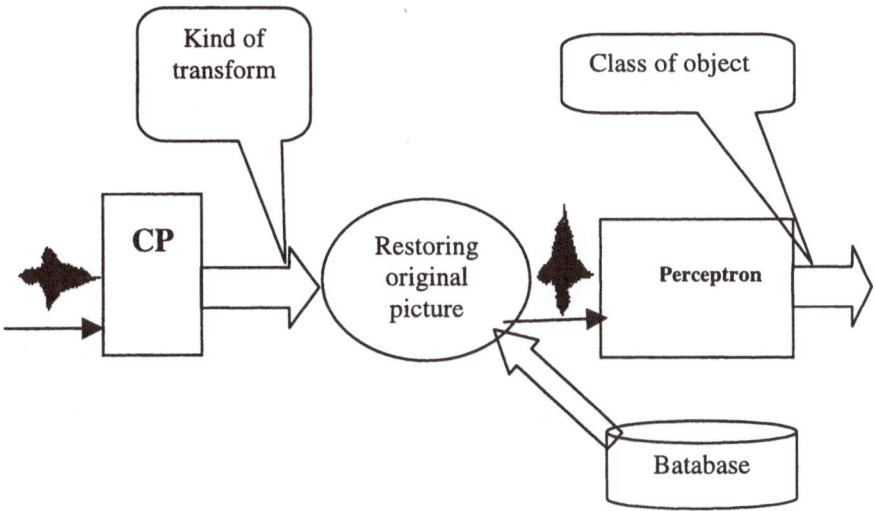

Fig. 1. The data flow in process recognition

In this way number of neurons in hidden and output layers is rising. Too many neurons makes a time of processing input signals longer and requires more computing outlays.

To avoid remembering all images of one object it is better to determine a kind of transform of input data and restore original picture of the object.

Author has decided to use CP network for this purpose. It is one of the ways to determine the angles of the recognized objects.

The input data are obtained from video camera and are transferred into CP neural network. The CP network is determining the kind of the transformation (angle). On the base of these issues the separate unit is restoring original picture of the flying object. And then perceptron is recognizing object presented in original form.

3 Work of the system

First set in data flow is determined by the kind of transform. The CP network was used for this purpose. The output of this network is a kind of transform. Afterwards follows the restoring stage. The output from restoring stage is the original picture of the object. The restored picture is presented to a perceptron. The output of the perceptron is a particular class of recognized flying objects.

Fig. 2. The data flow in process recognition

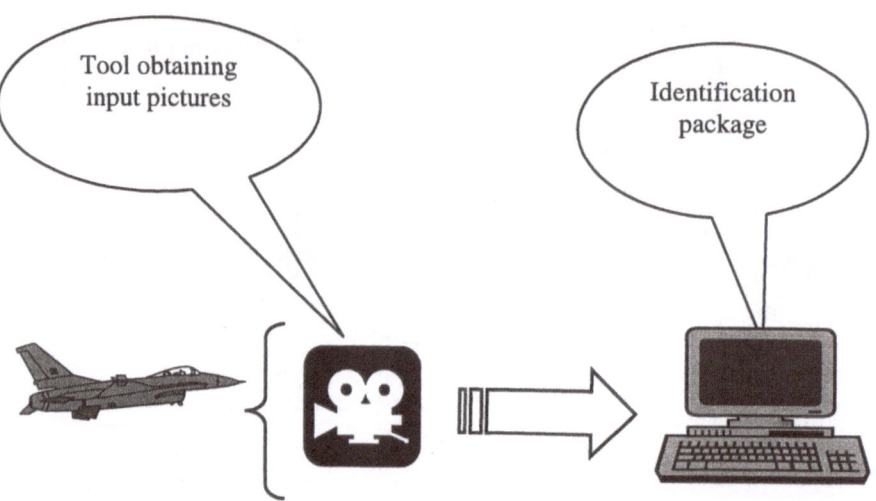

In this way, data flow allows us to avoid remembering all the images of the object, which have to be recognized. Time of recognition is longer but the perceptron consist of fewer neurons.

Fig. 3. The examples of input data

4 Conclusions

This paper presents the way to avoid remembering many images of the same object. On the basis of experiments advantages and disadvantages of this solution have been checked and presented. Author did a few tests to obtain a system that is useful for flying objects recognition. The aim of these tests was checking the influence parameters of the structure on the effectiveness of work and length of learning process. The purpose of the experiments was to check the influence of the way data flow on the efficiency of flying object recognition in military application. It was the network designed for flying object recognition based on their pictures. Although author has tested and proved that this solution is useful for speeding up the object recognition, it is not obvious whether it is efficient to the same extent for other applications.

Authors built a prototype model of the system, which requires some changes to be applied in external conditions. Presented neural network cannot be used as a single tool, so authors created the hybrid expert system, which integrates the two directions of the artificial intelligence research: pragmatical and bionical. This system links these two directions of the artificial intelligence research together. Author hopes that this work will result in creating system which could be used in military application.

References

[1] Hertz J., Krogh A., Palmer R.: Introduction to the Theory of Neural Computing, WNT, Warsaw 1993

[2] Jouny I., Garber F., Ahalt S. Classification of Radar Targets Using Synthetic Neural Networks, IEEE Transactions on Aerospace and Electronic System, vol. 29, No. 2, April 1993

[3] Semkło R. Using Neural Networks to Analyze Radar Signals, Military Academy of Technology Pub, Warsaw, July 1996

[4] Świątnicki Z., Semkło R. The Radar Signal Processing Using Neural Networks, Proceedings of Conference "New Trends in Signal Processing" Liptovsky Mikulas, May 1996

[5] Świątnicki Z., Semkło R. Computational Intelligence and Applications. Springer-Verlag, Berlin 1998

Personal Verification with Hand Shapes Using a Modular-Type Neural Network with RBF Output Units

Seiji Ishihara and Takashi Nagano

Department of Industrial and Systems Engineering, Faculty of Engineering, Hosei University, 3-7-2 Kajino-cho, Koganei, Tokyo 184-8584, Japan
E-mail:nagano@k.hosei.ac.jp

Abstract: There are increasing needs of personal verification technologies using physical characteristics of humans for automatic gate control systems. In this paper, we propose a personal verification system with hand shapes using a modular-type neural network with RBF output units. We extracted many features from a hand image with a simple algorithm, and then selected 20 features among them based on the results of the statistical analysis. These features are lengths of fingers and the area of a palm, etc. We used a set of the selected features as an input pattern to the modular-type neural network. Each module of the modular-type neural network is a three-layered neural network that has one RBF output unit. The modular-type neural network with RBF output units can achieve high rejection rates on patterns of unlearned classes. This is its advantage over the conventional modular-type neural networks with sigmoidal output units. We show that our system achieves both high verification rates on patterns of 40 learned persons and high rejection rates on patterns of 20 unlearned persons.

1   Introduction

Personal verification technologies for automatic gate control systems become more and more important. Needs for them are increasing in many cases, for example, access to electric databases, entrance into buildings and rooms, etc. Various personal verification systems using physical characteristics of humans have been developed. Hand shape is thought to be one of the useful physical characteristics [1][2]. It can be taken easily by using a usual image scanner, and is little influenced by scanning environments. Moreover, the use of hand shapes gives less mental and physical loads to users than the use of fingerprints[3] or iris patterns[4] used in the usual verification systems.

We propose a simple and easy method to take hand images with an image scanner and to extract features from them. We also propose a personal verification system using such features. The system is composed of a modular-type neural network

(MNN) with radial basis function (RBF) units in its output layer [5]. The system is shown to achieve both high verification rates on patterns of learned classes and high rejection rates on patterns of unlearned classes.

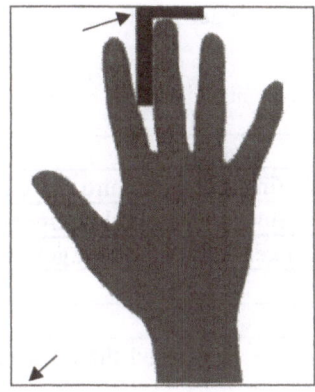

Fig. 1. The way of putting the right hand on an image scanner.

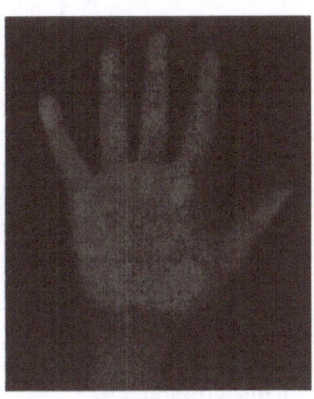

Fig. 2. An original image of the right hand.

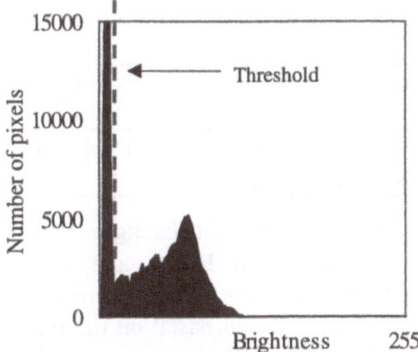

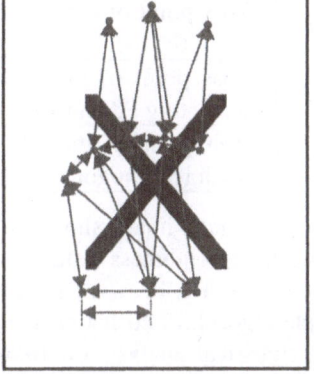

Fig. 3. Histogram of brightness of an original image. The original image is segmented at the threshold between the two neighboring brightness values which give the maximum difference of pixel numbers. The broken line shows the threshold.

Fig. 4. 11 feature points ($P1, P2, ..., P11$) and adopted 20 features represented by arrows and by the white area ($D_{1,2}$, $D_{1,3}$, $D_{1,9}$, $D_{2,5}$, $D_{2,7}$, $D_{2,10}$, $D_{3,4}$, $D_{3,6}$, $D_{3,7}$, $D_{3,10}$, $D_{4,5}$, $D_{4,9}$, $D_{4,10}$, $D_{4,11}$, $D_{6,7}$, $D_{8,9}$, $D_{8,10}$, $D_{8,11}$, $D_{9,11}$, and F). $D_{i,j}$ and F denote feature values defined by the length between Pi and Pj and by the white area respectively.

2 Pre-Processing

Images of right hands were taken by using an image scanner (716×573 pixels, 256 gray levels and 75dpi). As shown in Fig.1, the top and the left side of the middle finger were fitted to the guide bars, and five fingers were separated freely each other when a user put the right hand on a scanner. No other positional restrictions were imposed.

Table 1. Definition of 11 feature points.

P1	Top of the middle finger.
P2	Bottom of the trough between the middle finger and the third finger.
P3	Bottom of the trough between the index finger and the middle finger.
P4	Bottom of the trough between the third finger and the little finger.
P5	Top of the third finger.
P6	Top of the index finger.
P7	Cross point of the right outline of the index finger and the horizontal line crossing P4.
P8	Cross point of the left outline of the palm and the bottom horizontal line of the hand part. The bottom horizontal line is defined by the vertical position at which the horizontal width of hand image is equal to 0.9 × (length of the middle finger) around the wrist.
P9	Cross point of the right outline of the palm and the bottom horizontal line of the hand part.
P10	Cross point of the vertical line crossing P1 and the horizontal line connecting P8 and P9.
P11	Cross point of the left outline of the palm and the line crossing P7 which is orthogonal to the line connecting P3 and P9.

The original hand image shown in Fig. 2 was segmented from its background with the threshold brightness value shown by the broken line in Fig. 3, and then 11 feature points (P1, P2, ..., P11, see Fig.4 and Table 1) were extracted from it with a simple algorithm. 20 features shown in Fig.4 were selected based on the results of the statistical analysis on 1920 images of 40 persons. Their variances within classes (denoted by V_W) were small, and their variances between classes (denoted by V_B) were large.

3 Modular-Type Neural Network with RBF Output Units

We used the MNN shown in Fig. 5 for verifying persons. The MNN uses the same number of modules as that of classes. Each module is a three-layered neural network that has one RBF output unit and corresponds to each class. In training stage, each module is trained independently to divide each corresponding class from all the other classes.

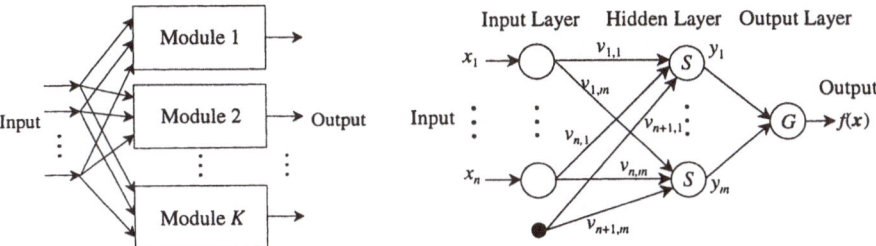

Fig. 5. Architecture of the modular-type neural network.

Fig. 6. Architecture of the module with an RBF output unit. A solid circle is a dummy unit with output 1 representing the bias term.

The architecture of the module with an RBF output unit is shown in Fig. 6. The input vector is $x=(x_1, x_2, ..., x_n, 1)$. The matrix of the connection weights from the input layer to the hidden layer is denoted by

$$
V = \begin{bmatrix} v_{1,1} & \cdots & v_{1,m} \\ \vdots & \ddots & \vdots \\ v_{n+1,1} & \cdots & v_{n,m} \end{bmatrix} .
$$

The output vector $y=(y_1, y_2, ..., y_m)$ of the hidden layer is given by

$$
y = S(xV) , \tag{1}
$$

where S denotes the sigmoidal output function. The output value $f(x)$ of the module is given by

$$
\begin{aligned}
f(x) &= G\left(\|y - t\|_w^2\right) \\
&= \exp\left(-(y-t)W^T W(y-t)^T\right) ,
\end{aligned} \tag{2}
$$

where G is the Gaussian output function, the vector $t=(t_1, t_2, ..., t_m)$ and the matrix W are the center of the Gaussian distribution and the weight matrix of the norm respectively. The weight matrix W is denoted by

$$
W = \begin{bmatrix} w_{1,1} & \cdots & w_{1,m} \\ \vdots & \ddots & \vdots \\ w_{m,1} & \cdots & w_{m,m} \end{bmatrix} .
$$

In training stage, parameters V, t and W are changed by the back-propagation algorithm. The error function E is defined by

$$
E = \frac{1}{2} \sum_i (d_i - f(x_i))^2 , \tag{3}
$$

where d_i is the target value for the i-th input vector x_i. Each change of the parameters is given by

$$\Delta \mathbf{V} = -\eta_V \frac{\partial E}{\partial \mathbf{V}} \quad ,$$

$$\Delta \mathbf{t} = -\eta_t \frac{\partial E}{\partial \mathbf{t}} \quad ,$$

$$\Delta \mathbf{W} = -\eta_W \frac{\partial E}{\partial \mathbf{W}} \quad ,$$

where h_V, h_t and h_W represent learning rates and are small positive numbers.

4   Experimental Results and Discussion

There were 1920 patterns of 40 learned classes (48 patterns per class) and 560 patterns of 20 unlearned classes (28 patterns per class). We used the first 20 patterns in each learned class for training and the rest 28 patterns for test. Each pattern consists of n (=11, 12, ..., 20) features. These features have the n largest values of V_B/V_W. Each module was trained until the mean square error was reduced to 0.001 or the number of iterations exceeded 50,000. Target values were 0.95 or 0.05. Learning rates were h_V=0.005, h_t=0.0001, and h_W=0.005. The number of hidden units m in each module was the smallest integer which satisfied the restriction: $n \leq 2m$.

We examined two criteria for correct verification. The first one is that an input pattern is accepted if the module corresponding to the correct person gives the maximum output value. Results are shown in Table 2. The second one is that an input pattern is accepted only if only the output value of the module corresponding to the correct person exceeds a fixed threshold. Results are shown in Table 3. We obtained zero misverification rate at the threshold of 0.65. The second criterion is practically more useful than the first one because misverification must be strictly avoided in personal verification for security systems. It can be said that we realized zero misverification rate keeping verification rate relatively high. Correct verification under the second criterion can be obtained by repeating trials again even if the first trial is rejected.

Table 2. Verification and misverification rates on test patterns of learned classes under the first criterion (%).

	Number of features (n)									
	11	12	13	14	15	16	17	18	19	20
Verification	97.7	98.8	99.0	99.2	99.4	99.1	99.1	99.1	99.2	99.2
Misverification	2.3	1.2	1.0	0.8	0.6	0.9	0.9	0.9	0.8	0.8

Table 3. Verification and misverification rates on test patterns of learned classes under the second criterion (%).

Thre-shold		Number of features (n)									
		11	12	13	14	15	16	17	18	19	20
0.5	Verification	93.6	95.3	95.9	98.4	98.0	97.9	98.0	98.0	98.2	98.2
	Misverification	1.6	1.0	0.7	1.1	1.1	1.2	1.6	1.6	1.3	1.4
0.6	Verification	90.6	91.9	93.6	96.1	95.1	96.0	95.6	95.5	95.9	96.0
	Misverification	0.7	0.3	0.3	0.1	0.4	0.6	0.5	0.8	0.6	0.9
0.65	Verification	87.3	88.2	90.7	93.7	93.2	93.2	93.8	94.0	94.2	94.2
	Misverification	0.6	0.3	0.1	0.1	0.4	0.4	0.0	0.5	0.5	0.5

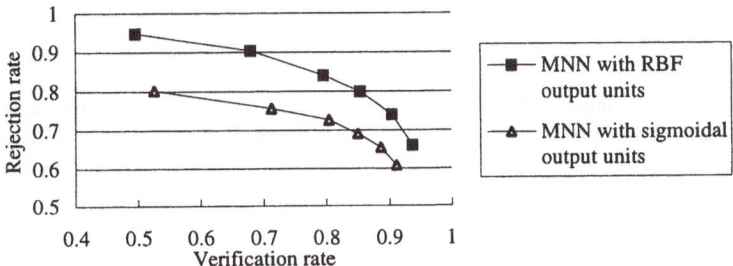

Fig. 7. Relations between verification rates on test patterns of learned classes and rejection rates on patterns of unlearned classes.

Next, we made comparison between rejection rates for unlearned classes of the MNN with RBF output units and those of the MNN with sigmoidal output units. Results in the case of n=17 are shown in Fig. 7. Each point plotted in Fig. 7 corresponds to each threshold value. In the case that the two systems achieved the same verification rate for learned classes, the rejection rate for unlearned classes of the first system was higher than that of the second system. The results of these simulations show the effectiveness of the system with RBF output units.

Acknowledgment

This research was supported by Grant-in-Aid #08279102 for Scientific Research on "Research (1)", the Ministry of Education, Science and Culture of Japan. We are thankful to Mr. Hideo Eguchi for his help in data collection.

References

1. Nagano T. and Hirai Y. (1998): Personal verification with palm print and hand shape by utilizing neural network techniques. International ICSC / IFAC Symposium on Neural Computation, Vienna, Austria, pp. 398-404
2. Nagano T., Ishihara S. and Eguchi H. (1999): Hand shape has sufficient information for personal verification. 7th European Congress on Intelligent Techniques & Soft Computing, Aachen, Germany, pp. 271
3. Wegstein J. H. (1982): An automatic fingerprint identification system. NBS Special Publication, pp. 500-589
4. Rosen J. (1990): Biometric system opens the door. Mechanical Engineering, vol. 112, no. 11, pp. 58-60
5. Ishihara S. and Nagano T. (1999): A modular neural network with RBF output units. 1999 IEEE International Conference on Systems, Man, and Cybernetics, Tokyo, Japan, vol. 2, pp. V-344-349

A Soft Measurement Technique for Searching Significant Subsets of Prostate Cancer Prognostic Markers

Huseyin Seker[1], Michael O. Odetayo[1], Dobrila Petrovic[1], Raouf Naguib[1], and Freddie Hamdy[2]

[1] BIOCORE, MIS, Coventry University, Coventry, UK

[2] Royal Hallamshire Hospital and Sheffield University, UK

Abstract: We propose a soft measurement computed by means of the Fuzzy K-Nearest Neighbor (FK-NN) algorithm to determine the degree of importance of subsets of the prostate cancer prognostic markers for prognostic analysis. A class membership degree of each vector for each class was considered rather than its crisp assignment. We present results that indicate that some specific subsets are very capable of prediciting prostate cancer and therefore we do not need to use all prognostic markers. The results also show that the soft measurement can give an idea of the level of importance of each subset rather than ranking, and its outcomes are more flexible and interpretable.

1 Introduction

Feature selection has been one of the main problems in pattern recognition since all features may not yield a better result and some of them may cause interference affecting outcomes in positive and/or negative way. The importance of features for pattern recognition problem has generally been determined by means of classification rate, and not many researches have investigated features in terms of an individual class. Furthermore, considering only classification rate affects reliability of outcomes since it assigns a vector to a specific class and completely neglects its degree of membership of that class.

Prostate cancer is one of the most common malignancies in the world. Several prognostic markers have been developed and analyzed for diagnostic and prognostic purposes. Early research on prostate cancer prognostic markers has been mostly based on statistical analysis, and a few studies has published recently are based on applications of artificial neural networks, in which they either included novel prognostic markers (immunostaining for p53 and bcl-2) or omitted them in the data set that were investigated, but all possible combinations have not been analyzed [1].

This study deals with searching important subsets of prognostic features in terms of individual patient's prognosis using the proposed soft measurement computed by means of the Fuzzy K-Nearest Neighbor (FK-NN) algorithm.

2 A Soft Measurement

The proposed soft measurement is a function of a class membership computed by means of FK-NN algorithm that has been shown to be a powerful classifier [2]. Although the FK-NN algorithm is a classifier, it however deals with determining a class membership degree of a vector rather than assigning a vector to a specific class. A class membership can also be called a degree of reliability. For example in a 2-class model, if a vector's membership degrees for the two classes are 0.99 and 0.01, respectively, one can obviously be convinced that the class of 0.99 membership is the class to which the vector belongs. However, if a vector's membership degrees of classes are 0.51 and 0.49, respectively, one can obviously be confused as to which class the vector belongs. The implication is that the vector will need re-analyzing since the class it is assigned to might not be the correct one. The membership assignment can therefore be useful in the classification problem [2] as well as in selecting significant feature subsets. Detail of the algorithm can be found in [2].

The soft measurement of an individual class can be computed as

$$W_{fc} = \frac{\sum_{i=1}^{N} \mu_c(x_{fi}).u_c(x_i)}{\sum_{i=1}^{N} u_c(x_i)} \tag{1}$$

where f refers to a subset of features, $\mu_c(x_{fi})$ is a membership degree of x_{fi}, computed by means of FK-NN, and $u_c(x_i)$ is the actual output of class-c. W_{fc} is the soft measurement, called as "a weighted-average class membership (WACM)", of class-c for subset f showing a degree of how much subset f can represent class-c.

3 Prostate Cancer

Prostate cancer is one of the most common malignancies. While several conventional and novel prognostic markers have all been shown to correlate with prognosis and survival [1], [3], all possible combinations of the features have not been analyzed to elucidate their effects on prognosis.

The prostate cancer data set in this study consists of 41 patients with histologically proven prostate cancer, and each one is made of seven clinical and experimental features listed in Table 1. The outcomes are categorized as (1) no response to treatment, (2) relapse following initial successful treatment and/or disease progression in untreated patients, and (3) sustained complete response to treatment or no progression in untreated patients.

Table 1. Prognostic features of the prostate cancer

Description of the features	Index
Tumor Stage (T1 – T4)	1
Skeletal Metastatis (M0-M1)	2
Gleason Score (2-10)	3
Serum PSA (1.2 - >2000)	4
p53 immunostaining (positive or negative)	5
bcl-2 immunostaining (positive or negative)	6
Treatment (hormonal, radical surgery or observation)	7

4   Results and Conclusion

Experiments were conducted using K=1,2,3, m=2 [2], and "leave-one-out" technique. Ninety nine combinations from a seven-feature model to three-feature models for prostate cancer data set were investigated, and AWCM is computed for each combination. The results related to the maximum AWCMs for K=1,2,3 are given in table 2. A vector was assigned to a class of maximum membership for classification purposes. Its results are also included in table 2.

The analysis of the prostate cancer prognostic markers showed that the subset {2,3,4,5,7} is the common subset in which the maximum WACMs of 0.6585, 0.6312 and 0.6103 for K=1,2 and 3 respectively, for all classes were obtained. The subsets {2,3,4,5,7}, {1,3,4,5,7}, {1,2,3,4,7}, {2,3,4,7} for K=2 yielded the minimum number of misclassified vectors. Among these subsets, {2,3,4,5,7} was also found to have the maximum WACM and could be the most capable of and reliable for predicting cancer. Furthermore, feature 4, which is Serum PSA, seems to be more significant for prognostic analysis.

In conclusion, the proposed soft measurement can give an idea of the level of importance of subsets of all features rather than ranking them, and the outcomes are more flexible and interpretable. The outcomes can then be thought to be closer to human decision making.

Table 2. Results of the prostate cancer data set. The subsets that have the maximum WACM are given. W_f is an average soft measuremet over all classes. *Almost all combinations yielded almost the same WACM for class-1.

K & Subset f	Number of Misclassified Vectors & Subset f	W_{f1}	W_{f2} & Subset f	W_{f3} & Subset f	W_f & Subset f
K = 1	14	0.4000	0.7500	0.7000	0.6585
	{2,3,4,5,7}	*	{1,2,3,4,5,6,7}	{2,3,4,5,7}	{2,3,4,5,7}
	{1,3,4,5,7}		{2,3,4,5,6,7}	{1,3,4,5,7}	{1,3,4,5,7}
	{1,2,3,4,7}		{1,3,4,5,6,7}	{1,2,3,4,7}	{1,2,3,4,7}
	{2,3,4,7}		{1,2,4,5,6,7}	{3,4,5,7}	{2,3,4,7}
			{1,2,3,4,6,7}	{2,3,4,7}	
			{1,2,3,4,5,6}	{3,4,7}	
			{3,4,5,6,7}		
			{1,4,5,6,7}		
			{1,3,4,6,7}		
			{1,3,4,5,6}		
			{1,2,4,6,7}		
			{1,4,6,7}		
K = 2	13	0.3500	0.7037	0.6774	0.6312
	{2,3,4,5,7}	*	{1,2,4,6,7}	{2,3,4,5,7}	{2,3,4,5,7}
	{1,3,4,5,7}				
	{1,2,3,4,7}				
	{2,3,4,7}				
K = 3	14	0.3600	0.6714	0.6630	0.6103
	{1,2,3,4,7}	*	{1,2,4,6}	{2,3,4,5,7}	{2,3,4,5,7}

References

[1] Naguib RNG, Neal DE and Hamdy FC (1998) "Neural Network Analysis of Combined Conventional and Experimental Prognostic Markers in Prostate Cancer: A Pilot Study", Br. J. Cancer, 78 (2): 246-250.

[2] Keller JM, Gray MR and Givens JA (1985) "A Fuzzy K-Nearest Neighbor Algorithm", IEEE SMC-15(4):580-585.

[3] Naguib RNG and Hamdy FC (1998) "A General Regression Neural Network Analysis of Prognostic Markers in Prostate Cancer", Neurocomputing, 19 (1-3): 145-150.

Application of an Adaptive Hybrid Neural Network to Medical Diagnosis

Chee Peng Lim[1*], Poh Suan Teoh[1], Phaik Yean Goay[1], and Robert F. Harrison[2]

[1] School of Industrial Technology, Universiti Sains Malaysia
  11800 Penang, Malaysia

[2] Department of Automatic Control and Systems Engineering
  University of Sheffield, Mappin Street, Sheffield S1 3JD, United Kingdom

Abstract: We have previously devised a hybrid neural network, based on the synergism of the Fuzzy ARTMAP and Probabilistic Neural Networks, for on-line pattern classification and probability estimation tasks. In this paper, we investigate the applicability of the hybrid network to medical diagnosis problems. In particular, the network was employed to predict and classify Myocardial Infarction patients into two categories (positive and negative cases) using a database of real records collected from a hospital. A number of experiments was conducted to evaluate the effects of several network parameters on its performance. The results are discussed and compared with those from the Fuzzy ARTMAP network.

1   Introduction

Neural networks have emerged as a practical tool to solve many real world problems. Perhaps the most widely used networks have been the feedforward type of neural networks, such as the Multi-layer Perceptron (MLP) and Radial Basis Function (RBF) networks. These networks possess some attractive properties when the objective is to develop a classifier to operate in a probabilistic environment. It has been shown that network architectures using logistic functions are able to approximate any smooth function to an arbitrary degree of accuracy [1]. A similar finding is also concluded for RBF networks [2]. Thus, it is likely that feedforward networks can offer a direct solution to the problem of developing a useful classifier. However, such an approach is only viable when there is good reason to believe that the data environment is stationary and that the samples used in training are sufficiently representative. In cases where learning takes place in a non-stationary environment, it is either necessary to allow the feedforward networks to carry on learning or to re-train them off-line.

---

* Corresponding author: Dr. CP Lim, School of Industrial Technology,
  Universiti Sains Malaysia, 11800, Penang, Malaysia.
  Tel: +604-6577888 Ext 2200, Fax: +604-6573678, Email: cplim@usm.my

In this paper, we describe a case study on medical diagnosis using a hybrid adaptive network based on the combination of Fuzzy ARTMAP (FAM) [3] and Probabilistic Neural Network (PNN) [4]. The FAM network offers an alternative to solving the stability-plasticity dilemma—how a learning system can absorb new information without forgetting previously learned information [5]. It is able to recruit nodes on-line and thus eliminate the need to pre-specify a fixed network structure before learning ensues. By incorporating the PNN into its framework, the hybrid network is able to operate in probabilistic environments. Several experiments have been conducted to assess the effectiveness of this hybrid network in a medical pattern classification task.

2 Probabilistic Fuzzy ARTMAP — A Hybrid Network

It is well documented that Adaptive Resonance Theory (ART) [5, 3] offers a family of incremental learning neural networks that can overcome the stability-plasticity dilemma. Among them, FAM is a supervised network synthesizing ART properties and fuzzy logic in a common platform. The FAM architecture comprises two unsupervised Fuzzy ART, ART_a and ART_b, modules, interlinked by a map field [3]. The key feature of FAM is its inclusion of a novelty detector to measure, against a threshold called the vigilance parameter, the similarity between the prototype patterns stored in the network and the input patterns. When the vigilance test is not satisfied, a new node is created, and the input is coded as its prototype pattern. As a result, the number of nodes grows with time, subject to the novelty criterion, in an attempt to learn a good network size autonomously and on-line. As different tasks demand different network structures, this learning approach thus avoids the need to specify a pre-defined static network size, or to re-train the network off-line.

On the other hand, the PNN is a neural network model that implements Bayes' theorem in its learning methodology. It learns instantaneously in one-pass through the data samples, and is able to form complex decision boundaries that approximate asymptotically the Bayes optimal limits. In addition, the decision boundaries can be modified on-line when new data become available without having to re-train the network. The PNN consists of four layers of nodes: the input layer, pattern layer, summation layer, and output layer. Nodes in the pattern layer are organized in groups corresponding to different target classes. The pattern nodes belonging to the same output are then linked to a summation node dedicated to that particular target class. The key feature of the PNN is its ability to estimate the probability density functions based on the data samples by using the Parzen-window technique. One disadvantage of the PNN is that it encodes every input pattern as a new node in the network, thus increases the network complexity and computational cost if large or unbounded data sets are used. However, this problem can be alleviated by using a clustering technique such as FAM.

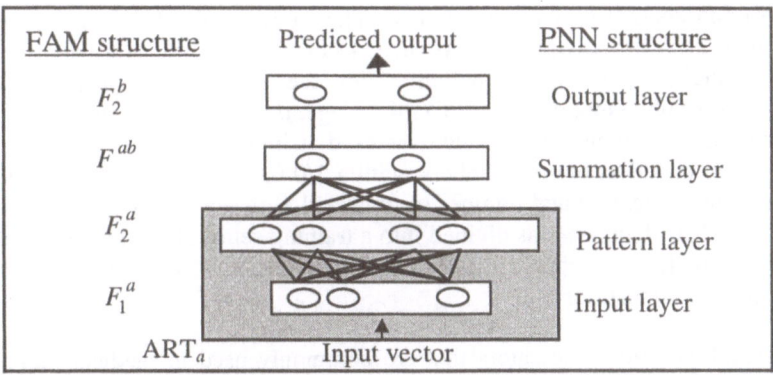

Fig. 1 A schematic diagram depicting the similarity between the network structures of FAM and PNN.

We have previously devised a hybrid network, known as Probabilistic Fuzzy ARTMAP (PFAM) [6], combining the FAM and PNN algorithms into a common framework. There is a close similarity in the network topology between FAM and the PNN, as depicted in Figure 1. The F_1^a and F_2^a layers of FAM correspond to the input and pattern layers of the PNN, respectively, whereas the map field layer, F^{ab}, corresponds to the summation layer. In essence, in one-from-N classification, each node in F_2^a is permanently associated with only one node in F^{ab} which is then linked to the target output in F_2^b. Thus, the F^{ab} nodes can be used to sum outputs from all the F_2^a nodes connected to a particular target category, taking the role of the summation nodes in the PNN. Then, F_2^b operates as the output layer of the PNN where the highest activated node is selected as the predicted class. The PFAM learning algorithm, in general, can be divided into two phases. First, the FAM clustering procedure is used for classifying the input patterns into different categories (learning phase). Subsequently, the PNN probability estimation procedure is used to predict a target output (prediction phase). The advantage of this integration is two-fold: (i) a probabilistic interpretation of output classes is established which enables the application of Bayes, risk-weighted, classification in FAM; (ii) the number of pattern nodes in the PNN is reduced by the clustering procedure of FAM. The above account provides a conceptual description of the synergism of FAM and the PNN into a hybrid network. Details of the PFAM network can be found in [6].

3   A Case Study in Medical Diagnosis

The objective of this paper is to study the usefulness of the PFAM classifier as a clinical decision support tool in the diagnosis of Myocardial Infarction (MI), commonly known as heart attack. Given the clinical data of patients with symptoms of the disease, PFAM has to classify the patients into two categories, MI (positive) and non-MI (negative) patients. The study involved a database of 500 patient records collected from the Medical Department of the Northern General Hospital, Sheffield, United Kingdom. For the experiments, a total of 26 measurements and symptoms, e.g. ECG data, age, description of chest pain, chest wall tenderness, sweating, nausea etc. was used as inputs to PFAM. All the input features were coded as binary numbers, with a 1/0 indicating presence/absence of symptoms, and a real-valued number (normalized between 0 and 1) for the input feature *age*. The database was divided into a training set of 300 samples and a test set of 200 samples with approximately equal proportions of MI and non-MI cases in the training and test sets.

We employed three indicators that are commonly used in medical diagnosis, i.e. accuracy, sensitivity, and specificity, to assess the performance of PFAM. They are defined as follows:

(i)   Accuracy—ratio of the number of correct predictions to the total number of cases;

(ii) Sensitivity—ratio of the number of correct positive predictions to the total number of patients having a positive outcome;

(iii) Specificity—ratio of the number of correct negative predictions to the total number of patients having a negative outcome

3.1   Vigilance Parameter

In PFAM, the role of the ART_a baseline vigilance parameter, $\bar{\rho}_a$, is to form prototype patterns with varying degrees of granularity. A high value of $\bar{\rho}_a$ leads to fine prototypes with narrow generalization, whereas a low value of $\bar{\rho}_a$ leads to coarse prototypes with broad generalization. In this experiment, the PFAM network was operated in conservative mode ($\alpha_a = 0.00001 \approx 0.0$) with fast learning ($\beta_a = 1.0$). After several trials, the smoothing parameter was set to 0.5. To determine a good setting of ART_a category granularity, the value of $\bar{\rho}_a$ was first changed from 0.0 to 0.9 with an increment of 0.1. The best range of $\bar{\rho}_a$ (between 0.60 and 0.80) was then altered with an increment of 0.01. Each test was repeated 10 times, with the results averaged. Figure 1 shows the overall results graphically.

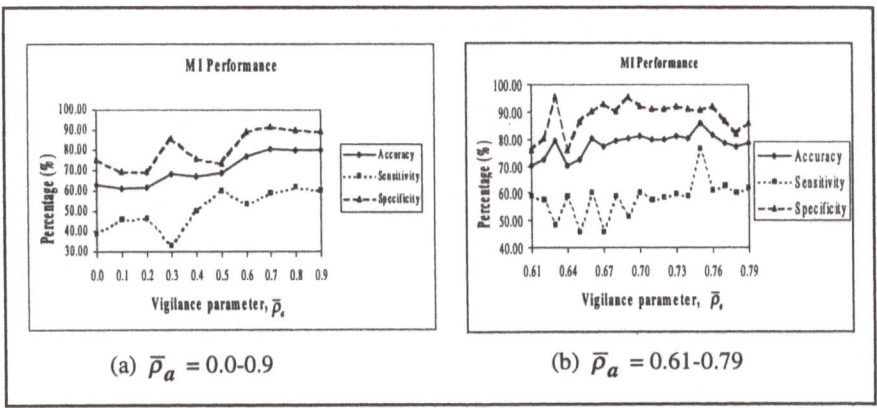

(a) $\overline{\rho}_a = 0.0\text{-}0.9$ (b) $\overline{\rho}_a = 0.61\text{-}0.79$

Fig. 2. The effect of $\overline{\rho}_a$ on the performance of PFAM for the MI database

As we can see from Figure 2, accuracy, sensitivity, and specificity were separately distributed. It is clearly shown that the PFAM network achieved the best performance for specificity, followed by accuracy and sensitivity. The value of $\overline{\rho}_a = 0.75$ yielded the best results, with 86.2% accuracy, 76.5% sensitivity, and 90.9% specificity.

3.2 Learning Mode

There are two learning modes: (i) *fast learning* corresponds to setting $\beta_a = 1$ for all times; (ii) *fast-commit and slow-recode learning* corresponds to setting $\beta_a = 1$ for an uncommitted node, and $\beta_a < 1$ for a committed node. The former rule allows the weight vector to converge to the asymptotic category boundary in one attempt; whereas the latter rule slowly varies the weight vector to make the system more resistant to noise [3]. Here we set $\overline{\rho}_a = 0.75$, and examined the effects of the learning rate on the network performance. The average results of 10 runs are plot in Figure 2.

From Figure 3, we can see that the PFAM network yielded the most acceptable performance in the fast learning mode ($\beta_a = 1$) with an average of 86.2% accuracy (highest), 76.5% sensitivity (highest), and 90.9% specificity (2.3% lower than the best specificity). Thus, we used fast learning in our subsequent experiments.

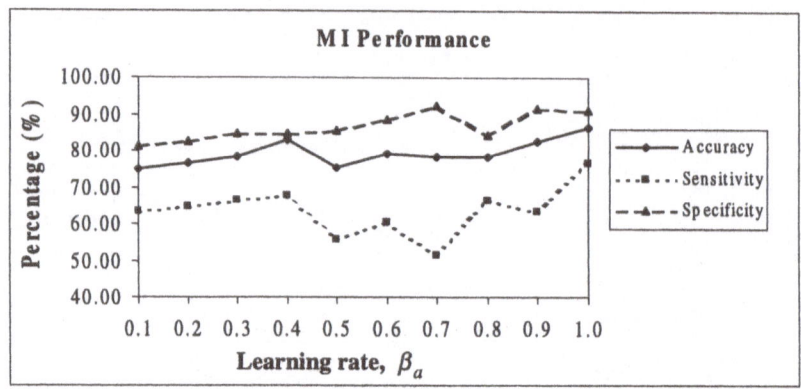

Fig. 3. The effect of β_a on the performance of PFAM for the MI database

3.3   Voting Strategy

The voting strategy was first introduced in [3] for the FAM network. It is based on the observation that FAM leads to different adaptive weights and recognition categories for different orderings of inputs. The different category structures cause the cases in the test set where errors occur to vary from one run to the next. To implement the voting strategy, a pool of networks was created; each trained on a different ordering of inputs. The outputs from the networks were combined by using a majority-voting scheme to produce an overall prediction. As an example, if we had 9 networks with 5 votes for MI and 4 votes for non-MI, then the prediction would be MI. Since erroneous predictions vary from one run to the next, voting cancels many of the errors [3].

In this experiment, an ensemble of 9 networks was created; each trained on different orderings of the inputs using parameters $\overline{\rho}_a = 0.75$ and $\beta_a = 1$. The accuracy, sensitivity, and specificity of the networks were averaged. In addition, for each test sample, the outputs from these 9 networks were combined using majority voting to produce a combined prediction, and compared with the target class to yield the voting results. The above procedure was repeated 12 times. Table 1 summarizes the overall average results and voting results, with indications of the maximum and minimum results.

Table 1 Overall average and voting results of PFAM for the MI database

	Voting	Average
Accuracy (%)	91 (89.0—92.0)	86 (84.9—85.8)
Sensitivity (%)	80 (73.5—83.8)	72 (70.1—74.0)
Specificity (%)	97 (95.5—98.5)	93 (91.6—93.5)

Clearly, voting is a good strategy for enhancing the performance of ART-based networks. A significant improvement for all the three performance indicators was achieved using voting. Note that the minimum voting results were better compared with the maximum average results, except for sensitivity with a marginal difference of 0.5%. The highest percentages of 91% accuracy, 80% sensitivity, and 97% specificity were the best results achieved in this study.

3.4   Comparison with FAM

This MI database has previously been investigated using FAM [7], and the best results are summarized in Table 2. The voting and average results from PFAM were higher by 1-2% and 7-8% for accuracy and specificity, respectively, compared with those from FAM. However, FAM was more sensitive towards the diagnosis of positive MI cases, with an improvement of 10% for both voting and average results from PFAM.

Note that in the database the number of MI cases is about 40% more than the number of non-MI cases. Since the specificity rate from PFAM is higher than that of sensitivity, this might imply that PFAM could classify dominant patterns more effectively compared with less frequent ones. FAM, on the other hand, could maintain its discriminatory ability in categorizing either common or uncommon patterns. This is evident from its approximately balanced accuracy, sensitivity, and specificity rates for both voting and average results.

Table 2 Best average and voting results of FAM for the MI database

	Voting	Average
Accuracy (%)	90	84
Sensitivity (%)	90	82
Specificity (%)	90	85

4   Summary

We have investigated the effectiveness of a hybrid adaptive network for a medical pattern classification task. The PFAM network is able to complement the drawbacks of FAM and the PNN, and to implement an incremental learning algorithm in probabilistic domains. From the medical diagnosis case study, the PFAM network was able to classify patients into MI and non-MI categories with satisfactory performance. Several experiments were conducted to fine-tune the parameters of PFAM, and to combine predictions from an ensemble of PFAM networks in order to enhance its performance. The results were comparable with those from FAM. Further work will concentrate on how to extract rules from the PFAM network in order for it to justify and to explain its predictions.

Acknowledgement. The first author acknowledges the research grants provided by Universiti Sains Malaysia as well as the Ministry of Science, Technology, and the Environment Malaysia (No. 06-02-05-8002) that have in part resulted in this article.

References

1. Cybenko, G. (1989). Approximation by Superposition of a Sigmoidal Function. Mathematics of Control, Signals and Systems, **2**, 303-314.

2. Poggio, T., Girosi, F. (1990). Network Approximation and Learning. Proc. of IEEE, **78**, 1481-1497.

3. Carpenter, G.A., Grossberg, S., et al. (1992). Fuzzy ARTMAP: A neural network architecture for incremental supervised learning of analogue multidimensional maps. *IEEE Trans on Neural Networks*, **3**, 698-712.

4. Specht, D.F. (1990). Probabilistic neural networks. *Neural Networks*, **3**, 109-118.

5. Carpenter, G.A., and Grossberg, S. (1987). A massively parallel architecture for a self-organising neural pattern recognition machine. *Computer Vision, Graphics and Image Processing*, **37**, 54-115.

6. Lim, C.P., and Harrison, R.F. (1997). An incremental adaptive network for on-line, supervised learning and probability estimation. *Neural Networks*, **10**, 925-937.

7. Harrison, R.F., Lim, C.P., and Kennedy, R.L. (1994). Autonomously learning neural networks for clinical decision support. In Ifeachor, E.C., and Rosen, K.G. (Eds.), Proceedings of the International Conference on Neural Networks and Expert Systems in Medicine and Healthcare (NNESMED-94), (pp. 15-22). Plymouth: University of Plymouth.

Reliability of Artificial Neural Network Predictions — A Case Study in Drug Release Profile Predictions

Siow San Quek[1], Chee Peng Lim[1*], and Kok Khiang Peh[2]

[1] School of Industrial Technology, Universiti Sains Malaysia,
11800 Penang, Malaysia.

[2] School of Pharmaceutical, Sciences Universiti Sains Malaysia,
11800 Penang, Malaysia.

Abstract: Artificial neural networks have been widely used in pharmaceutical research such as for estimation of process coefficients and pharmacokinetic parameters. In this paper, we present a study on the use of the Radial Basis Function-based Gaussian mixture model to predict dissolution profiles of a matrix controlled release theophylline pellet preparation. Performance of the network has been assessed using similarity factor—an index for profile comparison in pharmaceutical research. In addition, we also investigate the phenomena of interpolation and extrapolation of the test data sets that will affect the reliability of network predictions. The Parzen-window approach has been employed to determine, based on the calculated data densities, whether the trained network produces interpolated or extrapolated predictions. The experimental results are discussed and analyzed.

1   Introduction

Artificial Neural Networks (ANNs) are data-driven learning systems. They are capable of gathering their knowledge by learning relationships from the data samples collected from the problem domain. In addition, ANNs offer several other useful properties such as non-linearity, universal mapping, adaptability, and fault tolerance [1]. All these properties make ANNs suitable for solving a variety of practical problems such as pattern recognition, function approximation, forecasting, and control.

Recently, ANNs have been applied to solve problems in the pharmaceutical industry such as estimation of process coefficients and pharmacokinetic parameters [2-3]. The Multilayer Perceptron (MLP) [4] network is one of the most widely used networks in this area. It has been proven to be a universal function approximator and, therefore, can approximate any non-linear function with arbitrary accuracy when a sufficient number of neurons is provided [5]. However, one of the weaknesses of an MLP network is it has no inherent ability to indicate

* Corresponding author: Dr. CP Lim, School of Industrial Technology,
Universiti Sains Malaysia, 11800, Penang, Malaysia.
Tel: +604-6577888 Ext 2200, Fax: +604-6573678, Email: cplim@usm.my

when it is functioning outside the domain over which it has been trained. This is because the contours of constant hidden node activation are hyperplane and infinite in length, and their activations do not represent proximity to training data [6]. Therefore, it is impossible to identify the predictions from a trained MLP network are produced by whether interpolating or extrapolating the training input data.

Generally, extrapolation can be defined as any local region of the input space with little or no training data to support a model prediction [6]. Conversely, interpolation can be defined as any local region of the input space with enough training data to support a model prediction [6]. Typically, ANNs (and other empirical based models such as non-linear regression and multiple regression) are much more accurate in interpolation compared with extrapolation [7]. Therefore, it may be dangerous to accept blindly the predicted results from ANNs without knowing the trained network is operating in interpolation or extrapolation conditions. As a result, understanding the distinction between interpolation and extrapolation is important to evaluate the reliability of predictions from the trained network.

In the present paper, instead of using the MLP network, we use a variant of the Radial basis function (RBF) network as an alternative to evaluate the reliability of the network predictions. This is because the RBF network has also been proven to be a universal function approximator [8]. In addition, a method based on the Parzen-window approach for computing the reliability (extrapolation or interpolation) of the RBF network directly from the network architecture has been proposed in [6], and implemented in our studies.

2 RBF-Based Gaussian Mixture Model

Fig. 1 depicts the basic architecture of an RBF-based Gaussian mixture model. The network consists of input, hidden, and output layers. Each radial basis function unit (hidden unit) has a vector of center, c. The connection from the hidden layer to the output layer is weighted by w. The output of the network is

$$y(\overline{x}) = \sum_{i=0}^{H} w_i \phi(a_i) \tag{1}$$

where H is to the number of hidden nodes, vector a is the distance of the input vector x to each of the centers in the hidden layer. The Euclidean norm is used to compute distance

$$a_i = \sqrt{\sum_{j=1}^{d} (x_j - c_{ij})^2} \tag{2}$$

where d is the dimension of the input vector x.

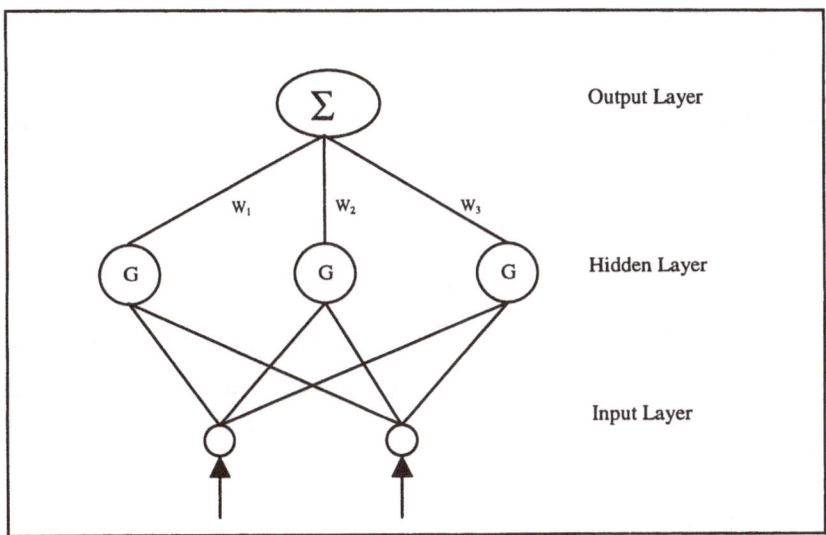

Fig. 1. An RBF-based Gaussian mixture network with activation function, G

The radial basis function, $\phi(a)$ is a Gaussian function

$$\phi(a) = \exp^{-(a^2/\sigma^2)} \tag{3}$$

where σ is the width of the basis function.

Basically, the RBF-based Gaussian mixture model uses a two-stage training algorithm to set the corresponding network parameters based on the training data. In the first stage, a K-means clustering algorithm [9] is used to determine the initial center points. After initialization, the Expectation Maximization (EM) algorithm [10] is then used to estimate the centers of the RBF-based Gaussian mixture model. The basis function widths, σ_i, are determined by setting to the maximum inter-center square distance after training the network. In the second stage, the pseudo-inverse method [11] is used to determine the weights and biases of the connection between the hidden and output layers. Note that the first stage of training is termed unsupervised learning because only the input vectors are provided for the training process, whereas the second stage of training is considered as supervised learning because the desired output vectors are specified for each input vector.

2.1 The Parzen-Window Estimation of Network Reliability

A method based on the Parzen-window approach for computing the reliability (extrapolation or interpolation) of the predictions directly from the network architecture has been proposed in [6]. This is according to the fact that the RBF network gives satisfactory results for test input data which are similar to its training data but poor results for test input data that are not similar. Here, the Parzen-window approach has been applied to the RBF-based Gaussian mixture model to generate reliability measurement for the network predictions.

The formula for computing the Parzen-window estimate for an input vector x to the RBF-based Gaussian Mixture model is given by

$$\rho(\overline{x}) = \frac{\sum_{i=1}^{H} \phi(a_i)\rho_i}{\sum_{i=1}^{H} \phi(a_i) + 1 - \max(\phi(a_i))} \qquad (4)$$

where H is the number of hidden nodes, and $\phi(a)$ is the output of the hidden nodes after applying equations (1) and (2), respectively. The H values of ρ_i are computed, after the RBF-based Gaussian mixture model network is trained, by using the formula

$$\rho_i(\overline{x}) = \frac{\sum_{v=1}^{V} \phi(a_i)}{V(\pi^{1/2}\sigma_i)^d} \qquad (5)$$

where V is the number of vectors used to train the network, d is the dimension of vector x, and σ_i is the width of the hidden node. It is suggested in [6] that the minimum ρ value of the training data from equation (4) can be used as a threshold value. When the estimated ρ value of an unknown input vector x is higher than the threshold, the network output can be considered as reliable (interpolation). On the other hand, when ρ is lower than the threshold, then the network output can be considered as unreliable (extrapolation). Therefore the network can automatically indicate a warning statement (extrapolation or interpolation) of its prediction for each of the test data samples.

3 A Case Study

In this case study, we utilized a RBF-based Gaussian mixture model to predict the dissolution profiles of a matrix controlled release theophylline pellet preparation. Different matrix ratios of microcrystalline cellulose (MCC) and glyceryl monostearate (GMS) were used to control the release rate of theophylline (10:0, 8:2, 7:3, 6:4, 5:5 and 4:6 of MCC:GMS).

The objective of this study was to predict the dissolution profiles as a time-series curve for a given matrix ratio of MCC and GMS. Motivation of our investigation is as follows. Instead of determining the dissolution profile of each matrix ratio by conducting actual physical experiments, a suitable ANN system can be developed and used to predict the trend of the profiles. Based on the recorded data, the ANN system can predict release profiles of pellet preparation containing various compositions of MCC and GMS that have yet been determined. When a satisfied release profile is obtained, a confirmation test can be carried out experimentally to verify the predicted profiles. By using this approach, a lengthy and time-consuming experimentation to decide on the appropriate matrix ratios of preparation can be reduced. In addition, the reliability of the network predictions can be directly measured by using the method describe in section 2.1.

Each of the six experiments with different proportions of MCC and GMS was repeated six times, giving a total number of thirty-six data samples. The percentage of dissolution was measured at times 0, 0.25, 0.5, 1.0, 1.5, 2.0, 3.0, 4.0, 6.0, 8.0, and 10 hours. The leave-one-out method was used to validate the network performance for each matrix ratio. Thus, 5 sets of experimental data were used for training except 1 set, which was used as reference profiles to be compare with the predicted profiles. . For example, 5 sets of data samples from MCC and GMS at ratios of 10:0, 8:2, 7:3, 6:4, and 5:5 were used to trained the network. Then, the trained network was used to predict the dissolution profile of MCC and GMS at ratio of 4:6. There were three inputs to the network. The first two inputs represented the matrix ratios of MCC and GMS, and the third input encoded the time point. The output was the predicted percentage of drug dissolution.

Performance of the network was assessed by comparing the predicted dissolution profiles with those obtained from actual experiments using similarity factor (f_2)—a similarity measurement in the percent rate of drug release between two dissolution profiles recommended by the United States Food and Drug Administration (FDA) [12]. The equation of f_2 is as follows.

$$f_2 = 50 \times \log \left\{ \left[1 + (1/P) \sum_{i=1}^{P} \left(\mu_{ti} - \mu_{ri} \right)^2 \right]^{-1/2} \times 100 \right\} \qquad (6)$$

The minimum requirement of f_2 by the FDA is equal or more than 50 [12].

3.1 Results and Discussion

Table 1 depicts the f_2 values for each matrix ratio of MCC and GMS. We can see that the network performs well in predicting the dissolution profiles, and all the f_2 values are above the minimum requirement of 50. Figure 2a depicts an example of interpolation condition, where the Parzen values from the test data is higher than the threshold value. Conversely, Figure 2b shows an example of extrapolation condition, where the Parzen values from the test data is lower than threshold value. Note that each ratio of matrix consists of 10 time points therefore there are 10 Parzen values. Therefore, the network outputs can be considered as interpolation or extrapolation predictions when the minimum or maximum Parzen values are higher or lower, respectively, than the threshold values. In addition, Table 1 shows the threshold values, and the maximum or minimum Parzen values for each of matrix ratios that are used to distinguish between interpolation and extrapolation of the test data by to the network. As might be expected, the performance of the network is relatively better for those from interpolation (8:2, 7:3, 6:4, 5:5) compared with those from extrapolation (10:0, 4:6) of test data.

Table 1 The Parzen values as well as the f_2 values of various matrix ratios of MCC and GMS for network predictions

MCC: GMS	Parzen Values		Network Indication	Similarity Factor, f_2
4:6	Threshold	0.2260	Extrapolation	66.2
	Test data (maximum)	0.2117		
5:5	Threshold	0.2298	Interpolation	76.0
	Test data (minimum)	0.2355		
6:4	Threshold	0.1040	Interpolation	75.2
	Test data (minimum)	0.1078		
7:3	Threshold	0.1053	Interpolation	75.9
	Test data (minimum)	0.1090		
8:2	Threshold	0.0801	Interpolation	72.3
	Test data (minimum)	0.0826		
10:0	Threshold	0.2820	Extrapolation	51.4
	Test data (maximum)	0.2409		

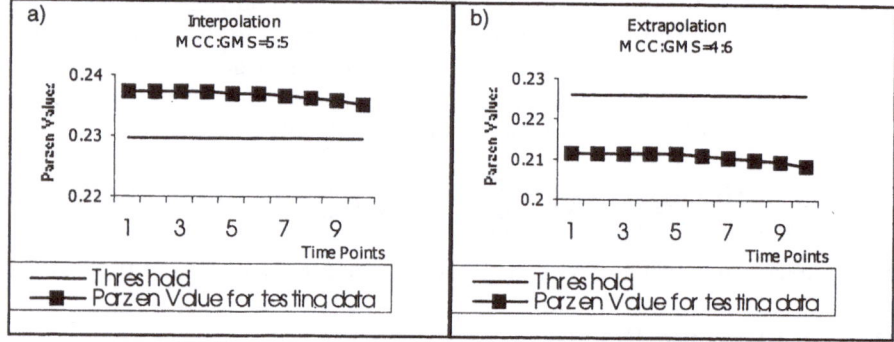

Fig.2. . Comparisan between the threshold and Parzen values at matrix ratio of MCC:GMS at 5:5 (Interpolation) and 4:6 (Extrapolation).

4 Summary

Based on the results obtained, the benefit of using ANNs in product formulation especially in the prediction of dissolution profiles is evident. By using this approach, a lengthy and time-consuming experimentation to decide on the appropriate matrix ratios of preparation can be reduced. On the other hand, the Parzen-window method is suitable to distinguish between interpolation and extrapolation of the data samples directly from the network computation. Therefore this would help develop a useful, valid, and reliable ANN-based intelligent software for pharmaceutical product development.

Acknowledgment. The authors acknowledge the research grants provided by Universiti Sains Malaysia as well as the Ministry of Science, Technology, and the

Environment Malaysia (No. 06-02-05-8002) that have in part resulted in this article.

References

1. Haykin, S. (1994) Neural network: A comprehensive foundation foundation. New York, NY: Macmillan.
2. J. Takahara, K. Takayama, and T. Nagai. (1997) Multi-objective simultaneous optimization based on artificial neural network in sustained released formulations. *J. Contr. Rel.* **49**:11-20.
3. A.S. Hussian, R.D. Johnson, N. Vachhrajani, and W.A. Ritshel. (1993) Feasibility of developing a neural network for prediction of human pharmacokinetic parameters from animal data. *Pharm. Res.* **10**:466-469.
4. D.E. Rumelhart, G.E. Hinton, and R.J. Williams, R.J. (1986) Learning internal representation by error propagation. In D.E. Rumelhart, and J.L. McLelland, J.L. (Eds.), *Parallel Distributed Processing*, I, (pp. 318-362). Cambridge, MA: MIT Press.
5. G. Cybenko. (1989) Approximation by superposition of a sigmoidal function. *Mathematics of Control, Signals and Systems*, **2**, 303-314.
6. J.A. Leonard, M.A. Kramer , L.H. Unger. (1992) A neural network architecture that computes its own reliability, Comput. Chem. Eng. 16 (9) 819-835.
7. Ian T. Nabney et al. (1997) Practical Assessment of Neural Network Applications. In SafeComp 97, Proceedings of the 16th International Conference on Computer Safety, Reliability and Security, ed. P. Daniel, pp. 357-368. Springer Verlag.
8. Girosi F., Poggio T. (1990) Networks and the Best Approximation Property, *Biological Cybernetics* **63**, 169-176.
9. Lloyd, S.P. (1982). Least squares quantization in PCM. *IEEE Transactions on Information Theory* **28** (2), 129-137.
10. Dempster, A.P., N.M. Laird, and D. B. Rubin (1977). Maximum likelihood from incomplete data via the EM algorithm. *Journal of the Royal Statistical Society*, B 39 (1), 1-38.
11. Bishop Christopher M. (1995) *Neural Networks for Pattern Recognition.* Clarendon Press, Oxford (UK).
12. FDA Guidance for Industry: Modified release solid dosage forms: Scale-up and Post Approval Changes (SUPAC-MR): Chemistry, Manufacturing and Controls. In vitro dissolution testing and in vivo bioequivalence documentation, September, (1997).

An Island-Based Evolutionary Algorithm for Maximizing Schedule Reliability

Piotr Jędrzejowicz[1] and Aleksandr Skakovski[1]

[1] Gdynia Maritime Academy, Computer Science Department, Morska 83, 81-225 Gdynia, Poland, {*pj, askakow*}*@wsm.gdynia.pl*

Abstract: The paper investigates the problem of scheduling multiple-variant (m-v) tasks on multiple processors with a view to maximize schedule reliability. Schedule reliability is understood as the probability that all tasks within schedule are executed without failures. It is proposed to manage complexity issues of the m-v tasks not at a single task level, but from the point of view of the whole set of tasks to be run under some time constraints. Because the problem is NP-hard, two evolutionary algorithms - an island based and a traditional population based algorithm to solve the problem have been proposed. The approach seems promising and the algorithms produce good to satisfactory solutions.

Keywords: schedule reliability, multiple-variant tasks, island based evolutionary algorithm

1   Introduction

There exist numerous situations where performing repeatedly a task or executing a number of its multiple redundant variants, increases chances for a successful task completion. The paper investigates the problem of scheduling multiple-variant (m-v) tasks with a view to maximize schedule reliability. Schedule reliability is understood as the probability that all tasks within schedule are executed without failures. The considered problem is based on the following assumptions: 1) tasks belonging to a set of m-v independent tasks, are to be scheduled on multiple processors under some, possibly hard, time constraints; 2) variants of a task can be run in parallel or in sequence; 3) variants of each task are also independent and their successes/failures are not correlated. The goal is to allocate m-v tasks to processors in such a way that schedule reliability is maximized and time constraints are kept. One of the potential application areas for m-v task scheduling algorithms is a fault-tolerant computing under time constraints. The best known techniques achieve software fault tolerance, for example N-version programming (NVP) [2], by increasing the number of independently developed program variants, which in turn leads to higher reliability at a cost of the additional resources used. Typical for classic scheduling criteria are, for example, schedule length, maximum tardiness or lateness, total lateness, etc. All of these could be also used in case of m-v tasks.

To improve efficiency of genetic algorithms (GA) several distributed GA's were proposed, for example in [1], [3]. The idea included an island-based approach where a set of independent populations of individuals evolves on cooperating with each other "islands". This approach brings two benefits: a model that maps easily onto the parallel hardware and extended search area (due to multiplicity of islands) what possibly prevents from sticking in local optima.

In this paper two evolutionary algorithms for scheduling m-v tasks to maximize schedule reliability are proposed. The first one - an island-based evolutionary algorithm (**IBEA**), belongs to the distributed algorithms class. The second one - a population based evolutionary algorithm (**PBEA**) – a classic evolutionary algorithm, is used within **IBEA** and serves as the reference algorithm.

2   Problem Formulation

The problem of scheduling a set N of n m-v tasks under hard time constraints is considered. It is assumed that the following information with respect to each m-v task j in N is available: ready time - a_j, deadline - d_j, number of available variants – NV_j, variant processing times - p_{ji}, variant reliabilities - r_{ji}, $j = 1, \dots, n$, $i = 1, \dots, NV_j$. According to Graham notation [4] the considered problem of scheduling m-v tasks can be denoted as $P|m\text{-}v,a_j|R$. $P|m\text{-}v,a_j|R$ is characterized by a set of multiple, identical processors P, and a set of multiple-variant tasks N. For each task there is the available number of variants NV_j. Tasks are independent and non-preemptable, with ready times and deadlines differing per task. Variants have arbitrary and possibly differing processing times. Variant reliabilities are statistically independent and known. Optimization criterion is schedule reliability calculated as:

$$R = \Pi R_j, \tag{1}$$

$$R_j = 1 - \prod_{i \in V_j} (1 - r_{ji}). \tag{2}$$

where V_j is a subset of variants of the task j used to construct a schedule, $1 \le |V_j| \le NV_j$. Decision variables include assignment of variants to processors and determination of V_j for each task. Tasks, i.e. their scheduled variants, can not be delayed.

3 Island Based Evolutionary Algorithm

The proposed Island Based Evolutionary Algorithm **IBEA** works on two levels with the two corresponding types of individuals. The following assumptions are made:

- an upper level individual is an island I_k, $k = 1, 2, ..., K$, (K- is the number of islands) that is represented by a set (population) of the lower level individuals (solutions) S_u, i.e. $I_k = \{S_u | u = 1, 2,..., PS\}$, PS – the size of a population

- all islands are located on the directed ring

- populations of lower level individuals evolve on each island independently

- each island I_k regularly sends its best solution to the successor $I_{(k \bmod K)+1}$ in the ring

- the algorithm stops when an optimality criterion is satisfied or the preset number of generations on each island have been generated

- when **IBEA** stops the best solution yielded across all islands is the final one

- the lower level of the **IBEA** is based on applying **PBEA**

IBEA includes performing the following steps:

Begin {IBEA}

Set the number of islands K, number of generations NG to be generated on each island, the size of a population on each island PS, the interval for solution interchange between islands - ng. On each island I_k generate an initial population PP_0, in which one part of individuals has random task order and the other part - fixed task order, that is tasks has to be ordered by non-decreasing ready time as the first criterion and non-decreasing deadlines as the second. In both cases subsets of task variants V_j generate at random, $1 \leq |V_j| \leq NV_j$.

While no stopping criteria is met **do**

    For each island I_k **do**

        Evolve ng generations with the help of **PBEA**

        Send the best solution to $I_{(k \bmod K) + 1}$

        Incorporate the best solution from $I_{((K+k-2) \bmod K) + 1}$ instead of the worst one

EndWhile

Find the best solution across all islands and save it as the final one

End {IBEA}

PBEA algorithm is based on the following assumptions:

- an individual is represented by subsets of variants V_j of each task j, i.e. $S_u = \{ V_j | 1 \leq | V_j | \leq NV_j; 1 \leq j \leq n \}$

- an initial population is composed in part of individuals of random task order and in part of individuals of fixed task order, that is tasks are ordered by non-decreasing ready time as the first criterion and non-decreasing deadlines as the second. In both cases subsets of task variants V_j are generated at random, $1 \leq |V_j| \leq NV_j$

- each individual can be transformed into a solution by applying list scheduling algorithm (**LSA**), which is a specially designed algorithm for scheduling multiple-processor tasks

- each solution produced by the **LSA** can be directly evaluated in terms of its fitness, that is schedule reliability

- new generation is formed by applying four evolution operators: selection and transfer of some more 'fit' individuals, random generation of new individuals, crossover, and mutation

- the algorithm stops when the optimality criterion has been satisfied or the preset number of generations has been generated

- when the algorithm stops the best yielded solution is the final one

PBEA includes performing the following steps:

Begin {PBEA}

Set $ic := 0$; (ic - iteration counter)

   While no stopping criteria is met **do**

      Set $ic := ic + 1$

      Calculate fitness factor for each individual in PP_{ic-1} using **LSA**

      Form new population PP_{ic}

      Select randomly a part of PS individuals from PP_{ic-1} (probability of selection depends on fitness of an individual)

      Produce a part of PS individuals by applying crossover operator to previously selected individuals from PP_{ic-1}

Produce a part of *PS* individuals by applying mutation operators to previously selected individuals from PP_{ic-1}

Generate a part of *PS* individuals from the set of potential individuals (random task order and V_j)

Generate a part of *PS* individuals from the set of potential individuals (fixed task order and random V_j)

EndWhile

End {PBEA}

To transform individual into a solution and estimate its fitness use **LSA**.
Begin {LSA}

Set a loop over the tasks variants ordered as they appear in an individual

Within the loop, allocate current variant to multiple processors in a way that minimizes the beginning time of its processing. Continue with variants until all have been allocated

If the resulting schedule has task delays, the fitness factor of the individual (ff_u) is set to $ff_u = -(1 - \Pi R_l)$ of all late tasks *l*. Otherwise $ff_u = \Pi R_j$ of all scheduled tasks *j*

End {LSA}

4   Experimental Results and Conclusions

To verify and evaluate the presented evolution-based algorithms several computational experiments have been carried out. The experiment included 50 randomly generated scheduling problems belonging to the $P|m\text{-}v,a_j|R$ class. Problems involved scheduling 10 - 29 tasks, each task 3 - 5 variants, on 2 - 7 processors. The solutions obtained by the proposed algorithms and three other approximation algorithms [5] have been compared with the best solutions found for $P|a_j,m\text{-}v|R$ problem by branch-and-bound algorithm. The respective relative errors were calculated and presented in Table 1. Parameter settings for **PBEA**: $PS = 28$, $NG = 2000$; for **IBEA**: $K = 27$, $PS = 28$, $ng = 25$, $NG = 2000$. For both algorithms the probability of: crossover operator $p_c = 1$, each mutation operator $p_m = 1/n_m$, n_m – the number of mutation operators ($n_m = 5$). **IBEA**'s overall mean relative errors are less about 2-3 times than corresponding **PBEA**'s. It took about 9-10 times more time for **IBEA** to find a solution than for **PBEA** (it has taken about 1-1,5 minutes for **PBEA** to find a solution on Pentium II-MMX CPU, 300MHz). In case of the **IBEA** much more computer memory (proportionally to the number of islands) is required. Thus, **PBEA** as a quicker and less memory-demanding algorithm can be used in case computational resources are limited. On the other hand, the **IBEA** could be useful when higher quality solutions are required and there are no strict constraints on time and memory resources. Although both algorithms are capable of finding good solutions it is still possible to improve their quality by designing genetic operators specific to the problem, or generating more fit individuals for the initial population, or, finally, including some intensification strategies based on other meta-heuristics to improve fitness of individuals during their evolution.

Table 1. Mean relative errors (%) from the best solutions found for Pla_j,m-$v|R$ problem

Number of processors	IBEA	PBEA	EA[a]	HETSA[b]	NNA[c]
2	3.17	7.25	54.33	14.33	8.33
3	7.12	19.41	40.14	18.43	9.17
4	8.46	11.85	34.31	14.31	12.83
5	10.23	17.57	29.67	10.67	14.75
6	9.65	27.89	20.87	8.13	9.00
7	11.62	30.21	19.50	8.5	11.00
Overall	8.24	19.05	32.26	12.62	11.63

[a] Evolutionary algorithm of another author
[b] Hybrid Evolutionary-Tabu Search Algorithm
[c] Neural Network Algorithm

References

[1] Alba E., Troya J. (1999) Analysis of Synchronous and Asynchronous Parallel Distributed Genetic Algorithms with Structured and Panmictic Islands. Proc. of the 10th Symp. on Par. and Dist. Proc., 248-256

[2] Avizienis A., L.Chen. (1977) On the implementation of the N-version programming for software fault tolerance during execution, Proc. IEEE COMPSAC 77, 149 - 155

[3] Belding T.C. (1995) The Distributed Genetic Algorithm Revisited, Proc. of the Sixth Int. Conf. on Genetic Algorithms, 114-121

[4] Graham R.L., E.L. Lawler et al. (1979) Optimization and approximation in deterministic sequencing and scheduling, Surv., Annals Discrete Math. **5**, 287 - 326

[5] Jedrzejowicz P., Skakovski A. et al. (2000) Maximizing Schedule Reliability in Presence of Multiple-Variant Tasks, to appear in Proc. of the Conf. on Foresight and Precaution, ESREL 2000, SARS and SRA-EUROPE Annual Conference, Edinburgh

Using of Genetic Algorithms (GA) in the Operating Control in Power System of Slovak Republic.

Ľuboslav Pribičko, Michal Kolcun

Department of Electro-Power Engineering, Technical University of Košice, Faculty of Electrical Engineering and Informatics, Vysokoškolská 4, 041 20 Košice, Slovakia. E-mail: pribicko@tuke.sk, kolcun@tuke.sk

Abstract: This article deals with the use of genetic algorithms (GA) in the electroenergetic field. These approaches are suitable for finding the extrems of optimalization problems. For this reason they were applied in control of power system which is a vast optimization problem from the aspect of economy of production, transmission and distribution of electric energy.

Keywords: Genetic Algorithm, Operating Control, Optimization

1 Introduction

The condition of regular and economical power supply of good quality is managing control of constantly spreading electrical framework. For this reason increase in quality of control is needed. One possibility to achieve this is to use modern approaches directly in power control as well as in preparing in all levels of dispatching control. Recently in the world and in Slovakia for solving of the recollection problems are used different techniques of artificial intelligence, among which the are Genetic Algorithms (GA), too. GA are used for the solving of the optimization problems from the aspect of economy of production, transmission and distribution of electric energy. The application of GA was used for these energetic problems:

- Optimization of steady running condition from the aspect of minimal active power losses.[1]

- Optimal fitting of power stations from the aspect of minimal costs.[2]

2   Optimization of Active Losses in Electrical Network

The problem of optimization of active power losses lies in finding optimal voltages in individual nodes of electrical network, so that an active power is minimal and the steady running conditions are observed. 110 kV node area Moldava was optimized which consists of 10 nodes where one of them is a balance node. Nodes area Moldava is supplied from the superior framework from the transformer 400/110 kV. The voltage of a balance node is considered 119 kV.

2.1   Description of the Optimization Problem

We consider kinked electrical network with n nodes. These nodes are connected with each other by m arms, which have known parameters. The active power ΔP in electrical network is calculated:

$$\Delta P = \sum_{i=1}^{N} U_i^2 g_{i,i} + \sum_{i=1}^{N} \sum_{j=i+1}^{N} 2 U_i U_j \cos(\delta_i - \delta_j) g_{i,j} \tag{1}$$

where U_i, U_j are the modules of voltages in i-th and j-th node of the network,

δ_i, δ_j are the angles of voltages in i-th and j-th node towards the angle on a balance node,

$g_{ii,} g_{ij}$ are real parts of a nodes admittance matrix $\dot{Y} = G - jB$

2.1.1   The Solving of Optimization Problem Using GA

Input ranges of an optimization function are between 109-119 kV for absolute value of voltages and 1,75π-2π for angle value of voltages δ. These ranges were chosen to obtain more quickly the convergency of GA. This way we obtain the value of minimal active power in node network Moldava which is equal to 1,2972 MW (fig.1). In this case the initial values were generated by GA [1]. When we select as a starting point values taken from optimization toolbox [2], we obtain value of losses $\Delta P = 1.0679 MW$. This results in fast convergency and lower losses (first population was more close to optimal result).

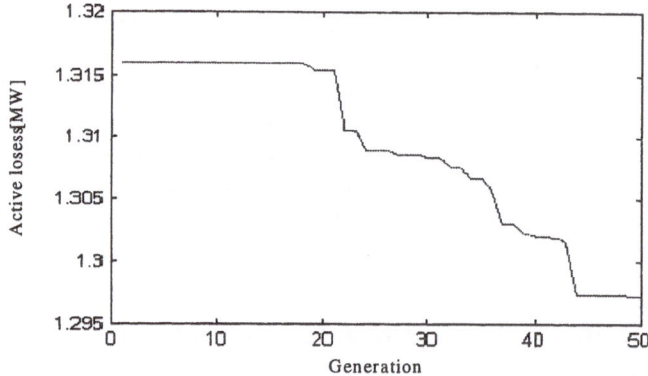

Fig. 1 Curve of searching minimal active losses

3 Optimal Fitting of Power Stations from the Aspect of Minimal Cost

Optimization of power stations fitting means the choice of power stations so that the daily diagram of loads is covered considering the individual limitations. This problem was solved in two ways:

- only thermal power stations (TP).

- thermal power stations and pumped storage power station (PSP).

To solve these problems we accept two simplifying conditions. In the first one do not consider the operation costs. In the second one we do not consider losses by transport and also optimization of reactive power.

3.1 Thermal Power Station

For concrete solution, the following thermal block combination was selected: EVO1/BL1, ENOB/BL1, 4 blocks from EVO2 (on gas) and 2 blocks from EVO2 (on mazut).In this model we do not shutting down or starting the blocks. Total costs of fuel represent $14,798596*10^6$ SKK/day.

3.2 Thermal Power Stations and Pumped Storage Power Station

For practical reasons, this model is the most useful in electrical network of Slovak Republic. In the future we assume its practical exploitation in Slovak

Energy Dispatching (SED) in Žilina. The model considers several TP blocks and one PSP. In PSP we know the consumption function of turbine and pumped storage operation. Power regulation in turbine operation is in the range 0 - P_{max}. PSP are setting on maximal pumped storage power or small range of power near the maximum (it is given by character of PSP). In pumped storage operation we consider constant head H. For calculation was used PSP Čierny Váh, which is a normal PSP without natural feed to lower tank, so total amount of water in the tanks is constant during the day. The remaining part of DDL must be divided between PSP Čierny Váh and thermal blocks as is shown in tab. 1.

Total costs of fuel represents $14,765583*10^6$ SKK/day. Total cost of fuel were therefore lower when PSP Čierny Váh was included in the DDL. In a specific example total cost of fuel were decreased by 33012,75 SKK (0,2357%) It follows from the achieved results that from the point of view of fuel costs it is convenient to use PSP even in a case when the remanent DDL can be covered by active blocks of TPS

4 Conclusion

GA are a relatively new proposed method in calculating and searching tasks. In spite of the quasi-coincidental solutions which they put forward they can be a promising alternative to classic calculating methods. They easily incorporate limitations of the set tasks. They are therefore suitable for solving discontinuous and non-linear functions.

References

[1] Ľ Pribička.: Optimization of steady states by using of GA, Diploma work, 1999

[2] Z Hogya.: Optimization fitting of power stations by using of GA, Diploma work, 1999

[3] J.H Holand.: Adaptation in Natural and Artificial Systems, MIT Press, 1975

[4] D. Goldberg : Genetic Algorithm in Search, Optimization, and Machine Learning, Addison -Wesley, 1989

time	TG1 [MW]	TG2 [MW]	TG3 [MW]	TG4 [MW]	TG5 [MW]	TG6 [MW]	TG7 [MW]	PSP [MW]
1.	106.9460	110.0000	74.6930	93.0066	79.8363	94.1233	97.8642	21.5307
2.	101.2897	110.0000	70.0895	91.8557	79.3248	88.8856	96.5547	0.0000
3.	88.2877	110.0000	59.5076	89.2102	78.1490	76.8457	93.5448	22.4550
4.	86.8957	110.0000	58.3748	88.9270	78.0231	75.5568	93.2225	0.0000
5.	93.6333	110.0000	63.8583	90.2979	78.6324	81.7958	94.7823	0.0000
6.	77.7901	108.7322	50.9640	87.0743	77.1997	67.1250	91.1146	0.0000
7.	106.8023	110.0000	74.5760	92.9773	79.8233	93.9902	97.8309	-102.000
8.	75.0000	90.0000	50.0000	79.9531	74.0347	60.0000	83.0122	0.0000
9.	92.8859	110.0000	63.2500	90.1458	78.5648	81.1037	94.6093	43.4405
10.	79.8519	110.0000	52.6420	87.4938	77.3862	69.0342	91.5919	0.0000
11.	99.5829	110.0000	68.7004	91.5084	79.1704	87.3051	96.1596	26.5731
12.	109.8648	110.0000	77.0685	93.6005	80.1002	96.8261	98.5399	0.0000
13.	103.3888	110.0000	71.7979	92.2828	79.5146	90.8294	97.0407	30.1459
14.	103.0613	110.0000	71.5314	92.2162	79.4850	90.5261	96.9648	58.2153
15.	110.0000	110.0000	79.2959	94.1573	80.3477	99.3604	99.1734	50.6653
16.	110.0000	110.0000	94.7998	98.0333	82.0703	105.0000	103.5834	33.5131
17.	110.0000	110.0000	83.6451	95.2446	80.8309	104.3088	100.4105	62.5600
18.	109.6375	110.0000	76.8836	93.5542	80.0797	96.6157	98.4873	83.7421
19.	88.7333	110.0000	59.8703	89.3009	78.1893	77.2583	93.6479	0.0000
20.	109.8648	110.0000	77.0685	93.6005	80.1002	96.8261	98.5399	0.0000
21.	104.6585	110.0000	72.8313	92.5412	79.6294	92.0051	97.3346	-102.000
22.	110.0000	110.0000	85.9871	95.8301	81.0912	105.0000	101.0767	-203.985
23.	75.0000	94.6866	50.0000	84.7216	76.1541	60.0000	88.4377	0.0000
24.	104.5527	110.0000	72.7452	92.5196	79.6198	91.9071	97.3101	-101.654

Tab.1. Economical distribution of power between thermal blocks and PSP
Čierny Váh.

A Population Learning Algorithm for Solving the Generalized Segregated Storage Problem

Dariusz Barbucha and Piotr Jedrzejowicz

Dept. of Computer Science
Gdynia Maritime Academy
Morska 83, 81-225 Gdynia, Poland
e-mail:{barbucha, pj}@wsm.gdynia.pl

Abstract: The paper presents a new population-based method, called population learning algorithm (PLA) for solving the Generalized Segregated Storage Problem (GSSP). PLA is an extension of population-based methods and adaptive memory programming techniques. It has been inspired by analogies to a social phenomenon rather than to a natural process. The paper introduces the GSSP, describes the concept of PLA and presents the application of PLA for solving GSSP. Computational experiment results are discussed in the final part of the paper.

1 Introduction

Generalized Segregated Storage Problem (GSSP) is a combinatorial optimization problem that involves allocation of certain number of goods (or cargoes) to available compartments subject to segregation (physical separation) constraints. GSSP was introduced in [1,2] and is a generalization of well known Segregated Storage Problem (SSP) considered for example in [4,7].

Generalized Segregated Storage Problem is characterized by: a set of goods (for each element of this set total quantity is known), a set of compartments or transportation means (capacities of compartments are known) and a unit costs of storing cargoes in compartments. Constraints are related to payloads or capacities of compartments, vehicles, etc., proper segregation of goods (some of them are allowed to be stowed together other are not) and geometry and structure of compartments. A goal is to find consignment and its allocation which satisfies segregation requirements and generates minimum cost.

Solving the Generalized Segregated Storage Problem is of practical importance, especially in maritime transportation of some cargoes including dangerous goods.

GSSP belongs to NP-hard class, so a population learning approximate algorithm solving this problem is proposed and presented in this paper.

2 Problem Formulation

Let m be a number of goods (cargoes), n - a number of available (internal) compartments. Storage demand - a_i $(i = 1...m)$ of each cargo and capacity of each compartment - b_j $(j = 1...n)$ are known. Let c_{ij} be a unit cost of storing cargo i in compartment j $(i = 1...m, j = 1...n)$. For a given set of goods a *segregation matrix* S is introduced. Element $s_{ij} \in Z^+$ of S matrix $(i, j = 1...m)$ defines required segregation distance between goods: s_{ij} is equal to 0 if and only if cargo i can be stowed together with j one without any restrictions and element s_{ij} is greater than 0 if some segregation conditions between cargos i, j $(i, j = 1...m)$ are required (for example $s_{ij} = 2$ says that cargoes i and j must be stored in two separated compartments). On the other hand, for a given set of compartments an additional *compartment segregation matrix* CS is defined. Element $cs_{ij} \in Z^+$ of CS matrix $(i, j = 1...n)$ says what kind of segregation is satisfied by a bulkhead between compartments i, j $(i, j = 1...n)$. It is also assumed that all demand for storage will be met. To meet this condition, it is assumed that external (virtual) storage space (denoted by $(n+1)^{st}$ compartment) is also available. It can accommodate any cargo at a higher unit cost $c_{i,n+1}$ $(i = 1...m)$. In this compartment segregation requirements do not have to be satisfied. Let x_{ij} be amount of cargo i stored in compartment j $(i = 1...m, j = 1...n+1)$.

GSSP can be formulated as follows:

$$Z = min \sum_{i=1}^{m} \sum_{j=1}^{n+1} c_{ij} x_{ij} . \tag{1}$$

subject to

$$\sum_{j=1}^{n+1} x_{ij} = a_i \quad for \ all \ i = 1...m . \tag{2}$$

$$\sum_{i=1}^{m} x_{ij} \le b_j \quad for \ all \ j = 1...n+1 . \tag{3}$$

$$\sum_{i=1}^{m} \sum_{j=1}^{m} x_{ik} x_{jl} h_{ijkl} = 0 \quad for \ all \ k,l = 1...n . \tag{4}$$

$$x_{ij} \ge 0 \quad for \ all \ i = 1...m, j = 1...n+1 . \tag{5}$$

where

$$h_{ijkl} = \begin{cases} 0 & if & s_{ij} \le cs_{kl} \\ 1 & if & s_{ij} > cs_{kl} . \end{cases} \tag{6}$$

Elements h_{ijkl} constitues a matrix H, which is a binary matrix (its elements are equal to 0 or 1). Each element of H is defined for two pairs of elements of (cargo, compartment) type - (i, k) and (j, l), where $i, j = 1 \dots m$, $k, l = 1 \dots n$.

Constraints (2) guarantee that availability of goods is not violated. Constraints (3) guarantee that compartment capacities are not exceeded. Constraints (4) ensure that goods are properly stored in compartments taking into account segregation requirements related to a set of goods and a set of compartments (see (6)).

3 Population Learning Algorithm

Population learning algorithm (PLA), originally introduced under the name social learning algorithm in [5,6], is an extension of population-based methods and adaptive programming techniques. It has been inspired by analogies to a social phenomenon rather than to a natural process. Whereas evolutionary algorithms emulate basic features of natural evolution, population learning algorithms could be designed to take advantage of features that are common to social education systems.

PLA, as all other population-based methods, handles population of individuals. An individual could be a solution of the considered problem or any other object that can be somehow transformed into solution. Initially, a massive population of individuals is generated. Generating the initial population could be, simply, based on some random mechanism. Once the initial population has been generated its individuals enter the first learning stage. It involves applying some, possibly basic and elementary, improvement schemes or conducting learning sessions. The improved individuals are then evaluated and better ones pass to the subsequent stage. A strategy of selecting better or more promising individuals must be defined and applied. At the following stages the whole cycle is repeated. Individuals are subject to improvement and learning, either individually or through information exchange, and the selected ones are again promoted to the higher stage and the remaining are dropped from the process. At the final stage the "best and the brightest" are evaluated in order to select a solution to the problem at hand. Basic idea of a population learning algorithm is shown in pseudo-code as Algorithm 1.

```
Algorithm 1. PLA (Population Learning Algorithm)
Begin
   Choose the number of stages - ST
   For each stage i=1...ST
      set the selection criterion SC(i)
   For each stage i=1...ST
      design the learning-improvement procedure L(i)
   Generate the initial population of individuals - P
   For each stage i=1...ST
   Begin
      For each individual in P
         apply the learning-improvement procedure L(i)
      Remove from P all individuals
         who do not pass the selection criterion SC(i)
   End
End
```

Therefore, any population learning algorithm applied to a particular problem must include such elements as definition of individuals, procedure for generating the initial population of individuals, size of the initial population, number of learning stages, learning/improvement procedures for each stage and promotion strategy.

4 Elements of PLA for GSSP

It was shown that PLA could be useful to solve some difficult scheduling problems [6]. In this paper the possibility of using PLA to GSSP is explored.

Let $I = \{1, 2, \ldots, m\}$ be a set of cargos and $J = \{1, 2, \ldots, n\}$ - a set of internal compartments. Let g be a function $g : \{1, \ldots, mn\} \to I \times J$ defined as follows:

$$g(v) = (\lfloor (v-1)/n \rfloor + 1, (v-1) \bmod n + 1) \qquad (7)$$

An ordered pair (p, q) is called *allocation (distribution)* of some units of cargo p to compartment q.

PLA for GSSP is based on the following assumptions:

- **Number of stages** - ST is equal to 3.
- **Individuals** are represented by a permutation of numbers from the $\{1, \ldots, mn\}$ set where each number can be transformed to an allocation of some cargo to a compartment using (7).
- Each solution represented by an individual is directly evaluated in terms of its **fitness** by decoding procedure $(decode(k))$. This procedure takes successive elements of individual and determines an allocation using (7). The fitness of the individual (f) reflects cost of allocating all cargoes to available compartments $(f(k) = \sum_{i=1}^{m} \sum_{j=1}^{n+1} c_{ij} x_{ij}^k$ and $x_{ij}^k = decode(k))$.
- **Initial population** is created randomly with an assumption, that individuals have suitable form, i.e. permutation.
- **Learning-improvement procedure for stage 1** - $L(1)$:
  1. For each individual $j \in P$ two strings are created: Z_j - string which contains elements related to allocations (p, q) used during the loading process $(x_{pq}^k > 0)$ and N_j - string which contains elements related to allocations (p, q) not used during the mentioned process $(x_{pq}^k = 0)$.
  2. New individual is created from an old one in such way that element related to "the most expensive allocation" (i.e. allocation (p, q) for which expression $x_{pq}^k(c_{p,n+1} - c_{pq})$ has the greatest value) is exchanged with element randomly chosen from N_j string.
  3. If the created individual is better, it is accepted, otherwise the individual is recovered.
- **Learning-improvement procedure for stage 2** - $L(2)$:
  1. For each individual $j \in P$ let t_j be a randomly choosen position from string representing j $(t_j \in \{1, \ldots, mn\})$
  2. New individual is created from an old one in such way that elements of string representing an individual is cyclically shifted to the left by t_j number of positions.

    3. If the created individual is better, it is accepted, otherwise the individual is recovered.
- **Learning-improvement procedure for stage 3 - $L(3)$:**
  1. For each individual $j \in P$ two strings are created in the same way as in $L(1)$.
  2. New individual is created from an old one by randomly changing position of each element of the Z_j string.
  3. If the created individual is better, it is accepted, otherwise the individual is recovered.
- **Selection criterion - $SC(i)$,** $i = 1, 2, 3$ for each intermediate stage requires that individuals with fitness below an average are rejected. At the final stage, selection criterion requires that the best individual only (the one with the smallest cost) is selected.

5 Computational Experiments

A number of computational experiments have been carried out to compare solutions generated by proposed algorithm to optimal solution and solution obtained by other algorithms (greedy heuristic, evolutionary programs) [2,3]. Presented algorithms have been implemented in C++ language and have been run on SUN Enterprise 4000. Optimal solutions have been obtained by a CPLEX solver.

For the purpose of testing, two data sets have been randomly generated. They was based on data used by Neebe [7]. A number of goods and a number of compartments were within the range [5, 20]. In data set 1 the internal storage costs c_{ij} were randomly drawn drawn from $U[10, 19]$ (the discrete uniform distribution between 10 and 19, inclusivly), the external storage costs $c_{i,n+1}$ from $U[20, 24]$. In data set 2 the internal storage costs c_{ij} were randomly drawn from $U[100, 199]$, the external storage costs $c_{i,n+1}$ from $U[200, 249]$. Quantities of cargos - a_i and capacities of compartments - b_j were randomly generated from $U[1, 9]$ in both data sets. Elements of segregation matrices S and CS were generated from $U[0, 5]$ and $U[0, 4]$, respectively in both data sets, too. Ten problems of various dimensions have been generated for each data set.

Results of computational experiments are given in Table 1. Three different algorithms have been used to solve GSSP: a dedicated heuristic (H-ABA) [3], an evolutionary program (EP) [2] a population learning algorithm (PLA) described above. In Table 1 mean relative errors from the optimum solution are shown. It is easy to see that PLA produces good solution (its mean relative error is equal to 2-3%) and could be used as a practical tool for solving GSSP.

6 Conclusions

A new population-based algorithm, called population learning algorithm has been used to solve Generalized Segregated Storage Problem. The paper in-

Table 1. Mean relative eroor from the optimum solution (in %) of H-ABA, EP and PLA algorithms for problems of various dimensions (data sets 1 and 2)

m	n+1	Data set 1 H-ABA	EP	PLA	Data set 2 H-ABA	EP	PLA
5	5	3.97	0.02	0.00	3.92	0.17	0.00
5	10	9.25	0.73	0.17	9.25	1.29	0.24
5	15	16.75	1.68	1.80	10.77	1.89	1.60
5	20	14.52	2.63	3.04	10.41	2.95	3.52
10	5	3.38	0.66	0.07	3.90	0.85	0.14
10	10	7.10	2.81	1.72	6.73	2.43	1.41
10	15	10.69	5.18	5.24	9.77	6.42	5.56
10	20	10.55	5.87	5.81	11.18	8.18	7.06
15	5	2.37	0.63	0.21	1.39	0.55	0.14
15	10	5.37	2.74	1.91	5.98	3.93	3.14
15	15	8.18	5.62	4.95	6.71	3.38	3.52
20	5	1.67	0.72	0.31	1.85	0.78	0.29
20	10	4.55	2.48	2.29	5.27	3.33	2.36
Average		7.57	2.44	2.12	6.70	2.78	2.23

troduces the GSSP, describes the concept of PLA and presents application of PLA to GSSP. The results of computational experiments have proved that algorithm described in this paper can produce competitive result comparing to other methods.

References

1. Barbucha, D., Filipowicz, W. (1997): Segregated Storage Problems in Maritime Transportation. In: Papageorgiou, M., Pouliezos, A. (Eds.): Proceedings of the 8th IFAC Symposium in Transportation Systems'97, Chania, Vol. II, 569-573
2. Barbucha, D. (1999): Evolution-based algorithm to solve the Generalized Segregated Storage Problem. In: Adamski, A., Rudnicki, A., Zak, J., (Eds.): Modeling and Management in Transportation, Poznan-Krakow, Vol. 1, 159-164
3. Barbucha, D. (1999): A few effective heuristics to solve the Generalized Segregated Storage Problem. EURO PRIME I Conference, 1st Meeting of Young Europeans on Operational Research, Warsaw
4. Evans, J.R., Tsubakitani, S. (1993): Solving the Segregated Storage Problem with Benders' Partitioning. Journal of the Operational Research Society Vol. 44, No. 2, 175-184
5. Jedrzejowicz, P. (1998): Social Learning Algorithm. Research Report 7/KI/98, Chair of Computer Science, Gdynia Maritime Academy, Gdynia
6. Jedrzejowicz, P. (1999): Social Learning Algorithm as a Tool for Solving Some Difficult Scheduling Problems. Foundation of Computing and Decision Sciences, Vol. 24, No 2, 51-66
7. Neebe, A.W. (1987): An Improved, Multiplier Adjustment Procedure for the Segregated Storage Problem. Journal of the Operational Research Society, Vol. 38, No. 9, 815-825

Using Support Vectors Machine for Classification of Remotely Sensed Images

M. Bundzel, P. Sinčák, N. Kopčo

Computational Intelligence Group, Laboratory of AI, Department of Cybernetics and AI, Faculty of Electrical Engineering and Informatics, TU Košice, Slovakia E-mail: cig@neuron-ai.tuke.sk, http://neuron-ai.tuke.sk/cig

Abstract: The paper deals with a comparison study of support vector machines classification approach and ARTMAP neural classifiers. SVM provides very interesting mathematical methods based on virtual transformation of input space into a multidimensional space. The high degree of nonlinear discrimination hyperplane is aproximated by task tranformation into dichotmial classification with the aim to achieve the best classification results. SVM was used with RBF kernel and experiments were done on benchmark data as well as on real-world datellite images over Slovakia. Comparisons with Fuzzy Artmap and Gaussian Artmap on these data were accomplished. Adaptive kernel function based on neural network is proposed for future reserach in this area.Classification is evaluated using contigency tables for multiclass classification problems. The aim was to develop a classification tool with the highest accuracy on the tested images.

Keywords: Support Vector Machines, VC dimension, RBF kernel function, Fuzzy Artmap, Gaussian Artmap, accuracy assessment, contigency tables

1 Introduction

Support Vectors Machines (SVMs) represent a powerfull tool in the field of pattern recognition and regression. Introduced by Vapnik in 1979 SVMs have received increasing attention only in last few years. For further research it is important to evaluate the power of SVMs with different kernels and compare it to existing methods. In this work, Gaussian ARTMAP was choosen to be a competitor of SVM with RBF kernel. The motivation of the project is to acomplish a comparison study between SVM type of classifiers and ARTMAP family classifiers on test and on real world data.

2 Support Vector Machine as a classifier

2.1 Basic description of a SVM principles

Following description is possible to find in extended version in [1].

Let us have the training data in the form: $\{\vec{x}_i, y_i\}$, $i = 1, ..., l$, $y_i \in \{-1, 1\}$, $\vec{x}_i \in R^d$. Let us assume that there is a hyperplane that separates positive examples from the negative examples (separating hyperplane). The points lying on the hyperplane satisfy $\vec{w} \cdot \vec{x} + b = 0$, where $\vec{w}$ is normal to the hyperplane and $|b|/\|\vec{w}\|$ is a perpendicular distance from the hyperplane to the origin ($\|\vec{w}\|$ is the Euclidean norm of $\vec{w}$). Let d_+ and d_- be the shortest distance from the separating hyperplane to the closest positive (negative) example. Define the "margin" of the separating hyperplane to be $d_+ + d_-$. For, linearly separable case the algorithm looks for the separating hyperplane with the largest margin. This situation is illustrated in the folowing figure.

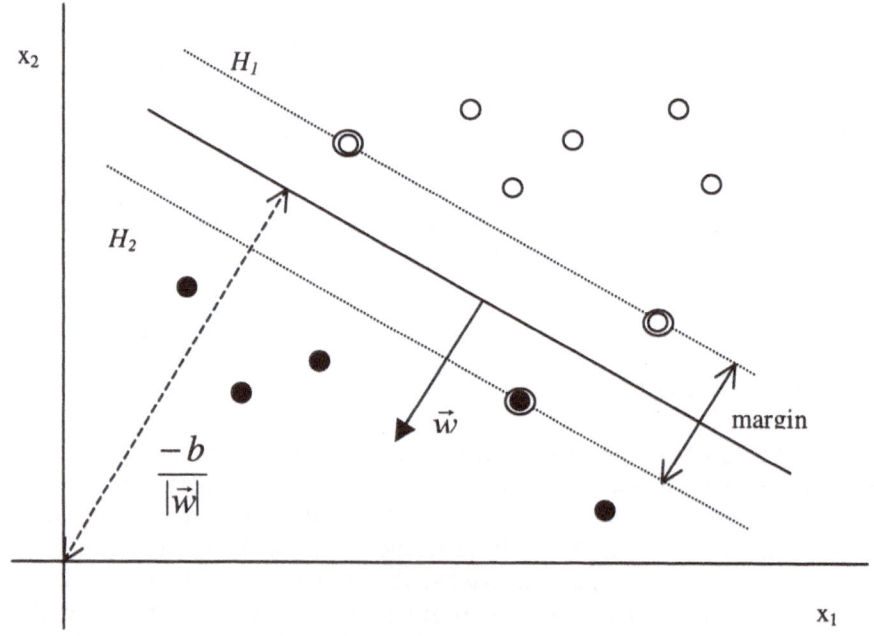

Figure 1 Linear separation with SVM, support vectors are circled.

Constraints for this optimization problem are following:

$$\vec{x}_i \cdot \vec{w} + b \geq +1 \ for \ y_i = 1 \tag{1}$$

and also

$$\vec{x}_i \cdot \vec{w} + b \leq -1 \ for \ y_i = -1 \tag{2}$$

or:

$$y_i \left(\vec{x}_i \cdot \vec{w} + b \right) - 1 \geq 0 \ \forall i \tag{3}$$

If the examples are linearly separable, it is always possible to find $\vec{w}$ and b, such that the inequalities (1) and (2) will hold. Hyperplanes

$H_1 : \vec{x} \cdot \vec{w} + b = 1$

and

$H_2 : \vec{x} \cdot \vec{w} + b = -1$

represents the margin with the width $2/\|\vec{w}\|$. H_1, and H_2 are parallel and no training examples fall between them. Optimal hyperplane will be determined by $\vec{w}$ and b for which is $\|\vec{w}\|^2$ maximal (or $2/\|\vec{w}\|$ minimal) subject to constraints (1) and (2). As can be seen on the **Figure 1** it illustrates the typical two dimensional case of an optimal hyperplane. Points lying on one of the hyperplanes H_1, H_2 are called support vectors. All other points could be removed from the training set and it would not change the solution. The optimization problem is switched to the Lagrangian formulation. Kuhn-Tucker (or Karush-Kuhn-Tucker) theorem for so-called convex optimization is used for this purpose. The most important reason of this reformulation is that the training data will appear only in the form of **dot product**. This is a crucial feature that allows generalizing the procedure to the nonlinear case.

Reformulated problem:

Maximize:

$$L_d \equiv \sum_{i=1}^{l} \alpha_i - \frac{1}{2} \sum_{i,j=1}^{i,j=l} \alpha_i \alpha_j y_i y_j \left(\vec{x}_i \cdot \vec{x}_j \right) \tag{4}$$

subject to:

$$0 \leq \alpha_i \leq C \tag{5}$$

$$\sum_{i=1}^{l} \alpha_i y_i = 0 \tag{6}$$

Where $\alpha_{i,j}$ are so called Lagrangian multiplyers and C is a user set constant determining the required calculation accuracy.

2.1 SVM Kernel functions

The above methods can be generalized to the case, where the decision function is not a linear function of the data. In some cases it might not be possible to separate training data with hyperplane and relaxing constraints because this would lead to a poor classification. Possible solution is to map the data to some other (multidimensional, even infinite dimensional) Euklidian space H, where it is possible to separate the data with a hyperplane. Let assume the mapping Φ:

$$\Phi : R^d \mapsto H \tag{7}$$

where R^d is the space of training data and H is the transformed (Hilbert) space. Please note, that data appears in the training problem only in the form of a dot product, Eqs.(4), (5), (6). Let us introduce a "kernel function" K such that $K(\vec{x}_i, \vec{x}_j) = \Phi(\vec{x}_i) \cdot \Phi(\vec{x}_j)$. Now it is possible to replace usual dot products by K everywhere in the algorithm without knowing what Φ is. One example is:

$$K_{ex}(\vec{x}_i, \vec{x}_j) = e^{-\|\vec{x}_i - \vec{x}_j\|/2\sigma^2} \tag{8}$$

In this particular example, H is infinite dimensional. It would not be possible to work with Φ explicitly. If $\vec{x}_i \cdot \vec{x}_j$ is replaced with $K_{ex}(\vec{x}_i, \vec{x}_j)$ everywhere in the algorithm, SVM lives in an infinite dimensional space. The training time is roughly the same as that by un-mapped data. All the considerations of the previous section hold, since linear separation is still done, but in the different space. Using Φ is also avoided in the test phase.

3 ARTMAP family neural networks

ARTMAP neural networks belong to the class of neural networks called Adaptive Resonance Theory (ART), a theory of cognitive information processing in the human brain. Based on this theory, a whole family of neural network algorithms was developed. These neural networks were shown to give a very good performance in applications involving clustering, classification, and pattern recognition. When compared to statistical and other neural-network-based clustering/classification algorithms, these networks usually obtain very good classification accuracy, while securing proven stability and a high level of compression in the system.. From the point of view of this study, the currently available ARTMAP classification systems can be divided into two groups. First, systems based on (or systems that are a modification of) fuzzy ARTMAP algorithm (e.g., ARTMAP-IC, ART-EMAP, etc). All these systems share the property that they prefer data clusters distributed into hyper-rectangles in feature space. In these systems the basic properties of the original ARTMAP design (stability, proven convergence, fast on-line learning) are preserved, but they also have well-known disadvantages, e.g., noise sensitivity and tendency to category proliferation. The other group is based on the Gaussian ARTMAP neural network. In this group of networks, preferably identifying Gaussian-shaped clusters, the stability and fast on-line learning properties of the fuzzy ARTMAP networks are traded for an emphasis on the ability of the system to generalize and for its decreased sensitivity to noise in the input data. Structurally, every ARTMAP network (fuzzy ARTMAP or Gaussian ARTMAP) can be divided into two parts. The first part, represented by an ART module, dynamically generates units, each identifying a single data cluster in feature space. This part can be used autonomously for cluster analysis of a given data set. The second part serves to identify each of the clusters found in the data with one of the classes defined on the data set. A detailed description of fuzzy ARTMAP (FA), first of the algorithms analyzed in this study, can be found in many previously published studies. From the point of view of this study, the most important property of this system is that the subsystem identifying clusters in feature space preferably identifies the clusters in which patterns are distributed as hyper-rectangles as illustrated in the following figure.

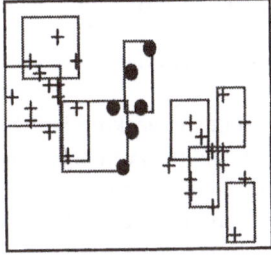

Figure 2 Distribution of discrimination rectangles defined by fuzzy ARTMAP in the feature space.

4 Experimental results

Experiments were done on benchmark and real-world data. Thorsten Joachims implementation of SVM was used ([2]). Simple extension to the algorithm was done in order to achieve multiclass classification. In all cases Radial Basis Function (RBF) kernel was used Classification accuracy was assessed by a contingency table approach. There were 2-benchmark datasets prepared for classification purposes. "Circle in the square" and "double spiral" were used for dichotomous classification purposes. The results of both Fuzzy ARTMAP and the SVM approach are presented in Table 1and Table 2

"Circle in the square"			"Double spiral"		
Predicted	Actual Class		Predicted	Actual Class	
Class	A	B	Class	A	B
A'	99.54%	0.68%	A'	93.25%	57.24%
B'	0.46%	99.32%	B'	6.75%	42.76%

Table 1 SVM results on benchmark datasets

"Circle in the square"			"Double spiral"		
Predicted	Actual Class		Predicted	Actual Class	
Class	A	B	Class	A	B
A'	98.34%	2.80%	A'	87.59%	9.26%
B'	1.66%	97.20%	B'	12.41%	90.74%

Table 2 Fuzzy ARTMAP results on benchmark datasets

As shown in Table 1, otherwise properly working SVM failed to classify class B of "double spiral" dataset. Reason of this phenomenon remained unclear - increasing error intolerance constant lead to an unaffordable long training time and manipulation with RBF coefficient didn't help eithter.

4.1 Experiments on real-world data

Experiments were done on benchmark and also real-world data. Basicly the behaviors of the methods were observed on multispectral image data with the aim to obtain the best classification accuracy on the test data subset. The Košice data consists of a training set of 3164 points in the feature space and of a test set of 3167 points of the feature space. A point in the feature space has 7 real-valued coordinates of the feature space normalized into the interval (0,1) and 7 binary output values. The class of a fact is determined by the output which has a value of one; the other six output values are zero. The data represents 7 attributes of the color spectrum sensed from Landsat satellite. The representation set was determined by a geographer and was supported by ground verification procedure. The main goal was landuse identification using the most precise classification procedure for achieving accurate results. The image was taken over the eastern Slovakia region particularly from the City of Kosice region. There were seven classes of interest picked up for classification procedure as it can be seen in Figure 3. Results of classification procedures are depicted in the form of contingence table 4 SVM with RBF kernel function was used.

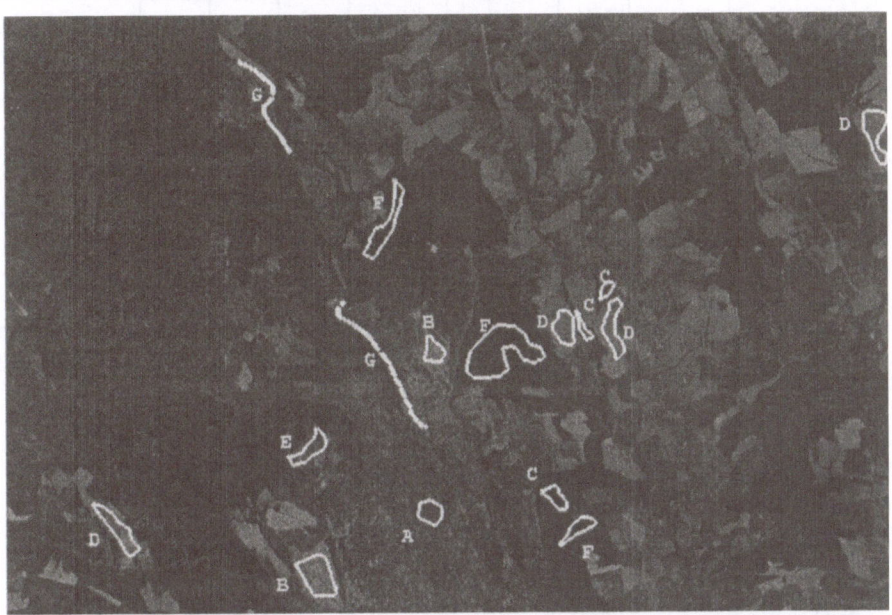

Figure 3 Original image. Highlighted areas were classified by expert (A – urban area, B – barren fields, C – bushes, D – agricultural fields, E – meadows, F – forests, G – water)

Predicted	Actual Class						
Class	A	B	C	D	E	F	G
A'	93.51	0.84	0.00	0.00	3.32	0.00	1.34
B'	0.61	88.30	0.00	3.56	12.76	0.00	1.34
C'	0.00	0.00	100.00	0.00	2.27	0.00	0.00
D'	0.00	8.45	0.00	96.33	0.52	0.00	0.00
E'	3.25	2.47	0.00	0.11	79.55	0.16	5.80
F'	0.00	0.00	0.00	0.00	0.00	98.97	2.68
G'	2.64	0.00	0.00	0.00	1.57	0.87	88.84

Predicted	Actual Class						
Class	A	B	C	D	E	F	G
A'	**96.15**	0.00	0.00	0.00	2.76	0.00	1.41
B'	0.00	**87.68**	0.00	3.01	6.08	0.00	0.00
C'	0.00	1.64	**100.0**	0.11	1.10	0.00	0.00
D'	0.00	7.60	0.00	**96.88**	0.00	0.09	1.41
E'	0.64	2.05	0.00	0.00	**83.98**	0.34	8.45
F'	3.21	1.03	0.00	0.00	6.08	**99.49**	1.41
G'	0.00	0.00	0.00	0.00	0.00	0.09	**87.32**

Tables 3 and 4 : Confusion matrix for fuzzy Artmap neural network with voting from 5 networks. The overall weighted PCC is 93.95 %. ;Confusion matrix for SVM. The overall weighted PCC is 95.64 %.

A B C D E F G

Figure 4 SVM classified image of the City of Kosice area. Shadows are sometimes classified as urban area which decreases classification accuracy significantly.

5 Conclusion

The paper delas with comparison study of Support Vector machine classifier with RBF kernel and fuzzy ARTMAP aproach. Both of the tested classifiers showed very good classification and generalization abilities. Experimental results indicate that certain datasets could cause problems to SVMs with RBF kernel function.

6 References

[1] Burges, CH.,1999 ,*Tutorial on Support Vector Machines for Pattern Recognition.*,http://svm.research.bell-labs.com/SVMdoc.html

[2] T. Joachims, Making large-Scale SVM Learning Practical. Advances in Kernel Methods - Support Vector Learning, B. Schölkopf and C. Burges and A. Smola (ed.), MIT-Press, 1999.

[3] Anthony M., Bartlett P. L. Neural Network Learning: Theoretical Foundations, ISBN 0 521 57353, Cambridge University Press 1999

[4]. G. A. Carpenter, M. N. Gjaja, S. Gopal, and C. E. Woodcock. Art neural networks for remote sensing: Vegetation classification from landsat tm and terrain data. IEEE Transactions on Geoscience and Remote Sensing, 35(2):308-325, 1999.

[5]. G.A. Carpenter and S. Grossberg. A massively parallel architecture for a selforganizing neural pattern recognition machine. Computer Vision, Graphics, and Image Processing, 37:54-115, 1987.

[6]. G.A. Carpenter, S. Grossberg, N. Markuzon, J.H. Reynolds, and D.B. Rosen. Fuzzy ARTMAP: A neural network architecture for incremental supervised learning of analog multidimensional maps. IEEE Transactions on Neural Networks, 3(5):698- 713, 1992.

[7] N. Kopčo, P. Sinčák, and H. Veregin, "Extended Methods for Classification of Remotely Sensed Images Based on ARTMAP Neural Networks," in *Computational Intelligence – Theory and Applications (Lecture Notes in Computer Science 1625), Proceedings of International Conference "The 6-th Fuzzy days,"* Dortmund, Germany, May 1999, pp. 206-219.

[8] P. Sinčák, H. Veregin, and N. Kopčo, "Conflation techniques in multispectral image processing," *Geocarto Int,* March, pp. 11-19. 2000.

[9] G.A. Carpenter, B.L. Milenova, and B.W. Noeske, "Distributed ARTMAP: a neural network for fast distributed supervised learning," *Neural Networks,* vol. 11, no. 5, Jul. 1998, pp. 793-813.

[10] J.R. Williamson, "Gaussian ARTMAP: A neural network for fast incremental learning of noisy multidimensional maps," *Neural Networks,* vol. 9, 1996, pp. 881-897.

Part 6

Posters

Application of Neural Network for Stress Classification

Milan Šorf, Vladimír Eck, Ladislava Janku, Lenka Lhotska

Czech Technical University in Prague, Faculty of Electrical Engineering, Department of Cybernetics, Technická 2, 16627 Praha 6, Tel. No.: +420 2 24357325, e-mail:sorf@lab.felk.cvut.cz

In this paper we describe application of neural network for stress classification [1] of a tested person whose physiological parameters [4] are measured. We have used hypothetical data at first. For neural network (NN) training we have used two training sets one for supervised learning and one for unsupervised learning. For supervised learning, the inputs of NN are three physiological parameters, namely diastolic blood pressure, heart frequency and skin resistance [2]. The output of NN is degree of stress that can have one of three values (no stress, medium stress, high stress) (see Table 1). Training set for unsupervised learning contains much more parameters so that the resulting network covers the whole input space. Input data form clusters around values for which the degree of stress is the same. Then of course there are cases lying between individual degrees of stress.

Table 1. Training set

Parameter	Degree of stress					
	0-no	0-no	0,5-medium	0,5-medium	1-high	1-high
Diastolic blood pressure (mm/Hg)	70	80	90	95	100	110
Heart frequency (tep/min)	60	80	90	100	110	120
Skin resistance (%, max.=30kΩ)	10	20	30	40	50	60

We have used two classifiers, namely Kohonen self-organising network and Learning Vector Quantization (LVQ) [3]. Kohonen network is a network that does not need a supervisor for learning process. It is based on cluster analysis algorithm and has two layers only. Number of inputs is equal to dimension of input space, in our case it is equal to three. Neurons do not have their own tunable "threshold" or bias. The neurons perform single operation in the network, namely calculation of distance between presented example and a pattern encoded in weights of the given neuron according to the formula

$$d = \sum_{i=0}^{N-1}\left[x_i(t)-w_i(t)\right]^2 \tag{1}$$

where $x_i(t)$ - individual elements of the presented example,
  $w_i(t)$ - corresponding weights of the neuron representing encoded pattern,
  d - neuron output.

Each neuron in output layer represents direct output. Learning process is performed in the following way. The algorithm tries to organise neurons in the grid into certain areas so that they are able to classify presented input data. In our case, the input space is a "3D noodle" (see Figure 1). The learning process is autonomous and runs iteratively. Output layer neurons have occupied locations around clusters of input space according to cluster analysis algorithm. They form network outputs. It is obvious from figure 1 that we can distinguish five degrees of stress in this case.

LVQ (Learning Vector Quantization) is a modified Kohonen network. The modification enables to use supervised learning. Since the network knows classification into individual classes for training examples, it can classify correctly cases with unknown classes. LVQ method is based on following algorithm: At first classical Kohonen network is used for training examples without information about correct assignment to classes. In this way vectors of probable future location are roughly set. In the next step the vectors are assigned classes they represent. After that training examples, including information about class assignment, are used for more precise training. Then the distance between each vector and training examples of each class is calculated. Then the vector is labeled with that class that has occurred most frequently with the closest position. Finally we have to find the best division between classes. In figure 2 trained LVQ network is shown. Output of this network is discrete (1 = no stress, 2 = medium degree of stress, 3 = high degree of stress).

Fig.1: Learning state of Kohonen network after 2500 steps

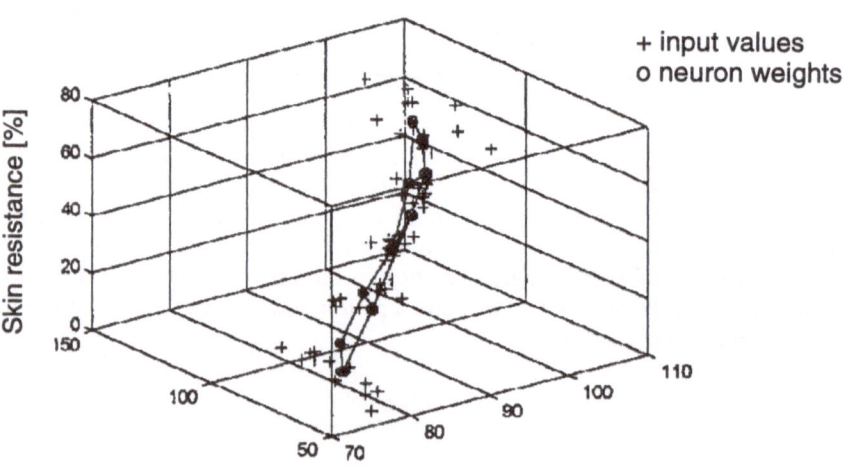

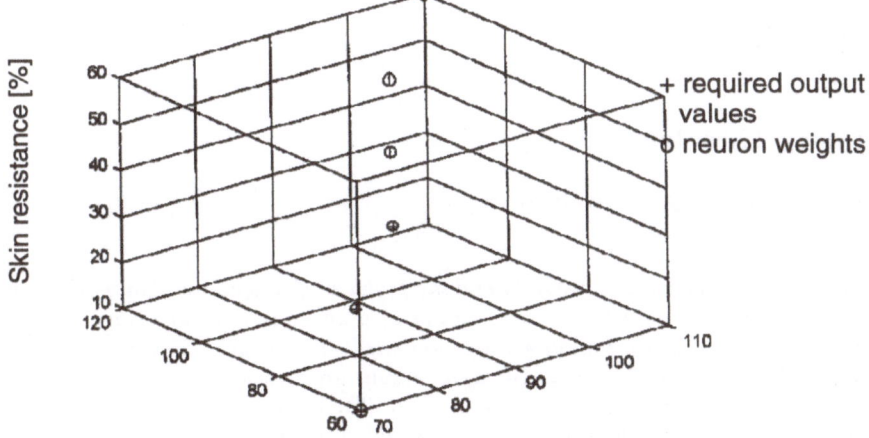

Fig.2: LVQ network state after 1000 steps

Presented two classifiers represent two different ways of training set processing with respect to the output. In case of self-organising network the output is represented by neurons in output layer and their neighbours. In case of LVQ method the output is one of three discrete values.

For comparison of accuracy of both networks a new example has been used as input. The example is represented by input vector $x^T=[92,83,22]$ ([diastolic blood pressure, heart frequency, skin resistance]). The expected degree of stress at the output is medium. In case of Kohonen network the output is given by reaction of neuron for medium degree of stress. In case of LVQ method the output value is 2 which corresponds to medium degree of stress. Results of tests have verified our presumption about application of NN for stress classification. The LVQ method is more advantageous because the learning process is faster (smaller number of steps required - 1/2 in comparison with Kohonen network) and the output is required state only, while at Kohonen network in some cases intermediate states are output as well.

References

[1] Novák, D., Eck, V.: Stress Classifiers Using Neural Networks [Research Report]. CTU FEE K333, Prague, 1999 (in Czech)

[2] Schreiber, V. et al.: Stress. Avincenum, Praha, 1985 (in Czech)

[3] Šnorek M., Jiřina M.: Neural Networks and Neurocomputers. CTU, Prague, 1996 (in Czech)

[4] Eck, V., Fejtová, M., Hlávková, J., Janků, L., Lhotská, L., Nejedlý, B., Šorf, M., Zavadil, P.:Intelligent Interface for Biomedical Systems. EUFIT 99, Aachen, 1999, s. 246-247 (in Czech)

Solvability and Stability of Fuzzy Relation Equations

Martin Gavalec

Technical University, Košice, Slovakia

Abstract: The problem of solvability and the problem of unique solvability of a fuzzy relation equation in an arbitrary max-min algebra are considered and corresponding necessary and sufficient conditions are presented. The results allow to solve both problems by an $O(n^3)$ algorithm. Analogous results are presented for the stability and periodicity problem of a fuzzy relation equation. The matrix period of a given square matrix is characterized by periods of non-trivial strongly connected components of associated threshold digraphs. The result enables to compute the matrix period in $O(n^3)$ time.

Fuzzy relation equations play important role in fuzzy control systems and in other applications, e.g. in discrete dynamic systems or in knowledge engineering [11], [12]. The question of solvability of a given fuzzy relation equation is closely connected with the solvability of a linear system of equations in fuzzy algebra. For max-min fuzzy algebra, the solvability and unique solvability of linear systems was studied in [1], [2], [3], [5], [6], [7], [8], [9], [10], where a number of interesting results are presented for special cases of max-min algebras, such as discrete, dense, bounded, or unbounded algebras. These results are generalized in [17], [18] for a general max-min algebra. The stability and periodicity questions on matrices in a max-min fuzzy algebra were investigated in [4], [13], [14], [15], [16], [19], [20] and [21].

1 Solvability and unique solvability

By a max-min fuzzy algebra $\mathcal{B}$ we mean any linearly ordered set with the binary operations of maximum and minimum, denoted as $\oplus$ and $\otimes$. For any natural $n > 0$, $\mathcal{B}(n)$ denotes the set of all n-dimensional column vectors over $\mathcal{B}$, and $\mathcal{B}(m,n)$ denotes the set of all matrices of type $m \times n$ over $\mathcal{B}$. The matrix operations over $\mathcal{B}$ are defined with respect to $\oplus, \otimes$, formally in the same manner as the matrix operations over any field. Matrices over $\mathcal{B}$ can be considered as finite fuzzy relations. We shall study the fuzzy relation equation of the form

$$A \otimes X = B$$

where $A \in \mathcal{B}(m,n)$, $B \in \mathcal{B}(m,p)$ are given fuzzy relations and the relation $X \in \mathcal{B}(n,p)$ is unknown.

If B is not bounded, then we extend B to $B^\star$ by adding the least element O, or the greatest element I, (or both, if necessary) to B. If B is bounded, then $B^\star = B$. To avoid the trivial case, we assume $O < I$. In notation $M = \{1, 2, \ldots, m\}$, $N = \{1, 2, \ldots, n\}$, $P = \{1, 2, \ldots, p\}$, we define a matrix $\bar{X} \in B^\star(n, p)$ by putting, for every $j \in N$, $k \in P$,

$$M_{jk} := \{i \in M; a_{ij} > b_{ik}\}, \qquad \bar{x}_{jk} := \min_{B^\star}\{b_{ik}; i \in M_{jk}\}$$

The minimum in the above definition is computed in $B^\star$. Therefore, $\bar{x}_{jk}$ is well-defined also in the case, when M_{jk} is an empty set, and then $\bar{x}_{jk} = \min_{B^\star} \emptyset = I \in B^\star$. Thus, the above definition of $\bar{X}$ is correct.

Theorem 1.1 Let $A \in B(m, n)$, $B \in B(m, p)$. The equation $A \otimes X = B$ has a solution $X \in B(n, p)$ if and only if the corresponding matrix $\bar{X} \in B^\star(n, p)$ fulfills $A \otimes \bar{X} = B$. If, moreover, $\bar{X} \in B(n, p)$, then $\bar{X}$ is the maximum solution, otherwise, there is no maximum solution in $B(n, p)$.

The theorem on unique solvability requires further notation. For every $j \in N$, $k \in P$, we define

$$I_{jk} := \{i \in M; a_{ij} \geq b_{ik} = \bar{x}_{jk}\}, \qquad \mathcal{I}_k := \{I_{jk}; j \in N\}$$

$$K_{jk} := \{i \in M; a_{ij} = b_{ik} < \bar{x}_{jk}\}, \qquad \mathcal{K}_k := \{K_{jk}; j \in N\}$$

Theorem 1.2 Let $A \in B(m, n)$, $B \in B(m, p)$. The equation $A \otimes X = B$ has a unique solution $X \in B(n, p)$ if and only if, for every $k \in P$, the system $\mathcal{I}_k$ is a minimal covering of the set $M - \bigcup \mathcal{K}_k$.

As a consequence of the previous two theorems we get an upper estimation for the computational complexity of the problems of solvability and unique solvability of fuzzy relation equation.

Theorem 1.3 Let $A \in B(m, n)$, $B \in B(m, p)$. Both questions, whether the equation $A \otimes X = B$ is solvable, or uniquely solvable, respectively, can be answered in $O(mnp)$ time.

Further related questions are studied in [17], where also the proofs of Theorems 1.1 – 1.3 can be found.

2 Stability and periodicity

In some applications, the powers of fuzzy relations are of great importance. For a given finite relation represented by a square matrix $A \in B(n, n)$, the convergence of the power sequence $(A^r; r = 1, 2, \ldots)$ is studied. We say that the sequence stabilizes, when $A^r = A^{r+1}$ holds true for every large enough r, and we say that the sequence is periodic with a period p, if p is the least positive integer such that $A^r = A^{r+p}$ for every large enough r. Thus, the power sequence of a matrix stabilizes if and only if it is periodic with period equal to 1. Although the period in general case can be exponentially large with respect to the size of A, the question of stability versus periodicity can be decided by computing the period in a polynomial time.

The formulation of the next theorem requires the notion of the threshold digraph (directed graph). If $A \in \mathcal{B}(n,n)$ is a square matrix and $h \in \mathcal{B}$ is a given threshold level, then the threshold digraph $\mathcal{G}(A,h)$ has n vertices denoted by $N = \{1,2,\ldots,n\}$. An ordered pair $(i,j) \in N^2$ is an arc in $\mathcal{G}(A,h)$ whenever $a_{ij} \geq h$. If $\mathcal{K}$ is a non-trivial strongly connected component in $\mathcal{G}(A,h)$, then the greatest common divisor of the lengths of all cycles in $\mathcal{K}$ is called the period of $\mathcal{K}$.

Theorem 2.1 *Let $A \in \mathcal{B}(n,n)$. The period of the power sequence of the matrix A is the least common multiple of the periods of all non-trivial strongly connected components in the threshold digraphs $\mathcal{G}(A,h)$ for all threshold levels $h \in \mathcal{B}$.*

The proof of Theorem 2.1 and an efficient algorithm for computing the matrix period are presented in [14].

Theorem 2.2 *Let $A \in \mathcal{B}(n,n)$. There is an algorithm for computing the period of the power sequence of A in $O(n^3)$ time.*

Further related questions, such as computing the orbit period of the matrix with respect to a given initial state vector, or some related *NP*-completeness results, are considered in [15], [16] and [19].

References

1. P. Butkovič, *Strong regularity of matrices – a survey of results*, Discrete Appl. Math. **48** (1994), 45-68.
2. P. Butkovič, K. Cechlárová, P. Szabó, *Strong linear independence in bottleneck algebra*, Lin. Algebra Appl. **94** (1987), 133-155.
3. P. Butkovič, F. Hevery, *A condition for the strong regularity of matrices in the minimax algebra*, Discrete Appl. Math. **11** (1985), 209-222.
4. K. Cechlárová, *On the powers of matrices in bottleneck/fuzzy algebra*, Lin. Algebra Appl. **246** (1996), 97-112.
5. K. Cechlárová, *Strong regularity of matrices in a discrete bottleneck algebra*, Lin. Algebra Appl. **128** (1990), 35-50.
6. K. Cechlárová, *Unique solvability of max-min fuzzy equations and strong regularity of matrices over fuzzy algebra*, Fuzzy Sets and Systems 75 (1995), 165-177.
7. K. Cechlárová, *Fuzzy discrete dynamic systems – efficient algorithms using digraphs*, Tatra Mt. Math. Publ. **6** (1995), 5-11.
8. K. Cechlárová, *On the powers of matrices in bottleneck/fuzzy algebra*, Lin. Algebra Appl. **246** (1996), 97-112.
9. K. Cechlárová, K. Kolesár, *Strong regularity of matrices in a discrete bounded bottleneck algebra*, Lin. Algebra Appl. **256** (1997), 141-152.
10. K. Cechlárová, J. Plávka, *Linear independence in bottleneck algebras*, Fuzzy Sets and Systems 77 (1996), 337-348.

11. R. A. Cuninghame-Green, *Minimax Algebra*, Lecture Notes in Econom. and Math. Systems **166**, Springer-Verlag, Berlin, 1979.

12. A. Di Nola, S. Sessa, W. Pedrycz, E. Sanchez, *Fuzzy Relation Equations and Their Applications to Knowledge Engineering*, Kluwer, Dordrecht, 1989.

13. M. Gavalec, *Periodicity of matrices and orbits in fuzzy algebra*, Tatra Mt. Math. Publ. **6** (1995), 35-46.

14. M. Gavalec, *Computing matrix period in max-min algebra*, Discr. Appl. Mathem. **75** (1997), 63-70

15. M. Gavalec, *Periods of special fuzzy matrices*, Tatra Mt. Mathem. Publ. **16** (1999), 47–60.

16. M. Gavalec, *Computing orbit period in max-min algebra*, Discrete Appl. Math. **100** (2000), 49–65.

17. M. Gavalec, *Solvability and unique solvability of max-min fuzzy equations*, Fuzzy Sets and Systems (submitted).

18. M. Gavalec, J. Plávka, *Strong regularity of matrices in general max-min algebra*, Lin. Algebra Appl. (submitted).

19. M. Gavalec, G. Rote, *Reachability of fuzzy matrix period*, Tatra Mt. Mathem. Publ. **16** (1999), 61–79.

20. Li Jian-Xin, *Periodicity of powers of fuzzy matrices (finite fuzzy relations)*, Fuzzy Sets and Systems **48** (1992), 365-369.

21. M. G. Thomason, *Convergence of powers of a fuzzy matrix*, J. Math. Anal. Appl. **57** (1977), 476-480.

Hybrid Evolutionary – Tabu Search Algorithm for Scheduling Multiple-Variant Tasks

Piotr Jedrzejowicz, Ewa Ratajczak, Henryk Szreder

Chair of Computer Science, Gdynia Maritime Academy
ul. Morska 83, 81-225 Gdynia, Poland, fax: +4858 620 6701
{pj, ewra, hsz}@wsm.gdynia.pl

1 Introduction

There exist numerous situations where performing repeatedly a task or executing a number of its multiple redundant variants, increases chances for a successful task completion. The paper investigates the problem $P|r_j, m\text{-}v|R$ (see [1] for details), of scheduling multiple-variant (m-v) tasks with a view to maximizing schedule reliability. Variants of each task are independent and can be run in parallel or in sequence.

One of the potential application areas for m-v task scheduling algorithms is the fault-tolerant computing. To make simplex software units fault-tolerant, the corresponding solution is to add one, two or more program variants. It should be noted that the concept of the m-v task could be used to model variety of the fault-tolerant structures, since all require processing of redundant variants (see [1][2]).

2 Problem formulation

The problem $P|r_j, m\text{-}v|R$ of scheduling a set N of n m-v tasks under hard time constraints is considered. The following information for each task is available: ready time - a_j, $j = 1,...,n$; deadline - d_j, $j = 1,...,n$; number of available variants – NV_j, $j = 1,...,n$; variant processing times - p_{ji}, $j = 1,...,n$, $i = 1,..., NV_j$; variant reliabilities - r_{ji}, $j = 1,...,n$, $i = 1,..., NV_j$.

The problem is characterized by a set of multiple, identical processors P, and a set of m-v tasks N. For each task there is the available number of variants NV_j. Tasks are independent and non-preemptable, with ready times, deadlines and processing times differing per task. Variant reliabilities are statistically independent and known. Optimization criterion is schedule reliability calculated as $R = \Pi R_{ji}$, where R_{ji} is reliability of task j for which i variant is scheduled. Decision variables include

3 Hybrid evolutionary – tabu search algorithm (ETA)

The proposed hybrid algorithm (ETA) is based on two earlier algorithms developed for $P|r_j,m\text{-}v|R$ problem: evolutionary algorithm (EA) and tabu search algorithm (TSA) [3][4]. Many different hybrid combinations of these algorithms plus additionally implemented local search techniques have been investigated. The following three approaches turned out to be the most promising ones.

The first algorithm (ETA1) is using a quick local search technique within an evolutionary algorithm as a kind of mutation operator and at the final stage the exhaustive local search is applied. The ETA1 is not relaying on tabu search at all, but proves to be the most efficient among the presented algorithms with respect to computation time. The second algorithm (ETA2) is using the same quick local search as a kind of mutation operator and next short tabu search algorithm and the exhaustive local search at the final stage. The third algorithm (ETA3) relays on using short tabu search algorithm as a kind of mutation operator and the exhaustive local search in the final stage. In Table 1 computational experiment results for all of the described algorithms are presented.

Table 1. Mean relative percentage errors from the best solution known for $P|r_j,m\text{-}v|R$.

EA	TSA	ETA 1	ETA 2	ETA 3
20.89	8.07	9.80	3.87	3.53

It can be observed that the proposed approach is efficient and at a cost of additional resources (mainly time) provides good results. The next important point of the research is reducing computational time of the ETA2 and ETA3 algorithms.

References

1. Jędrzejowicz P., I.Czarnowski, H.Szreder, A.Skakowski: Evolution-based scheduling of fault-tolerant programs on multiple processors: Jose Rolim et al. (red.), Parallel and Distributed Processing, Lecture Notes in Computer Science nr 1586, Springer 1999, p.210-219.

2. Jędrzejowicz P.: Social learning algorithm as a tool for solving some difficult scheduling problems: Foundation of Computing and Decision Sciences, vol.24, nr 2, 1999, p.51-66.

3. Czarnowski I., P.Jędrzejowicz, E.Ratajczak, H.Szreder: Nowe algorytmy szeregowania zadań w wielu wersjach, Materiały II Krajowej Konferencji "Metody i systemy komputerowe w badaniach naukowych i projektowaniu inżynierskim", kraków, 1999, p.567-572.

4. Jędrzejowicz P., E. Ratajczak: Zastosowanie metody przeszukiwania Tabu do szeregowania programów tolerujących błędy, Materiały Krajowej Konferencji Bezpieczeństwo i Niezawodność, KONBiN'99, ITWL, Warszawa, 1999, p.89-96.

Self-Adaptation in Evolutionary Design of Neural Networks

Bohdan Macukow and Maciej Grzenda

Warsaw University of Technology, Pl.Politechniki 1, 00-661 Warsaw, Poland

Abstract: Evolutionary computation as an alternative to the traditional methods of multilayer neural networks design has been widely applied. The results of many simulations show that evolutionary algorithm can outperform standard training strategies, including back-propagation and its modifications.

The algorithm, described in this paper, summarises the results of our work both in the field of recurrent and feedforward networks. Its main feature is the self-adaptation procedure applied to make the search for the network weights and architecture both effective and precise.

1 Introduction

Evolutionary programming as a method of constructing neural networks has been widely used in recent few years. Not only does it allow for simultaneous architecture design and weight adjustment, but it enables much broader range of optimisation criterions as well.

Whenever evolutionary programming is applied to adjust the weights of the neural connections, the problem of weight encoding arises. The main drawback of the binary genotype is the limited precision of it. The latter suggests the use of real-valued genotype so as to assure adequate accuracy of weights.

However, the results of multiple simulations comprising on our work have shown that the convergence of the algorithm can be significantly improved by limiting the number of weights used in the genotypes during the first generations of the algorithm. Thus, the primary purpose of our work was to exploit the advantages of different genotype forms and mutation operators by means of the modified self-adaptive procedure. Thanks to this procedure, both the overall quality of the networks evolved and the algorithm convergence have been improved comparing to the standard methods based on evolutionary programming.

Finally, the role of self-adaptation should be emphasised. To make it possible for the computational intelligence and neural systems to work as a part of intelligent software packages, it is necessary to resign from all the settings that are both problem-dependant and require expert knowledge.

2 Algorithm and its applications

The algorithm presented in this section is based on evolutionary programming. The population of neural networks is evolved so as to increase their correct response rate. Both the number of hidden neurones and the weights are affected by the evolution.

The results of multiple simulations, comprising on our previous work in the field, show the trade-off between fast convergence characteristic for binary genotype and high quality of the networks built on real-valued genotype. The primary objective of the method described was to combine the advantages of both methods in one algorithm.

Assuming the initial population of the algorithm is based on binary genotypes and uniform mutation of weights, the following self-adaptive procedure has been applied:

- every population member is defined not only by its genotype, but also the learning rule, including
  - the form of the genotype - binary or real-valued
  - the weight mutation rate
  - the standard deviation of the Gaussian distribution (applies for real-valued genotypes only)
- the learning rules are mutated and further selected in accordance with the quality of the offspring created using them

As a consequence of this method, different forms of genotypes and mutation rates can coexist in the population. Moreover, it is the selection that eliminates ineffective learning rules, for instance very low standard deviation in the initial generations of the algorithm.

The main advantage of this form of self-adaptation is that mutation and selection operators are responsible for choosing appropriate problem and generation-related algorithm settings.

3 Results and conclusions

The results of the tests show that the algorithm using self-adaptation outperforms both methods based on binary and real-valued genotypes. The fact, the learning rule can be set by the evolution helps the search process to employ significant changes in the initial generations and narrow down the mutation significance when tuning the networks. In other words the self-adaptation enables automatic selection of the search strategy. The results obtained with cross-validation for a well-known Iris data set vary around 96% of correct classification.

Once again, it is the lack of the parameters that require expert knowledge that is the most important feature of the algorithm. The self-adaptation makes it possible to apply evolutionary artificial neural networks in different types of computer-assisted diagnosis and forecasting.

Genetic Algorithms Efficiency in Neural Network Learning

Radosław Semkło[1] and Zbigniew Światnicki[2]

[1] Air Force Information Centre, 02—800 Warsaw, POLAND,
semklo@ias.wat.waw.pl

[2] Military University of Technology, Kaliskiego 2, 01-489 Warsaw, POLAND,
swiat@wat.waw.pl

Abstract: The problem of neural network learning is presented in this paper. The backpropagation algorithm and the genetic algorithms were used. Tested neural network was used for the object recognition based on radar signals. The run of neural network learned with genetic algorithms has been discussed.

Keywords: Object recognition, neural networks, pattern capability

1 Introduction

Significance of the genetic algorithms follows from using them (with great achievements) to resolve problems where progress has been stopped. Because of these reasons, we have taken the trials of using genetic algorithms to learn neural network. We have decided to check, which operation is more effective.

2 Experiments

To test an efficiency of the genetic algorithms we have decided to check the percent degree's influence on speed of the neural network's learning process. These operations have been used during the learning of multilayer feedforward network. This neural network has had a fixed structure and has been used for object recognition. The percent of correct network answers and global network error have been taken as the learning efficiency criteria. We have tested neural network using mutation and crossing separately and then both of these operations concurrently. We have used: crossing, mutation, crossing and mutation.

During the tests we have observed that, the rising degree of the crossing makes the efficiency of learning neural network rise. Based on conducted tests we have concluded that the range <10% - 45%) makes the neural network's learning process most effective. After these tests we have concluded that neural network learnt with using operation of the crossing needs less outlay of the computing but the efficiency is not very high.

Rising of the percent degree of the mutated neurons has caused the efficiency of learning neural network to rise. After tests we have concluded that using operation of the mutation to learn neural network needs more outlay of the computing but the efficiency is very high. After conducted tests we have concluded that the range <5% - 50%) makes the neural network's learning process most effective.

We have increased the percent degree of the neurons, which has been modified from 0% to 50% mutation and 0% to 50% crossing. The increasing has been conducted concurrently. The rising of the percent degree of the mutated and crossing neurons has caused the efficiency of learning neural network to rise. After tests we have concluded that the range <10/10% - 30/30%) makes the neural network's learning process most effective. Based on results of our researches we have concluded that this is the best solution (for us) to speed up the neural network's learning process.

3   Conclusions

We have presented that operations of the genetic algorithms are useful for speeding up the neural network's learning process. We have proved that genetic algorithms are useful, however it is not obvious if all kinds of genetic algorithms are useful on the same level. The alternative solution is using both the mutation and the crossing with the neural network. It is not absolutely sure that in other kinds of neural network and their using, our results will have applications. In connection with it, it's necessary to check an influence of the neural networks' and genetic operations' kinds on an efficiency of neural network's work.

References

[1] Semkło R. (1996) Using neural networks to analyze radar signals. Military Academy of Technology Pub, Warsaw

[2] Świątnicki Z., Semkło R. (1996) The Radar Signal Processing Using Neural Networks, Proceedings of Conference "New Trends in Signal Processing" Liptovsky Mikulas

[3] Świątnicki Z., Semkło R. (1998) Computational Intelligence and Applications. Springer-Verlag, Berlin

Using Genetic Algorithm for Fuzzy Filter Optimisation

Csaba Stupák[1], Stanislav Marchevský[1]

[1] Department of Electronics and Multimedial Communications, FEI TU of Košice, Park Komenského 13, 040 21 Košice, Slovakia

Abstract: This paper deals with distribution of the input-output fuzzy sets and selection of appropriate rulebase for fuzzy filter. This filter is able to perform image smoothing and it is especially appropriate for impulse noise suppression and image edge preservation at same time. The parameters of the filter were chosen by genetic algorithm. The filter structure is based on fuzzy filter structure proposed by Russo et al.

Keywords: image filtering, impulse noise, fuzzy logic, genetic algorithm

1 Description of the Fuzzy Filter Optimisation

The principle of the fuzzy filter (FFL) is simple. An operation window (OW) slides over the whole image from the upper-left position to bottom-right position. At every step the fuzzy operator is applied on the data of the OW. Usually the square OW of dimension 3x3 is used.

Let x^* be the pixel to be processed and $x_1, x_2, \ldots, x_8$ the neighbouring pixels. The corresponding filtered output value of the FFL will be computed by $y = x^* + \Delta x$, where Δx is the correcting term yielded by the FFL. In order to obtain the correcting term Δx capable of cancelling the impulse noise, it can be used a simple set of fuzzy rules [2]. The basic principle is defined as follows: *"if x^* is darker than the neighbour pixels then make it much brighter and vice-versa."*. The detailed description of the fuzzy operator was described in [1]. The parameters, position and width of the fuzzy sets as well as the rulebase were designed by Russo et al. However, these parameters do not have to be optimal. This paper is oriented to found the optimal parameters by genetic algorithm (GA).

The chromosome of the FFL is divided into two parts (Fig.1). The first part describes the position and width of the input/output fuzzy sets. The second part of the chromosome describes the fuzzy rulebase. Similarly as in [1], in this case the rules were rotated by 90 degrees and the fuzzy sets were symmetrical, too.

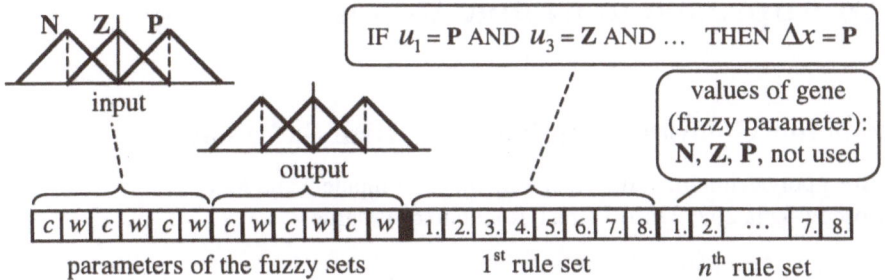

Fig.1   Chromosome description

There were 120 chromosomes in the population. The probabilities of crossover and mutation were 0.9 and 0.1, respectively. The elitism scheme was used, so the best chromosomes (30%) were passed to the next iteration without change. The simulation was performed for 10000 iteration. The manmade filter's error is $MSE = 445$, while by the proposed filter (Fig.2) $MSE = 257$ was obtained.

Input set:
$P = \{-182, 223, 628\}$
$Z = \{-346, 0, 346\}$
$N = \{-628, -223, 182\}$

Output set:
$P = \{137, 211, 285\}$
$Z = \{-48, 0, 48\}$
$N = \{-285, -211, -137\}$

Legenda: ■ P set   ☐ N set   ▨ Z set

input   output

Similarly for N set.

Fig.2   Parameters of the proposed filter

2   Conclusion

The designed FFL performed by GA overcomes the performance of the manmade FFL. Moreover the filter is robust because of symmetric constrains e.g. rulebase rotation and symmetry of fuzzy sets. Future research should be oriented to development of FFL with five input/output fuzzy sets and 5x5 operation window.

References

1. Russo, F., Ramponi, G. (1994) Introducing the Fuzzy Median Filter. Signal Processing VII: Theories and Applications, European Association for Signal Processing, 963-966

2. Vaščák, J (1996) Use of Fuzzy Logic for Control of Electrical Drives (text book). TEMPUS JEN 02177, Košice, (in Slovak)

An Approach to Mobile Robot Learning

Vladimir Golovko[1], Oleg Ignatiuk[1], Rauf Sadykhov[2]

[1] Brest polytechnic Institute, Department of Computers and Mechanics,
Moscowskaja 267, 224017 Brest, Republic of Belarus

[2] National Academy of Sciences,
Surganova 6, Minsk, Republic of Belarus

Abstract: Building autonomous mobile robots has been a primary aim of robotics and artificial intelligence. Artificial neural networks are capable of performing the different aspects of autonomous driving, such as collision-free motions, avoiding obstacles, mapping and planning of path. This paper describes the global architecture of the neural system for autonomous control of a mobile robot. Such neural system has the ability for self-training and self-organizing.

1   The Control System Architecture

The global architecture of the neural system is represented on Figure 1. It consists of different neural modules, which are combined in an intelligent system. The neural system solves the following tasks: performs data fusion; reactive control of the mobile robot while moving in the unknown environment; the formation of the global route map in the process of the motion in the unknown environment; the choice of the optimal route.

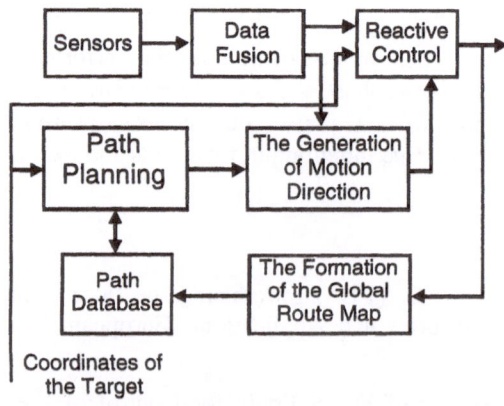

Figure 1. The Control System architecture

The neural system must provide the following demands: robust control in case of inexact information from sensors; training with the supervisor; self-training and self-organizing; capability for real time action

One can see on Figure 1 the information from different sensors is combined by data fusion module. As a result we have the local environment map. The local environment map is used for reactive control and for unpredicted obstacle avoidance, if the working environment is known. Reactive control takes place if the working environment is unknown. In this case, the planning stage has no sense. The inputs to the neural system are the final goal position and the sensor data. For this purpose the neural networks are used. If one trains a neural network by correct output data in case of inexact input information, it will provide the robust control of the robot. The neural system can itself collect the training data and learn during the interaction of a robot with the environment. As a result the self-organizing of a mobile robot is provided.

In the process of the robot motion the neural system memorizes the path. For this purpose is used the arrangement of the indicators from start point to target. Each indicator contains direction, which defines how the robot should reach next indicator, a distance between neighbor indicators etc. As a result of robot motion in the unknown environment mapping is performed. Mapping is the process of constructing a model of the environment during motion in the space. As a result of mapping the formation of the global route map and of path database takes place. The path database stores all possible paths and relevant environment data.

Now let's examine the case if the robot motion is performed in the known environment. In this case the path planning module identifies the optimal route for a specific motion action in the actual environment and generates the direction of the motion in the key points (indicators) of the path. For this purpose the path planning module uses a path database to form an optimal solution allowing to reach the target with minimal cost. The neural system performs the reactive control between the key points of the possible route.

In such a system self-training and self-organizing is realized both on the reactive level and on the level of path planning.

2 Conclusion

This paper is focused on description of an intelligent neural system for the control of a mobile robot. Such system is developed according to the INTAS project (Intelligent Neural System for autonomous control of a mobile robot). Compared to other project activities, the proposed neural system has the ability for self-training and self-organizing and behaves itself as a person during orientation in environment.

Reactive Agents Based Autonomous Transport System

Milan Schmotzer

Department of Cybernetics and AI, Technical University of Košice, Letná 9/B, 042 00 Košice, Slovak Republic, (schmotze@tuke.sk)

Abstract: The SRA–ATS (Simple Reactive Agent Based real-time Autonomous Transport System) was created in Prolog at the beginning of year 2000. It can easily be re-implemented to another computer language. It is based on the "new" alife-like AI paradigm – there is no scheduling or planning activity implemented in an agent. "Intelligence" of each agent is a result of agent's simple reactions.

Keywords: reactive, agent, transport, automatic, real-time, logic programming

1. SRA-ATS Based Application Characterisation

Because of its effective way for designing of complex systems (fast prototyping facility), the Prolog AI computer language was chosen. The SRA-ATS system was written for the Arity Prolog but it can easily be ported to another Prolog interpreter. (Only two small predicates need to be changed.)

The *new* artificial life like AI paradigm *"does not like"* planning, scheduling or hypothesis space searching. Instead of such *terrible* CPU-consuming algorithms, reactive (immediately reacting) techniques should be used. Moreover in SRA-ATS based applications no privileged agents are used (but they can be defined if one needs them).

SRA-ATS based application properties:

☐ It is rule-based. (Rules are greatly supported by Prolog.)

☐ It has easily understandable design.

☐ Therefore such system is good for teaching.

☐ There does not exist any special (privileged) agents in the system.

☐ Created software acts as a fully autonomous system (no human interaction is awaited/needed).

☐ It is a real-time system.

☐ There is no inter-agent communication (except for near agent position detection).

2. SRA Agents' Attributes

☐ Simple agent architecture.

☐ Module based (scheduling and/or other modules can easily be added).

☐ Therefore easily extendable agent design.

☐ Easily configurable.

☐ Easily re-programmable.

☐ Run-ready reactive modules:

    ☐ Immediate menacing collisions detection system.

    ☐ Anti-crash (logical rotation) module.

    ☐ Pseudo-intelligent moving module.

3. SRA Autonomous Storage System

A Simple Reacting Agent Based Autonomous Storage System prototype should work as an traditional storehouse with only one difference – there shall not be any human in an autonomous storage system. There can (logically) exist two basic versions of an autonomous storage system:

1. Agents will stay rather easy and a label matching algorithm will be used. At the store for certain number of pieces of each type of a commodity a special place should be reserved (and therefore the store space will not be optimally utilised most of the time).

2. Agents will be slightly more complex but they will be able to self-optimise the utilisation of store space. For example, a global list of positions can be used.

It depends on the user needs which model will be chosen. If he/she wants a fast storage system, the first type of proposed algorithms should be used. If the user wants a storage space optimised system, the second one should be chosen.

Mathematical Notes on Neural Networks

Ivan Daňo

Department of Mathematics, Faculty of Electrical Engineering and Informatics, Technical University, Hlavná 6, SK-04120 Košice, Slovakia

Abstract: Analog circuits have played a very important role in the development of modern electronic technology.Conventional digital computation methods have run into a serious speed bottleneck due to their serial nature. To overcome this problem, a new computation model, called "neural networks," has been proposed, which is based on some aspects of neurobiology and adapted to integrated circuits. In the present paper we investigate the properties of a class of artificial neural networks which can be characterized by a large system of ordinary diferential equations.

Keywords: artificial neural networks,differential equations, optimal solutions.

Consider an $M \times N$ artficial neural network, having $M \times N$ cells arranged in M rows and N columns. We call the cell on the i-th row and the j-th column cell (i, j), and denote it by $C(i, j)$.

Definition 1: The r-neighborhood of a cell $C(i, j)$, in a cellular neural network is defined by

$$O_r(i,j) = \{C(k,l) : \max\{|k - i|, |l - j|\} \leq r, 1 \leq k \leq M; 1 \leq l \leq N\}, \quad (1)$$

where r is a positive integer number. We will consider neural networks described by differential equations of the form

$$C\frac{du_{xij}(t)}{dt} = -\frac{1}{R_x}u_{xij}(t) + \sum_{C(k,l)\in O_r(i,j)} Q_1(i,j;k,l)u_{ykl}(t)+$$

$$+ \sum_{C(k,l)\in O_r(i,j)} Q_2(i,j;k,l)u_{wkl} + I ,$$

$$1 \leq i \leq M; \quad 1 \leq j \leq N , \qquad (2)$$

where

$$u_{yij}(t) = \frac{1}{2}(|u_{xij}(t) + 1| - |u_{xij} - 1|), \qquad (3)$$

$$u_{wij} = E_{ij}, \ |u_{xij}(0)| \leq 1, \ |u_{wij}| \leq 1, \ C > 0, \ R_x > 0, \qquad (4)$$

$$Q_1(i,j;k,l) = Q_1(k,l;i,j), \ 1 \leq i, \ 1 \leq j, \ k \leq M, \ l \leq N. \qquad (5)$$

The variable w, x, and y denote the input, state, and output, respectively. In particular, $I_{xy}(i,j;k,l)$ and $I_{xw}(i,j;k,l)$ are linear voltage controlled

current sources with the characteristics $I_{xy}(i,j;k,l) = Q_1(i,j;k,l)u_{ykl}$ and $I_{xw}(i,j;k,l) = Q_2(i,j;k,l)u_{wkl}$ for all $C(k,l) \in O_r(i,j)$ .The only nonlinear element in each cell is a piecewise-linear voltage-controlled current source $I_{yx} = (\frac{1}{R_y})f(u_{xij})$,
where

$$f(q) = \frac{1}{2}(|q+1| - |q-1|) \ .$$

All of the linear and piecewise-linear controlled sources used in our neural network can be easily realized using operational amplifiers. The dynamics of a neural network has both output feedback and input control mechanisms. The output feedback effect depends on the interactive parameter $Q_1(i,j;k,l)$ and the input control effect depends on $Q_2(i,j;k,l)$. Consequently, it is sometimes instructive to refer to Q_1 as a feedback operator and Q_2 as a control operator. Further we wil consider artificial neural networks described by differential equations of the form

$$C_i \frac{du_i}{dt} = \sum_{j=1}^{n} T_{ij}v_j - \frac{u_i}{R_i} + I_i \ , \ i = 1,...,n, \tag{6}$$

where for each i, C_i, R_i and I_i are constans, $T_{i,j}$ is an symmetric constant matrix, $u_i \in R, v_i \in (-1,1), v_i = g_i(\lambda u_i)$ where $\lambda > 0$ is a constant. We show that certain properties of systems of autonomous differential equations (6) can be extended to the class of nonlinear differential equation of the form

$$C_i \frac{du_i}{dt} = \sum_{j=1}^{n} s_{ij}(t)T_{ij}v_j(t) - \frac{1}{\tau_i(s_i)}u_i(t) + I_i(t), \ i = 1,...,n, \ t \in R_+. \tag{7}$$

or to a special case of that class.

References

1. GRUJI, L.T. - MICHEL, A.N.: Qualitative analysis of neural networks under structural perturbations. Proc. 1990 ISCAS, pp.391-394, May 1990.
2. Chua, L.O.: Cellular Neural Networks. Theory. IEEE Trans. Circuits Syst.,vol. 35, No.10, p. 1257-1272, 1988.
3. Li, J.H. - Michel, A.N.: Qualitative Analysis and Synthesis of a Class of Neural Networks. IEEE Trans. Circuits Syst., vo.35,No.8, pp. 976-986, 1988.
4. Dao, I.: Artificial Neural Networks. (submitted) .

Entropy of Fuzzy Dynamical Systems

Beloslav Riečan

Mathematical Institute, Slovak Academy of Sciences,
Štefánikova 49, 814 73 Bratislava, Slovakia
Faculty of Natural Sciences, Matej Bel University,
Tajovského 40, 974 01 Banská Bystrica, Slovakia

Abstract: Using fuzzy partitions instead of set partitions we have defined a new invariant of dynamical systems. In this communication we discuss the notion and show how it can be modified to be useful.

1 Fuzzy entropy

Entropy of dynamical systems has been introduced for distinguishing some non-isomorphic dynamical systems. The notion is based on the notion of the entropy

$$- \sum p_i \log p_i$$

of a set partition. Here we shall consider fuzzy dynamical systems defined by the following way.

Definition. Let $(\Omega, \mathcal{S}, P)$ be a probability space, $\mathcal{F}$ be the set of all $\mathcal{S}$-measurable functions from Ω to $[0,1]$. Fuzzy dynamical system is the triple $(\mathcal{F}, m, U)$, where $m : \mathcal{F} \to [0,1]$ is defined by the equality

$$m(f) = \int_{\Omega} f \, dP$$

and $U : \mathcal{F} \to \mathcal{F}$ is a maping satisfying
the following conditions:

(i) If $f + g \leq 1_{\Omega}$, then $U(f + g) = U(f) + U(g)$.
(ii) $U(1_{\Omega}) = 1_{\Omega}$.
(iii) $m(U(f)) = m(f)$ for any $f \in M$.
(iv) $U(f \cdot g) = U(f) \cdot U(g)$ for any $f, g \in \mathcal{F}$.

A fuzzy partition is a set $A = \{f_1, ..., f_n\} \subset \mathcal{F}$ such that

$$\sum_{i=1}^{n} f_i = 1_{\Omega}$$

If $A = \{f_1, ..., f_n\}$, then

$$U^i(A) = \{U^i(f_1), ..., U^i(f_n)\},$$

where $U^0(f) = f$, $U^{i+1}(f) = U(U^i(f))$.

It is easy to see that $U(A)$ is a partition for any partition A. As usual define the entropy function $\varphi : [0, 1] \to [0, 1]$ by the formula

$$\varphi(x) = -x \log x, \quad \text{if } x > 0,$$
$$\varphi(0) = 0.$$

If $A = \{f_1, ..., f_n\}, B = \{g_1, ..., g_k\}$ are two fuzzy partitions then we define

$$A \vee B = \{f_i \cdot g_j; i = 1, ..., n, j = 1, ..., k\},$$

the entropy

$$H(A) = \sum_{n=1}^{n} \varphi(m(f_i))$$

and the conditional entropy

$$H(A|B) = \sum_{i=1}^{n} \sum_{j=1}^{k} m(g_j) \varphi\left(\frac{m(f_i \cdot g_j)}{m(g_j)}\right),$$

where the summands with $m(g_j) = 0$ are ommited.

The entropy of a fuzzy dynamical system has been defined by the following formulas:

$$h(A, U) = \lim_{n \to \infty} \frac{1}{n} H\left(\bigvee_{i=1}^{n-1} U^i(A)\right).$$

Finally, if $G \subset \mathcal{F}$ and $\mathcal{P}$ is the family of all fuzzy partitions, then

$$h_G(U) = \sup\{h(A, U); A \in \mathcal{P}, A \subset G\}$$

The following generalization of the celebrated Kolmogorov - Sinaj theorem holds:

Theorem. Let $C = \{C_1, ..., C_n\}$ be a measurable set partition of Ω such that the σ-algebra S is generated by the set $\bigcup_{i=1}^{\infty} U^i(C)$. Then for every fuzzy partition $A = \{g_1, ..., g_k\}$ there holds

$$h(A, U) \leq h(C, U) + \int_{\Omega} \left(\sum_{i=1}^{k} \varphi(g_i)\right) dP.$$

Of course, the definition has the following defect: If G contains all constant functions, then $h_G(U) = \infty$. This defect is eliminated by the following correction.

2 Hudetz entropy

If $A = \{f_1, ..., f_n\}$ is a fuzzy partition, then we define its Hudetz entropy

$$H^b(A) = \sum_{i=1}^{k} \varphi(m(f_i)) - m\left(\sum_{i=1}^{k} \varphi(f_i)\right),$$

$$h^b(U) = \lim_{n \to \infty} \frac{1}{n} H^b\left(\bigvee_{i=0}^{n-1} U^i(A)\right),$$

and for any $G \subset \mathcal{F}$ we define

$$h_G^b(U) = \sup\{h^b(A, U); A \subset G, A \in \mathcal{Q}\}$$

where $\mathcal{Q}$ is the set of all fuzzy partitions. Then the following theorem holds:

Theorem. Let $(\Omega, \mathcal{S}, P, T)$ be a dynamical system, $\mathcal{F}$ be the set of all functions $f : \Omega \to [0,1]$ measurable with respect to $\mathcal{S}$, $U : \mathcal{F} \to \mathcal{F}$, $U(f) = f \circ T$. Let $C \subset G \subset \mathcal{F}$. Then

$$h_G^b(U) = h^b(C, U) = h(C, U).$$

References

1. Maličký, P., Riečan, B. (1987) On the entropy of dynamical systems. In: Proc. Ergodic Theory and Related Topics II, pp. 135–138. Taubner, Leipzig
2. Hudetz, T. (1993) Quantum topological entropy. In: Quantum Probability and related Topics VIII, pp. 237–261. World Scientific, Singapore
3. Riečan, B., Neubrunn, T. (1997) Integral, Measure, and Ordering. Kluwer, Dordrecht and Ister, Bratislava

Neural Extension of Fuzzy Prolog

Martin Lieskovský

Department of Computer Science, Faculty of Science, University of P.J.Šafárik,
041 54 Košice, Jesenná 5, Slovak Republic.
Lieskovsky@duro.science.upjs.sk

Abstract: We extend Fuzzy Prolog with Neural Network Selector to modify deduction strategy. Neural Network Selector helps to select rule to calculate better answers first and to avoid infinite branches of deduction tree. Fuzzy Prolog and Neural Network Selector are implemented as java objects. Object oriented approach allows to change type of the used neural network.

Keywords: neural network, Prolog, Fuzzy values, deduction strategy, object oriented approach

1 Background

In our previous papers [4] we dealt with Warren's implementation of Prolog. We introduced fuzzy modification, where clauses and facts can have fuzzy value associated, describing importance (trust, possibility). Our modification of Prolog incorporated fuzzy connectives. We allow arbitrary connectives fulfilling certain condition to be used in clause body (between predicates) and in the rule (between rule body and rule head). Well known are

Lukasiewicz:

$$\&^{\bullet}_L = \max(\,0,\, x+y-1\,)$$
$$\to^{\bullet}_L = \min(\,1,\, 1-x+y\,)$$
$$\vee^{\bullet}_L = \min(\,1,\, x+y\,)$$

Gödel:

$$\&^{\bullet}_G = \min(\,x,\, y\,)$$
$$\to^{\bullet}_G = y \text{ if } x > y \text{ else } 1$$
$$\vee^{\bullet}_G = \max(\,x,\, y\,)$$

Product logic:

$$\&^{\bullet}_P = x.y$$
$$\rightarrow^{\bullet}_P = \min(1, \frac{y}{x})$$
$$\vee^{\bullet}_P = x + y - xy$$

Either in implementation of this model, or in practical using of this model we found another important source of fuzziness – data. Fuzziness in data arises from unprecise specification, vague terms or linguistic notions. In large data sources, we found object-oriented approach as very useful to handle this phenomenon. We present two object-oriented approaches to fuzzy querying and unification. We choose Java language for implementation of our model. With SUN's sockets we realised resolution engine as distributed algorithm, where each branch of resolution is handled by independent object – engine. This allows execute resolution engines on several computers over network.

2   Motivation

In Prolog with two-valued logic, there is depth first search used mainly. In Fuzzy Prolog we have more and deeper branches of unification tree. If we want to calculate answers with higher (or lower) fuzzy value, we need some strategies to choose branch to continue in, because depth first strategy returns answers regardless to fuzzy value. We have introduced (see [5]) some strategies based on prediction of fuzzy value of computed answer: if we have two rules with different fuzzy value, that one with higher fuzzy value is used. For each rule is created own engine object, which execute this branch of computing. Engines are ordered by upper bound of fuzzy value of answer computed in this branch. Engine with highest fuzzy value are executed first.[1] Unfortunately there is no guarantee that computed answer will really have higher fuzzy value. By ordering engines we guarantee that answers will be reported in correct order, but engine (branch) with high predicted fuzzy value can decrease fuzzy value dramatically in last unification or with last fact used. To protect against such time wasting computing we incorporate Neural Network Selector.

---

[1] These strategies are based on monotonicity of connectives used. If rule has fuzzy value 0.8, then fuzzy value of answer to this rule cannot have fuzzy value grater than 0.8. If conjunction used in rule body is min (from Goedel's logic) then fuzzy value of whole rule body cannot be greater than fuzzy value of any atom in the rule body.

3 Our approach

As mentioned above, every branch is executed in different object of class engine. Engine is fully functioning prolog engine with only limitation: there are no choice points and no backtracking at all. In every choice point new engines are created for every choice-branch of computing. Every engine has method to return predicted fuzzy value of answer.

```
class Engine {

    float get_prediction()

    ...

}
```

Simple change allows us to use several values to order engines by.

```
class Engine {

    float[] get_prediction()

    ...

}
```

This change allows us to use not only predicted fuzzy value of answer to order engines, but any value (e.g. number of bound and/or unbound variables).

Which engine should be preferred one? How to choose? As the neural networks are suitable to categorise unprecise data, we implemented Neural Network Selector as support tool to select the computational branch in which the answer with higher fuzzy value should be computed. Fuzzy Prolog is designed in objects, so Neural Network Selector is implemented as object and its method think is invoke from get_prediction method of main object of Fuzzy Prolog – engine. Type of neural network is not restricted to concrete one. Fuzzy Prolog expects object of class Selector and any object (any type of neural network, as long as any type of training or training method) can be used. Moreover we can use selector to predict depth of branch (length of computing – number of used rules to compute answer) or work around infinite branches.

```
class Neural_selector extends Selector {

        float Think( arguments )

        ...

}
```

There can be arbitrary number of Neural Selector as long as they are childs of Selector class, moreover we can combine Neural Selectors with other types also.

Arguments passed to think method depends on Neural Network implemented in selector and goal that is Selector used for. E.g. if we want discover (detect) infinite branches we always pass number[2] of predicate and information about bound and unbound variables. Bound and unbound variables are passed as vector of binary values (0-unbound, 1-bound). Answer of this selector is 0 for infinite and 1 for finite.

For depth prediction we can use same arguments passed to selector also, but answer is depth of branch.

4   Results

The best results we got in detection of infinite branches (rules generating infinite subtree). These results we got with unsupervised concurrent learning method with twolayer perceptron network with one output neuron. Input was composed from rule number and number of bound variables in rule head. This network model can be used in estimating of number of unbound variables after rule using. For other (more complex task we use feed forward neural network with back-propagation learning method and one hidden layer. The best results we got in prediction of depth of branch. Predicate ordering in rule body needs some improvements. Prediction of fuzzy value of answers requires facts with fuzzy value equal to one, and rules with fuzzy values less than one. Otherwise there was no reasonable results.

5   Discussion

Neural Network selector can work on various inputs and may return different answers. E.g. it can work on estimated fuzzy value of answer and it can return computed value of answer. It can work on number of unbound or bound variables in rule head and after using rule. From predicates in resolventa it can compute their order to improve performance, etc. E.g. if we use predicates with smallest depth of branch first, we can get more bound variables and decrease depth of branch of other predicates. Neural Network Selector is trained with computed answers and their fuzzy values or with depth of branches, in training phase. Different types of neural networks can be used as long as different types of training methods.

---

[2] Every predicate has assigned unique number which identify them – it is unusefull to pass names of predicates. Predicates with different arity have assigned different numbers.

6 References

[1] H. Aït-Kaci:Warren Abstract Machine, A Tutorial Reconstruction, MIT Press, Cambridge, MA, 1991

[2] D.Dubois, H.Prade: Fuzzy Sets and Systems:Theory and Applications, Academic Press, New York, 1980

[3] M.H. van Emden: Quantitative deduction and its fixpoint theory, The Journal of Logic Programming, Elsevier Science Publishing, 1986

[4] M.Lieskovský: Fuzzy WAM for Expert Systems, J.Žižka ed.:Proc. of AIT'96, Technical University Brno, 1996.

[5] M.Lieskovský: Quantitative Search Strategies for Prolog-based Expert Systems, Proc. of Practical Application of Prolog 1997, p.353-367, PA Company, London, 1997

[6] D. Meritt : Building Expert Systems in Prolog, Springer Verlag, Berlin, 1988

[7] B. Meyer: Object Oriented Software Construction, Prentice Hall, 2nd edition, 1997

[8] W.Pedrycz: Fuzzy Neural Networks and Neurocomputations, Fuzzy Sets and Systems, 56, p.1-28,1993

[9] P. van Roy:1983-1993:The Wonder Years of Sequential Prolog Implementation, Journal of Logic Programming, Volume 1912 p.385-442, Springer Verlag 1994

[10]L. Sterling, E. Shapiro : The Art of Prolog, MIT Press, Cambridge MA, 1986.

[11] P. Vojtáš: Fuzzy reasoning with flexible selection of t-operators. Proceedings of IFSA'97, vol. I, p.345-352, ACADEMIA, 1997